WADSWORTH
CENGAGE Learning™

WRITE 1: Sentences and Paragraphs
Dave Kemper, Verne Meyer, John Van Rys,
and Pat Sebranek

Publisher: Lyn Uhl

Director, Developmental English and College Success:
Annie Todd

Development Editors: Leslie Taggart, Karen Mauk

Assistant Editor: Melanie Opacki

Editorial Assistant: Matthew Conte

Media Editor: Amy Gibbons

Marketing Manager: Kirsten Stoller

Marketing Coordinator: Ryan Ahern

Marketing Communications Manager: Stacey Purviance
Taylor

Content Project Manager: Rosemary Winfield

Art Director: Jill Ort

Print Buyer: Susan Spencer

Rights Acquisition Specialist, Image: Jennifer Meyer Dare

Rights Acquisition Specialist, Text: Katie Huha

Production Service: Sebranek, Inc.

Text Designer: Sebranek, Inc.

Cover Designer: Hannah Wellman

Cover Image: Gettyimages.com

Compositor: Sebranek, Inc.

Sebranek, Inc.: Steven J. Augustyn, April Lindau,
Colleen Belmont, Chris Erickson, Mariellen Hanrahan,
Dave Kemper, Tim Kemper, Rob King, Chris Krenzke,
Lois Krenzke, Mark Lalumondier, Jason C. Reynolds,
Janae Sebranek, Lester Smith, Jean Varley

For product information and technology assistance, contact us at
Cengage Learning Customer & Sales Support, 1-800-354-9706.

For permission to use material from this text or product,
submit all requests online at **www. cengage.com/permissions.**
Further permissions questions can be emailed to
permissionrequest@cengage.com.

Library of Congress Control Number: 2010935707

Student Edition:
ISBN-13: 978-0-618-64219-9
ISBN-10: 0-618-64219-6

Annotated Instructor's Edition:
ISBN-13: 978-0-618-64220-5
ISBN-10: 0-618-64220-X

Wadsworth
20 Channel Center Street
Boston, MA 02210
USA

Cengage Learning is a leading provider of customized learning solutions with office
locations around the globe, including Singapore, the United Kingdom, Australia,
Mexico, Brazil, and Japan. Locate your local office at:
international.cengage.com/region.

Cengage Learning products are represented in Canada by Nelson Education, Ltd.

For your course and learning solutions, visit **www.cengage.com.**

Purchase any of our products at your local college store or at our preferred online
store **www.cengagebrain.com.**

Printed in the United States of America
1 2 3 4 5 6 7 14 13 12 11 10

WRITE 1:
Sentences and Paragraphs

CONTENTS

Inti St. Clair/Digital Vision/Getty Images

visionandimagination.com/Flickr/Getty Images

Ilja Mašík, 2010/used under license from www.shutterstock.com

"Easy writing makes hard reading, but hard writing makes easy reading."
—Florence King

Part 7: Readings   396

ULTRA.F/Photodisc/gettyimages

Preface

Our objective with *WRITE 1: Sentences and Paragraphs* and its companion *WRITE 2: Paragraphs and Essays* is to help you function, and even flourish, in college and in the workplace. Now more than ever, you need effective communication skills in order to take your place in our information-driven world. There really is no alternative. Writing, speaking, collaborating, thinking critically—these are the survival skills for the twenty-first century. We have kept this crucial directive clearly in mind during the development of *WRITE 1* and *WRITE 2*.

Overview of *WRITE 1*

WRITE 1 covers all of the essential communication skills needed to succeed in the college classroom:

Part 1 features **writing to learn**, **reading to learn**, and making the **writing-reading** connection.

Part 2 helps you learn about using the **writing process** and the **traits of effective writing**.

Part 3 covers **the forms of paragraph and essay writing** that you will be expected to develop in the college classroom: description, illustration, definition, narration, classification, process, comparison, cause-effect, and argumentation.

Part 4 provides in-depth **sentence workshops** to help you master sentence basics and overcome sentence challenges.

Part 5 offers many **word workshops** to help you understand and master using the parts of speech in your writing.

Part 6 includes **punctuation and mechanics workshops** that cover commas, apostrophes, semicolons, colons, hyphens, dashes, quotation marks, italics, and capitalization.

Part 7 is **a reader with short, medium, and long professional essays** for the major forms of paragraph writing covered in part 3.

Research-Based Approach

■ **The Writing Process** *WRITE 1* presents writing as a process rather than an end product. Too often, writers try to do everything all at once and end up frustrated, thinking that they can't write.

WRITE 1 shows you that writing must go through a series of steps before it is ready to submit. As you work on the various writing tasks, you will internalize strategies that you can employ in all of your future writing, whether analytical essays in college or quarterly reports in the workplace.

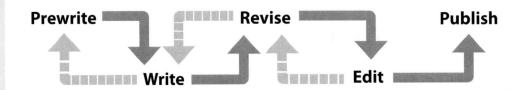

Prewrite → Write → Revise → Edit → Publish

■ **The Traits of Writing** *WRITE 1* not only explains the steps you should take during a writing project but also tells you what to include—the traits. These traits comprise *ideas, organization, voice, word choice, sentence fluency, conventions,* and *design.*

Working with the traits helps you in two important ways: It (1) identifies the key elements of successful paragraphs and essays and (2) provides a vocabulary for discussing writing with others. This information will give you the background knowledge you need to engage thoughtfully with writing.

■ **Connecting the Process and the Traits** *WRITE 1* helps students address the appropriate traits at different points during the writing process. For example, during your prewriting, or planning, you should focus on the ideas, organization, and intended voice in your writing.

The traits are especially useful when revising an initial draft because they help you know what to look for. All of the revising checklists in *WRITE 1* are traits based.

> **Revise** Improve your writing, using your partner's comments on the response sheet and the following checklist. Continue working until you can answer yes to each question.
>
> **Ideas:**
> 1. Do I compare two subjects—myself and another person? _____
> 2. Do I use three points of comparison? _____
> 3. Do I include details that show instead of tell? _____
>
> **Organization:**
> 4. Do I have a topic sentence, middle, and a closing sentence? _____
> 5. Have I used a point-by-point organizational plan? _____
> 6. Have I used transitions to connect my sentences? _____
>
> **Voice:**
> 7. Do I sound knowledgeable and interested? _____

■ **The Writing-Reading Connection** *WRITE 1* provides you with accessible and exemplary models of sentences, paragraphs, and essays. Before you begin to write, you read and respond both verbally and on the page. And as you write, you will read and respond to other students' works. Numerous activities throughout *WRITE 1* support the writing- reading and speaking-listening connections.

■ Grammar in Context *WRITE 1* is designed to provide grammar instruction, as much as possible, within the context of your own writing—to merge skills with craft. Study after study has shown this to be the most effective approach to teaching grammar.

In a typical writing chapter, you are introduced to two or three new grammar skills or concepts. After practicing each skill, you apply what you have learned as you edit your own writing. Additional practice activities are provided in the workshop section of the text.

Developmental Design

WRITE 1 employs the following proven strategies:

■ Helpful Visuals Research shows that visuals help writers learn new concepts and processes. As a result, charts, graphs, and illustrations are used throughout each chapter; and you are encouraged to use graphic organizers as you develop your own writing.

■ Structured Instruction Each chapter in *WRITE 1* is carefully structured and easy to follow, guiding you through the writing process and helping you produce writing that reflects your best efforts. This approach is essential to help you stay with a piece of writing until it is truly ready to submit.

After completing the work in *WRITE 1,* you will have internalized key strategies for producing effective writing.

■ Clear Format Objectives, explanations, and directions in *WRITE 1* are clearly marked so you know what you are expected to do and why. In addition, each two-page spread offers definite starting and ending points for your work, eliminating the necessity to page back and forth within a chapter.

Because *WRITE 1* is so easy to follow, it lends itself to small-group work and independent study.

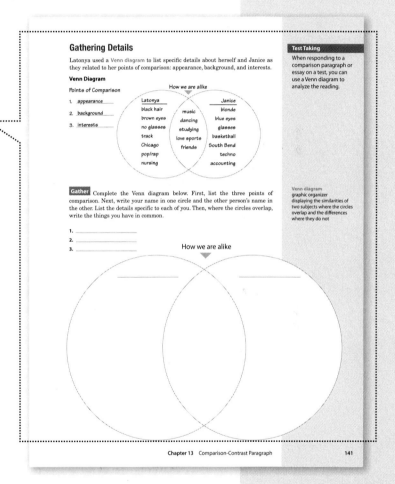

"Students need opportunities to think for themselves, to build intellectual confidence as well as intellectual competence."
—Dave Kemper

■ Reflection and Reinforcement

WRITE 1 asks you to reflect on your writing after completing the various paragraph and essay assignments. This self-assessment or reflection is a critical activity, helping you to internalize the different forms and strategies.

■ Familiar Connections

WRITE 1 compares new, perhaps difficult concepts with old familiar ones, establishing a comfortable context.

■ Vocabulary Key terms related to instruction are defined.

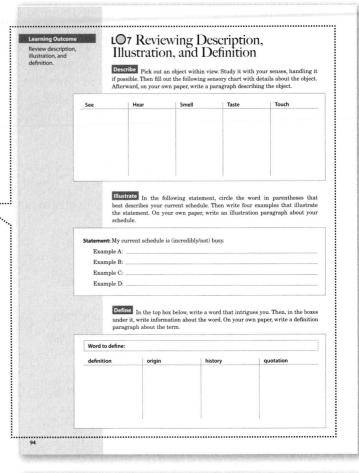

Learning Outcome
Review description, illustration, and definition.

LO7 Reviewing Description, Illustration, and Definition

Describe Pick out an object within view. Study it with your senses, handling it if possible. Then fill out the following sensory chart with details about the object. Afterward, on your own paper, write a paragraph describing the object.

See	Hear	Smell	Taste	Touch

Illustrate In the following statement, circle the word in parentheses that best describes your current schedule. Then write four examples that illustrate the statement. On your own paper, write an illustration paragraph about your schedule.

Statement: My current schedule is (incredibly/not) busy.

Example A: _____

Example B: _____

Example C: _____

Example D: _____

Define In the top box below, write a word that intrigues you. Then, in the boxes under it, write information about the word. On your own paper, write a definition paragraph about the term.

Word to define:			
definition	origin	history	quotation

94

Learning Outcome
Read to learn.

"The books that help you the most are those that make you think the most."
—Theodore Parker

Traits

Effective writing has strong ideas, clear organization, appropriate voice, precise words, smooth sentences, correct conventions, and a strong design. Use these traits to understand what you read.

LO1 Reading to Learn

Thoughtful, active reading encompasses a number of related tasks: previewing the text, reading it through, taking notes as you go along, and summarizing what you have learned. Active reading gives you control of reading assignments and makes new information part of your own thinking.

Effective Academic Reading

Follow the guidelines listed below for all of your academic reading assignments. A few of these points are discussed in more detail later in the chapter.

1. **Know the assignment:** Identify its purpose, its due date, its level of difficulty, and so on.
2. **Set aside the proper time:** Don't try to read long assignments all at once. Instead, try to read in 30-minute allotments.
3. **Find a quiet place:** The setting should provide space to read and to write.
4. **Gather additional resources:** Keep on hand a notebook, related handouts, Web access, and so on.
5. **Study the "layout" of the reading:** Review the study-guide questions. Then skim the pages, noting titles, headings, graphics, and boldfaced terms.
6. **Use proven reading strategies:** See pages 10–13.
7. **Look up challenging words:** Also use context cues to determine the meaning of unfamiliar terms.
8. **Review difficult parts:** Reread them, write about them, and discuss them with your classmates.
9. **Summarize what you learned:** Note any concepts or explanations that you will need to study further.

using the words surrounding an unfamiliar term to help unlock its meaning

Reflect Circle the star that best identifies your study-reading skills. Then explain your choice on the lines below. In your explanation, consider which of the above guidelines you do or do not follow. Weak ★ ★ ★ ★ ★ Strong

8

xiv

Additional Special Features

The following features appear as side notes or special call-outs to help you develop your communication skills and to connect your work with other learning situations—both in school and in the workplace.

Traits

The traits are used for writing and reading.

Test Taking

When appropriate, tips for taking exams are provided.

Speaking & Listening

Optional oral activities complement the writing instruction.

WAC

Special notes connect your work to writing in different classes.

Workplace

Special notes connect your work to writing in the workplace.

ESL Support

These features will help those who speak English as a second language to improve their understanding as they complete the activities in *WRITE 1*.

Insight

The insights explain or reinforce concepts for students who are just learning English.

Vocabulary

Challenging words and idioms are defined throughout, helping ESL students—or any student.

Insight

As you've seen, commas are needed to set off extra information in a sentence. Sometimes the extra information comes between the subject and the verb:

Lupe, who is a great singer and dancer, loves theater.

Commas are needed in the sentence above. But when there is no extra information to set off, do not separate the subject and verb with a comma.

Incorrect: Lupe, loves theater.
Correct: Lupe loves theater.

"I hear and I forget; I see and I remember;
I write and I understand."
—Proverb

Inti St. Clair/Digital Vision/Getty Images

1 Writing and Learning

Why should you care about writing? The answer is simple: You'll be doing a lot of it in college and in the world beyond. Today's technology, in fact, has made writing more important than ever before. Just ask anyone in the workplace. In one respect, writing is an invaluable learning tool because it helps you **sort out** your thoughts about new ideas and concepts. In another respect, it is an essential communication tool because you write to pass on what you have learned.

This chapter serves two important functions: (1) It introduces you to "writing to learn"—a way to use writing to succeed in college, and (2) it **initiates** the discussion of writing to share—developing paragraphs, essays, and other forms of writing.

Please know that there are no secrets or shortcuts to becoming an effective writer and learner. But also know that if you sincerely try, you will succeed.

What do you think?

What does the quotation on the previous page say about the learning process? And how does it match up with your own learning process?

Vocabulary

sort out
make clear

initiates
starts, begins

Answers will vary.

Learning Outcomes

LO1 Write to learn for yourself.

LO2 Write to share learning.

LO3 Consider the range of writing.

LO4 Review writing and learning.

LO1 Writing to Learn

Gertrude Stein made one of the more famous and unusual statements about writing when she said, "To write is to write is to write is to write . . . ." The lofty place that writing held in her life echoes in the line. As far as she was concerned, nothing else needed to be said on the subject.

What would cause a writer to become so committed to the process of writing? Was it for fame and recognition? Not really. The real fascination that experienced writers have with writing is the frame of mind it puts them in. The act of filling up a page stimulates their thinking and leads to exciting and meaningful learning.

Changing Your Attitude

If you think of writing in just one way—as an assignment to be completed—you will never discover its true value. Writing works best when you think of it as an important learning tool. It doesn't always have to lead to an end product submitted to an instructor.

A series of questions, a list, or a quick note in a notebook can be a meaningful form of writing if it helps you think and understand. If you make writing an important art of your learning routine, two things will happen: (1) You'll change your feelings about the importance of writing, and (2) you'll become a better thinker and learner.

Speaking & Listening

As a class, discuss this writing experience: Did it help you focus your thinking on the topic? Did you surprise yourself in any way? Could you have written more? If so, about what?

Reflect Write nonstop for 5 minutes about one of the topics below. Don't stop or hesitate, and don't worry about making mistakes. You are writing for yourself. Afterward, checkmark two things that you learned about yourself.

My Expectations About College   (or)   **My Goals in Life**

Answers will vary.

Keeping a Class Notebook

Keeping a class notebook or journal is essential if you are going to make writing to learn an important part of your learning routine. Certainly, you can take notes in this notebook, but it is also helpful to reflect on what is going on in the class. Try these activities:

- Write freely about anything from class discussions to challenging assignments to important exams.
- Discuss new ideas and concepts.
- Argue for and against any points of view that came up in class.
- Question what you are learning.
- Record your thoughts and feelings during an extended lab or research assignment.
- Evaluate your progress in the class.

WAC

Note taking is a common form of writing to learn in most classes. Always try to explore your thoughts and feelings alongside the basic notes. This makes note taking more meaningful. (See page 12.)

Special Strategies

Writing or listing freely is the most common way to explore your thoughts and feelings about your course work. There are, however, specific writing-to-learn strategies that you may want to try:

Sent or Unsent Messages	Draft messages to anyone about something you are studying or reading.
First Thoughts	Record your first impressions about something you are studying or reading.
Role-Play	Write as if you are someone directly involved in a topic you are studying.
Nutshelling	Write down in one sentence the importance of something you are studying or reading.
Pointed Question	Keep asking yourself why? in your writing to sort out your thoughts about something.
Debate	Split your mind in two. Have one side defend one point of view, and the other side, a differing point of view.

"You never really understand something until you can explain it to your grandmother."

—Albert Einstein

Practice In a notebook, explore your thoughts throughout a unit of study in one of your courses. Use a few of the strategies discussed above, starting with basic free writing. Afterward, assess the value of this writing.

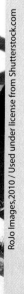

RoJo Images,2010 / Used under license from Shutterstock.com

Note:

Writing is called a process because it must go through a series of steps before it is ready to share. (See pages 24–79.)

Speaking & Listening

As a class, explore the following question: Why is writing often called "thinking on paper"?

LO2 Writing to Share Learning

The other important function of writing is to share what you have learned. When you write to learn, you have an audience of one, yourself; but when you write to share learning, you have an audience of many, including your instructors and classmates.

All writing projects (paragraphs, essays, blog entries) actually begin with writing to learn, as you collect your thoughts about a topic. But with a first draft in hand, you turn your attention to making the writing clear, complete, and ready to share with others.

A Learning Connection

As the graphic below shows, improved thinking is the link between the two functions of writing. Writing to learn involves exploring and forming your thoughts; writing to share learning involves clarifying and fine-tuning them.

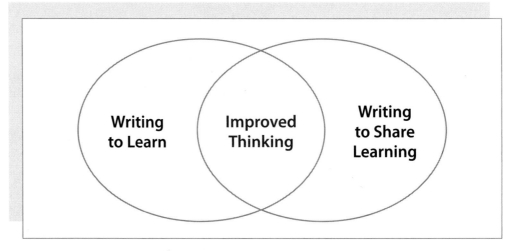

Writing to Learn | **Improved Thinking** | **Writing to Share Learning**

Identify Label each scenario below as an example of writing to learn (WL) or writing to share learning (WSL).

___WL___   **1.** Carlos is freely exploring his thoughts about a reading assignment.

___WSL___   **2.** Oki is making a paragraph clearer before turning it in.

___WL___   **3.** Ferrin is listing his early thoughts about a topic for a blog entry.

___WSL___   **4.** Thea is adding more information to an e-mail message she will send to her instructor.

___WSL___   **5.** Steve is developing a letter to the editor to submit to the college newspaper.

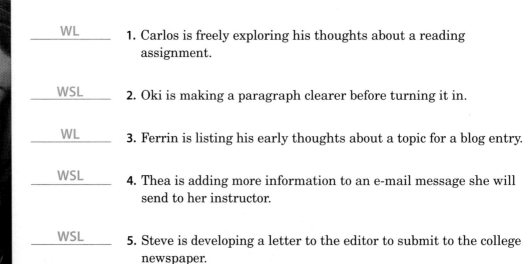

LO3 Considering the Range of Writing

The forms of writing to share cover a lot of territory as you can see in the chart below. Some of the forms are quick and casual; others are more thoughtful and formal. As a college student, your writing may cover this entire spectrum, but the instruction you receive will likely focus on the more formal types.

The Writing Spectrum

Formal and Thoughtful

Multimedia Reports

Research Papers

Stories/Plays/Poems

Responses to Literature

Persuasive Paragraphs and Essays

Expository Paragraphs and Essays

Business Letters

Personal Narratives

Blogs

E-Mails

Microblogs

Casual and Quick　Text Messages

Insight

Completeness and correctness are not critical in quick and casual writing, but they are important for all of the other forms on the chart.

React After studying the chart, answer the following questions. Then discuss your responses as a class.

1. How many of these forms of writing have you used?

   Answers will vary.

2. Which ones have you never used?

   Answers will vary.

3. How has technology affected the way you write?

   Answers will vary.

LO4 Reviewing Writing and Learning

Writing to Learn Answer the following questions about writing as a learning tool. (See pages 2–3.)

1. What is the difference between writing to learn and the writing that you have traditionally done in school?

   (AWV) Example: Usually you are supposed to hand in your writing for a grade, but writing to learn is writing for yourself.

2. Name two different ways to use a classroom notebook or journal.

   (AWV) Example: To discuss new ideas and concepts; to evaluate your progress in class; to question what you are learning.

3. What is meant by nutshelling? By pointed questions?

   Nutshelling involves writing down in one sentence the importance or significance of something you just learned. Pointed questions involve asking *why?* in your writing to sort out your thoughts.

Writing to Share Learning Answer the following questions about writing to share learning. (See page 4.)

1. What is the difference between writing to learn and writing to share learning?

   Writing to learn involves uncovering your thoughts and feelings; your audience is yourself. Writing to share learning involves sharing your thoughts with an audience.

2. How can writing to share learning help you form your thoughts?

   Writing to share learning clarifies and fine-tunes your thoughts by making them clear, complete, and readable.

The Range of Writing Identify the function or reason for using each of the following forms of writing. (See page 5.)

Text Messages An informal way to communicate with your friends and family

E-Mails A more formal means of communicating with friends, family, and co-workers

Business Letters A formal and thoughtful means of business correspondence, best for long or serious messages

Persuasive Essays A formal and very thoughtful form of academic writing. Its purpose is to persuade or convince an audience.

> "To read without reflecting is like eating without digesting."
> —Edmund Burke

Fuse/Getty Images

2

Reading and Learning

Reading and learning just naturally go hand in hand. You read to learn about new concepts and ideas; you read to learn how to do something or how something works; you read to better understand the past, the present, and the future. In most of your college classes, of course, reading is an essential learning tool.

Your instructors will expect you to become thoughtfully involved in each of your reading assignments, not only to gain a basic understanding of the material, but also to compare it with what you already know and to reflect on its importance. The guidelines and strategies presented in this chapter will help you become an active, thoughtful reader—someone engaged in the material rather than someone simply "reciting" the words.

Learning Outcomes

LO1 Read to learn.

LO2 Use reading strategies.

LO3 Read graphics.

LO4 Review reading and learning.

What do you think?

What does the quotation above have to say about becoming thoughtfully involved in reading?

Answers will vary.

LO1 Reading to Learn

Thoughtful, active reading encompasses a number of related tasks: previewing the text, reading it through, taking notes as you go along, and summarizing what you have learned. Active reading gives you control of reading assignments and makes new information part of your own thinking.

Effective Academic Reading

Follow the guidelines listed below for all of your academic reading assignments. A few of these points are discussed in more detail later in the chapter.

1. **Know the assignment:** Identify its purpose, its due date, its level of difficulty, and so on.
2. **Set aside the proper time:** Don't try to read long assignments all at once. Instead, try to read in 30-minute allotments.
3. **Find a quiet place:** The setting should provide space to read and to write.
4. **Gather additional resources:** Keep on hand a notebook, related handouts, Web access, and so on.
5. **Study the "layout" of the reading:** Review the study-guide questions. Then skim the pages, noting titles, headings, graphics, and boldfaced terms.
6. **Use proven reading strategies:** See pages 10–13.
7. **Look up challenging words:** Also use context cues to determine the meaning of unfamiliar terms.
8. **Review difficult parts:** Reread them, write about them, and discuss them with your classmates.
9. **Summarize what you learned:** Note any concepts or explanations that you will need to study further.

Reflect Circle the star that best identifies your study-reading skills. Then explain your choice on the lines below. In your explanation, consider which of the above guidelines you do or do not follow.   Weak ★ ★ ★ ★ ★ Strong

Answers will vary.

> "The books that help you the most are those that make you think the most."
> —Theodore Parker

Traits

Effective writing has strong ideas, clear organization, appropriate voice, precise words, smooth sentences, correct conventions, and a strong design. Use these traits to understand what you read.

Using a Class Notebook

To thoughtfully interact with a text, you need to write about it, so reserve part of your class notebook for responses to your readings. Certainly, you can take straight notes on the material (see page 12), but you should also personally respond to it. Such writing requires you to think about the reading—to agree with it, to question it, to make connections. The following guidelines will help you get started:

Insight

If you are a visual person, you may understand a text best by mapping or clustering its important points. (See page 39 for a sample cluster.)

- **Write whenever you feel** a need to explore your thoughts and feelings. Discipline yourself to write multiple times, perhaps once before you read, two or three times during the reading, and one time afterward.

- **Write freely and honestly** to make genuine connections with the text.

- **Respond to points of view** that you like or agree with, information that confuses you, connections that you can make with other material, and ideas that seem significant.

- **Clearly label and date your responses.** These entries will help you prepare for exams and other assignments.

- **Share your discoveries.** Think of your entries as conversation starters in discussions with classmates.

Special Strategies

Here are some specific ways to respond to a text:

Discuss Carry on a conversation with the author or a character until you come to know him or her and yourself a little better.

Illustrate Use graphics or pictures to help you think about a text.

Imitate Continue the article or story line by trying to write like the author.

Express Share your feelings about a text in a poem.

Practice Follow the guidelines on this page to explore your thoughts about one of your next reading assignments. Afterward, assess the value of responding in this way to the text.

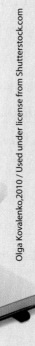

Olga Kovalenko,2010 / Used under license from Shutterstock.com

LO2 Using Reading Strategies

To make sure that you gain the most from each reading assignment, employ the additional strategies on the next four pages.

Annotating a Text

Annotating a text allows you to interact with the writer's thoughts and ideas. Here are some suggestions:

- Write questions in the margins.
- Underline or highlight important points.
- Summarize key passages.
- Define new terms.
- Make connections to other parts.

Annotating in Action

Note:
Annotate reading material only if you own the text or if you are reading a photocopy.

annotating
the process of underlining, highlighting, or making notes in a text

---

Los Chinos Discover el Barrio
by Luis Torres

He's contrasting the colorful art with the drab surroundings.

There's a colorful mural on the asphalt playground of Hillside Elementary School, in the neighborhood called Lincoln Heights. Painted on the beige handball wall, the mural is of life-sized youngsters holding hands. Depicted are Asian and Latino kids with bright faces and ear-to-ear smiles.

The mural is a (mirror) of the makeup of the neighborhood today: Latinos
reflection
living side by side with Asians. But it's not all smiles and happy faces in the *contrast* Northeast Los Angeles community, located just a couple of miles up Broadway from City Hall. On the surface there's harmony between Latinos and Asians. But there are indications of simmering ethnic-based tensions.

personal connection

That became clear to me recently when I took a walk through the old neighborhood—the one where I grew up. As I walked along North Broadway, I thought of a joke that comic (Paul Rodriguez) often tells on the stage. He paints a
Who?
picture of a young Chicano walking down a street on L.A.'s East Side. He comes upon two Asians having an animated conversation in what sounds like babble. "Hey, you guys, knock off that foreign talk. This is America—speak Spanish!"

Ha! This shows how two different immigrant groups struggle to fit in.

Annotate Carefully read the excerpt below from an essay by Stephen King. Then annotate the text, according to the following directions:

- Circle the main point of the passage.
- Underline or highlight one idea in the first paragraph that you either agree with, question, or are confused by. Then make a comment about this idea in the margin.
- Do the same for one idea in the third paragraph and one idea in the final paragraph.
- Circle one or two words that you are unsure of. Then define or explain these words in the margin.

Why We Crave Horror Movies
by Stephen King

I think that we're all mentally ill; those of us outside the asylums only hide it a little better—and maybe not all that much better, after all. We've all known people who talk to themselves, people who sometimes squinch their faces into horrible grimaces when they believe no one is watching, people who have some hysterical fear—of snakes, the dark, the tight place, the long drop . . . and, of course, the final worms and grubs that are waiting so patiently underground.   1   5

When we pay our four or five bucks and seat ourselves at tenth-row center in a theater showing a horror movie, we are daring the nightmare.

Why? Some of the reasons are simple and obvious. To show that we can, that we are not afraid, that we can ride this roller coaster. Which is not to say that a really good horror movie may not surprise a scream out of us at some point, the way we may scream when the roller coaster twists through a complete 360 or plows through a lake at the bottom of the dip. And horror movies, like roller coasters, have always been the special province of the young; by the time one turns 40 or 50, one's appetite for double twists or 360-degree loops may be considerably depleted.   10   15

We also go to re-establish our feelings of essential normality; the horror movie is innately conservative, even reactionary. Freda Jackson as the horrible melting woman in *Die, Monster, Die!* confirms for us that no matter how far we may be removed from the beauty of a Robert Redford or a Diana Ross, we are still light-years from true ugliness.   20

And we go to have fun.

Ah, but this is where the ground starts to slope away, isn't it? Because this is a very peculiar sort of fun, indeed. The fun comes from seeing others menaced—sometimes killed. One critic suggested that if pro football has become the voyeur's version of combat, then the horror film has become the modern version of the public lynching. . . .   25

Taking Effective Notes

Taking notes helps you focus on the text and understand it more fully. It changes information you have read about to information that you are working with. Personalizing information in this way makes it much easier to remember and use.

Note-Taking Tips

- Use your own words as much as possible.

- Record only key points and details rather than complicated sentences.

- Consider boldfaced or italicized words, graphics, and captions as well as the main text.

- Employ as many abbreviations and symbols as you can (vs., #, &, etc.).

- Decide on a system for organizing or arranging your notes so they are easy to review.

An Active Note-Taking System

To make your note taking more active, use a two-column system, in which one column (two-thirds of the page) is for your main notes and another column (one-third of the page) is for comments, reactions, and questions.

Two-Column Notes

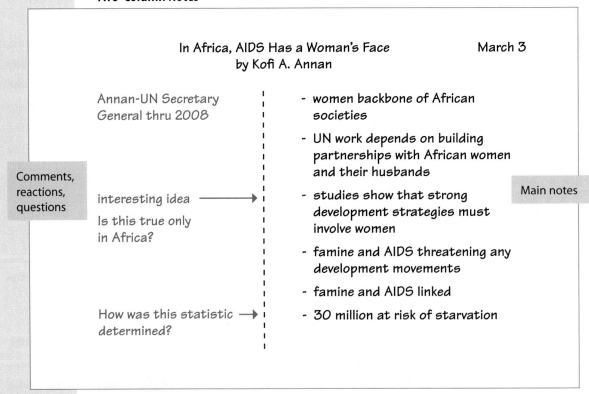

In Africa, AIDS Has a Woman's Face   March 3
by Kofi A. Annan

Comments, reactions, questions

Annan-UN Secretary General thru 2008

interesting idea →

Is this true only in Africa?

How was this statistic → determined?

Main notes

- women backbone of African societies
- UN work depends on building partnerships with African women and their husbands
- studies show that strong development strategies must involve women
- famine and AIDS threatening any development movements
- famine and AIDS linked
- 30 million at risk of starvation

Practice Use the two-column note system for one of your next reading assignments. Use the left-hand column to react with questions, comments, and reflections about the information that you record.

Summarizing a Text

Summarizing a reading assignment is an effective way to test how well you understand the information. **Summarizing** means to present the main points in a clear, concise form using your own words (except for those few words from the original text that can't be changed). Generally speaking, a summary should be no more than one-third as long as the original.

Summarizing Tips

- Start with a clear statement of the main point of the text.
- Share only the essential supporting facts and details (names, dates, times, and places) in the next sentences.
- Present your ideas in a logical order.
- Tie all of your points together in a closing sentence.

Example Summary

The example below summarizes a two-page essay by Kofi A. Annan concerning the suffering caused by AIDS and famine in southern Africa.

Main points (underlined)

Essential supporting facts

Closing sentence (underlined)

Famine and AIDS are threatening the agricultural societies in southern Africa. Tragically, women, the main unifying force in African societies, make up 59% of individuals worldwide infected by the HIV virus. With so many women suffering from AIDS, the family structure and the agricultural infrastructure are suffering severely. These conditions have significantly contributed to the famine conditions and resulting starvation. Any traditional survival techniques used by African women in the past won't work for these twin disasters. International relief is needed, and it must provide immediate food and health aid. A key focus of health aid must be the treatment of women infected with HIV and preventative education to stop the spread of the disease. The future of southern Africa depends on the health and leadership of their women.

iofoto, 2010/used under license from www.shutterstock.com

Practice Summarize the information in one of the essays on pages 397–463 or in an essay provided by your instructor. Use the tips and sample above as a guide.

summarizing
presenting the main points of a text in a clear, concise form using, for the most part, your own words

LO3 Reading Graphics

In many of your college texts, a significant portion of the information will be communicated via charts, graphs, diagrams, and drawings. Knowing how to read these types of graphics will help you become a more effective and informed college student. Follow the guidelines listed below when you read a **graphic**.

- **Scan the graphic.** Consider it as a whole to get an overall idea about its message. Note its type (bar graph, pie graph, diagram, table, and so forth), its topic, its level of complexity, and so on.

- **Study the specific parts.** Start with the main heading or title. Next, note any additional labels or guides (such as the horizontal and vertical guides on a bar graph). Then focus on the actual information displayed in the graphic.

- **Question the graphic.** Does it address an important topic? What is its purpose (to make a comparison, to show a change, and so on)? What is the source of the information? Is the graphic dated or biased in any way?

- **Reflect on its effectiveness.** Explain in your own words the main message communicated by the graphic. Then consider its effectiveness, how it relates to the surrounding text, and how it matches up to your previous knowledge of the topic.

Vocabulary

graphic
a visual representation of information that reveals trends, makes comparisons, shows how something changes over time, and so on

horizontal
parallel to ground level, at right angles to the vertical

vertical
straight up and down, at right angles to the horizontal

Analysis of a Graphic

Review the vertical bar graph below. Then read the discussion to learn how all of the parts work together.

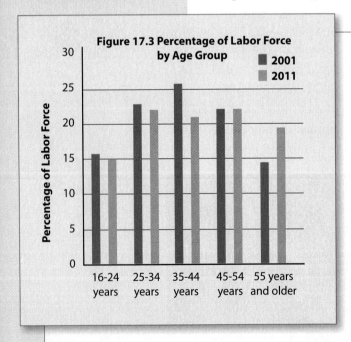

Discussion: This bar graph compares the labor force in 2001 to the labor force in 2011 for five specific age groups. The heading clearly identifies the subject or topic of the graphic. The **horizontal** line identifies the different age groups, and the **vertical** line identifies the percentage of the labor force for each group. The key in the upper right-hand corner of the graphic identifies the purpose of the color coding used in the columns or bars. With all of that information, the graphic reads quite clearly—and many interesting comparisons can be made.

React Read and analyze the following graphics, answering the questions about each one. Use the information on the previous page as a guide.

Graphic 1

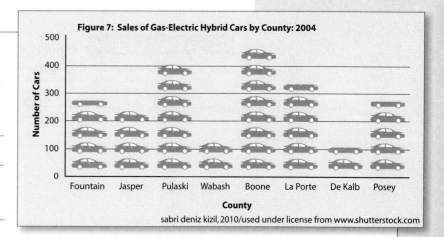

Figure 7: Sales of Gas-Electric Hybrid Cars by County: 2004

sabri deniz kizil, 2010/used under license from www.shutterstock.com

1. This graphic is called a pictograph rather than a bar graph. What makes it a "pictograph"?

   A pictograph uses pictures to

   represent numerical data.

2. What is the topic of this graphic?

   Sales of Gas-Electric

   Hybrid Cars by County

3. What information is provided on the horizontal line? On the vertical line?

   HL: Counties   VL: Number of gas-electric hybrid cars

4. What comparisons can a reader make from this graphic?

   The reader can compare counties by number of sales and number of sales by county.

Graphic 2

Figure 36.2 Complex Web Site Map

1. This graphic is called a line diagram, mapping a structure. What structure does this diagram map?

   A Web site

2. What two working parts are used in this diagram: *words, lines,* and *symbols?* Circle the appropriate choices.

3. How are the different navigational choices on a complex Web site shown on this graphic?

   The choices are shown by using branches and arrows to connect different levels of

   the Web site.

LO4 Reviewing Reading and Learning

Complete these activities as needed to help you better understand the concepts covered in this chapter.

Using a Class Notebook Explain why responding in writing to your reading assignments is valuable. (See page 9.)

Responding in writing helps you interact with text, think about the reading, and form an

opinion about it.

Annotating a Text Explain what it means to annotate a text; also identify the main value of this reading strategy. (See pages 10–11.)

Annotating means underlining, highlighting, or making notes in a text. It allows you to

interact with the writer's thoughts and ideas.

Taking Effective Notes Identify three note-taking tips that you find the most helpful. (See page 12.)

1. Answers will vary.

2.

3.

Reading Graphics Answer the following questions about a graphic in *WRITE 1*. (See pages 14–15.)

1. The graphic on page 14 is a basic type of graph containing columns of information. What is the topic of this graph?

   Percentage of Labor Force by Age Groups in 2001 and 2011

2. How is the information arranged?

   Information appears in a bar graph comparing amounts in two years.

3. Identify one main point represented in this graphic.

   (AWV) Example: More people 55 years and older are working in 2011 than in 2001.

> "There are some things you learn best in calm, and some in storm."
>
> —Willa Cather

Donovan Reese/Photodisc/Getty Images

3

Making the Writing-Reading Connection

One obvious conclusion can be drawn from the first two chapters in *WRITE 1*: Writing and reading are really **two sides of the same coin**. You write to learn, and you read to learn. You use writing to help you understand your reading. You use reading to help you with your writing. Writing is thinking; reading is thinking. The connections go on and on.

This chapter provides three common strategies that enhance college-level writing and reading: (1) using questions to analyze writing and reading assignments, (2) using the traits of effective writing to analyze your writing and reading, and (3) using graphic organizers to arrange ideas in your writing and reading.

Learning Outcomes

LO1 Analyze the assignment.

LO2 Use the traits of writing.

LO3 Use graphic organizers.

LO4 Review the writing-reading connection.

Vocabulary

two sides of the same coin
an idiom meaning "different but closely related"

What do you think?

In the quotation above, what distinction is Cather making about learning? How would you apply her point to reading and writing?

Answers will vary.

LO1 Analyzing the Assignment

At the start of any writing or reading assignment, you should analyze the **dynamics** of the situation to make sure that you fully understand what is expected of you. The dynamics of an assignment are similar to the key ingredients in a recipe. If you forget any one of them, the final product will suffer.

The STRAP Strategy

You can use the **STRAP strategy** to analyze your writing and reading assignments. The strategy consists of answering questions about these five features: *subject, type, role, audience,* and *purpose*. Once you answer the questions, you'll be ready to get to work. This chart shows how the strategy works:

For Writing Assignments		For Reading Assignments
What specific topic should I write about?	**Subject**	What specific topic does the reading address?
What form of writing *(essay, article)* will I use?	**Type**	What form *(essay, text chapter, article)* does the reading take?
What position *(student, citizen, employee)* should I assume?	**Role**	What position *(student, responder, concerned individual)* does the writer assume?
Who is the intended reader?	**Audience**	Who is the intended reader?
What is the goal *(to inform, to persuade)* of the writing?	**Purpose**	What is the goal of the material?

The STRAP Strategy in Action

Suppose you were given the following reading assignment in a sociology class:

> Read the essay "Fatherless America" in your text. Then prepare a summary paragraph, highlighting the author's main claim and key supporting points.

Here are the answers to the STRAP questions for this assignment:

Subject:	U.S. society becoming "fatherless"
Type:	Persuasive essay
Role:	Concerned citizen/advocate
Audience:	Americans in general
Purpose:	To persuade or take a stand

Test Taking

The STRAP questions help you quickly understand a writing prompt or a reading selection on a test.

Respond Use the STRAP strategy to analyze the two assignments that follow.

Think about it...

Assignment 1: Read "From 'How to Handle Conflict'" starting on page 416 in *WRITE 1*. Then, in your class notebook, respond to the reading, noting its key features and your reactions to them.

Subject: What specific topic does the reading address?
Conflict resolution

Type: What form *(essay, text chapter)* does the reading take?
Article / Essay

Role: What position does the writer assume?
Educator / Instructor / Professional

Audience: Who is the intended audience?
Workers / Businesspeople / Employees

Purpose: What is the goal of the material?
To teach the reader how to deal with conflict

Before you begin any reading assignment, you should also consider these issues:

• The importance of the assignment

• The time you have to complete it

• The way the assignment fits into the course as a whole

Assignment 2: Analyze a reading assignment provided by your instructor or given in one of your other classes.

Subject: What specific topic does the reading address?
Answers will vary.

Type: What form *(essay, text chapter)* does the reading take?
Answers will vary.

Role: What position does the writer assume?
Answers will vary.

Audience: Who is the intended audience?
Answers will vary.

Purpose: What is the goal of the material?
Answers will vary.

LO2 Using the Traits

Chapter 4 in *WRITE 1* goes into great detail about using the **traits** to help you with your writing. (See pages 25–34.) You can use these same traits to help you analyze and discuss your reading assignments.

Previewing the Traits

The traits of writing are highlighted below. Each one addresses an important feature in a reading selection, whether an essay, a chapter, an article, or a piece of fiction. (The questions will help you analyze a reading selection for the traits.)

- **Ideas** The information contained in reading material
  What is the topic of the reading?
  What main point is made?
  What supporting details are provided?

- **Organization** The overall structure of the material
  How does the reading selection begin?
  How is the middle part arranged?
  How does the selection end?

- **Voice** The personality of the writing—how the writer speaks to the reader
  To what degree does the writer seem interested in and knowledgeable about the topic?
  To what degree does the writer engage the reader?

- **Word Choice** The writer's use of words and phrases
  What can be said about the nouns, verbs, and modifiers in the reading? (Are the words too general, or are they specific and effective? Does the writer use **figurative language**?)

- **Sentence Fluency** The flow of the sentences
  What stands out about the sentences? (Are they varied in length, do they flow smoothly, do they seem stylish, and so on?)

- **Conventions** The correctness or accuracy of the language
  To what degree does the writing follow the conventions of the language?

- **Design** The appearance of the writing
  What, if anything, stands out about the design? (Does it enhance or take away from the reading experience?)

Vocabulary

traits
the key elements found in effective writing

figurative language
metaphors, personification, or other creative comparisons used to describe something or to make a point

Tatiana Popova,2010 / Used under license from Shutterstock.com

A Sample Analysis of a Reading Selection

Here is a traits analysis of "Two Views of the Same News Find Opposite Biases," a comparison essay on pages 425–426 in *WRITE 1*.

■ Ideas

The essay focuses on biased behavior—more specifically, why people reach different conclusions about the same event. The writer refers to an experiment that analyzes and compares pro-Arab and pro-Israeli responses to the reporting of the 1982 war in Lebanon. (The experiment shows that both sides feel that the reporting was biased against them.)

■ Organization

The first three paragraphs establish the main point (thesis) of the essay.

The middle paragraphs cite and analyze the main findings of the experiment, following a point-by-point pattern of organization.

The closing paragraph provides a quotation by an authority and sums up the essay.

■ Voice

The writer seems knowledgeable about and interested in his topic. He speaks to the reader in a friendly but professional way. The opening line—"You could be forgiven . . ." —draws the reader into the essay.

■ Word Choice

The writer uses some technical or unfamiliar terms—*recursive, partisan, raison d'etre,* and so on. However, these terms are defined for the reader. Otherwise, the word choice reflects the vocabulary of an educated and informed writer.

■ Sentence Fluency

The sentences are, for the most part, on the long side. A few of them require a second or third reading to pick up all of the information they contain. Overall, however, the sentences flow smoothly. Most of the paragraphs are brief (one or two sentences), which adds to the readability of the essay.

■ Conventions

The writer clearly follows the conventions, presenting error-free writing.

■ Design

The brief paragraphs give the essay a somewhat unusual appearance. Headings may have made the essay more readable.

Respond Analyze "From 'How to Handle Conflict' " on pages 416–418 for the traits. To develop your analysis, ask and answer each of the trait questions on page 20, or use the questions as an overall response guide, as is done in the analysis above. (Use your own paper.)

Speaking & Listening

Work on this activity with a partner or a small group of classmates if your instructor allows it.

WAC

See page 48 for six common graphic organizers that you can use to organize ideas in any class.

LO3 Using Graphic Organizers

Graphic organizers visually represent ideas or concepts and are commonly used to organize the ideas that you collect for your writing. You can use the same organizers to "chart" the key information in reading assignments.

Charting a Reading Assignment

Provided below is a line diagram that charts the key points in the definition essay on page 180 in *WRITE 1*. (A line diagram shows the logical relationships between the main ideas.)

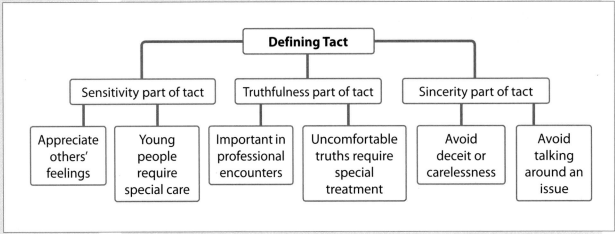

Respond   In the space below, create a line diagram to chart the information in the classification paragraph on page 114. (Ignore the errors in the sample.)

Answers will vary.

LO4 Reviewing the Writing-Reading Connection

Learning Outcome
Review the writing-reading connection.

Complete these activities as needed to help you better understand the writing-reading connection.

Analyze the Assignment Use the STRAP strategy to analyze the following reading assignment: (See pages 18–19.)

Read "What Adolescents Miss When We Let Them Grow Up in Cyberspace" starting on page 441 in your text.

Subject: "What Adolescents Miss When We Let Them Grow Up in Cyberspace"

Type: Article—cause-effect essay

Role: Student reader

Audience: General

Purpose: To show the causes and effects of using the Internet

Use the Traits Analyze "What Adolescents Miss When We Let Them Grow Up in Cyberspace" for the following traits. (See pages 441–442.)

Ideas: Answers will vary.

_____

_____

_____

_____

_____

Organization: _____

_____

_____

_____

_____

Voice: _____

_____

_____

"I tell them [writing a novel is] like driving a car at night. You never see farther than your headlights, but you can make the whole trip that way."

—E. L. Doctorow

4 Using the Writing Process and the Traits

Have you ever taken a nighttime trip in a remote area? The headlights of your car carve out a cave of light in an otherwise dark world. That sensation might be a little disconcerting, but, as Doctorow says in the quotation on the previous page, you can make the whole journey that way.

With writing, you have two similar lights—the writing process and the traits of writing. They illuminate the way for you, helping you get where you need to go. This chapter tells how.

What do you think?

How has your writing experience been like driving at night? What has lit your path?

Answers will vary.

Learning Outcomes

LO1 Think about writing as a process.

LO2 Learn about the steps in the writing process.

LO3 Learn about the traits of effective writing.

LO4 Connect the process and the traits.

LO1 Understanding the Writing Process

Few things in life can be as unpleasant as having a root canal. All of the drilling, scraping, pulling, pushing, cracking—please! Unfortunately, for some of you, writing can also be unpleasant, not for any physical discomfort, but because you struggle with it.

Part of the problem may be your approach. You may think that you should know everything you want to say before you get started. Well, writing doesn't work that way. Certainly, you should do some planning before you get started, but as the quotation on the part-opening page says, "You never [have to] see farther than your headlights." That is why writing is called a **process:** You often discover what you want to say while writing. Knowing this can make writing a lot easier— and help you do your best work.

The Process in Action

Read/React Read the following quotations by experienced writers who describe different aspects of the writing process. Discuss these quotations with a partner or a small group of classmates. Then explain below what one or two of the statements mean to you.

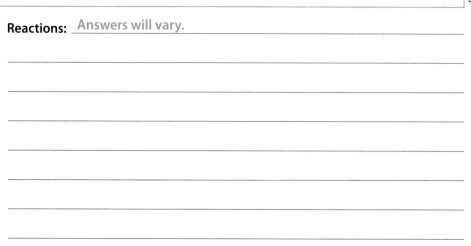

"The inspiration comes while you write."

—Madeleine L'Engle

"In writing, the more a thing cooks, the better."

—Doris Lessing

"Easy writing makes hard reading, but hard writing makes easy reading."

—Florence King

"The best advice on writing I've ever received was, 'Rewrite it!' A lot of editors said that. They all were right."

—Robert Lipsyte

Reactions: Answers will vary.

_____

_____

_____

_____

_____

_____

Vocabulary

writing process
the process a writer uses to develop a piece of writing, from planning through publishing

Thinking About Your Own Writing

Respond Answer the following questions about your writing experiences. Be sure to explain each of your answers.

1. Rate your experience as a writer by circling the appropriate star:

   negative ★ ★ ★ ★ ★ positive

   Explain. *Answers will vary.*

   _____

   _____

   _____

2. What is the easiest part of writing for you? _____

   _____

   _____

3. What is the hardest part of writing for you? _____

   _____

   _____

   _____

4. What types of writing assignments challenge you the most? _____

   _____

   _____

   _____

5. What is the best thing you have ever written? _____

   _____

   _____

6. What is the most important thing you have learned about writing?

   _____

   _____

   _____

   _____

Marc Brasz/Corbis

Spotlight on Writing

"If not for writing, I would have been shut behind a wall of silence."

Edwidge Danticat was born in Haiti, a small, impoverished Caribbean country bordering the Dominican Republic. She came to New York City as a shy young lady of 12, having to deal with a new language, new schools, new everything.

As a high school student, Danticat began writing for a citywide newspaper called *New Youth Connections* and soon realized that writing was something she had to do—for the rest of her life. What she has accomplished has been extraordinary.

Danticat has published several books, including *Krik? Krack!* (1996), a National Book Award finalist, and *Brother, I'm Dying* (2007), a National Book Critics Circle Award winner.

Today, she is recognized as the most significant writer of the modern Haitian experience, all because she had the courage to put pen to paper.

LO2 The Steps in the Process

The writing process helps you pace yourself. When you try to do everything all at once, writing becomes a real struggle; but by following the steps that are explained below, you can do one thing at a time.

Process	Activities
Prewriting	Start the process by (1) selecting a topic to write about, (2) collecting details about it, and (3) finding your focus, the main idea or thesis.
Writing	Then write your first draft, using your prewriting plan as a general guide. Writing a first draft allows you to connect your thoughts about your topic.
Revising	Carefully review your first draft and have a classmate review it as well. Change any parts that could be clearer and more complete.
Editing	Edit your revised writing by checking for style, grammar, punctuation, and spelling errors.
Publishing	During the final step, prepare your writing to share with your instructor, your peers, or another audience.

Explain In the space provided, tell how the writing process above compares with how you complete your writing assignments. Consider what you usually do first, second, third, and so on.

Answers will vary.

_____

_____

_____

_____

_____

_____

_____

_____

_____

_____

> "Writing should be seen from the inside, as a process, rather than from the outside, as a product."
> —Donald Murray

Think about it.

Writing leads to making discoveries, forming new understandings, and analyzing information—the types of thinking so essential to doing well in college.

The Process in Action

As the chart indicates, you will likely move back and forth between the steps in the writing process. For example, after writing a first draft, you may decide to collect more details about your topic—a prewriting activity.

Process Chart

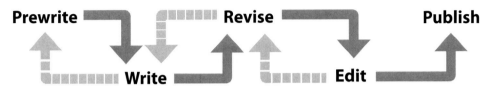

Create In the space provided below, create a chart that shows your own process—the one you described on page 28. Discuss your chart with a partner or small group of classmates.

> Answers will vary.

Reasons to Write

The four main reasons to write are given below. Always use the writing process when **writing to show learning** and when **writing to share**.

Reason	Forms	Purpose
Writing to show learning	Summaries, informational essays	To show your understanding of subjects you are studying
Writing to share	Personal essays, blog postings, short stories, plays	To share your personal thoughts, feelings, and creativity with others
Writing to explore	Personal journals, diaries, unsent letters, dialogues	To learn about yourself and your world
Writing to learn	Learning logs, reading logs, notes	To help you understand what you are learning

Explain Why is using the writing process unnecessary for **writing to explore** and **writing to learn**?

(AWV) Example: Writing to explore and to learn do not produce finished

pieces of writing. They use writing to help the writer understand.

Speaking & Listening

If you are having trouble explaining your process, talk about it with a partner.

Test Taking

When you respond to a prompt on a test, use an abbreviated form of this process. Spend a few minutes gathering and organizing ideas, then write your response. Afterward, read what you have done and quickly revise and edit it.

LO3 Understanding the Traits of Writing

What makes one particular pizza your favorite? It's all in the ingredients, isn't it? The crust might be crispy and light; the toppings, fresh; the spices, perfect.

It's all in the ingredients with effective writing, too. The ingredients, or **traits**, that you find in the best articles and essays are described below.

■ **Strong Ideas** Good writing contains plenty of good information (ideas and details). And all of the information holds the reader's interest.

> The University of Tennessee's most notorious farm doesn't specialize in grain, livestock, or milk production. It deals with bodies—dead ones, to be exact. Technically speaking, the 2.5-acre wooded plot is called the Anthropological Research Facility, but it's more commonly referred to as the Body Farm. It hosts more than 150 decomposed corpses. Since 1971, research on the Body Farm has led to many critical breakthroughs in forensic science and crime-scene investigation.
>
> — Zackary Dean

1. Rate the passage for ideas by circling the appropriate star:

   weak ★ ★ ★ ★ ★ strong

   Explain. Answers will vary. _____

   _____

2. What is the main point? _____

   _____

3. What is the most interesting detail in the passage? _____

   _____

   _____

■ **Logical Organization** Effective writing has a clear overall structure—with a beginning, a middle, and an ending. Transitions (*first, later on, for a brief time*) link the ideas.

> For five years, I have worked in one of the busiest emergency rooms in southeastern Michigan. For the last two years, I have picked up overtime by working in four other hospitals, including the busiest emergency room in inner-city Detroit. No matter where I am, I experience the same problem—too many patients and not enough staff.
>
> — Paul Duke

1. Rate the passage for organization by circling the appropriate star:

   weak ★ ★ ★ ★ ★ strong

   Explain. Answers will vary. _____

   _____

2. How is this passage arranged—by time, by location, by logic? _____

   _____

3. What transitional phrases does the writer use? _____

   _____

■ **Fitting Voice** In the best writing, you can hear the writer's voice— her or his special way of saying things. It shows that the writer cares about the subject.

Speaking & Listening

Read this model aloud to a partner. Then have the partner read the model. How do your different voices and expression affect the overall impact of the model?

> Snake haters beware: Scientists in Colombia unearthed a prehistoric snake fossil so large it makes a cobra look like an earthworm. How large? Try 42 feet. That's longer than a school bus! Researchers concluded this snake species would have weighed up to one ton. With proportions so colossal, no wonder scientists named it *Titanoboa*.
>
> — Amira Halper

1. Rate the passage for voice by circling the appropriate star:

   weak ★ ★ ★ ★ ★ strong

   Explain. Answers will vary. _____

   _____

2. Does the writer seem to care about the topic? Explain. _____

   _____

   _____

3. How would you identify the voice in this passage—sincere, silly, bored?

   _____

   _____

■ **Well-Chosen Words** In strong writing, nouns and verbs are specific and clear, and the modifiers add important information.

> She strutted to the microphone with the swagger of a rock star. The sparse crowd, busy with their coffee and crosswords, offered her a polite smattering of applause. This was it. For four months, she had poured her private feelings into poetry. For the next four minutes, she would reveal those feelings to twenty-some odd strangers. But before she could begin, a woman interrupted: "Excuse me, miss," she said. "You wouldn't happen to know a four-letter word meaning 'obstruct'?"
>
> — Latisha Jones

1. Rate the passage for word choice by circling the appropriate star:

   weak ★ ★ ★ ★ ★ strong

   Explain. Answers will vary. _____

   _____

2. Which, if any, specific verbs stand out for you? _____

   _____

   _____

3. What other words do you find interesting? (Name two.) _____

   _____

   _____

■ **Smooth Sentences** The sentences in good writing flow smoothly from one to the next. They carry the meaning of the essay or article.

> On any given day in Delaware's Wilmington State Park, rock climbers safely glide down treacherous 40-foot cliff faces as if they're riding invisible elevators. The technique is known as *rappelling*. Adventure enthusiasts and rescue teams alike use harnesses, gears, anchors, and ropes to descend slopes that are too dangerous to travel down on foot. Make no mistake; rappelling can be dangerous without proper training and equipment.
>
> — Reid Haywood

1. Rate the sentences in the passage by circling the appropriate star:

weak ★ ★ ★ ★ ★ strong

Explain. Answers will vary. _____

_____

2. In what ways does the writer vary the sentences she uses?

_____

_____

3. Which sentence do you like best? Why? _____

_____

_____

■ **Correct Copy** Strong writing is easy to read because it follows the conventions or rules of the language.

> Have you ever wondered who owns Antarctica? You might ask who would want the earth's coldest, driest, and least hospitable continent? The truth is that seven different countries claim areas of the continent. In accordance with the 1959 Antarctic Treaty, though, the land mass remains a politically neutral space for scientific exploration and environmental conservation.
>
> — Emila Carmen

1. Rate the conventions in the passage by circling the appropriate star:

weak ★ ★ ★ ★ ★ strong

Explain. Answers will vary. _____

_____

2. What punctuation marks, other than periods, are used in this passage?

_____

_____

3. How is one of these other punctuation marks used? _____

_____

_____

■ **Appropriate Design** In the best academic writing, the design follows the guidelines established by the instructor or school.

LaShawna Wilson
Ms. Davis
Forces in Science
February 11, 2011

Physics of Rainbows

"Why are there so many songs about rainbows?" asks the old tune. Perhaps it's because rainbows are beautiful, multicolored, and huge, arching over cities and mountains. But rainbows have captured human imagination as much because of their mystery as their beauty. In his work with prisms, Sir Isaac Newton demonstrated that something as beautiful and mysterious as a rainbow could be created through the simple property of refraction.

Basics of Refraction

The key to understanding rainbows is refraction. When light passes from one medium to another, it bends. Simply look at a straw in a glass, and the apparent break in the straw when it enters the water demonstrates refraction. Light is bending as it passes through the water, showing the straw in a different place.

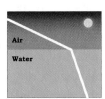

Figure 1: Basic refraction. Light moving from one medium to another slows down. When entering at an angle, the light is more sharply refracted.

When light enters a new medium at a sharp angle, the refraction is stronger. That's because one side of the light beam is entering the medium first, thereby slowing down, as the other side of the light beam continues longer at its previous speed. The result is a turn in the angle of the light ("Prism" 13). This effect is demonstrated in Figure 1.

Wilson 2

Frequencies and Refraction

Different frequencies of light bend at different angles. The relatively long wavelengths of red light do not bend as much as the relatively short wavelengths of purple light, which is why a prism splits white light into its colors.

A raindrop can do the same thing. Figure 2, derived from the Web site "How Stuff Works," shows how white light is bent when passing through a raindrop.

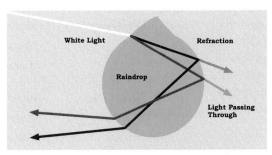

Figure 2: Refraction of light through a raindrop. Note that the purple light exits at a higher angle than the red. Drops lower in the air will reflect violet light to viewers' eyes, while higher drops reflect red light. (Source http://science.howstuffworks.com/rainbow2.htm.)

Bands of Color

The reason that a rainbow looks like bands of color is that the observer sees only one color coming from each droplet. As Figure 2 shows, a droplet that is higher in the sky will refract red into the eyes of the viewer. A droplet that is lower in the sky will refract violet into the viewer's eyes. This same pattern holds for all of the colors in between—orange, yellow, green, blue, and indigo. This effect creates the bands of color that the person sees when looking at the rainbow.

1. Circle the appropriate star to rate the headings, margins, and graphics on these pages: weak ★ ★ ★ ★ ★ strong

   Explain. Answers will vary. _____

   _____

2. What one design feature stands out for you? _____

   _____

3. Why is format and design important for a finished piece of writing? _____

   _____

   _____

Workplace

Design becomes especially important when you create a workplace document. Using correct format for letters, memos, and reports helps readers understand the content and projects a professional image.

LO4 Connecting the Process and the Traits

The writing process guides you as you form a piece of writing. The writing traits identify the key elements to consider in the writing. This chart connects the two. For example, it shows that during prewriting, you should focus on ideas, organization, and voice.

Process	Traits
Prewriting	**Ideas:** selecting a topic, collecting details about it, forming a thesis **Organization:** arranging the details **Voice:** establishing your stance (objective, personal)
Writing	**Ideas:** connecting your thoughts and information **Organization:** following your planning **Voice:** sounding serious, sincere, interested, . . .
Revising	**Ideas:** reviewing for clarity and completeness **Organization:** reviewing for structure/arrangement of ideas **Voice:** reviewing for appropriate tone
Editing	**Word choice:** checking for specific nouns, verbs, and modifiers **Sentences:** checking for smoothness and variety **Conventions:** checking for correctness
Publishing	**Design:** evaluating the format

Think Critically Team up with a classmate to discuss the following questions. Record your answers in the spaces provided below.

1. Which writing trait interests you the most? Why?

   Answers will vary.

2. Which step in the writing process should probably take the most time? Explain. Answers will vary.

3. How could you use this chart during a writing project? Answers will vary.

Monkey Business Images, 2010/used under license from www.shutterstock.com

Martin Child/Photographer's Choice/Getty Images

5

Prewriting

Who doesn't enjoy a spellbinding movie, an awesome concert, a nail-biting championship game? Witnessing great performances is one of life's great pleasures, and we remember each one for a long, long time.

What most of us don't think about is all the **behind-the-scenes** work that makes such a performance possible. Consider moviemaking. Among other things, there's a script to craft, a cast to pick, a filming location to select, a budget to establish, and on and on.

There is a lot of behind-the-scenes work that goes into effective writing, too. This work is called **prewriting**, and it consists of, among other things, selecting a writing idea, gathering details, and establishing a focus. In this chapter, you will learn about and practice important prewriting strategies.

What do you think?

Do you agree with the Edison quotation above? Why or why not? What percentages would you give to inspiration and perspiration?

Answers will vary.

Learning Outcomes

LO1 Analyze the assignment.

LO2 Select a topic.

LO3 Gather details about a topic.

LO4 Establish a writing focus.

LO5 Identify a pattern of organization.

LO6 Organize your information.

LO7 Review prewriting.

Vocabulary

behind-the-scenes
an idiom meaning "out of public view"

prewriting
the first step in the writing process, the preparation leading to the actual writing

LO1 Analyzing the Assignment

The writing process starts as soon as one of your instructors makes a writing assignment. And, of course, each assignment will call to mind many questions—the first one being *What will I write about?* You can use the STRAP strategy to help first answer your questions about the assignment and begin your preparation.

How the Strategy Works

The STRAP strategy consists of key questions that you answer about a writing assignment.

Subject:	What specific topic should I write about?
Type:	What form of writing (*essay, article, report*) will I use?
Role:	What position (*student, citizen, employee, family member*) should I assume?
Audience:	Who (*classmates, instructor, government official, parent*) is the intended reader?
Purpose:	What is the goal (*to inform, to analyze, to persuade, to share*) of the writing?

The STRAP Strategy in Action

Suppose you were given the following assignment in a sociology class:

> Write a personal essay or blog post in which you analyze a common expression that you find bothersome.

Here are the answers to the STRAP questions for this assignment:

Subject:	a common, bothersome expression
Type:	a personal essay or blog post
Role:	student
Audience:	classmates
Purpose:	to analyze

Ingvar Bjork, 2010/used under license from www.shutterstock.com

Respond Analyze the two writing assignments below using the STRAP strategy. Refer to the previous page to help you complete your work.

Think about it...

Assignment 1: In a letter to the editor suitable for a community publication, take a stand on a relevant environmental issue. Be sure to select an issue that deserves immediate attention.

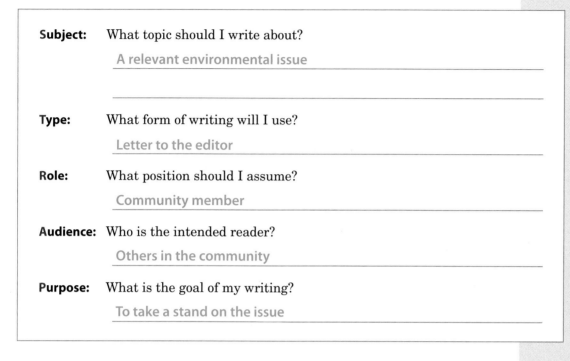

Subject:	What topic should I write about?	
	A relevant environmental issue	
Type:	What form of writing will I use?	
	Letter to the editor	
Role:	What position should I assume?	
	Community member	
Audience:	Who is the intended reader?	
	Others in the community	
Purpose:	What is the goal of my writing?	
	To take a stand on the issue	

Before you begin any writing assignment, you should also consider these issues:

- How the writing will be assessed
- How much time you have to complete your work
- How much importance the assignment carries

Assignment 2: As part of your take-home exam, write an informational essay explaining the main characteristics of a stress-related condition.

Subject:	What topic should I write about?	
	The main characteristics of a stress-related condition	
Type:	What form of writing will I use?	
	Informational essay	
Role:	What position should I assume?	
	Student taking an exam	
Audience:	Who is the intended reader?	
	The instructor	
Purpose:	What is the goal of my writing?	
	To explain / to get a good grade	

Tip

Look for key words in an assignment—*explain, compare, analyze*—so you know exactly what you should do.

LO2 Selecting a Topic

Novelist Kurt Vonnegut gave good advice for selecting a writing idea. He said, "Find a subject you care about and which you in your heart feel others should care about." Having strong feelings about a writing idea makes it that much easier to produce a finished piece that you feel good about and that your reader will enjoy.

The Narrowing Process

Typically, when your instructors make assignments, they provide a starting point for your topic search. Suppose you were given this assignment from page 37:

As part of your take-home exam, write an informational essay explaining the main characteristics of a stress-related condition.

The general subject area, "a stress-related condition," serves as the starting point for a topic search. However, to identify a topic limited enough for an informational essay, a writer would first have to narrow the subject, perhaps to stress-related *physical* conditions. With this focus in mind, a writer could then identify a specific topic like *dehydration*.

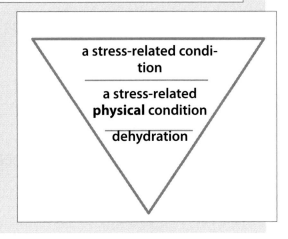

a stress-related condition

a stress-related **physical** condition

dehydration

Tip

When evaluating a possible topic, always ask yourself if it is too general or too specific for the assignment.

Choose Identify a specific writing idea by filling in the inverted pyramid for the following assignment. (Use the example above as a guide.)

Writing assignment: In a letter to the editor suitable for your community newspaper, take a stand on a relevant environmental issue.

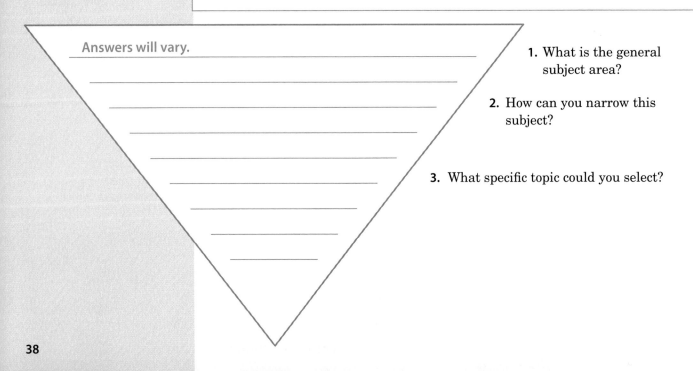

Answers will vary.

1. What is the general subject area?

2. How can you narrow this subject?

3. What specific topic could you select?

Selecting Strategies

If you have trouble identifying a specific topic for an assignment, first review your notes, text, and appropriate Web sites for ideas. Also consider using one of these selecting strategies:

■ **Clustering** Begin a cluster (or web) with a nucleus word or phrase related to the assignment. (The general subject area or narrowed subject would work.) Circle it and then cluster related words around it. As you continue, you will identify possible writing ideas.

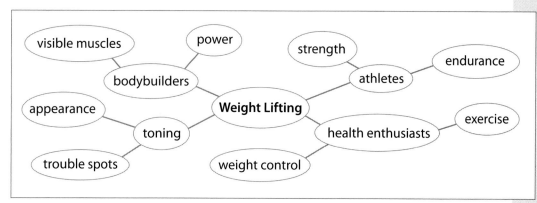

Extend

If one of the clustering ideas truly interests you, write freely about it for 5 minutes to see what you can discover.

■ **Listing** Freely list ideas as you think about your writing assignment. Keep going as long as you can. Then review your list for possible topics.

■ **Freewriting** Write nonstop for 5–10 minutes about your assignment to discover possible topics. Begin by writing down a particular thought about the assignment.

Practice Use one of the strategies explained above to identify possible topics related to one of the following general subject areas:

exercise	popular music	careers	freedom/rights	technology

Answers will vary.

_____

_____

_____

_____

_____

_____

_____

_____

_____

_____

_____

_____

"Knowledge is of two kinds. We know subjects ourselves, or we know where we can find information [about] it."

—Samuel Johnson

At this stage, the most important trait is ideas. Hunt them down, gather them up. More is better.

LO3 Gathering Details

Once you identify a specific writing topic, you need to gather information about it. Obviously, if you already know a lot about a topic, you may not need to do much collecting. For other topics, however, try the following strategies.

Gathering Your First Thoughts

Use one of these strategies to find out what you already know about the topic.

- **Clustering** Create a cluster with your specific topic as the nucleus word. (See page 39.)

- **Listing** List thoughts and ideas about your topic as well as questions about it that come to mind. Record as many ideas as you can.

- **Focused Freewriting** Write nonstop for at least 5–8 minutes to see what ideas you unlock about your topic. Do not stop to think what to say next; simply go where your writing takes you.

Collect Use one of the strategies above to gather your first thoughts about a topic you identified on page 39. (Select an activity different from the one you used on the previous page.)

Answers will vary.

Freerk Brouwer, 2010/used under license from www.shutterstock.com

Learning More About a Topic

For most college writing assignments, you will need more than your own thoughts to develop an effective piece of writing. To gather additional information about a topic, try these activities.

■ **Analyzing** Explore your topic from a number of different angles by answering the following questions:

> • What parts does my topic have? *(Break it down.)*
> • What do I see, hear, or feel when I think about my topic? *(Describe it.)*
> • What is it similar to and different from? *(Compare it.)*
> • What value does it have? *(Evaluate it.)*
> • How useful is it? *(Apply it.)*

■ **Imagining** Think creatively about a topic by writing and answering **unconventional** questions. Note these examples:

Writing About an Important Issue

> • What game would this issue enjoy?
> • What type of clothing does it resemble?

Writing About a Person

> • What type of food is this person like?
> • What type of book do you associate with the person?

Collect In the space provided below, use the analyzing or imagining strategy to discover more about the topic you worked with on page 40. (If you choose the imagining strategy, ask and answer at least three questions about the topic.)

Answers will vary.

WAC

Conducting **primary** and **secondary** research is another important way to learn more about a topic. Common methods of research include reading, exploring Web sites, consulting experts, and so on.

Vocabulary

unconventional
out of the ordinary, unusual, or offbeat

primary sources
original sources of information such as participating or interviewing

secondary sources
secondhand sources of information such as reading an article about a topic

LO4 Finding a Focus

Selecting a topic and collecting information about it are important first steps. But you still have some important decisions to make, the first of which involves finding a focus for your writing.

Choosing a Focus

An effective **focus** establishes boundaries for your writing and helps you decide what information to include about your topic. Let's say you are writing an editorial about the food in your school cafeteria and want to make the point that a huge amount of food is wasted during each meal. This particular feeling could serve as a focus for an editorial because it is reasonable, clear, and worthy of discussion.

Topic: food in your school cafeteria

Focus: amount of food that is wasted

Review Rate the effectiveness of each focus below by circling the appropriate star. Consider whether the focus is clear, reasonable, and worth developing. Then explain your rating.

1. **Topic:** sports drinks
   Focus: the best choice during long workouts

   weak ★ ★ ★ ★ ★ strong

   Answers will vary.
   _____

2. **Topic:** society's view of beauty
   Focus: seems good

   weak ★ ★ ★ ★ ★ strong

   Answers will vary.
   _____

3. **Topic:** cultural comparisons between Korea and the United States
   Focus: contrasting views on cleanliness

   weak ★ ★ ★ ★ ★ strong

   Answers will vary.
   _____

4. **Topic:** lacrosse
   Focus: a fast-growing sport

   weak ★ ★ ★ ★ ★ strong

   Answers will vary.
   _____

Forming a Thesis Statement

For most of your college writing, you will state your focus in a **thesis statement** (or in a **topic sentence** if you are writing a paragraph). A strong thesis statement highlights a special part or feature of a topic or expresses a particular feeling about it. You can use the following formula to write a thesis statement or topic sentence.

A specific topic	**+**	A particular feeling, feature, or part	**=**	An effective thesis statement or topic sentence
arrival of Hernán Cortés in Mexico		marked the beginning of the end of the Aztec empire		The arrival of Hernán Cortés in Mexico marked the beginning of the end of the Aztec empire.

Tip

Keep working with a thesis statement or topic sentence until it accurately expresses the main point of your writing.

Create Identify a focus and then write a topic sentence or thesis statement for each of the following assignments. The first one is done for you.

1. **Writing assignment:** Paragraph describing a specific style of clothing

   Specific topic: Zoot suit

   Focus: Popular during the swing era

   Topic sentence: The zoot suit *(specific topic)* became a popular fashion symbol in the swing era *(a particular feature)*.

2. **Writing assignment:** Paragraph explaining how to do something

   Specific topic: Using chopsticks

   Focus: Answers will vary.

   Topic sentence: _____

   _____

3. **Writing assignment:** Essay analyzing a popular type of cooking

   Specific topic: Cajun cooking

   Focus: Answers will vary.

   Thesis statement: _____

   _____

4. **Writing assignment:** Essay exploring technology and education

   Specific topic: Electronic textbooks

   Focus: Answers will vary.

   Thesis statement: _____

   _____

Vocabulary

thesis statement
the controlling idea in an essay, highlighting a special part or feature of a topic or expressing a particular feeling about it

topic sentence
the controlling idea in a paragraph

LO5 Choosing a Pattern of Organization

Once you've established a focus or thesis, you must identify an appropriate pattern of organization for the information you plan to include in your writing. Here's how to proceed:

1. **Study your thesis statement or topic sentence.** It will usually indicate how to organize your ideas. For example, consider the following thesis statement:

> Eating locally grown produce will improve the local economy.

This thesis suggests arranging the information by order of importance, because you are trying to prove a point.

2. Then **review the information you have gathered**. Decide which ideas support your thesis and arrange them according to the appropriate method of organization. For the thesis statement above, you would either arrange your reasons from most important to least important or vice versa.

Patterns of Organization

Listed below are some common patterns of organization that you will use in your writing.

Traits

Think about your purpose as you choose a pattern of organization. Often, your working thesis statement will suggest how you should organize details.

- Use **chronological order** (time) when you are sharing a personal experience, telling how something happened, or explaining how to do something.

- Use **spatial order** (location) for descriptions, arranging information from left to right, top to bottom, from the edge to the center, and so on.

- Use **order of importance** when you are taking a stand, arguing for or against something, and so on. Either work from most important to least important or the other way around.

- Use **deductive** organization if you want to follow your topic sentence or thesis statement with supporting reasons, examples, and facts.

- Use **inductive** organization when you want to present specific details first and conclude with your topic sentence or thesis statement.

- Use **compare-contrast** organization when you want to show how one topic is different from and similar to another one.

Study each of the following thesis statements. Then choose the method of organization that the thesis suggests. Explain each of your choices. The first one is done for you.

1. **Thesis statement:** The bottom of the hill in my childhood neighborhood offered everything young boys wanted.

   Appropriate method of organization: spatial order

   Explain: The thesis statement suggests that the writer will describe the area at the bottom of the hill, so using spatial order seems appropriate.

> "An effective piece of writing has focus. There is a controlling vision which orders what is being said."
> —Donald Murray

2. **Thesis statement:** In most cases, people involved in recreational fishing should use barbless hooks.

   Appropriate method of organization: Order of importance

   Explain: Order of importance works well for showing the reasons in the persuasive writing.

3. **Thesis statement:** To become an effective leader, a person must develop three main traits.

   Appropriate method of organization: Deductive / Order of importance

   Explain: Deductive organization provides supporting details for the main point. Order of importance features the main traits in order.

4. **Thesis statement:** Meeting my grandmother for the first time rates as one of my most important personal encounters.

   Appropriate method of organization: Chronological order

   Explain: Chronological order works well for narratives.

5. **Thesis statement:** (Choose one that you wrote on page 43.)

   Appropriate method of organization: Answers will vary.

   Explain:

LO6 Organizing Your Information

After selecting an appropriate method of organization, you're ready to arrange the supporting information for your writing. Here are three basic strategies for doing that:

- **Make a quick list** of main points.
- **Create an outline** or organized arrangement of main points and subpoints.
- **Fill in a graphic organizer**, arranging main points and details in a chart or diagram.

Using a Quick List

A quick list works well when you are writing a short piece or when your planning time is limited. Here is a quick list for a descriptive paragraph about zoot suits. (The list organizes details in spatial order, from top to bottom.)

Sample Quick List

Topic sentence: The zoot suit became a popular fashion symbol in the swing era.
- begins with a stylish wide-brimmed hat turned down
- follows with an oversized, tapered long jacket
- under jacket, a dress shirt with a tie
- pleated pants taper to narrow bottoms
- ends with two-tone, thin-soled shoes

Create Write a topic sentence and a quick list for a narrative paragraph about a funny, scary, or otherwise significant personal experience. Include four to six details in your list, organized chronologically.

Topic sentence: Answers will vary.

Quick list:

Answers will vary.

Using an Outline

An effective outline shows how ideas fit together and serves as an effective blueprint for your writing. You may be familiar with topic and sentence outlines, which follow specific guidelines: If you have a "I," you must have at least a "II." If you have an "A," you must have at least a "B," and so on. You can also make up your own kind of outline to put your ideas in order.

Sample Customized Outline

What follows is the first part of a **customized** outline that includes main points stated in complete sentences and supporting details stated as phrases.

WAC

For research papers and other formal pieces of writing, you may be expected to complete a traditional topic or sentence outline.

> **Thesis statement:** Humpback whales are by far the most playful and amazing whale species.
>
> 1. Most observers note that humpbacks appear to enjoy attention.
>   - lift bodies almost completely out of water (breaching)
>   - slap huge flippers against the water
>   - thrust their flukes (tail portion) straight out of water
>
> 2. Humpback whales "sing" better than other whales.
>   - song lasts up to 30 minutes
>   - head pointed toward ocean floor when singing
>   - seem to engage in group singing

Create Using the sample above as a guide, develop a customized outline for an essay about becoming a leader. A thesis statement and three main points are identified for you. Put the main points in the most logical order and make up two or three details to support each main point. (Work on this activity with a partner if your teacher allows it.)

Vocabulary

customized
changed or altered to meet individual or personal needs

Thesis statement: To become an effective leader, a person must develop three main traits.

Main points: Leaders must earn the respect of others. Leaders must display good work habits. Leaders must be confident.

1. Answers will vary. _____
   - _____
   - _____
   - _____

2. Answers will vary. _____
   - _____
   - _____
   - _____

3. Answers will vary. _____
   - _____
   - _____
   - _____

Using Graphic Organizers

Note: A cluster is another type of graphic organizer. (See page 39.)

Graphic organizers are charts or diagrams for arranging information. You can use them either to collect information or to organize the supporting facts and details you have already gathered.

Sample Graphic Organizers

Time Line Use for personal narratives to list actions or events in the order they occurred.

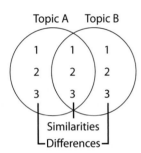

Subject: _____
1.
2.
3.
4.
5.

Process Diagram Use to collect details for science-related writing, such as the steps in a process.

Topic: _____

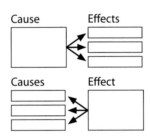

Step 1
Step 2
Step 3

Line Diagram Use to collect and organize details for academic essays.

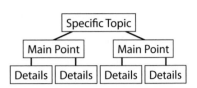

Specific Topic

Main Point   Main Point

Details Details Details Details

Venn Diagram Use to collect details to compare and contrast two topics.

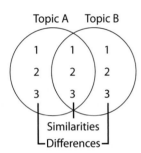

Topic A   Topic B
1   1   1
2   2   2
3   3   3
Similarities
Differences

Cause-Effect Organizer Use to collect and organize details for cause-effect essays.

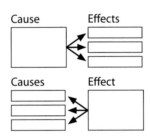

Cause   Effects

Causes   Effect

Problem-Solution Web Use to map out problem-solution essays.

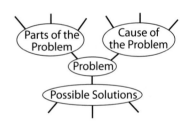

Parts of the Problem   Cause of the Problem
Problem
Possible Solutions

Create Use the appropriate graphic organizer to organize the information for an essay about becoming an effective leader.

Answers will vary.

_____

_____

_____

_____

_____

_____

L𝗢7 Reviewing Prewriting

Prewriting is the planning step in the writing process. Here is a quick overview of key prewriting strategies covered in this chapter.

▪ Using the STRAP Strategy

This strategy helps you to analyze the following parts of an assignment:

Subject:	What specific topic should I write about?
Type:	What form of writing will I use?
Role:	What position should I assume?
Audience:	Who is the intended reader?
Purpose:	What is the goal of the writing?

▪ Selecting a Topic

Choosing a topic for a paragraph or an essay involves selecting a specific topic related to the general subject area identified in the assignment.

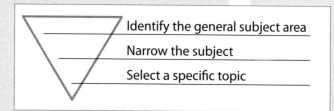

Identify the general subject area

Narrow the subject

Select a specific topic

▪ Gathering Details

Gathering involves discovering what you already know about a topic and what you need to find out. Here are some of the strategies that you can use to collect information.

- ▪ Listing
- ▪ Clustering
- ▪ Freewriting
- ▪ Analyzing
- ▪ Researching

▪ Forming a Topic Sentence or Thesis Statement

A topic sentence (for a paragraph) or a thesis statement (for an essay) provides a focus for writing. The following formula can be used to create either one.

A specific topic **+** A particular feeling, feature, or part **=** An effective topic sentence or thesis statement

▪ Organizing Information

A writer can use a quick list, an outline, or a graphic organizer to arrange supporting information for writing. Here is a list of common graphic organizers.

- ▪ Time Line
- ▪ Process Diagram
- ▪ Line Diagram
- ▪ Venn Diagram
- ▪ Cause-Effect Organizer
- ▪ Problem-Solution Web

Reflect Think of two of the most important things you learned about prewriting in this chapter. Explain your choices below.

Answers will vary.

Reinforcement

Complete these activities as needed to help you better understand key strategies covered in this chapter.

Analyze an Assignment Use the STRAP questions (see pages 36–37) to analyze the following writing assignment:

Write an informational blog essay suitable for a school publication in which you introduce the reader to an important new form of physical training.

Subject:	What topic should I write about?
	Answers will vary.
Type:	What form of writing will I use?
	Answers will vary.
Role:	What position should I assume?
	Answers will vary.
Audience:	Who is the intended reader?
	Answers will vary.
Purpose:	What is the goal of my writing?
	Answers will vary.

Selecting a Topic Select a specific topic for the following general subject area (or a subject of your own choosing): *green energy sources*. (See page 38.)

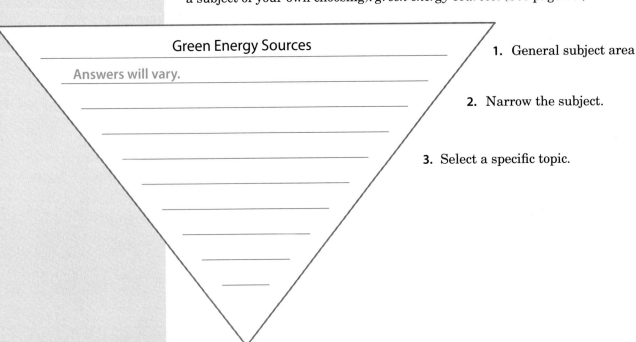

Green Energy Sources

Answers will vary.

1. General subject area

2. Narrow the subject.

3. Select a specific topic.

"Writing and rewriting is a constant search for what one is trying to say."

—John Updike

6

Drafting

The word "draft" as related to writing means "a preliminary or early version." So developing a draft is your first (or early) attempt to connect your thoughts about a writing idea. This writing should go smoothly if you have completed the necessary prewriting.

Writing a first draft becomes difficult only if you try to get everything just right. By all means, follow your plan and refer to your notes, but don't get bogged down with the wording of every single sentence. The purpose of drafting is simply to get your ideas on paper, to see what you have to work with. Think of a first draft as an **emerging** piece of writing.

The advice and strategies provided in this chapter will help you develop effective first drafts. Among other things, you'll learn how to avoid writer's block and how to include different levels of detail in your writing.

Learning Outcomes

LO1 Follow a drafting plan.

LO2 Form a meaningful whole.

LO3 Develop your ideas in different ways.

LO4 Use different levels of detail.

LO5 Review drafting.

visionandimagination.com/Flickr/Getty Images

Vocabulary

emerging
coming into being, still forming

What do you think?

How is writing, as John Updike says, "a constant search for what one is trying to say"?

Answers will vary.

LO1 Following a Drafting Plan

You're ready to develop a first draft once you have completed the necessary prewriting: gathering enough information about your topic, establishing a focus or thesis, and organizing your supporting ideas. (See pages 35–50.)

How you approach this writing is up to you. You may want to spend a little extra time with your opening paragraph. Then, with the beginning set, you may find it easier to complete the draft. Or you may want to get all your thoughts on paper right away—beginning, middle, and ending.

A Writing Plan

Use the following points as a guide when developing a first draft:

Traits

Focus first on your ideas, pouring them out into the paragraph or essay structure. As you work, let your voice develop.

- Focus on developing your ideas, not on trying to produce a final copy.

- Follow your prewriting and planning notes, but also feel free to include new ideas as they come to mind during your writing.

- Continue writing until you cover all of your main points or until you come to a logical stopping point.

- Express yourself honestly and sincerely, using other sources of information to support what you have to say.

- If you get stuck, employ one of the strategies covered on the next page.

React Explain the meaning of the following idea: *When writing a first draft, focus on producing possibilities rather than perfection.*

(AWV) Example: Instead of worry about finishing or reaching a certain

word count, the writer should focus on developing ideas, discovering new

connections, and expressing thoughts honestly and sincerely.

Avoiding Writer's Block

Writer's block is the condition of not knowing what to say in a piece of writing. You've got pen in hand or fingers on the keyboard, but the words just won't come. It's quite natural to experience writer's block every once in a while. But your chances of facing this condition are greatly reduced if you know a lot about your topic and have strong feelings about it. That is why prewriting is so important.

Strategies to Try

When writer's block strikes, try one of these strategies to get the words flowing.

1. **Write as if you are in a conversation with the reader.** Don't worry about sounding academic or correct. Instead, talk to the reader.

> Liz, I want to tell you about . . .

2. **Write nonstop in short, fluid bursts of 3–5 minutes.** Don't worry about making mistakes, or you'll stop the flow of ideas.

> Dehydration occurs when the body loses more fluids than it takes in. When the body doesn't have these fluids . . .

3. **Start in the middle.** The traditional Latin term for such a beginning is *in media res* (literally, "in the middle of things"). Don't waste time with building an elaborate opening. Just identify your topic or focus, if necessary, and go from there.

> I was an eyewitness to a drug deal at work. I was at work about 20 feet from the alley when I heard . . .

Speaking & Listening

Exchange your writing with a classmate and discuss the effectiveness of the strategy that you used.

Write Develop the first part of a draft in which you discuss something in everyday life that bugs you *(noisy eaters, sniffers and coughers, braggarts, barking dogs, and so on)*. Use one of the strategies above to get started.

Answers will vary.

"If you want to write, you must begin by beginning, continue by continuing, finish by finishing. This is the great secret. . . . Tell no one."

—Jack Heffron

LO2 Forming a Meaningful Whole

Novelist John Steinbeck said, "throw the whole thing on paper" when it comes to drafting. By "the whole thing," he meant connecting all of your thoughts and feelings about your topic. You should also think in terms of forming a meaningful whole, a complete draft with a beginning, a middle, and an ending. Until you do that, you won't know how to proceed.

Forming a meaningful whole for a paragraph means including a topic sentence, body sentences, and a closing sentence. For an essay, it means including an opening part (including a thesis statement), a number of supporting paragraphs, and a closing paragraph. (See pages 179–193.)

Graphically Speaking

The graphics below show the structure of both basic forms of writing.

Paragraph Structure

Topic Sentence

A **topic sentence** names the topic.

Detail Sentences

Detail sentences support the topic.

Closing Sentence

A **closing sentence** wraps up the paragraph.

Essay Structure

Opening Paragraph

The **opening paragraph** draws the reader into the essay and provides information that leads to a thesis statement. The thesis statement tells what the essay is about.

Middle Paragraphs

The **middle paragraphs** support the thesis statement. Each middle paragraph needs a topic sentence, a variety of detail sentences, and a closing sentence.

Closing Paragraph

The **closing paragraph** finishes the essay by revisiting the thesis statement, emphasizing an important detail, providing the reader with an interesting final thought, and/or looking toward the future.

Review Study each of these writing samples. Put a plus (+) next to the sample if it forms a meaningful whole; put a minus (−) next to the sample if it doesn't. Explain what is missing if you label a sample with a minus.

In first grade, I found out that circuses don't necessarily live up to all of the hype. We were going to the circus for our class trip, and I was really excited about it. Our class had worked for weeks on a circus train made of shoe boxes, and Carrie Kaske told me her mom had fainted when she saw the lion tamer perform. When the day finally came, the wonderful circus turned out to be one disappointment after another. We were so high up in the arena, I had a hard time making out the performers scurrying around in the three rings, and the lion tamer was so far away that I didn't even try to watch him. After the first half hour, all I wanted to do was buy a soda and a monkey-on-a-stick and get out of there. Of course, nothing in life is that easy. We weren't allowed to buy anything, so I couldn't have my souvenir. And instead of a cold soda, I had a carton of warm milk the room mothers had so thoughtfully brought along. I returned to school tired and a little wiser. I looked at our little circus train and thought I'd rather play with it than go to another circus.

1

5

10

Explanation: Answers will vary.

_____

_____

_____

_____

_____

Uncle John is normally a likeable man, except at family reunions when he appoints himself official photographer. He spends the whole time with one eye looking through a lens and the other scoping out potential victims for his photographs. Uncle John doesn't believe in candids, so he insists upon interrupting all activity to persuade his prey to pose for his pictures. In return he gets photographs of people arranged in neat rows smiling through clenched teeth. We've told him time and time again to chill out with the staged photos, but he continues to insist that we, "Come over here, so I can take your picture."

1

5

Explanation: Answers will vary.

_____

_____

_____

_____

_____

LO3 Developing Your Ideas

As you develop your ideas in a first draft, you are consciously or unconsciously describing, explaining, analyzing, comparing, defining, classifying, reflecting, and so on. Think of these as your basic writing moves.

In most pieces of writing, you will employ a variety of these moves. For example, when writing a descriptive paragraph or essay, you might *describe* a favorite place in your childhood, *reflect* on its importance, and then *compare* it to other places. In an essay of definition, you might *define* the subject, *compare* it to something similar, and *share* a brief story about it.

Basic Writing Moves

If for some reason you get stuck during a draft, try one or more of these moves to unlock some new ideas.

Narrating — sharing an experience or a story

Describing — telling how someone or something appears, acts, or operates

Explaining — providing important facts, details, and examples

Analyzing — carefully examining a subject or breaking it down

Comparing — showing how two subjects are similar and different

Defining — identifying or clarifying the meaning of a term

Reflecting — connecting with or wondering about

Evaluating — rating the value of something

Arguing — using logic and evidence to prove something is true

Workplace

Workplace documents
require each of these
moves in different
situations. That's because
each of these basic
writing moves reflects a
different purpose.

Respond Review the list of writing moves and then answer the following questions. Work on this activity with a classmate if your instructor allows it.

1. Which writing move would be very easy to employ and why?

   Answers will vary.

2. Which one would be very challenging to employ and why?

   Answers will vary.

3. Which of these writing moves have you used most often in the past?

   Answers will vary.

4. Which ones do you have little experience with and why?

   Answers will vary.

Identify Name the main writing move exhibited in each of these writing samples and briefly explain your choice.

1. My grandmother's rose garden was a symphony of color, and she was the conductor. Shears in hand, she would step confidently toward the rose trellis and spread her hands before the bushes. With a quick downbeat her sheers sliced through the sharp thorns. . . .

   Main writing move: _Describing_

   _____

   _____

2. Most people think of smokestacks and car fumes when they think of air pollution. However, individuals are exposed to more air pollution when they are inside their own homes than when they are outside. The biggest reason for in-home air pollution is the lack of air circulation. As people make their houses airtight, they trap dirty air inside. . . .

   Main writing move: _Explaining_

   _____

   _____

3. In *Native Son* by Richard Wright and *Equus* by Peter Schaffer, the two main characters, Bigger and Alan, struggle to take control of their lives. Both boys are entering adulthood and realize that what they do and say is severely restricted by the workplace, the media, and religion. Because of his family's desperate financial situation, Bigger is forced to . . . Alan experiences the pressure of working . . .

   Main writing move: _Comparing_

   _____

   _____

4. *Webster's* defines *eclectic* as selecting or choosing elements from different sources or systems. *Eclectic* implies variety. But what a great way of saying variety. Variety sounds so generic, so Brand X. But *eclectic* is rich with imaginative sound. . . .

   Main writing move: _Defining_

   _____

   _____

5. Throughout life, we meet individuals that move us, shape us, affect the way in which we go about life. Many people have influenced my life, but none more than Mr. Schneider, one of my high school English teachers. You always had a way of making me feel good about myself. The little talks you had with all of us brought up important things that I needed to hear. For example, . . .

   Main writing move: _Reflecting_

   _____

   _____

LO4 Using Levels of Detail

Your college instructors will require a certain level of **depth** in your writing. When you make a point, they will expect you to fully explain it with specific examples and details before you make another. The process of making important points and supporting them with details is at the core of most writing.

To write with depth, you should include different levels of detail. Here are three basic levels.

> **Level 1:** A **controlling sentence** names a topic (usually a topic sentence) or makes a main point.
>
> **Level 2:** A **clarifying sentence** explains a level 1 sentence.
>
> **Level 3:** A **completing sentence** adds details to complete the point.

Details in Action

The passage that follows uses three different levels of detail. Notice how each new level adds depth to the writing.

> **(Level 1)** Louis Braille, a blind French student, developed a system of communication for people with this handicap. **(Level 2)** The system consists of an alphabet using combinations of small raised dots. **(Level 3)** The dots are imprinted on paper and can be felt, and thus read, by running the fingers across the page.

Here's another passage containing a combination of the three levels of detail.

> **(Level 1)** Cartoons helped to shape the way I think. **(Level 2)** Most of them taught me never to take life too seriously. **(Level 3)** Many of the characters made their way through life with smirks on their faces. **(Level 3)** And all but a few of them seized the day, living for the moment. **(Level 2)** In an offhanded way, cartoons also provided me with a guide on how to act. **(Level 3)** Good versus evil was usually clearly defined. **(Level 3)** Other cartoons stressed the importance of loyalty.

Note:
To "complete" this passage, the writer could add another level of detail (level 4) by including references to specific cartoon characters.

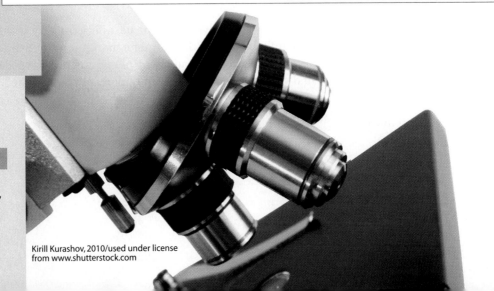

Kirill Kurashov, 2010/used under license from www.shutterstock.com

Identify Carefully read the following passage; then label its levels of details. (Work on this activity with a partner if your instructor allows it.)

(_____L1_____) Jim Thorpe was one of the star athletes representing the United States in the 1912 Summer Olympics in Sweden. (_____L2_____) Thorpe, a Native American, was an extremely versatile athlete, but he was especially skilled in track and field. (_____L3_____) He won a gold medal in the pentathlon, a track-and-field event of five parts. (_____L3_____) He also won a gold medal in the decathlon, a ten-part track-and-field event.

Create Write a brief paragraph about one of the following topics (or a topic of your own choosing): *types of friends, the causes of good (or poor) grades, your definition of courage, a favorite Web site, an interesting career.* Be sure that your paragraph includes at least five or six sentences.

Answers will vary.

Identify Label the sentences in your paragraph with the numbers 1, 2, or 3, depending on the level of detail they include. Then in the space below, explain where you could add even more detail in your paragraph.

Answers will vary.

"The writer writes with information, and if there is no information there will be no effective writing."
—Donald Murray

Note: Your paragraph will surely contain level 1 (the topic sentence) and level 2 details. It may also contain level 3 details to support or illustrate the nearest level 2 sentence, and so on.

LO5 Reviewing Drafting

Here is a quick review of drafting, the second step in the writing process.

Follow a drafting plan.

Focus on developing your ideas, not on producing a final copy, and use your prewriting and planning notes as a general writing guide.

Form a meaningful whole.

A complete first draft includes a beginning, a middle, and an ending. Until you complete all three parts, you won't know how to proceed.

A complete paragraph:	A complete essay:
Topic Sentence	Thesis Statement
Body	Supporting Paragraphs
Closing Sentence	Closing Paragraph

Develop your ideas in different ways.

In most pieces of writing, you will make a variety of writing moves. You may start with some **description**, add some **reflection**, then make a **comparison**, and so on.

Use different levels of detail.

In your college writing, you will be expected to include at least three different levels of detail.

Level 1: Controlling sentences name a topic or make a main point.
Level 2: Clarifying sentences explain level 1 sentences.
Level 3: Completing sentences add details to complete the point.

Reflect Look at the picture on the left. Then explain how writing a first draft is like or unlike traveling into the unknown with only a map as a basic guide.

Answers will vary.

Dave & Les Jacobs/Blend Images/
Getty Images

> "The first draft is the down draft—you just get it down.
> The second draft is the up draft—you fix it up."
> —Anne Lamont

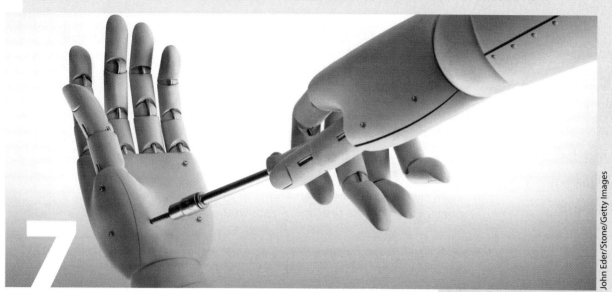

John Eder/Stone/Getty Images

7 Revising

Someone once said, "Hard writing makes easy reading." In this context, "hard writing" refers to writing that is strong from start to finish because of the effort put into it. And "easy reading" refers to the pleasurable (informative, stimulating) reading experience such writing provides.

Revising is really **synonymous** with hard writing because when you revise, you improve a first draft until it says what you want it to say. The amount of time spent revising is directly related to the quality of the finished piece. If you put in the necessary time, the results will please both you and your instructors.

This chapter provides guidelines and strategies for revising your first drafts. You will learn, among other things, the traits of strong writing and how they can direct the changes you make.

Learning Outcomes

LO1 Understand the revising process.

LO2 Recognize the traits of strong writing.

LO3 Understand the basic revising moves.

LO4 Learn the basics of peer reviewing.

LO5 Review the revising process.

Vocabulary

synonymous
alike in meaning or significance

What do you think?

In the quotation above, what does Lamont mean by the second draft being the "up draft"?

Answers will vary.

LO1 Understanding Revising

Revising is the process of improving your message—the ideas, organization, and voice in your writing. To make the best revising decisions, follow these guidelines:

■ **Take some time away from your writing.** This will help you see your first draft more clearly, and with a fresh outlook.

■ **Read your first draft a number of times,** silently and out loud, to get an overall impression of your work.

■ **Have a trusted peer or two react to your writing.** Their questions and comments will help you decide what changes to make.

■ **Check your overall focus or thesis.** Decide if it still works and if you have provided enough support for it.

■ **Then review your work, part by part.** Pay special attention to the opening, since it sets the tone of your writing, and the closing, since it serves as your final word on the topic.

■ **Plan a revising strategy** by deciding what you need to do first, second, and third.

> "It would be crazy to begin revising immediately after finishing the first draft, and counter to the way the mind likes to create."
> —Kenneth Atchity

Traits

Don't pay undue attention to surface issues—usage, spelling, punctuation—at this point in the process. Instead, focus on the ideas, organization, and voice of your writing.

Select Checkmark the statements below that clearly refer to revising. Work on this activity with a classmate if your instructor allows it.

   ✓   **1.** Reviewing the opening part to make sure it effectively introduces your thesis

       2. Looking up a specific comma rule

   ✓   **3.** Adding supporting details in one of your paragraphs

   ✓   **4.** Changing the order of two parts to strengthen your message

       5. Replacing one word with a synonym

   ✓   **6.** Deleting a part that is not really related to your thesis

       7. Moving a prepositional phrase from the beginning to the end of a sentence

   ✓   **8.** Rewriting the closing part so it more effectively **ties everything together**

Vocabulary

ties everything together
an idiom meaning "to make important connections"

tan4ikk, 2010/used under license from www.shutterstock.com

Review Carefully read the following first draft at least two times. As you read, notice parts that you like and parts that need work.

> When I was a kid, there was this guy who used to hang around all the time. My father built houses and fixed up people's kitchens and stuff. Ted worked for my father for about five years. He would work until he had enough money for awhile, then he'd come back for more work. Beats me what he did when he wasn't working for us. He scraped and painted and hauled equipment and other stuff. He was about 60 and lived in a Crown Victoria car with maroon leather upholstery. He had a funny patchwork quilt and lace pillows in the backseat. It looked just like a living room for little people. He even had a little TV that hooked up to his car's lighter. He parked the car on his brother's farm. On sunny days, he'd open up the trunk where he kept a cooler, take out a lawn chair, and sit there sipping root beer. I don't know what else he did. It was funny to see him pull up in his house every morning, his Cubs hat pushed back on his balding head. After a cup of coffee, he'd say, "Well I guess I need a few more chores, Tony."

(Line numbers: 1, 5, 10)

Respond React to this writing by answering the following questions. Try to make specific references to the text in your explanations.

Speaking & Listening
Discuss your responses with a classmate. Did each of you react in the same way to the writing?

1. Are the contents interesting and worth sharing? Explain.

   Answers will vary.

2. Does the paragraph begin with a clearly expressed topic sentence? If not, what is wrong with it?

   Answers will vary.

3. How effective is the middle part? Explain.

   Answers will vary.

4. Does the paragraph have a strong ending? Explain.

   Answers will vary.

5. If you were revising this paragraph, what change would you be sure to make?

   Answers will vary.

LO2 Recognizing Strong Writing

What traits or elements make writing strong? Most writing experts would agree on the list that follows. You will find this list helpful when you review and revise your first drafts. If your writing doesn't "pass" certain descriptors, then you should make the necessary improvements.

Tip

Here's another important point to consider: Does your writing meet the requirements of the assignment? To check for this, revisit your answers to the STRAP questions. (See pages 18–19.)

Traits

Word choice and sentence fluency are not as important as the other traits at this point. But they become very important during the editing step.

Revising Checklist

Ideas

☐ 1. Does an interesting and relevant topic serve as a starting point for the writing?

☐ 2. Is the writing focused, addressing a specific feeling about or a specific part of the topic? (The focus is usually expressed in the thesis statement.)

☐ 3. Are there enough specific ideas, details, and examples to support the thesis?

☐ 4. Overall, is the writing engaging and informative?

Organization

☐ 5. Does the writing form a meaningful whole—with beginning, middle, and ending parts?

☐ 6. Does the writing follow a logical pattern of organization?

☐ 7. Do transitions connect ideas and help the writing flow?

Voice

☐ 8. Does the writer sound informed about and interested in the topic?

☐ 9. In addition, does the writer sound sincere and genuine?

Word Choice

☐ 10. Does the word choice clearly fit the purpose and the audience?

☐ 11. Does the writing include specific words as much as possible?

Sentence Fluency

☐ 12. Are the sentences clear and do they flow smoothly?

☐ 13. Are the sentences varied in terms of their beginnings and length?

React Carefully read the passages below. Then answer the questions dealing with ideas in the first passage, organization in the second, and voice in the third.

Ideas As a wrestling cheerleader in high school, I witnessed many meets and many matches. But one meet, in particular, really stands out. Just as the meet against Parkview was to start, the 98-pounder from the other school came out on the mat. He was small and narrow in every way, except for his oversized shoulder muscles. But it wasn't the boy's build that shocked me as much as the way he moved. He could barely walk, even with the help of crutches. And once on the mat, he had to drag himself into position. We all were in awe; we couldn't believe that this boy was going to wrestle. The next year, he wrestled again. He lost both matches that I saw, but he didn't quit. . . .

1. Is the topic relevant and interesting? Explain.

   Yes. The idea of a disabled wrestler is interesting.

2. Is the writing focused? Explain.

   Yes. The writing focuses on one particular match.

3. Does the writing contain plenty of detail? Explain.

   Yes. The disabled wrestler is clearly described.

Organization Being vice president of the United States is not necessarily the road to the presidency. In fact, fewer than half of our country's vice presidents have gone on to the Oval Office. To be exact, 14 vice presidents have become president, while 30 have not. At certain times in our history, a number of consecutive terms have expired before a vice president followed a president into office. Between 1805 and 1837, seven consecutive terms passed before a vice president—Martin Van Buren—was elected president. . . .

1. What transitions are used in this passage? Underline two or three of them.

2. What do the transitions add to or do for the writing?

   Transitions connect ideas together and show how sentences relate to each other.

Voice The appearance of comets in the night skies has puzzled people for thousands of years. The first stargazers thought they were distant planets. Aristotle and the astronomers of his time theorized that they were the result of air escaping from the earth's atmosphere and catching fire. It wasn't until the fifteenth and sixteenth centuries that scientists realized comets were unique heavenly bodies. But that didn't change the long-standing myth that the sighting of a comet meant impending disaster. . . .

Does the writer sound informed about and interested in the topic? Explain.

Yes. The writer provides a variety of interesting details about the topic.

Word choice also shows interest.

"By the time I reach a fifth version, [my writing] begins to have its own voice."

—Ashley Bryan

LO3 Understanding the Basic Moves

You have four basic moves that you can make when you are ready to improve your writing. Depending on the situation, you can add, cut, rewrite, or reorder your ideas.

Add information if . . .

- your beginning or ending lacks **impact**.
- additional main points are needed.
- you need to clarify or complete a main point.

> The cinder-block walls of the living room were cold and unfriendly, and to a homesick girl they held no holiday promise. The forlorn evergreen stood in the corner like a misbehaving child . . .

Cut information if . . .

- it doesn't support or explain your main points (including your thesis).
- it simply repeats what has already been said.

> Quietly I tiptoed into the room, my eyes darting like water bugs, searching for lizards. ~~I looked left and right for the bugs.~~ What a strange, silent Christmas it was going to be. . . .

Rewrite information if . . .

- it isn't clear and easy to follow.
- the level of language (voice) doesn't fit with the rest of the writing.

> Slowly I crept toward the electrical outlet and inserted the plug. ~~To my utter amazement the lights illuminated the room quite impressively.~~ A thousand brilliant lights danced upon the tree. And in the darkness beyond the window . . .

Reorder information if . . .

- it is out of logical order.
- it would make a clearer impact in another spot.

> The villagers stood hand in hand by the living room window. I found out that I wasn't alone. I could see the wonder and delight in each of their eyes.

Test Taking

For some prompted writing tasks, you may be expected to revise your work. For others, you may not. Make sure you understand the way the test will be graded.

66

Write Develop the first draft of a paragraph in which you describe a favorite class or instructor or a favorite job or employer. Include at least six or seven sentences.

Answers will vary.

React Evaluate your writing using pages 64 and 65 as a guide. Then, in the space provided below, identify two or three changes that you would make to improve the paragraph.

1. Answers will vary.

2.

3.

> "What you say must be honest, but you don't have to say everything you feel."
>
> —Ken Macrorie

Working with your writing peers may be one of the most important strategies that you can use to improve your writing. So get into the habit of sharing your work.

Andresr, 2010/used under license from www.shutterstock.com

constructively
in a helpful manner

LO4 Reviewing with Peers

It always helps to have your peers review your work during the revising process. Their reactions can help you find ways to strengthen your writing. The following guidelines tell you how to conduct peer-review sessions, whether you are working with one partner or in a small group.

The Role of the Writer

1. **Have a complete piece of writing to share.** Make a copy for each group member.

2. **Set the scene** by making a few introductory comments about your work. But don't say too much.

3. **Read your work out loud.** Don't stop for explanations; just read the text as clearly as you can.

4. **Afterward, listen carefully to the reactions,** and answer any questions. Don't try to defend yourself or your writing. Just listen and take notes on important points.

5. **Ask for help** if you have concerns about certain parts.

The Role of the Listeners/Responders

1. **Pay careful attention during the reading.** Take brief notes if you think it would help. Then read the text silently.

2. **React positively and constructively.** Instead of saying "Nice start," for example, say something more exact, such as "Sharing that dramatic story in the beginning really made me take notice."

3. **Comment on specific things you noticed.** Saying, "It would be good to add more style to your writing" isn't very helpful. But saying, "Many of the sentences start in the same way" gives the writer a specific idea for improving the writing.

4. **Question the writer** if you are unsure of something. "What is the purpose of . . . ?" or "Why did you start the . . . ?"

5. **Show that you are really interested in helping.** Have at least one positive comment and one suggestion to offer. Also listen to others' comments and add to them.

Share Following the guidelines on the previous page, conduct a peer-responding session for the first draft you wrote on page 67. (Work with one partner or a small group of your peers.) List one or two helpful suggestions that were made about your work.

1. Answers will vary.
_____
_____
_____

2. _____
_____
_____
_____

Revise In the space below, write another draft of your paragraph based on your own review and the response of your peers.

Answers will vary.
_____
_____
_____
_____
_____
_____
_____
_____
_____
_____
_____
_____
_____
_____
_____
_____
_____
_____
_____

LO5 Reviewing Revision

Complete these activities as needed to help you better understand the revising process.

Understanding Reviewing and Revising Number these revising steps so they are in the correct order. (See page 62.)

> <u>2</u> Read your first draft a number of times.
>
> <u>1</u> Take some time away from your writing.
>
> <u>6</u> Lastly, plan your revising strategy.
>
> <u>3</u> Have a trusted peer or two react to your writing.
>
> <u>4</u> Check your overall focus or thesis.
>
> <u>5</u> Then review your work, part by part.

Recognizing Strong Writing Donald Murray said that without good information there can be no good writing. So how can you tell if a piece of writing contains good ideas or information? Name two things that you will find. (See pages 64–65.)

1. Answers will vary.

2. _____

Understanding the Basic Moves Fill in the blank with the appropriate revising move—adding, cutting, rewriting, or reordering information—for each of the following situations. (See page 66.)

Adding _____   1. A main point needs more support.

Rewriting _____   2. The language doesn't fit the rest of the draft.

Cutting _____   3. An idea is unrelated to your focus or thesis.

Reviewing with Peers The first responsibility of a peer reviewer is to carefully listen to or read a writer's draft. What are two additional responsibilities for a reviewer? (See page 68.)

- React positively and constructively

- Comment on specific things you noticed

- Question the writer

- Show that you are really interested in helping

masahiro Makino/Flickr/Getty Images

"Grammar is the piano I play by ear."
—Joan Didion

8

Editing

Editing is the process of checking the style and accuracy of your writing. You're ready to focus on this step once you have completed all of your major revisions. Think of editing as the process of **fine-tuning** your writing before sharing it.

The first part of this chapter covers style, with special attention given to word choice and sentence **fluency**. The second part covers correctness, offering strategies for finding and fixing errors, an explanation of the common editing symbols, and information about editing academic writing. When you are ready to edit for correctness, be sure to refer to pages 194–394 in *WRITE 1* for explanations and examples of the rules or conventions of the language.

What do you think?

How can grammar be "played by ear"?

Answers will vary.

Learning Outcomes

LO1 Understand the basics of word choice.

LO2 Learn about sentence fluency.

LO3 Learn how to check for correctness.

LO4 Edit academic writing.

LO5 Review editing.

Vocabulary

fine-tuning
making small changes or adjustments

fluency
smooth expression or flow of ideas

LO1 Understanding Word Choice

When it comes to word choice, the first **rule of thumb** is to use words that fit the audience and purpose of your writing. For example, the words used in a personal essay would not necessarily be appropriate for a report or research paper.

Pay special attention to the nouns and verbs you use since they carry and influence much of the meaning and style of your writing. The information that follows serves as a guide to using nouns and verbs.

Using Specific Nouns

Nouns name people, places, ideas, and objects, and they range from the very general (*man* or *drink*) to the very specific (*Barack Obama* or *mango juice*). Notice how the nouns become more specific in the chart below. When it comes to your writing, specific nouns almost always work better than general ones.

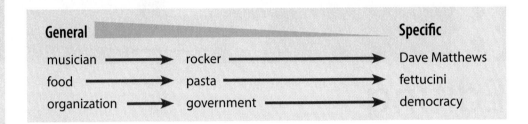

General		Specific
musician	→ rocker →	Dave Matthews
food	→ pasta →	fettucini
organization	→ government →	democracy

Complete Fill in the blanks below with nouns that become more specific.

General ————————————————————— Specific

People:

Answers will vary. _____ _____

_____ _____ _____

Objects:

_____ _____ _____

_____ _____ _____

Ideas:

_____ _____ _____

_____ _____ _____

Using Specific Verbs

Action verbs tell what is happening in a sentence. A specific action verb like *examine* will usually work better than a general one like *look* because it is more exact. Listed below are a few additional **synonyms** for *look*; each one is more exact and interesting.

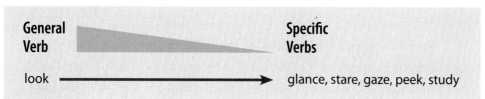

General Verb	Specific Verbs
look →	glance, stare, gaze, peek, study

Complete List three or four specific verbs for two of the following general verbs: *give, laugh, think,* or *make*. Use the example above as a guide.

General verb:	Answers will vary.	Specific verbs:
General verb:		Specific verbs:

"It is with words as with sunbeams—the more they are condensed, the deeper they burn."
—Robert Southey

Watch for "Be" Verbs

Overusing "be" verbs (*is, are, was,* and *were*) can weaken your writing, so always look for ways to use action verbs.

Sentence with a "be" verb:

Maria Posada **is** the supervisor of the nursing trainees.

Sentence with an action verb:

Maria Posada **supervises** the nursing trainees.

Revise Rewrite each of the following sentences so that it contains a specific action verb rather than a linking verb. (You can often form an action verb from another word in the sentence.)

Sentence with a "be" verb: Ben Franklin was a promoter of free access to books.

Sentence with an action verb: Ben Franklin promoted free access to books.

Sentence with a "be" verb: Scooters are a dominant feature of modern European traffic.

Sentence with an action verb: Scooters dominate modern European traffic.

Extend

Circle the main verbs that you used in the sentences that you wrote for the Extend feature on the previous page. Replace at least two or three of these verbs (including linking verbs) with more specific action verbs.

Vocabulary

synonyms
words having similar meaning

LO2 Writing Fluent Sentences

Your writing will be stylistic if the sentences are fluent, or flow smoothly from one idea to the next. To achieve sentence fluency, vary your sentences in terms of their length and beginnings. Note how the sentences in the following passage flow smoothly:

Traits

Sentences that all sound the same become too predictable and are actually hard to read.

> Fred's Sandwich Shop opens in the back onto an alley. Last night, while cutting veggies in the kitchen, I happened to see a man in a tailored suit and a typical looking townie in a T-shirt and jeans meet in the alley behind our dumpster. They were not more than 20 feet away from me. Without any real caution, the townie handed the man a roll of bills, and in return, received a package wrapped in brown paper. A quick examination of the goods and a simple nod signaled the end of the transaction, and they both went their separate ways. This whole drug deal took less than 45 seconds.
>
> **Discussion:** The passage reads smoothly because, among other things, no two sentences start in the same way, and the sentences vary in length from 9 to 35 words.

Create In the space provided below, describe an exciting or surprising event that you witnessed. Try to write at least five or six sentences.

Answers will vary.

Phecsone, 2010/used under license from www.shutterstock.com

Review Circle the first two or three words in each of your sentences. Also count the number of words in each sentence. Then decide if you need to vary some of the beginnings or lengths of your sentences to make them more fluent. If so, rewrite the passage on your own paper.

A Closer Look at Fluency

One way to achieve sentence fluency is to combine series of shorter sentences into longer ones that read more smoothly. Combining sentences is one of the keys to becoming a better writer, helping you to present your ideas in a more **sophisticated** way.

Read Study the three short sentences that follow. Then notice how the ideas flow more smoothly when they are combined.

Shorter Sentences

Last weekend, Moira prepared lunches at Brighton Hall.
Brighton Hall is a local community center.
The lunches consisted of soup and sandwiches.

Combined Sentence

Last weekend, Moira prepared lunches of soup and sandwiches at Brighton Hall, a local community center.

Create Follow the directions below to combine the following sentences in various ways. (Add, delete, or change words as necessary.)

1. There was a power failure.
2. The power failure hit the school.
3. The power failure hit without warning.
4. The failure left the lower-level classes completely in the dark.
5. The failure left the tech-ed classes without operable equipment.
6. The failure left the cafeteria with half-cooked food.

1. Combine the first three sentences.

   A power failure hit the school without warning.

2. Combine the last three sentences.

   The failure left the lower-level classes completely in the dark, the tech-ed classes without operable equipment, and the cafeteria with half-cooked food.

3. Combine sentences three and four using the word *which* to introduce one of the ideas.

   The power failure, which left the lower-level classes completely in the dark, hit without warning.

4. Complete this sentence:

   When the power failure hit, Answers will vary.

"Putting style in almost always clutters up writing; removing clutter gives writing style."
—William Zinsser

Traits

If you pay too much attention to correctness too soon, you may ignore the most important part of your writing—your ideas. Think ideas before conventions, always.

LO3 Checking for Correctness

You're ready to focus on correctness once you have edited your writing for style. When editing for correctness, you check your writing for punctuation, capitalization, spelling, and grammar errors.

Strategies for Editing

There are many different types of errors to look for. This means you must examine your writing word for word and sentence by sentence. The following strategies will help you edit thoroughly and effectively.

- If possible, first set your writing aside for a day or two.
- Work with a clean copy of your writing, one that incorporates your revisions and stylistic changes.
- Check one element at a time—spelling, punctuation, subject-verb agreement, and so on.
- For spelling, start at the bottom of the page to force yourself to look at each word. (Remember that your spell-checker will not catch all types of spelling errors.)
- For punctuation, circle all the marks to force yourself to look at each one.
- Read your work aloud at least once, noting any errors as you go along.
- Refer to a list of common errors or a personal list of errors you often make.
- Have an editing guide (see pages 194–394 in this text) and a dictionary handy.
- Also ask a trusted classmate to edit your work.

Respond In the space provided below, identify three of these strategies that you think would be most helpful. Explain your choices. Afterward, share responses with your classmates.

Answers will vary.

Using Editing Symbols

You, as well as an instructor or a writing tutor, can use editing symbols to mark errors in your writing. Listed below are some of the most common symbols.

Symbol	Meaning	Symbol	Meaning
C̲ chicago	Capitalize a letter.	first my ∧ speech	Insert here.
F̶all	Make lowercase.	∧ ∧ ∧	Insert a comma, a colon, or a semicolon.
Mr⊙Ford	Insert (add) a period.	∨ ∨ ∨	Insert an apostrophe or quotation marks.
Sp. or (recieve)	Correct spelling.	? ! ∧ ∧	Insert a question mark or an exclamation point.
Mr. Lott ~~he~~	Delete (take out) or replace.	(possible͡worst)	Switch words or letters.

Edit Use the editing symbols above to mark the errors in the following piece and show how they should be corrected. The first error has been marked for you.

> When we lived on Maple s̲treet, we had a neighbor who seemed to have two   1
>
> personalities ∧ his name was Mr. Bunde. I worked for him one S̶ummer while I
>
> was in grade school, cutting his lawn and doing other yard work. After a few
>
> months of working for him ∧ I'd had more than enough. In general, he was a nice
>
> enough guy ∧ and he ~~likes~~ liked to joke around some of the time. Unfortunately, it   5
>
> was hard to tell if he was really kidding or if his mood was suddenly changing.
>
> When he was in one of his moods ∧ I couldn't do anything (rite). Sometimes ∧ he
>
> would complain about other neighbors ∧ and he would expect me to agree with
>
> him, even though he (new) they were my friends. I not only ~~have~~ had to concentrate
>
> on my work ∧ but I also had to be on my guard, trying to predict Mr. Bunde ∨ s   10
>
> mood. Why did I have to work for him ? ∧

Traits

The second part of *WRITE 1* provides grammar, punctuation, capitalization, and spelling practice to help you improve your editing skills.

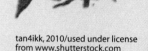

LO4 Editing Academic Writing

Everyday writing may have an informal style, but academic writing should have a semiformal writing style. The following information identifies the basics of these two styles.

Informal

This is a somewhat relaxed style of writing often used when communicating via e-mail, letters, blogs, narratives, personal essays, and so on. This style is often signaled by . . .

- **contractions** (*I'll, she's, can't*),
- **popular expressions** (*Can you believe that!*),
- **cliches** (*blew his top*),
- **first-person references** (*It took me a long time . . .*), **and**
- **occasional fragments** (*Not if I can help it*).

Semiformal

This is a careful, all-purpose style of writing that you will use in most of your academic essays, articles, reports, and papers. This style is signaled by . . .

- **few contractions** (*A strict vegetarian will not . . .*),
- **carefully chosen words** (*The recycled lumber can withstand . . .*),
- **few, if any, cliches,**
- **few, if any, first-person references** (*The election proved . . .*) **and**
- **carefully constructed sentences.**

Insight

The level of language used by your friends may be much different from the level of language expected in academic writing. Develop the ability to shift into semiformal language as needed.

Extend

On your own paper, write the same brief message twice, using a different writing style for each version. You can choose between these three styles: very personal, informal, or semiformal.

Respond Decide if each of the following passages demonstrates an informal or a formal style of writing. Explain each of your choices.

1. Science fiction is not always, as some people believe, a second-rate, comic-book literary **genre**.

    _____ Informal   ✓ Semiformal

    The sentence is carefully constructed, with well-chosen words and no contractions.

2. We were really scared when the cops pulled us over on I-65. Who wouldn't be?

    ✓ Informal   _____ Semiformal

    The example includes first-person references and a popular expression.

3. Elderly people in Milwaukee often struggle to pay their utility bills during the coldest months of the year. One utility advocacy group reports that . . .

    _____ Informal   ✓ Semiformal

    This carefully constructed example could be a part of a newspaper article.

    It includes no contractions or cliches.

cliches
overused expressions or ideas, such as *sharp as a tack*

genre
category, type, or class

LO5 Reviewing Editing

Complete these activities as needed to help you better understand the editing process.

Word Choice In the space provided below, write two or three sentences about your favorite restaurant. Afterward, underline the nouns and circle the verbs in your writing. Replace any general words with more specific ones. (See pages 72–73 for help.)

> Answers will vary.

Sentence Fluency Explain, in the space below, two ways that you can vary your sentences and make them read more smoothly. (See pages 74–75 for help.)

> Answers will vary.

Editing for Correctness Edit the following sentences using the symbols on page 77 to mark the errors and show how they should be corrected.

have you ever traveled to another Country I no from personal experience that it can be an exciting experience. I spent six moths in london England.

Academic Writing Style There are two basic writing styles—informal and semiformal. Explain the differences between the two styles. (See page 78 for help.)

Informal style

This relaxed style of writing is marked by first-person references, contractions, popular expressions, and so on. It is used for casual communication.

Semiformal style

This careful, purposeful style of writing is found in academic essays and articles. The style uses few contractions, cliches, or first-person references.

"Art is the imposing of a pattern on experience, and our aesthetic enjoyment is recognition of the pattern."

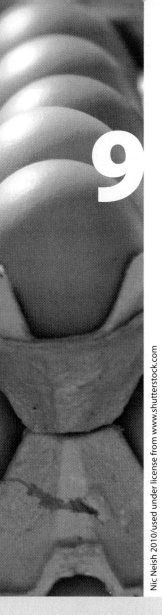

9 Description, Illustration, and Definition

Consider the lowly egg carton. It has a very simple pattern—a series of hollows designed to preserve eggs in their dozens. A milk carton has a different pattern—rectangular, with a cardboard spout for pouring. And a Chinese-food carton has another pattern, a single piece of waxed cardboard folded into a trapezoid and clasped at the top.

Paragraphs have different patterns, too, based on what they hold. Some paragraphs hold descriptions, others illustrations, and others definitions. This chapter provides models and prompts to help you develop these basic patterns of paragraphs. Later chapters guide you through developing even more advanced patterns. Each is designed to hold a certain kind of thinking.

What do you think?

What would happen to eggs in a milk carton, or Chinese food in an egg carton, or milk in a cigarette carton?

Answers will vary.

Learning Outcomes

LO1 Analyze a descriptive paragraph.

LO2 Write a descriptive paragraph.

LO3 Analyze an illustration paragraph.

LO4 Write an illustration paragraph.

LO5 Analyze a definition paragraph.

LO6 Write a definition paragraph.

LO7 Review description, illustration, and definition.

LO1 Analyzing a Descriptive Paragraph

A descriptive paragraph paints a word picture. It uses strong sensory details—
sights, sounds, smells, tastes, and textures—to describe its subject. Descriptive
writing is often used in narratives.

Read/React Read the following descriptive paragraph and answer the questions
at the bottom of the page.

A Quixotic Statue

The **topic sentence** identifies the subject and expresses the writer's thought about it.

Body sentences provide an overall impression and specific sensory details.

The **closing sentence** describes the importance of the object.

The **Don Quixote** statuette my dad gave me isn't worth much. *1*
It stands about a foot high and depicts a gaunt old man in battered
armor sitting astride a swayback horse. The helmet on Quixote's
head is dented, its visor bent above bushy eyebrows, squinting
eyes, a wide wedge of a nose, and a rampant mustache and beard. *5*
His breastplate and shield are so worn that whatever emblems
they once held have been pummeled into obscurity. The statue
looks like rough-cast pewter, but when I accidentally knocked it
over, it smashed on the floor, revealing itself to be painted plaster.
I scooped up the jaggy chunks and did my best to stick them back *10*
together. Now seams of seeping glue and off-color paint crisscross
the figure, and electrician's tape clings to the bent lance. Despite
these flaws, despite dust and cobwebs, Quixote still manages to
stare out with a look of inexhaustible hope. The statuette wasn't
worth much when Dad gave it to me, and it's worth even less now. *15*
But somehow, after all this time and all this glue and tape, the
statue means even more to me.

1. What does the paragraph describe?

A foot-high Don Quixote statue

2. Write down key details from the model:

Sights	Sounds	Textures
one foot high	pummel	bushy eyebrows
old man	smash	worn-down armor
swayback horse		jagged chunks
large beard and		
mustache		
off-color paint		

3. How does the writer organize the details of this description?

The writer first identifies the object and expresses a thought about it.

Next, the writer describes the object before reflecting on the importance

of the object.

Vocabulary

quixotic
idealistic; unrealistic

Don Quixote
(Don Kee-HOE-tee)
an idealistic man who
thinks he is a knight
of old and battles
windmills, thinking
they are dragons;
from Cervantes' book
of the same name

LO2 Writing a Descriptive Paragraph

To write your own descriptive paragraph, follow these guidelines for prewriting, writing, revising, and editing.

Prewriting

List/Select Under each category, list favorite objects. Then choose one object you know well and could describe in a paragraph.

Clothes	Foods	Decorations
Answers will vary.		

Gather Write down key sensory details about the object you have chosen.

See	Hear	Smell	Taste	Touch
Answers will vary.				

Create Answer the following questions to create a topic sentence for your essay.

1. What is your topic? Answers will vary.

2. What interesting thought or feeling do you have about it?

3. Write a sentence that names the topic and expresses the thought or feeling.

Write Create a first draft of your description paragraph, following the paragraph outline below:

Paragraph Outline

Topic Sentence: Begin with the topic sentence you wrote on the previous page.

Body Sentences: Write a sentence that provides an overview of the favorite object. Follow with sentences that provide sensory details in a reasonable order (top to bottom, left to right, outside to inside).

Closing Sentence: Write a sentence that sums up the object's meaning to you.

Answers will vary.

Revising

Revise Read your paragraph and, if possible, have someone else read it as well. Then use the following checklist to guide your revision. Keep revising until you can check off each item in the list.

Ideas

☐ **1.** Does my paragraph describe an interesting object?

☐ **2.** Do I provide an overview of the object?

☐ **3.** Do I include a variety of sensory details—sights, sounds, smells, and so on?

Organization

☐ **4.** Does my topic sentence name the object and provide an interesting thought or feeling about it?

☐ **5.** Do the body sentences provide sensory details in a logical order (top to bottom, left to right, outside to inside)?

☐ **6.** Does my closing sentence tell what the object means to me?

Voice

☐ **7.** Does my writing voice reflect the object's meaning to me?

☐ **8.** Does my voice engage the reader?

Editing

Edit Create a clean copy of your paragraph and use the following checklist to check it for words, sentences, and conventions.

Words

☐ **1.** Have I used specific nouns and verbs? (See page 103.)

☐ **2.** Have I used more action verbs than "be" verbs? (See page 73.)

Sentences

☐ **3.** Have I varied the beginnings and lengths of sentences? (See pages 226–231.)

☐ **4.** Have I combined short choppy sentences? (See page 232.)

☐ **5.** Have I avoided shifts in sentences? (See page 278.)

☐ **6.** Have I avoided fragments and run-ons? (See pages 261–266, 270–271.)

Conventions

☐ **7.** Do I use correct verb forms (*he saw,* not *he seen*)? (See pages 320, 324.)

☐ **8.** Do my subjects and verbs agree (*she speaks,* not *she speak*)? (See pages 245–260.)

☐ **9.** Have I used the right words (*their, there, they're*)?

☐ **10.** Have I capitalized first words and proper nouns and adjectives? (See page 386.)

☐ **11.** Have I used commas after long introductory word groups? (See page 358.)

☐ **12.** Have I carefully checked my spelling?

LO3 Analyzing an Illustration Paragraph

An illustration paragraph provides examples to support a main point. Many types of college writing require the use of illustrations and examples.

Read/React Read the following illustration paragraph and answer the questions at the bottom of the page.

The Elsewhere Generation

The **topic sentence** provides the main point.

Body sentences give examples that illustrate the main point.

The **closing sentence** recasts the main point in an interesting way.

With their immersion in social media, **millennials** are being called the "Elsewhere Generation." Quite often, a millennial will ignore people in the same room while virtually interacting with people elsewhere. A teenage boy plays a massively multiplayer online role-playing game with people in a different country while his brothers beg him to play basketball outside. A group of friends sits in a cafe, but instead of talking to each other, they are texting people who are miles away. A student is listening to a lecture while typing a status update on Facebook. Two joggers run side by side, but each is talking on a headset to someone elsewhere. This constant **multitasking** means that millennials can interact with many people in many places at once. Sometimes, though, millennials seem to be everywhere and nowhere at the same time. *1* *5* *10*

1. What is the main point of the paragraph?

   Millennials are connected with people around the world, but often ignore people close to them.

2. List examples that illustrate the main point:

   Example A: A teenage boy playing a role-playing game with a foreigner

   Example B: A group texting others while they sit with each other

   Example C: A student on Facebook during a lecture

   Example D: Two joggers running together but talking to others on headsets

3. How does the writer sum up the main point of this paragraph?

   Millennials interact with many people in many places at once but sometimes ignore what's going on in front of them.

Bakaleev Aleksey/iStockphoto.com

Vocabulary

millennial
a person born between the mid 1970s and the early 2000s

multitasking
doing many things simultaneously

L○4 Writing an Illustration Paragraph

To write your own illustration paragraph, follow these guidelines for prewriting, writing, revising, and editing.

Prewriting

Answer Respond to the following questions to select a topic and gather details about it.

1. What is the best thing about your generation? _Answers will vary._

2. What is the worst thing about your generation? _Answers will vary._

3. How is your generation unique? _Answers will vary._

4. Which observation above could you write about in an illustration paragraph?
   Answers will vary.

5. Considering your chosen observation, write a topic sentence that states this idea and expresses a thought or feeling about it.
   Answers will vary.

6. Write four examples that illustrate the main point you have made in your topic sentence.
   Example A: _Answers will vary._

   Example B: _____

   Example C: _____

   Example D: _____

Write Create a first draft of your illustration paragraph, following the paragraph outline below:

Paragraph Outline

Topic Sentence: Begin with the topic sentence you wrote on the previous page.

Body Sentences: Write sentences that provide examples that illustrate the main point you made about your generation. Use transitions as needed to connect your ideas.

Closing Sentence: Write a sentence that sums up your main point or recasts it in an interesting way.

Answers will vary.

Revising

Revise Read your paragraph and, if possible, have someone else read it as well. Then use the following checklist to guide your revision. Keep revising until you can check off each item in the list.

Ideas

- ☐ **1.** Do I make an interesting observation about my generation?
- ☐ **2.** Do I provide a number of examples that illustrate the observation?

Organization

- ☐ **3.** Does my topic sentence state the observation and a thought or feeling about it?
- ☐ **4.** Do the body sentences give examples that illustrate my main point?
- ☐ **5.** Does my closing sentence reflect on my main point?

Voice

- ☐ **6.** Does my writing voice sound knowledgeable and interested?
- ☐ **7.** Do I share ideas in a way that engages the reader?

Editing

Edit Create a clean copy of your paragraph and use the following checklist to check it for words, sentences, and conventions.

Words

- ☐ **1.** Have I used specific nouns and verbs? (See page 103.)
- ☐ **2.** Have I used more action verbs than "be" verbs? (See page 73.)

Sentences

- ☐ **3.** Have I varied the beginnings and lengths of sentences? (See pages 226–231.)
- ☐ **4.** Have I combined short choppy sentences? (See page 232.)
- ☐ **5.** Have I avoided shifts in sentences? (See page 278.)
- ☐ **6.** Have I avoided fragments and run-ons? (See pages 261–266, 270–271.)

Conventions

- ☐ **7.** Do I use correct verb forms (*he saw,* not *he seen*)? (See pages 320, 324.)
- ☐ **8.** Do my subjects and verbs agree (*she speaks,* not *she speak*)? (See pages 245–260.)
- ☐ **9.** Have I used the right words (*their, there, they're*)?
- ☐ **10.** Have I capitalized first words and proper nouns and adjectives? (See page 386.)
- ☐ **11.** Have I used commas after long introductory word groups? (See page 358.)
- ☐ **12.** Have I carefully checked my spelling?

Insight

If you speak a language other than English, you could write a definition paragraph based on an English word that comes from your home language.

LO5 Analyzing a Definition Paragraph

A definition paragraph explores the meaning of a word, using the dictionary definition, origin, history, and other details. Definition writing is important in many forms of academic writing.

Read/React Read the following definition paragraph and then fill in the graphic organizer with details from the paragraph.

Looking for Utopia

The **topic sentence** identifies the term and gives a basic definition.

Body sentences explore the term in a number of ways.

The **closing sentence** leaves the reader with a final thought.

Everyone wishes to find a perfect place—a utopia that has no crime and no disease, where everyone is happy, healthy, wealthy, and wise. In fact, the word "utopia" would seem to mean "good place," coming from the Greek "eu" (good) and "topos" (place). However, the prefix in Greek is not "eu" but "ou," which means "not" or "no." That's right; "utopia" means "no place." Sir Thomas More coined the term in 1516, writing a book about a perfect place that didn't exist. His book was a satire, trying to show that a utopia wasn't possible. That didn't stop a number of utopian movements from springing up. In fact, one utopian community established in New Harmony, Indiana, proudly announced that it was based on ideas commended by Sir Thomas More. This 2,000-person communal city banned money but quickly dissolved due to quarrelling. Nathaniel Hawthorne tells in *The Scarlet Letter* why such utopias are bound to fail: "The founders of any new colony, whatever Utopia of human virtues and happiness they originally project, have invariably recognized it among their earliest practical necessities to allot a portion of the virgin soil as a cemetery, and another portion as the site of a prison." In other words, no utopia can exist as long as any humans are in it.

Utopia			
definition	origin	history	quotation
no place	the Greek prefix "ou," which means "not" or "no" and "topos," which means "place"	Sir Thomas More coined the term in a 1516 satire. A community in Indiana once termed itself a "utopian community."	"The founders of any new colony, whatever Utopia of human virtues and happiness they originally project, they invariably . . ." —Nathaniel Hawthorne

Elenamiv, 2010/used under license from www.shutterstock.com

LO6 Writing a Definition Paragraph

To write your own definition paragraph, follow these guidelines for prewriting, writing, revising, and editing.

Prewriting

Associate Read each word below and write down the first word that occurs to you. Then choose one of the words you thought of as the subject of a definition essay.

Eat _Answers will vary._	Paint _____	Crab _____
Hand _____	Man _____	Goof _____
Heal _____	Light _____	Water _____
Leaf _____	Hook _____	Heap _____
Lie _____	Mistake _____	Lucky _____

Gather In the top box below, write the word you will define in your paragraph. Then research the term and write notes about its definition, origin, and history. Also find and record a quotation that uses the term.

Word to define: Answers will vary.

definition	origin	history	quotation
Answers will vary.			

Write Create a first draft of your definition paragraph, following the paragraph outline below:

Paragraph Outline

Topic Sentence: Write a topic sentence that names the term and gives a basic definition.

Body Sentences: Write sentences that explore the meaning and history of the term. Provide a quotation that uses the term.

Closing Sentence: Write a sentence that leaves the reader with an interesting final thought about the term.

Answers will vary.

Revising

Revise Read your paragraph and, if possible, have someone else read it as well. Then use the following checklist to guide your revision. Keep revising until you can check off each item in the list.

Ideas

☐ **1.** Does my paragraph focus on an interesting term?

☐ **2.** Do I explore the definition, origin, and history of the term?

☐ **3.** Do I include a quotation that uses the term?

Organization

☐ **4.** Does my topic sentence name the term and give a basic definition?

☐ **5.** Do the body sentences provide a variety of details about the term?

☐ **6.** Does my closing sentence leave the reader with a final interesting thought?

Voice

☐ **7.** Does my writing voice show my interest in the term?

☐ **8.** Does my voice engage the reader?

Editing

Edit Create a clean copy of your paragraph and use the following checklist to check it for words, sentences, and conventions.

Words

☐ **1.** Have I used specific nouns and verbs? (See page 103.)

☐ **2.** Have I used more action verbs than "be" verbs? (See page 73.)

Sentences

☐ **3.** Have I varied the beginnings and lengths of sentences? (See pages 226–231.)

☐ **4.** Have I combined short choppy sentences? (See page 232.)

☐ **5.** Have I avoided shifts in sentences? (See page 278.)

☐ **6.** Have I avoided fragments and run-ons? (See pages 261–266, 270–271.)

Conventions

☐ **7.** Do I use correct verb forms (*he saw,* not *he seen*)? (See pages 320, 324.)

☐ **8.** Do my subjects and verbs agree (*she speaks,* not *she speak*)? (See pages 245–260.)

☐ **9.** Have I used the right words (*their, there, they're*)?

☐ **10.** Have I capitalized first words and proper nouns and adjectives? (See page 386.)

☐ **11.** Have I used commas after long introductory word groups? (See page 358.)

☐ **12.** Have I carefully checked my spelling?

LO7 Reviewing Description, Illustration, and Definition

Describe Pick out an object within view. Study it with your senses, handling it if possible. Then fill out the following sensory chart with details about the object. Afterward, on your own paper, write a paragraph describing the object.

See	Hear	Smell	Taste	Touch
Answers will vary.				

Illustrate In the following statement, circle the word in parentheses that best describes your current schedule. Then write four examples that illustrate the statement. On your own paper, write an illustration paragraph about your schedule.

Statement: My current schedule is (incredibly/not) busy.

Example A: _Answers will vary._____

Example B: _____

Example C: _____

Example D: _____

Define In the top box below, write a word that intrigues you. Then, in the boxes under it, write information about the word. On your own paper, write a definition paragraph about the term.

Word to define: Answers will vary.

definition	origin	history	quotation
Answers will vary.			

> "I've never tried to block out the memories of the past, even though some are painful. I don't understand people who hide from their past. Everything you live through helps to make you the person you are now." —Sophia Loren

10

Narrative Paragraph

People are often inspired to *live in the now*. On this topic, American philosopher Ralph Waldo Emerson said, "With the past, I have nothing to do; nor with the future. I live now." In other words, what's done is done and your future is dependent on the opportunities you have today. Certainly this is worthy inspiration, but living in the moment doesn't mean you should let your past slip away.

Reflecting on a memorable past experience can give your life meaning as you discover how the experience shaped you to be the person you are today. A paragraph that shares such a memory is called a narrative paragraph.

This chapter will guide you through the process of writing a narrative paragraph about an unforgettable memory from your life. As well as sharing your story with others, be ready to relive it yourself.

What do you think?

What does living in the now mean to you? Do you subscribe to this lifestyle? Why or why not?

Answers will vary.

Learning Outcomes

LO1 Understand personal paragraphs.

LO2 Plan a personal paragraph.

LO3 Write the first draft.

LO4 Revise the writing.

LO5 Edit the writing.

LO6 Reflect on the experience.

Learning Outcome

Understand personal paragraphs.

LO1 Reviewing a Narrative Paragraph

Read/React Read the following paragraph. Then answer the questions below to identify your first impressions about it.

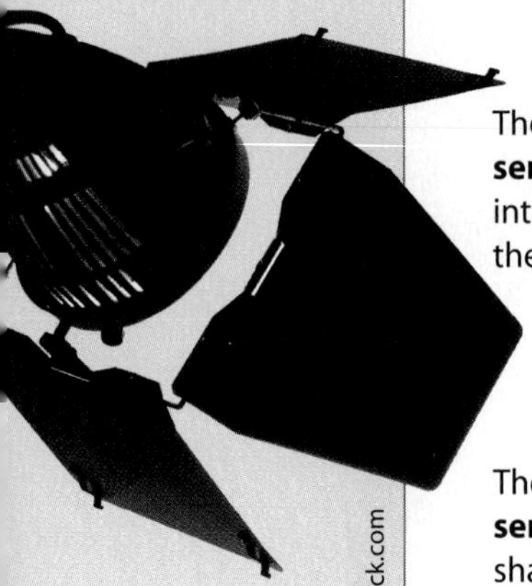

Ramzi Hachicho, 2010/used under license from www.shutterstock.com

Taking a Bow

The **topic sentence** introduces the subject.

The **body sentences** share details about the memory.

The **closing sentence** reflects on the memory.

My final moments on stage during the musical *Grease* are ones I'll never forget. It was a Saturday night, and my high school's matchbox-sized theater was filled to capacity, only no one was sitting. We had finished singing our closing number and the cast, crew, and I stood hand in hand, soaking in a standing ovation. I couldn't help but feel a supreme sense of satisfaction. This was the culmination of three months of hard work. Heck, *tonight* was hard work. My voice was shot. My hair was frizzy. And sweat beads trickled down my brow, streaking globs of black mascara under my eyes. I looked like a mess, but I didn't care. Four rows into the audience my family was going bonkers. Dad pumped his fist as if the Steelers won the Super Bowl, while mom waved her hands in the air wildly. Under normal conditions, this type of behavior would make me run for cover, but not tonight. Eventually the curtain closed and my special night was over. I never did pursue a career in theater, but on that night, in that moment, Broadway didn't seem so faraway.

1. Name two things that you like about the paragraph. (Consider specific details, main ideas, particular sentences, and so on.)

   a. Answers will vary.

   b.

2. List two questions that you have about the paragraph. (Is there something that you would like to know more about? Are there any words or phrases that you don't understand completely?)

   a. Answers will vary.

   b.

A Closer Look

Rochelle used **thought details** to reveal her personal insights and feelings about her theater experience. Such details add meaning and authenticity to a personal paragraph.

Identify This chart includes three different kinds of thought details—sensations, emotions, and reflections. Review Rochelle's personal paragraph to find the thought details. Then write them in the appropriate column of the chart.

Traits
This graphic organizer helps you analyze the ideas in the reading. A similar organizer will help you gather ideas for your own writing.

Thought Details

Sensations Think about sights, sounds, smells, tastes, feelings (touch).	Emotions Think of feelings—happiness, loneliness, indifference.	Reflections Think of opinions and conclusions.
match-box sized	supreme sense of satisfaction	The final moments on stage are ones I'll never forget.
frizzy hair		This type of behavior would make me run for cover, but not tonight.
Sweat beads trickled down by brow, streaking globs of black mascara under my eyes.		In that moment, Broadway didn't seem so far away.

Explain What type of thought detail are you most interested in hearing about from a writer? Why?

Answers will vary.

Vocabulary

thought details
details that explore a writer's impressions, emotions, and reflections

Traits

Transition words connect one sentence to another, strengthening organization. Narrative writing requires transitions that show time (see page 101).

LO2 Prewriting: Planning

In your own personal paragraph, you will write about an unforgettable memory. Think of a past time, place, or experience that holds significant meaning for you.

Selecting a Topic

Dan listed four experiences that he vividly remembers: the first day on his first job, his grandfather's funeral, his high school track championship, and his backpacking trip. He chose to write about his backpacking trip with his brother.

Select In the space below, list four unforgettable memories from your life. Then circle the one memory you would like to write about in a personal paragraph.

1. Answers will vary.   3. _____

2. _____   4. _____

Using Chronological Order

Once you have selected a topic, you should think closely about the order of events in your memory. In most cases, personal paragraphs are arranged according to time, or **chronological order**, placing events in the order in which they happened.

Identify Use the time line below to list the main events of your memory chronologically.

1. Answers will vary.

2.

3.

4.

Gathering Details

The most vivid personal paragraphs use plenty of sensory details. Such details allow the reader to picture, hear, and touch what you describe. Dan used a sensory chart to list specific sensory details about his backpacking trip.

Sensory Chart

Sights	Sounds	Smells	Tastes	Feelings (touch)
-forests of evergreens -dirt path -mountain ranges -thick fog	-talk with brother -birds chirping -crunching leaves	-fresh air -smell of rain	-peanut butter granola bar	-achy thighs -burning lungs

Gather Complete the sensory chart below. Collect any sights, sounds, smells, tastes, or feelings about your subject in the appropriate column.

Sights	Sounds	Smells	Tastes	Feelings (touch)
Answers will vary.				

LO3 Writing: Creating a First Draft

Provided below is Dan's personal paragraph about a special moment in his life. He uses sensory and other thought details to clearly describe the moment.

Read/React Carefully read Dan's paragraph, paying attention to the way he organizes his story into a beginning, a middle, and an ending. Afterward, answer the questions about the paragraph.

A Rugged Ride

Topic Sentence

Riding up the mountain trail, my thighs ached and my lungs burned, but I couldn't be happier. Fifty feet in front of me pedaled my brother, Keith, fresh off his tour with the Marines. This mountain biking adventure was his idea. The green, forest-lined trail was rugged, with sharp turns and steep descents. At one point we hit a patch of fog and I lost sight of Keith. It felt as if we were riding through clouds. The ghostly air was damp and smelled like rain. I slowed down and called for my brother, "Are you still up there?" "Would I be anywhere else?" he yelled back. When the fog disappeared, we stopped for a **breather** on a ridge that overlooked a vast valley. A sea of pointy **evergreens** stretched for miles, ending near the peak of a distant mountain. While I snacked on a peanut butter granola bar, Keith glanced over at me. "This is fun, isn't it," he commented. "It's good having you back, man," I responded. With that, we hopped on our bikes and continued our adventure.

Body Sentences

Closing Sentence

(line numbers: 1, 5, 10, 15)

1. What main feeling does Dan share in the topic sentence?

   happiness

2. Identify at least three sensory or other thought details in the paragraph. Write them down.

   (AWV) green, forest-lined trail; riding though fog clouds; damp, ghostly
   air; pointy evergreens; etc

3. What two things do you especially like in the paragraph? (Consider words, sentences, or ideas.)

   Answers will vary.

Write Create a first draft of your paragraph using the ideas and details from your sensory chart (page 99). Use the paragraph outline below and transition words as you need them.

Paragraph Outline

Topic Sentence: Write a topic sentence that sets the stage for the paragraph. To set the right course, you should identify your topic and put it in perspective in an interesting way.

Body Sentences: Write body sentences that share details (sensations as well as emotions and reflections) about the subject and each main point.

Closing Sentence: Write a closing sentence (or two) that captures the significance of your experience.

Transition words that show time: after / at / before / during / finally / first / later / next / next week / now / second / soon / suddenly / third / then / today / until / when / while / yesterday

Speaking & Listening

Have your partner read your paragraph aloud. Then complete the response sheet together.

LO4 Revising: Improving the Writing

Revising involves sharing your work with a peer and improving your writing by adding, cutting, reworking, or rearranging material.

Peer Review

Sharing your writing is especially important when you are revising a first draft. The feedback that you receive will help you improve your paragraph. Use a peer-response sheet to respond to a classmate's writing, or to have a classmate respond to yours.

Respond Complete this response sheet after reading the first draft of a classmate's paragraph. Then share the sheet with the writer. (Keep your comments helpful and positive.)

Paragraph title: _Answers will vary._ _____

Writer: _____ Reviewer: _____

1. Which part seems to work best: topic sentence, middle, or closing sentence?

   Why? _____

   _____

   _____

2. Which part needs some work? Why? _____

   _____

   _____

   _____

3. Does the piece include any sensations, emotions, or reflections? Name them.

   _____

   _____

   _____

4. Identify a portion of the paragraph that illustrates the writer's passion for the subject.

   _____

   _____

   _____

Specific Nouns and Verbs

You can strengthen your paragraph by substituting specific nouns and verbs for those that are too general. Thoughtful, vivid words will make your writing more interesting.

Insight

To learn new, more precise nouns and verbs, use a thesaurus to find new words, but then use a dictionary to understand the exact meaning of different words.

	General Noun	vs.	Specific Noun
	The **place** was beautiful.		The **valley** was beautiful.

	General Verb	vs.	Specific Verb
My thighs **hurt**.		My thighs **ached**.
My brother **rode** in front of me.		My brother **pedaled** in front of me.
There **were** evergreens everywhere.		The evergreens **stretched** for miles.
I **ate** a granola bar.		I **snacked** on a granola bar.

Revising in Action:

Read aloud the unrevised and then the revised version of the following excerpt. Note how the specific words energize the writing.

> ... we stopped for a ~~rest~~ *breather* on a ridge that overlooked ~~a large opening~~ *a vast valley*. *A sea of pointy evergreens stretched for miles* ~~There were evergreens everywhere~~, ending near the peak of a distant mountain. While I ~~ate~~ *snacked on* a peanut butter granola bar...

Revise Improve your writing, using the checklist below and your partner's comments on the response sheet. Continue working until you can check off each item in the list.

Ideas

☐ **1.** Do I focus on one specific memory?

☐ **2.** Is the memory meaningful to me?

☐ **3.** Do I include sufficient sensory and other thought details?

Organization

☐ **4.** Do I have a topic sentence, body sentences, and a closing sentence?

☐ **5.** Is the paragraph organized chronologically?

☐ **6.** Have I used transitions to connect my sentences?

Voice

☐ **7.** Do I sound interested and sincere?

Speaking & Listening

Direct quotations should sound natural, as if the person is speaking. Read direct quotations out loud to check the way they sound.

LO5 Editing: Punctuating Dialogue

Dialogue refers to the words spoken by people and set apart with quotation marks.

Quotation Marks and Dialogue

In some personal paragraphs, **dialogue** may be used to capture the unique voices of the people involved in the story. When you recall or create conversations between people, you must use quotation marks before and after the speaker's exact words, also called a **direct quotation**. However, when you use an **indirect quotation**—one that does *not* use the speaker's exact words—quotation marks are not needed. See the examples that follow.

Direct quotation:

Sitting in my one-room apartment, I remember Mom saying, **"Don't go to the party with him."**

Indirect quotation:

I remember Mom saying **that I should not go to the party with him.**

Note: The words *if* and *that* often indicate dialogue that is being reported rather than quoted.

Punctuation Practice Read the sentences below. Place quotation marks (" ") before and after the words in direct quotations. If the sentence contains no direct quotations, write *correct* next to the sentence.

1. "Christina, could you give me a ride to the airport?" I asked. _____

2. "You are one lucky guy," said Reid. _____

3. The tour guide said that we should get our cameras out. correct _____

4. "There's little chance I'll ever eat octopus," joked Hailey. _____

5. Before we left I said, "Don't forget your wallet and cell phone!"_____

6. Kyle said if he goes to the movie tonight, he will miss the party. correct _____

7. "Where did you get that dress?" asked Brianna. _____

8. Derrick says that he thinks your sweater shrunk in the dryer. correct _____

Apply Read your narrative paragraph. If you included any direct quotations, make sure they are properly marked with quotation marks. If you did not use any direct quotations, consider adding one or two to enliven and improve the voice of your writing.

Vocabulary

dialogue
a conversation between two people

direct quotation
a person's exact words

indirect quotation
a statement that reports a speaker's words

Punctuation Used with Quotation Marks

As you edit your narrative paragraph, pay special attention to the punctuation marks used with quotation marks. In general, there are three special rules to follow:

- When periods or commas follow the quotation, place them before the closing quotation mark.

  "Never be afraid to ask for help," advised Mr. Lee.

  "With the evidence we now have," Professor Howard said, "many scientists believe there could be life on Mars."

- When question marks or exclamation points follow the quotation, place them before the closing quotation mark if they belong with the quoted words. Otherwise, place them after the quotation mark.

  "Bill, do you want to go to the gym with me?" I asked.

  Were you telling the truth when you said, "Let's go home"?

- When semicolons or colons follow the quotation, place them after the quotation mark.

  He said, "Absolutely not"; however, he relented and left work early.

Insight

These rules for punctuating quotations reflect the U.S. standards. British English follows different rules.

Punctuation Practice In each sentence, correct the misplaced punctuation marks. (Use the transpose sign ∿.) Refer to the rules above for help.

1. "Please hand your papers in by the end of the week", advised Professor Hopkins.

2. Mark said, "See you soon;" however, he missed his flight.

3. "With everything that happened", my boss said ", it might be best to take Friday off."

4. "Don't be late"! exclaimed Lisa.

5. "Should we meet tomorrow"? asked Renee.

6. Did you really mean it when you said, "We are just looking?"

7. "Remember, you have a doctor appointment on Thursday", my mom reminded me.

8. "Can you pass me the ketchup?" I asked.

Apply Read your narrative paragraph. Check the punctuation of dialogue closely.

Marking a Paragraph

The model that follows has a number of errors.

Punctuation Practice Correct the following paragraph, using the correction marks to the left. One correction has been done for you.

Correction Marks

- ✠ delete
- d̲ capitalize
- ꞁᴅ lowercase
- ∧ insert
- ⌄ add comma
- ∧? add question mark
- word∧ add word
- ⊙ add period
- ⬭ spelling
- ∼ switch

Habits

People say I'm a creature of habit, but that's not entirely true. For instance,   1

to
I like ∧ try new foods. When I was in New hampshire, I ate raw oysters. People

say they taste like the ocean. Indeed, they are very salty. I do enjoy the thrill

of a new food, however, oysters will not become a staple of my diet. Besides

eating bizarre foods, I also enjoy going on weeknd adventures. Last saturday,   5

my friends and I went camping outside of the city. We didn't even set up tents,

opting to sleep under the stars. Unfortunately, the rising sun woke us up at

was
about 6:00 a.m. I only got about for hours of sleep, so I ∧ tired and crabby for

the rest of the day. I guess that's won way I am a creature of habit. I like my

sleep. Another unusual activity I enjoy is Pilates. For some reason my friends   10

think this makes me a wimp, but I bet they couldn't make it threw one class.

I would love to see them try⊙

Insight

You have seen how quotation marks are used before and after direct quotations. Quotation marks are also used around special words: (1) to show that a word is being discussed as a word, (2) to indicate that a word is slang, or (3) to point out that a word is being used in a humorous or ironic way.

(1) In our society, the word **"honesty"** is often preceded by the modifier **"old-fashioned."**

(2) You are wearing an **"old-school"** style of jeans.

(3) In an attempt to be popular, he works very hard at being **"cute."**

Correcting Your Paragraph

Now it's time to correct your own paragraph.

Apply Create a clean copy of your writing and use the following checklist to check for errors. When you can answer yes to a question, check it off. Continue working until all items are checked.

WAC

Use this checklist for editing writing assignments in all of your classes.

Editing Checklist

Words

☐ **1.** Have I used specific nouns and verbs? (See page 103.)

☐ **2.** Have I used more action verbs than "be" verbs? (See page 73.)

Sentences

☐ **3.** Have I varied the beginnings and lengths of sentences? (See pages 226–231.)

☐ **4.** Have I combined short choppy sentences? (See page 232.)

☐ **5.** Have I avoided shifts in sentences? (See page 278.)

☐ **6.** Have I avoided fragments and run-ons? (See pages 261–266, 270–271.)

Conventions

☐ **7.** Do I use correct verb forms (*he saw*, not *he seen*)? (See pages 320, 324.)

☐ **8.** Do my subjects and verbs agree (*she speaks*, not *she speak*)? (See pages 245–260.)

☐ **9.** Have I used the right words (*their, there, they're*)?

☐ **10.** Have I capitalized first words and proper nouns and adjectives? (See page 386.)

☐ **11.** Have I used commas after long introductory word groups? (See page 358.)

☐ **12.** Have I punctuated dialogue correctly? (See pages 104–105.)

☐ **13.** Have I carefully checked my spelling?

Adding a Title

Make sure to add an attention-getting title. Here are three simple strategies for creating one.

■ **Use a phrase or a word from the paragraph:** Habits
■ **Use a main idea from the paragraph:** Taking a Bow
■ **Use strong, colorful words from the paragraph:** A Rugged Ride

Create Prepare a clean final copy of your paragraph and proofread it.

Insight

Have a classmate, friend, or family member read your work to catch any missed errors.

LO6 Reviewing Narrative Writing

Complete these activities as needed to help you better understand writing narrative paragraphs.

Fill In Look closely at the photograph. Imagine you are the person on the beach with the red shoes. What sensory details—sights, smells, sounds, and so on—do you experience? Write as many as you can in the sensory chart. (See page 99.)

Sights	Sounds	Smells	Tastes	Feelings (touch)
Answers will vary.				

Define In your own words, define **chronological order**. (See page 98.)

Answers will vary.

Sort Circle the transitions that *show time:* (See page 101.)

(first)   above   (before)   near   (next)   (then)

"I want all my senses engaged. Let me absorb the
world's variety and uniqueness."
—Maya Angelou

Valentyn Volkov 2010/used under license from www.shutterstock.com

Classification Paragraph

The word *fruit* describes thousands of varieties, from cherries to blueberries to plums. But each of those varieties has subcategories. For example, there are two main types of cherries—sweet and sour—and within those categories are many, many varieties, including the two shown above. Believe it or not, those yellow cherries are maraschinos *before* being dyed and processed into that sweet thing in a Shirley Temple.

A classification essay explores the varieties of something. It breaks down a topic into categories and subcategories. In this chapter, you will be writing a classification paragraph about a topic of your own selection.

Learning Outcomes

LO1 Understand classification paragraphs.

LO2 Plan a classification paragraph.

LO3 Write the first draft.

LO4 Revise the writing.

LO5 Edit the writing.

LO6 Review classification writing.

What do you think?

What is you favorite type of apple? Is it tart or sweet, red or green, soft or crisp? Why is it your favorite?

Answers will vary.

LO1 Reviewing a Paragraph

A classification paragraph analyzes a subject by breaking it into different categories or types.

Read/React Read the following classification paragraph and answer the questions below.

A Question of Taste

The **topic sentence** introduces the categories.

The **body sentences** describe each category.

The **closing sentence** leaves the reader with a final thought.

> All the flavors that a person can taste are made up of a few ¹ basic taste sensations. In the Western world, people are used to thinking about four tastes: salty, sweet, sour, and bitter. The salty taste comes from substances that include sodium, such as snacks like potato chips or pretzels. The sweet sensation comes ⁵ from sugars, whether in processed foods like sweetened cereals or naturally occurring in fruit or honey. Sour tastes come from acidic foods (pH below 7) such as lemons and grapefruit, and bitter tastes come from alkaline foods (pH above 7) such as coffee or dark chocolate. But in the Eastern world, two other taste sensations are ¹⁰ recognized. A savory taste (**umami**) comes from amino acids, which are a basic part of meats and proteins. And a spicy taste (**piquancy**) comes from substances like the capsaicin in hot peppers. Given the savory and spicy nature of Indian, Thai, Chinese, and other Eastern foods, it's no wonder that these tastes are recognized. ¹⁵ But other nontaste sensations also add to the enjoyment of food— aroma, color, shape, temperature, texture, dryness, and sound, just to name a few. With all the senses to appeal to, chefs can make every dish a unique work of art.

1. Name two things that you like about the paragraph. (Consider specific details, main ideas, particular sentences, and so on.)

   a. Answers will vary. _____

   _____

   b. _____

   _____

2. Name two questions you have about the paragraph. (Is there something that you would like to know more about? Are there any words or phrases that you don't understand completely?)

   a. Answers will vary. _____

   _____

   b. _____

   _____

A Closer Look

List Complete the chart below by writing the name of each taste sensation, a definition of that sensation, and examples of foods that create the taste. The first one has been done for you.

Traits

This organizer helps you analyze the reading, and will help you write your own classification paragraph.

Type/Category	Definition	Examples
salty	a taste that contains sodium	potato chips or pretzels
sweet	a taste that contains sugar	cereal or fruit or honey
sour	a taste that comes from acidic foods	lemons
bitter	a taste that comes from alkaline foods	coffee or dark chocolate
umami (savory)	a taste that comes from amino acids	meats and proteins
piquancy (spicy)	a taste that comes from substances like capsaicin	hot peppers

Consider What nontaste sensations does the writer list? Why are these sensations not included in the main classification?

Aroma, color, shape, temperature, texture, dryness, and sound

Nontaste sensations do not fit as a category of basic taste sensations.

LO2 Prewriting: Planning

In your own classification paragraph, you will explore the categories or types of something. These two pages will help you select a topic and gather details about it.

Explore Read through the "Essentials of Life" list below. Select four general subject areas that you would like to explore. Then, for each subject area, write a possible topic. An example has been done for you.

Essentials of Life

food	intelligence	resources
clothing	personality	energy
shelter	senses	money
education	emotions	government
work	goals	laws
entertainment	health	rights
recreation	environment	science
religion	plants	measurement
family	animals	machines
friends	land	tools
community	literature	agriculture
communication	arts	business

Example Subject Area:

energy

Example Topic:

Types of solar energy

1. Subject Area:

Answers will vary.

Topic:

Types of

2. Subject Area:

Topic:

Types of

3. Subject Area:

Topic:

Types of

4. Subject Area:

Topic:

Types of

Select Review the topics listed above and select one that could be broken down into 3 to 6 types (a number you could cover in a single paragraph).

Researching Your Topic

Once you have selected a topic, you'll want to find out more about it. Search Internet sites, encyclopedias, school texts, and other sources as necessary. As you break your topic into types or categories, consider the following:

> **Types or categories should be . . .**
>
> - **exclusive**, which means that one example doesn't fit into more than one category
> - **consistent**, which means that examples of this category have the same traits

Organize In the chart below, list each type or category in the first column. In the second column, define the type or category. In the third column, write examples of the type or category.

Type/Category	Definition	Examples
Answers will vary.		

LO3 Writing: Creating a First Draft

As you prepare to write your own first draft, read the sample classification paragraph below, which focuses on different uses of solar power.

Read/React Carefully read the paragraph below, paying attention to the ways that the categories are named and defined as well as the examples that are provided. Afterward, answer the questions about the paragraph.

Plugging into Sunlight

Topic Sentence

Body Sentences

Closing Sentence

With fossil fuels running out, people are learning more and more ways to use the free energy of the sun. The simplest form of solar energy is solar lighting, which means designing buildings to take advantage of natural light. A more advanced form is solar heating, or gathering the sun's warmth and using it to heat a building. The sun heats up a "thermal mass"—whether stone, cement, or water—which then radiates the heat. A third use of solar energy is solar cooking. Box cookers are insulated boxes with clear tops, and parabolic cookers use solar rays to boil water or cook food. A fourth use of solar energy provides drinkable water to millions of people. Solar water treatment devices can turn salt water into fresh water and can disinfect water using the sun's rays. Photovoltaic cells produce a fifth type of solar energy, converting sunlight into electrical energy. The energy can power household devices and even electrical vehicles. Finally, solar chemical systems use the sun to power chemical reactions, from producing hydrogen to purifying natural gas. Of course, the oldest type of solar power was not invented by people but by plants. Photosynthesis turns sunlight, water, and minerals into food for plants and the whole world!

1

5

10

15

20

1. What six uses of solar power does the writer define?

   a. Solar lighting
   b. Solar heating
   c. Solar cooking
   d. Solar water treatment
   e. Solar energy
   f. Solar chemical systems

2. What transition words does the writer use to connect the sentences?

   A third, a fourth, finally, of course, a more advanced

Write Create a first draft of your paragraph using the ideas and details from your prewriting (pages 112–113). Consider the paragraph outline below:

Paragraph Outline

Topic Sentence: Write a topic sentence that introduces the subject and refers to the types or categories.

Body Sentences: Write body sentences that name each category, define it, and provide examples.

Closing Sentence: Write a closing sentence that leaves the reader with an interesting final thought.

Speaking & Listening

Have your partner read your paragraph aloud. Then complete the response sheet together.

LO4 Revising: Improving the Writing

Revising involves sharing your work with a peer and improving your writing by adding, cutting, reworking, or rearranging material.

Peer Review

Having a peer read and review your writing will help you revise. The following peer response sheet will guide the peer review process.

Respond Read a classmate's paragraph and complete the following response sheet. (Keep comments helpful and positive.) Share the sheet with the writer.

Paragraph title: _Answers will vary._____

Writer: _____ Reviewer: _____

1. Which part seems to work best: topic sentence, middle, or closing sentence? Why?

    _____

    _____

    _____

2. Which part needs some work? Why?

    _____

    _____

    _____

3. What types or categories did the paragraph explain?

    a. _____   d. _____

    b. _____   e. _____

    c. _____   f. _____

4. What two details did you like most?

    _____

    _____

5. Identify a phrase or two that shows the writer's level of interest in the topic.

    _____

    _____

    _____

Using Transitions

Transition words and phrases can help you identify each type or category and rank them, perhaps by complexity, rareness, age, or some other factor:

One type	The simplest	The most common	The earliest
A second	A more complex	A less common	A later
A third	An advanced	A rare	A recent
The last	The most complex	A very rare	The newest

Traits

Transitions help you organize your writing and improve sentence fluency.

Revising in Action

Read aloud the unrevised and then revised version of the following excerpt. Note how the transition words identify and rank the categories.

> The simplest form of solar energy is
> . . . people are learning more and more ways to use the free energy of the sun. Solar
> , which   A more advanced form is
> lighting means designing buildings to take advantage of natural light. Solar heating
> , or
> is gathering the sun's warmth and using it to heat a building. The sun heats up a
>
> "thermal mass"—whether stone, cement, or water—which then radiates the heat.
> A third use of solar energy is solar cooking.
> Box cookers are insulated boxes with clear tops, and parabolic cookers use solar rays
>
> to boil water or cook food. . . .

Revising

Revise Improve your writing, using the following checklist and your partner's comments on the response sheet. Continue working until you can check off each item in the list.

Ideas

☐ **1.** Do I identify my subject?

☐ **2.** Do I name and define the types or categories?

☐ **3.** Do I provide examples of each type?

Organization

☐ **4.** Do I have an effective topic sentence, body sentences, and a closing sentence?

☐ **5.** Do I use transition words and phrases to identify and rank the types?

Voice

☐ **6.** Does my voice sound knowledgeable and interested?

LO5 Editing: Subject-Verb Agreement

Subjects and verbs must agree in number. These two pages cover basic subject-verb agreement and agreement with compound subjects.

Basic Subject-Verb Agreement

A singular subject takes a singular verb, and a plural subject takes a plural verb:

One <u>type</u> of instrument <u>is</u> percussion.
  singular subject   singular verb

Two percussion <u>instruments are</u> drums and cymbals
             plural subject   plural verb

In order to identify the correct subject, disregard any words that come between the subject and verb.

<u>One</u> of the types of instruments <u>is</u> percussion.
  singular subject   singular verb

(*Types* and *instruments* are not subjects, but objects of the prepositions.)

Test Taking

Some tests require you to correct subject-verb agreement errors. For more practice, see pages 246–260.

Agreement Practice In each sentence, create subject-verb agreement by circling the correct verb in parentheses.

1. The percussion category (include/**includes**) instruments that make noise by striking something.

2. Pianos, by that definition, (is/**are**) percussion instruments.

3. The hammers inside a piano (**strike**/strikes) the strings to make the sound.

4. Of course, drums (is/**are**) also types of percussion.

5. The drumsticks, made of hardwood, (**hit**/hits) the skin of the drumhead.

6. Another of the instrument types (**is**/are) winds.

7. This family of instruments (include/**includes**) flutes, clarinets, and even brass.

8. When wind (produce/**produces**) the sound, the instruments (is/**are**) winds.

9. Some winds like the clarinet or oboe (**make**/makes) sound with a reed.

10. Other winds like the trumpet or trombone (**make**/makes) sound with the player's lips.

Apply Read your classification paragraph, making sure that your subjects and verbs agree.

Agreement with Compound Subjects

A compound subject is made of two or more subjects joined by *and* or *or*. When the subjects are joined by *and*, they are plural and require a plural verb:

A baritone and a trombone play the same range.
plural compound subject   plural verb

When the subjects are joined by *or*, the verb must match the number of the last subject.

Either the woodwinds or the brass plays the main theme.
singular subject   singular verb

Either the brass or the woodwinds play the main theme.
plural subject   plural verb

Agreement Practice In each sentence, create subject-verb agreement by circling the correct verb in parentheses.

1. Stringed instruments and their players (**fill out**/fills out) the orchestra.

2. Violins and violas (**play**/plays) the higher notes.

3. A cello or bass (handle/**handles**) the lower notes.

4. The horsehair bow and the string (**make**/makes) the sound.

5. Either music or screeches (emerge/**emerges**) depending on the player's talent.

6. A soloist or all the violins (**carry**/carries) the melody.

7. The conductor or the concertmaster (indicate/**indicates**) when to bow.

8. The concertmaster and the strings (**sit**/sits) closest to the audience.

9. The orchestra and any soloist (**perform**/performs) to packed audiences.

10. Either the musicians or their director (thank/**thanks**) the crowd.

Write Write the end of each sentence, matching the verb to the compound subject.

1. The director and the orchestra _Answers will vary._

2. The orchestra or the director _Answers will vary._

Apply Read your classification paragraph, making sure that your compound subjects and verbs agree.

Marking a Paragraph

The model classification paragraph that follows has a number of errors.

Editing Practice Correct the following paragraph, using the marks on the left. The first error has been corrected for you.

Correction Marks

 delete

d̲ capitalize

ɭ̸ lowercase

∧ insert

∧̒ add comma

?∧ add question mark

word∧ add word

⊙ add period

◯ spelling

∽ switch

My Condiments to the Chef

When most Americans talk about mustard, they mean a type of bright-yellow   *1*

goo that the rest of the world hardly recognizes as mustard. Actually, *there are* four basic

types of mustard. Yellow mustard *is* ~~are~~ the most common in America, made from

finely ground mustard seed, vinegar, and a bright yellow coloring called turmeric.

Yellow mustard is mild, a constant companion of hot dogs. For a spicier mustard,   *5*

people in the united states and outside as well enjoy brown mustard. it is made

from coarse-ground mustard seeds, ~~and~~ so it looks yellow and brown. For an even

stronger flavor, mustard lovers turn to the famous mustard called Dijon, named

after the French city where it *began* ~~begun~~ Dijon mustard is fine ground and most often

contains wine instead of ◯viniger. In addition to these basic types of mustard,   *10*

there ~~their~~ are all kinds of specialty mustards, mixed with everything from honey to

jalapenos, when it comes to taste, there's a mustard for just about anybody.

Insight

In academic writing, the pronouns *I* and *you* have special rules for subject-verb agreement:

- *I* takes the verb *am* instead of *is*: I *am* (**not** I *is*).
- *I* also takes plural action verbs: I *sit* (**not** I *sits*).
- *You* always takes a plural verb: You *are;* you *sit* (**not** You *is;* you *sits*).

For more information, see pages 250–251.

Correcting Your Paragraph

Now it's time to correct your own paragraph.

Apply Create a clean copy of your paragraph and use the following checklist to check for errors. When you can answer yes to a question, check it off. Continue working until all items are checked.

WAC

Use this checklist for editing writing assignments in all of your classes.

Editing Checklist

Words

☐ **1.** Have I used specific nouns and verbs? (See page 103.)

☐ **2.** Have I used more action verbs than "be" verbs? (See page 73.)

Sentences

☐ **3.** Have I varied the beginnings and lengths of sentences? (See pages 226–231.)

☐ **4.** Have I combined short choppy sentences? (See page 232.)

☐ **5.** Have I avoided shifts in sentences? (See page 278.)

☐ **6.** Have I avoided fragments and run-ons? (See pages 261–266, 270–271.)

Conventions

☐ **7.** Do I use correct verb forms (*he saw,* not *he seen*)? (See pages 320, 324.)

☐ **8.** Do my subjects and verbs agree (*she speaks,* not *she speak*)? (See pages 245–260.)

☐ **9.** Have I used the right words (*their, there, they're*)?

☐ **10.** Have I capitalized first words and proper nouns and adjectives? (See page 386.)

☐ **11.** Have I used commas after long introductory word groups? (See page 358.)

☐ **12.** Have I punctuated dialogue correctly? (See pages 104–105.)

☐ **13.** Have I carefully checked my spelling?

Adding a Title

Make sure to add a title that calls attention to your paragraph. Here are some simple strategies for coming up with a catchy title.

- **Use a number:** Four Types of Mustard
- **Use an expression:** A Matter of Taste
- **Think outside the box:** Plugging into Sunlight
- **Be clever:** My Condiments to the Chef

Insight

Have a classmate, friend, or family member read your work to catch any missed errors.

Create Prepare a clean final copy of your paragraph and proofread it.

LO6 Reviewing Classification Writing

Complete these activities as needed to help you better understand writing classification paragraphs.

Gather Think about the types of friends you have. Do you have different friends for different locations or experiences? List the types of friends and a definition for each type. Then list examples of each type. (See pages 111 and 113.)

Type/Category	Definition	Examples
Answers will vary.		

Correct For each sentence below, create subject-verb agreement by circling the correct verb in parentheses. (See pages 118–119.)

1. My friends Carl and Leon (is/**are**) what I call "football buddies."

2. Either Carl or Leon or both (**attend**/attends) every game at my house.

3. They or I (**provide**/provides) the food for the big game.

4. The Bears (is/**are**) my favorite, but the Packers (is/**are**) Carl and Leon's.

5. Either I or my friends (**get**/gets) humiliated when those two teams meet.

> "I am a woman in process. I'm just trying like everybody else. I try to take every conflict, every experience, and learn from it. Life is never dull."
>
> —Oprah Winfrey

Mark Yuill, 2010/used under license from www.shutterstock.com

12

Process Paragraph

Process writing answers practical questions: How can I jump-start my car? What's the best way to cook an omelet? What steps should I follow to tie a tie? When you answer such questions, you are analyzing a process, breaking it down into steps, and explaining how the process works.

In this chapter, your goal is to write a paragraph that clearly describes a process for the reader, who will then be able to follow or accomplish it. You will need to be well acquainted with this process so you can explain it with ease, including all the information your least knowledgeable reader will need to know.

Learning Outcomes

LO1 Understand process paragraphs.

LO2 Plan a process paragraph.

LO3 Write the first draft.

LO4 Revise the writing.

LO5 Edit the writing.

LO6 Reflect on the experience.

What do you think?

Read the quote from Oprah Winfrey above. Are you a woman (or man) in process? How so?

Answers will vary.

LO1 Reviewing a Process Paragraph

This chapter focuses on writing a process paragraph that explains how to do or how to make something. The paragraph that follows demonstrates this form.

Read/React Read the following process paragraph. Then answer the questions below to identify your first impressions about it.

Jump Start

The **topic sentence** introduces the process that will be discussed.

The **body sentences** explain the steps in the process.

The **closing sentence** wraps up the paragraph.

One of the most frustrating situations to deal with is a car with a dead battery. Fortunately, with a set of jumper cables and a little help, you can get back on the road in no time. To jump-start a car battery, you will need a set of jumper cables and a second car with a fully charged battery. First, line both cars up so the batteries are as close as they can be. Make sure both cars are turned completely off. Next, familiarize yourself with the positive (+) and negative (-) terminals of both car batteries. After you have done so, connect one end of the positive jumper cable (usually red or orange) to the positive terminal of the dead battery. Then connect the other end of the positive cable to the positive terminal of the live battery. Next, connect the negative cable (usually black) to the negative terminal of the live battery. Finally, clamp the other end of the negative cable to a solid nonpainted metal part of the engine on the dead car. From there, stand back and start the car that's providing the jump. Wait about five minutes, and then try to start the car with the dead battery. If it starts up, your last step is to remove the cables in the reverse order in which you put them on. And then you can hit the road.

1

5

10

15

1. Name two things that you like about the paragraph. (Consider specific details, main ideas, particular sentences, and so on.)

   a. Answers will vary.

   b. Answers will vary.

2. List two questions that you have about the paragraph. (Is there something that you would like to know more about? Are there any words or phrases that you don't understand completely?)

   a. Answers will vary.

   b. Answers will vary.

A Closer Look

In his process paragraph, Cedric explains how to jump-start a dead car battery. He discusses the steps in the process in chronological order, using transitions to move from one step to the next.

Identify Identify the six steps to jump-starting a dead battery, according to Cedric's paragraph. Then identify the transition word (or words) used at the beginning of each step. The first step has been completed for you.

Traits

Transition words used to show time: after / before / finally / first / later / next / second / third / then / when / while

Time Order (Chronological)	Transition	Steps
1	first	line both cars up so the batteries are close
2	next	familiarize yourself with the positive and negative terminals of the dead battery
3	after	connect one end of the positive cable to the positive terminal of the dead battery
4	then	connect the other end of the positive cable to the positive terminal of the live battery
5	next	connect the negative cable to the negative terminal of the live battery
6	finally	clamp the other end of the negative to a sold nonpainted metal part of the engine on the dead car

Traits

Choose a focused topic you can cover in one paragraph. A broad topic may require several paragraphs to explain.

Workplace

If you are describing a topic from a work environment, research by observing the process in action.

LO2 Prewriting: Planning

In your own process paragraph, you will explain how something is done or made. Consider practical topics that would be useful for your readers to know about.

Selecting a Topic

Laura began by listing two processes she was familiar with, changing a flat tire and training for a biathlon. Then she listed two processes she didn't know about but wanted to learn, applying for a passport and starting a blog.

Select In the space below, list four potential topics for your process paragraph. They may be processes you know a lot about or ones you need to research. Circle the topic you would like to write about.

> Answers will vary.

Researching a Process

Once you have selected a topic, you need to research it for information that thoroughly explains the process.

Identify Complete the research questions below.

What is the process? Answers will vary.

Why should my readers know about it?

What steps are required to complete it?

What tools or materials are needed to complete it?

What outcome does the process produce?

Gathering Details

After choosing her topic, Laura used a **process analysis diagram** to list the steps in the process in chronological order.

Process Analysis Diagram

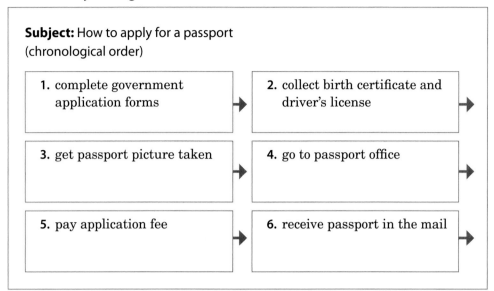

Subject: How to apply for a passport
(chronological order)

1. complete government application forms	**2.** collect birth certificate and driver's license
3. get passport picture taken	**4.** go to passport office
5. pay application fee	**6.** receive passport in the mail

Gather Complete the process analysis diagram below. Start by writing down the topic of your process paragraph. Then fill in the steps in the correct order. Note: If your process takes more than six steps to complete, continue on a separate sheet of paper.

Vocabulary

process analysis diagram
graphic organizer displaying the steps in a process in chronological order

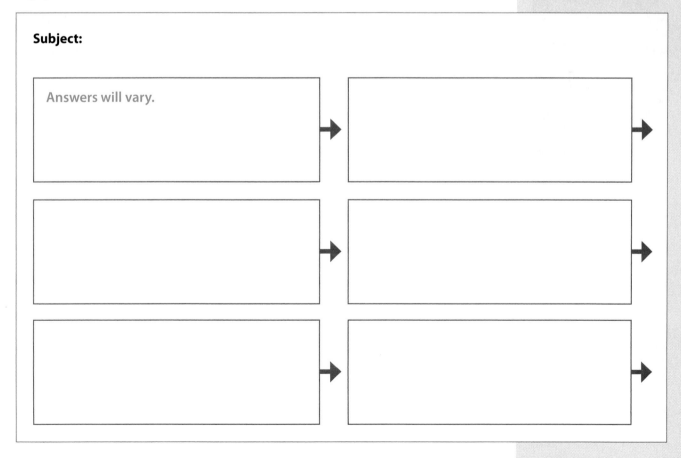

Subject:

Answers will vary.

LO3 Writing: Creating a First Draft

Provided below is Laura's paragraph describing how to apply for a passport. She uses transition words to move smoothly from one step in the process to the next.

Read/React Carefully read Laura's paragraph, paying attention to the way she organizes her steps. Afterward, answer the questions about the paragraph.

magicoven, 2010/used under license from www.shutterstock.com

How to Apply for a Passport

Topic Sentence

    If you plan on traveling outside the United States, you will need to obtain a passport before you leave. Applying for a passport is a relatively easy process but one that is time sensitive. The general rule is to apply at least six weeks before you plan to leave the country. Your first task then is to complete the government forms needed to start the application process. These forms can be downloaded online or filled out at a passport office. If you print out the applications, you will need to bring them to a passport office location near you, along with proof of your U.S. citizenship, proof of identification, and two passport photographs. A birth certificate (not a copy) is accepted proof of U.S. citizenship, while a driver's license or government ID are common proofs of identification. Once you arrive at the passport facility with all the necessary forms, you will need to provide your social security number and pay an application fee. Do all that, and you can expect to receive your passport in the mail in less than two months. One final reminder—when it finally does show up in your mailbox, store it in a safe place!

Body Sentences

Closing Sentence

(line numbers: 1, 5, 10, 15)

1. What is the purpose of the topic sentence?

   to introduce the topic and explain its importance

2. Do you think the organization of the steps makes the process easy to follow? Why or why not?

   Answers will vary.

3. What two things do you especially like in the paragraph? (Consider words, sentences, or ideas.)

   Answers will vary.

Write Create a first draft of your paragraph using the ideas and details from your research questions and process analysis diagram (pages 126–127). Refer to the transition words on page 125 for help with connecting your ideas. Finally, follow the paragraph outline below.

Paragraph Outline

Topic Sentence: Write a topic sentence that introduces the process you will discuss.

Body Sentences: Write body sentences that explain the steps in the process.

Closing Sentence: Write a closing sentence that sums up the paragraph.

LO4 Revising: Improving the Writing

Revising involves sharing your work with a peer and improving your writing by adding, cutting, reworking, or rearranging material.

Peer Review

Speaking & Listening

Have your partner read your paragraph aloud. Then complete the response sheet together.

Sharing your writing is especially important when you are revising a first draft. The feedback that you receive will help you improve your paragraph. Use a peer-response sheet to respond to a classmate's writing, or to have a classmate respond to yours.

Respond Complete this response sheet after reading the first draft of a classmate's paragraph. Then share the sheet with the writer. (Keep your comments helpful and positive.)

Paragraph title: ___Answers will vary._____

Writer: _____ Reviewer: _____

1. Which part seems to work best: topic sentence, middle, or closing sentence?

   Why? _____

   _____

   _____

2. Which part needs some work? Why? _____

   _____

   _____

3. Identify the steps of the process explained in the paragraph.

   a. _____ d. _____

   b. _____ e. _____

   c. _____ f. _____

4. Name two details you like the most.

   a. _____

   b. _____

5. Identify a phrase or two that shows the writer's level of interest.

   _____

   _____

   _____

Giving Commands

Since process paragraphs often offer instructions, consider using imperative sentences to improve your writing. Imperative sentences give commands and speak directly to the reader. Notice how the imperative sentences that follow contain an understood subject (you).

Insight

Command sentences are the only sentences in English that can have an understood subject.

Imperative Sentences

- **Line up** both cars so the batteries are as close as they can be.
- **Connect** the negative cable to the negative terminal.
- **Store** it in a safe place.

Revising in Action:

Read aloud the unrevised and then revised version of the following excerpt. Note how the imperative sentences prevent wordiness and improve the instructional voice of the writing.

. . . Then ~~you should~~ connect the other end of the positive cable to the positive terminal of the live battery. Next, ~~you will have to~~ connect the negative cable (usually black) to the negative terminal of the live battery. Finally, ~~you must~~ clamp the other end of the negative cable to a solid nonpainted metal part of the engine on the dead car . . . .

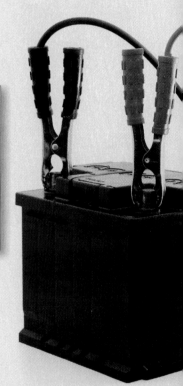

Dino O., 2010/used under license from www.shutterstock.com

Revise Improve your writing, using the following checklist and your partner's comments on the response sheet. Continue working until you can check off each item in the list.

Ideas

☐ **1.** Do I explain an interesting process?

☐ **2.** Do I include all the steps in the process?

Organization

☐ **3.** Do I have an effective topic sentence and closing sentence?

☐ **4.** Are the steps in a logical or time order?

☐ **5.** Have I used transitions to connect my ideas?

Voice

☐ **6.** Do I use command sentences to give instructions?

LO5 Editing: Sentence Errors

Some of the most common sentence errors writers make are fragments, comma splices, and run-ons.

Fragments and Run-Ons

Complete sentences help the reader to discern the writer's meaning. Fragments and run-ons, however, are errors that can derail a sentence's meaning. A **fragment** is a phrase or dependent clause that lacks a subject, verb, or some other essential part, making the thought incomplete. A **run-on sentence** is actually two sentences joined without adequate punctuation or a connecting word, resulting in the reader's confusion. See the fragment and run-on examples that follow and note how each is corrected.

Susan Fox, 2010/used under license from www.shutterstock.com

Fragment:	Raymond left his house. Forgetting the present for his mother.
Corrected:	Raymond left his house, forgetting the present for his mother.
Run-On Sentence:	Kate decided to wear shorts the weather was beautiful.
Corrected:	Kate decided to wear shorts because the weather was beautiful.

Sentence Practice On the short blank next to each example, identify the word group as a fragment (F), run-on (R), or complete sentence (C). Then rewrite the fragments and run-ons, making them correct, complete sentences.

1. Left the door open. ____F____

   Correction: (AWV) Example: Chris left the door open.

2. The water park was a blast the water was cold. ____R____

   Correction: (AWV) Example: The water park was a blast, but the water was cold.

3. The dog spun in circles. Not knowing he was chasing his tail. ____F____

   Correction: (AWV) Example: The dog spun in circles, not knowing he was chasing his tail.

4. I was late for the movie because my car ran out of gas. ____C____

   Correction: _____

Vocabulary

fragment
a group of words that is missing a subject or a predicate (or both) or that does not express a complete thought

run-on sentence
a sentence error that occurs when two sentences are joined without punctuation or a connecting word

Apply Read your process paragraph, making sure all your sentences are complete.

Comma Splice

A third common sentence error is the comma splice. **Comma splices** occur when two independent clauses are connected ("spliced") with only a comma. To correct a comma splice, either replace the comma with a period or a semicolon or add a coordinating conjunction (*and, but, or, nor, for, so, yet*) after the comma. Consider the examples that follow.

Insight

You can remember the coordinating conjunctions—*for, and, nor, but, or, yet, so*—by remembering that their first letters spell "fan boys."

Splice:	People speak of sporting events in the same way they discuss war, that's not a fair comparison.
Corrected with a period:	People speak of sporting events in the same way they discuss war. That's not a fair comparison.
Corrected with a semicolon:	People speak of sporting events in the same way they discuss war; that's not a fair comparison.
Corrected with a coordinating conjunction:	People speak of sporting events in the same way they discuss war, but that's not a fair comparison.

Sentence Practice Rewrite these examples to correct the comma splices.

1. Shelly compared her haircut to a natural disaster, I thought it looked good.

   (AWV) Example: Shelly compared her haircut to a natural disaster, but I thought it looked good.

2. My roommate won't stop talking, I don't understand why he says this stuff.

   (AWV) Example: My roommate won't stop talking; I don't understand why he says this stuff.

3. I hate when the dryer fails to fully dry my clothes, I need to find more quarters.

   (AWV) Example: I hate when the dryer fails to fully dry my clothes. I need to find more quarters.

4. I'm anxious for my test scores to arrive, my future depends on the outcome.

   (AWV) Example: I'm anxious for my test scores to arrive; my future depends on the outcome.

Apply Read your process paragraph and look for comma splices, correcting any that you find.

Vocabulary

comma splice
a sentence error that occurs when two sentences connected with only a comma

Marking a Paragraph

The model that follows has a number of errors.

Punctuation Practice Correct the following paragraph, using the marks on the left.

Correction Marks

ℒ delete

d̲ capitalize

⌀ lowercase

∧ insert

∧̦ add comma

?∧ add question mark

word∧ add word

⊙ add period

◯ spelling

∽ switch

The Amendment Process

Did you know ~~their~~ *there* are two ways to propose a new amendment to   1

the Constitution? The first method is the path each current amendment

has taken. For this process to work‚ an amendment must be proposed by a

two-⟨thrids⟩ vote in each house of Congress. Next, the proposed amendment

must be ratified by three-fourths of the states‚ Before it officially becomes   5

an amendment. The second way to amend the Constitution ~~are~~ *is* to calls for a

Constitutional Convention. For this to happen, two-thirds of the states would

have to demand the convention take place. s̲imilar to the first method, the

proposed amendment would then have to be ratified by a three-fourths vote

of the states. To date, this method has never been used *and* it is unlikely we will   10

see a constitutional C̲onvention anytime soon.

Insight

Avoid using two negative words to express a single negative idea. Double negatives are not accepted in academic writing.

Double Negative: I don't have no change for a $20 bill.

Standard: I don't have any change for a $20 bill.

I have no change for a $20 bill.

Amy Johansson, 2010/used under license from www.shutterstock.com

Correcting Your Paragraph

Now it's time to correct your own paragraph.

Apply Create a clean copy of your paragraph and use the following checklist to check for errors. When you can answer yes to a question, check it off. Continue working until all items are checked.

WAC

Use this checklist for editing writing assignments in all of your classes.

Editing Checklist

Words

- ☐ **1.** Have I used specific nouns and verbs? (See page 103.)
- ☐ **2.** Have I used more action verbs than "be" verbs? (See page 73.)

Sentences

- ☐ **3.** Have I varied the beginnings and lengths of sentences? (See pages 226–231.)
- ☐ **4.** Have I combined short choppy sentences? (See page 232.)
- ☐ **5.** Have I avoided shifts in sentences? (See page 278.)
- ☐ **6.** Have I avoided fragments and run-ons? (See pages 261–266, 270–271.)

Conventions

- ☐ **7.** Do I use correct verb forms (*he saw,* not *he seen*)? (See pages 320, 324.)
- ☐ **8.** Do my subjects and verbs agree (*she speaks,* not *she speak*)? (See pages 245–260.)
- ☐ **9.** Have I used the right words (*their, there, they're*)?
- ☐ **10.** Have I capitalized first words and proper nouns and adjectives? (See page 386.)
- ☐ **11.** Have I used commas after long introductory word groups? (See page 358.)
- ☐ **12.** Have I punctuated dialogue correctly? (See pages 104–105.)
- ☐ **13.** Have I carefully checked my spelling?

Adding a Title

Make sure to add a title that calls attention to the topic. Here are two simple strategies for creating one.

- ■ **How-to title:** How to Start a Nonprofit Corporation
- ■ **Point to the process:** Applying for a Passport

Create Prepare a clean final copy of your paragraph and proofread it.

Insight

Have a classmate, friend, or family member read your work to catch any missed errors.

LO6 Reviewing Process Writing

Complete these activities as needed to help you better understand writing process paragraphs.

Time Line Think about your morning routine. What steps do you take from the time you wake up until the time you get to school or work? In what order do you take the steps? Fill in the following time line, using chronological order to describe the steps you take to get ready in the morning. In the column marked "Transition," write down a transition word that could introduce this step. (See page 125.)

Time Order (Chronological)	Transition	Steps
1	Answers will vary.	
2		
3		
4		
5		
6		

Match Draw a line to connect each sentence error below to its description. (See pages 132–133.)

1. Fragment — two sentences joined without adequate punctuation or a connecting word

2. Run-on — a phrase or dependent clause that lacks a subject, verb, or some other essential part

3. Comma splice — two independent clauses that are connected with only a comma

Sort Circle transitions that *show time*. (See page 125.)

(before)   both   (later)   (then)   however   (finally)   though

"Shall I compare thee to a summer's day?"

—William Shakespeare

13

Comparison-Contrast Paragraph

Take a look at this photo. It is full of contrasts: a tree is contrasted with a power station, nature with technology, green with blue, horizontal with vertical. But the photo also contains some interesting comparisons. The water vapor from the power plant looks much like the clouds overhead. The green tree matches the green grass. And, moving beyond appearances, the plants and the power station are both involved with energy use and production.

By looking at the similarities and differences between two things, you can come to understand both things better. A paragraph that examines similarities and differences is called a comparison-contrast paragraph.

This chapter will guide you through the process of writing a paragraph that compares and contrasts two people—you and someone you know well.

Learning Outcomes

LO1 Understand comparison paragraphs.

LO2 Plan a comparison paragraph.

LO3 Write the first draft.

LO4 Revise the writing.

LO5 Edit the writing.

LO6 Reflect on the experience.

What do you think?

How are you similar to a summer's day? How are you different?

Answers will vary.

137

LO1 Reviewing a Comparison Paragraph

When you show how two things are similar, you are **comparing** them, and when you show how they are different, you are **contrasting** them. This chapter focuses on writing comparison-contrast paragraphs. The paragraph that follows demonstrates this form.

Read/React Read the following paragraph. Then answer the questions below to identify your first impressions about it.

Old Versus New

The **topic sentence** summarizes the comparison-contrast theme.

The **body sentences** share details about the subjects.

The **closing sentence** finishes the comparison.

   People often say I look like a younger version of my father, but ¹ in most ways, we are very different. Our appearance is similar in that I have Dad's brown eyes and black hair. We even have similar smiles, according to my mom. But no one would say we look the same in the clothes we wear. Dad dresses **old school** in work pants ⁵ and button-down shirts, always tucked in. For me, it's jeans and a Padres jersey, never tucked in. Our different dress shows our different personalities. Dad is quiet, shy, and hardworking, while I am very friendly and sometimes a little crazy. Neither of us, however, is interested in causing trouble. Most of our differences ¹⁰ come from our different backgrounds. Dad was born in Mexico in a small town south of Monterrey. He moved to San Diego as a young man and has worked very long hours as a cook ever since. It has taken him a long time to feel comfortable in this country, while the United States is all I have ever known. Dad's tough life has made ¹⁵ him more careful and serious than I am, but if he had lived my life, he would be much more like me.

1. Name two things that you like about the paragraph. (Consider specific details, main ideas, particular sentences, and so on.)

   a. Answers will vary.

   _____

   b. _____

   _____

2. List two questions that you have about the paragraph. (Is there something that you would like to know more about? Are there any words or phrases that you don't understand completely?)

   a. Answers will vary.

   _____

   b. _____

   _____

Monty Rakusen/Getty Images

Vocabulary

comparing
pointing out the similarities between two things

contrasting
pointing out the differences between two things

old school
an idiom meaning "traditional or following past practices"

A Closer Look

Miguel used a **point-by-point pattern of organization** to arrange the details in his paragraph. He discussed each point of comparison for both himself and his father before moving on to the next one.

Identify This chart shows the three points of comparison in Miguel's paragraph: *appearance*, *personality*, and *background*. Fill in the chart with specific details about Miguel and his father for each point of comparison.

Point of Comparison	Father	Miguel
Appearance Think of size, shape, hair color, eye color, skin color, gender, clothing, and so on.	brown eyes black hair similar smile work pants and button-down shirt	brown eyes black hair similar smile jeans and untucked jersey
Personality Think of attitude, outlook, feelings, actions, and so on.	quiet shy hardworking nonconfrontational	friendly outgoing a little crazy nonconfrontational
Background Think of place of birth, schooling, family, hometown, and so on.	born in Mexico	born in USA

Explain In your opinion, which point of comparison is the most interesting, and which is the least interesting? Why?

Answers will vary.

LO2 Prewriting: Planning

In your own paragraph, you, too, will compare and contrast yourself with a friend or relative. Think of someone that you know very well so that you have plenty of details to use in your writing.

Selecting a Topic

Latonya began by listing four people that she knew well: her sister, aunt, roommate, and father. She chose her roommate, Janice.

Select In the space below, list four people you know well. Then circle the one person you would like to compare and contrast in a paragraph.

Answers will vary.

Speaking & Listening

Complete the "Identify" activity with a partner. Ask your partner about the person he or she is writing about. Discuss physical appearance, personality, background, and interests. Then switch roles and have your partner ask you the same questions.

Selecting Points of Comparison

Once you have selected a topic, you need to decide on points of comparison.

Identify Complete the chart below. In the first column, list your characteristics for each point of comparison to the left. In the second column, list the characteristics of the person you have chosen. Finally, choose three points of comparison to use in your paragraph.

Point of Comparison	You	Other Person
Appearance Think of size, shape, hair color, eye color, skin color, gender, clothing, and so on.	Answers will vary.	
Personality Think of attitude, outlook, feelings, actions, and so on.		
Background Think of place of birth, schooling, family, hometown, and so on.		
Interests Think of favorite activities, friends, restaurants, and so on.		
(Other)		

Gathering Details

Latonya used a **Venn diagram** to list specific details about herself and Janice as they related to her points of comparison: appearance, background, and interests.

Venn Diagram

Points of Comparison

1. appearance

2. background

3. interests

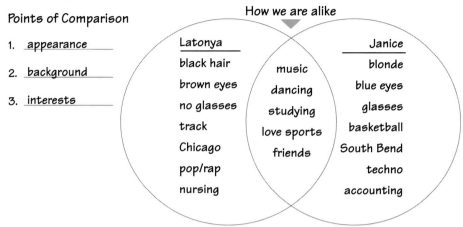

How we are alike

Latonya		Janice
black hair	music	blonde
brown eyes	dancing	blue eyes
no glasses	studying	glasses
track	love sports	basketball
Chicago	friends	South Bend
pop/rap		techno
nursing		accounting

Gather Complete the Venn diagram below. First, list the three points of comparison. Next, write your name in one circle and the other person's name in the other. List the details specific to each of you. Then, where the circles overlap, write the things you have in common.

1. Answers will vary.

2. _____

3. _____

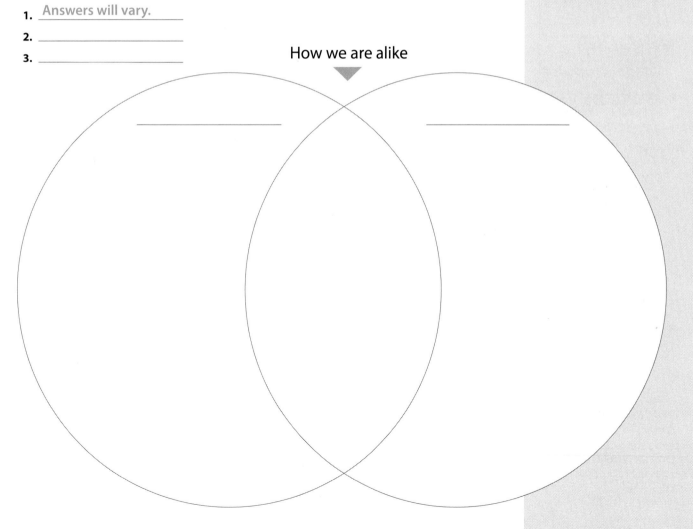

How we are alike

Workplace

In the workplace, you may need to compare two products, services, or bids. You'll need to choose points of comparison then, too.

LO3 Writing: Creating a First Draft

Provided below is Latonya's paragraph, comparing herself with her friend Janice. Latonya has used the point-by-point pattern of organization and her three points of comparison are *appearance, background,* and *interests.*

Read/React Carefully read Latonya's paragraph, paying attention to the way she organizes her ideas. The three points of comparison are labeled. Afterward, answer the questions about the paragraph.

We Can Dance

Appearance

To look at my roommate and me, you'd think we have 1 nothing in common. First of all, we look like complete opposites. Janice is tall, with long blonde hair and blue eyes, while I'm short, with black curly hair and brown eyes. Janice loves wearing her basketball jersey from her Indiana State 5 Championship team. I prefer dressing in my cross-country gear and taking off down the road. We're also from completely different places. I'm a city girl, born and raised on the south

Background

side of Chicago, right in the heart of Barack Obama country. Janice grew up on a farm in a sea of corn, near South Bend, 10 Indiana. So why do Janice and I get along so well? Some might think it is our interest in sports, but that's only a small part of it. When we first moved in together, I turned on some hip-hop,

Interests

and Janice started **popping and locking**. She was good! So I showed her some of my moves, and even tried the techno music 15 she likes. Before you know it, we came to be the best of friends, going to parties and dances together and having a blast.

1. What is the topic sentence in the paragraph? (Underline it.) What main feeling does Latonya state in that sentence?

   Latonya and her roommate don't look like they would have much

   in common.

2. Why do you think she talks about their mutual interests last in the paragraph?

   To show that despite coming from different backgrounds, these girls

   aren't all that different

3. What two things do you especially like in the paragraph? (Consider words, sentences, or ideas.)

   Answers will vary.

Write Create the first draft of your paragraph using the ideas and details from your chart and Venn diagram (pages 140–141). Follow the steps in the paragraph outline below, and use the transitional words to the right to make your writing flow.

Paragraph Outline

Topic Sentence: Write a topic sentence that tells who you are comparing yourself to.

Body Sentences: Write body sentences that share details about each subject for each point of comparison.

Closing Sentence: Write a closing sentence that sums up your comparison.

PeppPic, 2010/used under license from www.shutterstock.com

Traits

Transitions to compare:
as / as well / also / both / in the same way / much as / much like / one way / like / likewise / similarly

Transitions to contrast:
although / even though / by contrast / but / however / on the one hand / otherwise / though / still / while / yet

LO4 Revising: Improving the Writing

Revising involves sharing your work with a peer and improving your writing by adding, cutting, reworking, or rearranging material.

Speaking & Listening

Have your partner read your paragraph aloud. Then complete the response sheet together.

Peer Review

Sharing your writing is especially important when you are revising a first draft. The feedback that you receive will help you improve your paragraph. To help you respond to a classmate's writing or receive help with your own writing, use a peer-response sheet.

Respond Complete this response sheet after reading the first draft of a classmate's paragraph. Then share the sheet with the writer. (Keep your comments helpful and positive.)

Paragraph title: _Answers will vary._

Writer: _____   Reviewer: _____

1. Which part seems to work best: topic sentence, middle, or closing sentence?

   Why? _____

   _____

   _____

2. Which part needs some work? Why? _____

   _____

   _____

3. What are the three points of comparison in the paragraph?

   a. _____

   b. _____

   c. _____

4. Name two favorite details.

   a. _____

   b. _____

5. Identify a phrase or two that shows the writer's level of interest.

   _____

   _____

Show, Don't Tell

Your paragraph will be stronger if you **show** similarities and differences, not just **tell** about them. Consider the examples that follow. The improvement can be dramatic when you revise to "show."

Showing vs. Telling

Showing	Telling
She's popping and locking.	She likes to dance.
She lives on a farm in a sea of corn.	She is a country girl.
She lives in her championship jersey.	She is an athlete.
She has blonde hair and blue eyes.	She is white.

Revising in Action:

Read aloud the unrevised and then the revised version of the following excerpt. Note how much the first draft is improved by showing instead of telling. The writer provides more information, creates more interest, and gives the reader something to "see."

. . . First of all, we look like complete opposites. Janice is ~~white and~~ tall, with long blonde hair and blue eyes, wearing her basketball jersey from her Indiana State Championship team. while I'm ~~black and~~ short, with black curly hair and brown eyes. ~~We like different sports.~~ Janice loves ~~basketball,~~ I prefer dressing in my cross-country gear and taking off down the road. ~~and I like track.~~ We're also from completely different places. . . .

Revise Improve your writing, using the following checklist and your partner's comments on the response sheet. Continue working until you can check off each item in the list.

Ideas

- ☐ **1.** Do I compare two subjects—myself and another person?
- ☐ **2.** Do I use three points of comparison?
- ☐ **3.** Do I include details that show instead of tell?

Organization

- ☐ **4.** Do I have a topic sentence, middle, and a closing sentence?
- ☐ **5.** Have I used a point-by-point organizational plan?
- ☐ **6.** Have I used transitions to connect my sentences?

Voice

- ☐ **7.** Do I sound knowledgeable and interested?

R. Gino Santa Maria, 2010/used under license from www.shutterstock.com

Vocabulary

show
provide details that let the reader experience an idea or get a clear picture

tell
offer a general fact or circumstance without letting the reader experience it

LO5 Editing: Comma Use

Commas tell the reader when to pause, making the writing easy to follow.

Commas After Introductory Words

Many sentences naturally start with the subject. Some sentences, however, start with an introductory phrase or clause. A comma is used to separate a long introductory word group from the rest of the sentence. When you read sentences like these out loud, you will naturally pause after the introductory words. That tells you that a comma is needed to separate these words from the rest of the sentence. See the examples that follow.

> **Introductory Word Groups:**
>
> After my third birthday**,** my brother was born. (prepositional phrase)
>
> When he arrived on the scene**,** life changed for me. (dependent clause)

Phiseksit 2010/used under license from www.shutterstock.com

Punctuation Practice Read the sentences below, out loud. Listen for the natural pause after an introductory phrase or clause. Place a comma to set off the introductory words.

1. When my younger brother was born‚ I was jealous.

2. Before he showed up‚ I had Mom all to myself.

3. At the beginning of our relationship‚ we didn't get along very well.

4. As the years passed‚ my brother stopped being a pest and became a friend.

5. As a matter of fact‚ we both came to love basketball.

6. Without my younger brother‚ I wouldn't have anyone to push my basketball skills.

7. Taking that into account‚ our long rivalry has helped us both.

8. Since our teenage years‚ we've become best friends.

9. Although we still tease each other‚ we're not being vicious.

10. When we bump fists‚ I sometimes remember when we bumped heads.

Apply Read your comparison paragraph and look for sentences that begin with introductory phrases or clauses. If you do not find any, add an introductory phrase or clause to a few sentences to vary their beginnings. Does this help your writing read more smoothly? Remember to use a comma to separate a long introductory word group from the rest of the sentence. (For more information, see page 358.)

Commas with Extra Information

Some sentences include phrases or clauses that add information in the middle or at the end of sentences. This information should be set off with commas. You can recognize this extra information because it can be removed without changing the basic meaning of the sentence. When you read the sentence out loud, there's a natural pause before and after the phrase or clause. This indicates where you are to place the commas.

Insight

Commas are very important in written English. For more practice with comma use, see pages 357–366.

> **Extra Information:**
>
> I have a tough time waking up, not surprisingly.
>
> My mother, who works two jobs, makes me breakfast every morning.

Punctuation Practice In each sentence, use a comma or commas to separate extra information. Listen for the natural pause. Some sentences may not have extra information.

1. My mother works as a waitress which is a tough job.

2. She also works as a licensed practical nurse which is an even tougher job.

3. The nursing home the one on Main and 7th is strict.

4. A time card punched one second late is docked fifteen minutes an unfair policy.

5. A time card punched ten minutes early does not earn overtime. correct

6. The restaurant job pays minimum wage which is not much.

7. Tips from a good lunch not the busiest time can double Mom's pay.

8. What I've learned about determination real grit I learned from Mom.

9. She wants to help me qualify for a better job a selfless goal.

10. I want exactly the same thing no surprise there.

Apply Read your comparison paragraph and look for sentences that have extra information. If you haven't included any, add some extra information in a sentence or two. Do these additions make your writing more interesting? Remember to use commas to set off extra information in your sentences. (For more information, see page 364.)

Marking a Paragraph

The model that follows has a number of errors.

Editing Practice Correct the following paragraph, using the marks to the left. One correction has been done for you.

Into the Spotlight

My wife and I love each other but it's hard to imagine how we could be   *1*

more different. Lupe's a social butterfly. She been always meeting people for

coffee or talking to people on the phone. By contrast, I'm private. I work at

U.S. steel and come home. The only person I really want to be with is Lupe, but

she's always dragging me out to partys. Their is another big difference. Lupe,   *5*

who is a great singer and dancer loves theater. She's been in a dozen plays.

When it come to me the idea of being on stage is terrifying. She convinced me

once to be in a play I forgot my one line. so, is there anything Lupe and I have

in common? We love each other. Lupe needs me to keep her grounded, and

I need her to pry me out of the house. We've even figured out a way to work   *10*

around the theater thing. Next play she is in, I'll work set crew. That's how we

get along so well. I work backstage, set up props for her, and getting what she

needs. Then she walks into the spotlight and performs.

Correcting Your Paragraph

Now it's time to correct your own paragraph.

Apply Create a clean copy of your paragraph and use the following checklist to check for errors. When you can answer yes to a question, check it off. Continue working until all items are checked.

WAC

Use this checklist for editing writing assignments in all of your classes.

Editing Checklist

Words

☐ **1.** Have I used specific nouns and verbs? (See page 103.)

☐ **2.** Have I used more action verbs than "be" verbs? (See page 73.)

Sentences

☐ **3.** Have I varied the beginnings and lengths of sentences? (See pages 226–231.)

☐ **4.** Have I combined short choppy sentences? (See page 232.)

☐ **5.** Have I avoided shifts in sentences? (See page 278.)

☐ **6.** Have I avoided fragments and run-ons? (See pages 261–266, 270–271.)

Conventions

☐ **7.** Do I use correct verb forms (*he saw*, not *he seen*)? (See pages 320, 324.)

☐ **8.** Do my subjects and verbs agree (*she speaks*, not *she speak*)? (See pages 245–260.)

☐ **9.** Have I used the right words (*their, there, they're*)?

☐ **10.** Have I capitalized first words and proper nouns and adjectives? (See page 386.)

☐ **11.** Have I used commas after long introductory word groups? (See page 358.)

☐ **12.** Have I punctuated dialogue correctly? (See pages 104–105.)

☐ **13.** Have I carefully checked my spelling?

Adding a Title

Make sure to add an attention-getting title. Here are three simple strategies for creating one.

■ **Use a phrase from the paragraph:** Into the Spotlight
■ **Point to a similarity or difference:** We Can Dance
■ **Use the word "versus":** Old Versus New

Insight

Have a classmate, friend, or family member read your work to catch any missed errors.

Create Prepare a clean final copy of your paragraph and proofread it.

© Ocean/Corbis

L○6 Reviewing Comparison Writing

Complete these activities as needed to help you better understand how to write comparison-contrast paragraphs.

Compare/Contrast Consider this photograph. How are the two creatures represented in it alike? How are they different? Fill in the following Venn diagram, listing similarities and differences.

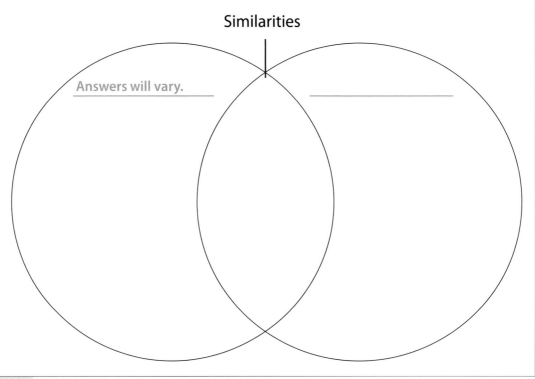

Similarities

Answers will vary.

Match Draw a line to connect each organizational pattern below to its description.

1. Point-by-point

2. Similarities-differences

3. Subject-by-subject

■ an organizational pattern focusing first on one subject and then on the other

■ a pattern in which one point of comparison is discussed for both subjects before moving on to the next point

■ an organizational pattern sharing how subjects are alike and how they are different

Sort Circle transitions that *contrast*:

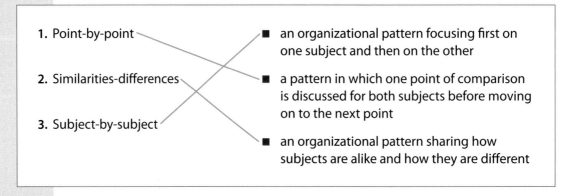

also   both   (but)   (however)   like   (otherwise)   (though)

"There is only one constant, one universal. It is the only real
truth. Causality. Action, reaction. Cause and effect."

—from *The Matrix Reloaded*

Mike Norton, 2010/used under license from www.shutterstock.com

14

Cause-Effect Paragraph

Studying the causes and effects of a phenomenon can help you better understand why and how things happen around you. Your work in a meteorology class may explain the causes and effects of forest fires, a discussion with a friend may reveal the impact of instant-replay technology on the NFL, and so on.

In this chapter, you will write a paragraph to explain the causes and effects of a past or present incident, event, or circumstance. And during the process, as you learn how one event leads to another, you will grasp the topic in a new way.

Learning Outcomes

LO1 Understand cause-effect paragraphs.

LO2 Plan a cause-effect paragraph.

LO3 Write the first draft.

LO4 Revise the writing.

LO5 Edit the writing

LO6 Reflect on the experience.

What do you think?

Read the quotation above from the movie *The Matrix Reloaded*. Briefly explain an action you have taken that had a cause and an effect.

Answers will vary.

LO1 Reviewing a Paragraph

When you think about the relationship between the causes and effects of an event, an incident, or a circumstance, you are practicing cause-effect reasoning. This chapter focuses on writing a paragraph that clearly explains a cause-effect relationship. The paragraph that follows demonstrates this form.

Read/React Read the following cause-effect paragraph. Then answer the questions below to identify your first impressions about it.

Cutting Down the Atmosphere

The **topic sentence** introduces the cause-effect relationship.

The **body sentences** explain the causes and effects.

The **closing sentence** restates the main point.

> Trees make up an essential part of the earth's ecosystem, *1* but rapid deforestation is having harmful effects on the planet. Deforestation refers to the clearance of forests through logging and burning. The main cause of deforestation is the use of trees for lumber and fuel. Forests are also cut down to make room for *5* farming. But while deforestation can boost struggling economies, it is also causing harm to the environment. Adverse effects of deforestation include erosion of soil, disruption of the water cycle, loss of biodiversity, and flooding and drought. The most harmful effect, though, may be on the climate. Deforestation leads to a *10* greater accumulation of carbon dioxide in the atmosphere, which in turn may warm the planet. Those who practice deforestation must determine if the economic benefits outweigh the negative impact on our earth.

1. Name two things that you like about the paragraph. (Consider specific details, main ideas, particular sentences, and so on.)

   a. Answers will vary. _____

   _____

   b. Answers will vary. _____

   _____

2. List two questions that you have about the paragraph. (Is there something that you would like to know more about? Are there any words or phrases that you don't understand completely?)

   a. Answers will vary. _____

   _____

   b. Answers will vary. _____

   _____

A Closer Look

Grant used an **effect-focused pattern of organization** to arrange the details in his paragraph. He briefly explains the main causes of deforestation before focusing on specific effects of the practice.

Vocabulary

effect-focused pattern of organization
a pattern of organization that focuses on the "effects" of a cause-effect relationship

Identify Grant used a cause-effect T-chart to organize his research about deforestation. Fill in the chart with the specific causes and effects of deforestation that are covered in Grant's paragraph.

Subject: The Causes and Effects of Deforestation

Causes	Effects
■ lumber	■ erosion of soil
■ fuel	■ disruption of the water cycle
■ farming	■ loss of biodiversity
■	■ flooding and drought
■	■ boost struggling economies

Explain In your opinion, should the writer have paid more attention to the causes of deforestation? Why or why not?

Answers will vary.

WAC

Cause-effect relationships are crucial to all areas of study, but especially the sciences and history.

LO2 Prewriting: Planning

In your own paragraph, you will explain the causes and effects of a phenomenon of your choice. Think of an event, a circumstance, or an incident—from the past or present—that has made a lasting impact on the world around you.

Selecting a Topic

If you are having trouble thinking of topics, consider the categories listed below.

Cause-Effect Categories

- Family Life
- Politics
- Society

- Environment
- Entertainment
- Workplace

Select List three or four possible topics on the blanks below. Then circle the topic you would like to write about in a paragraph.

Answers will vary.

Researching the Causes and Effects

Once you have selected a topic, you will need to research the causes and effects related to it.

Identify Complete the chart below to show the relationship between the causes and effects of your topic.

Topic: Answers will vary.

1. Cause: _____

1. Effect: _____

2. Cause: _____

2. Effect: _____

3. Cause: _____

3. Effect: _____

Gathering Details

As you research your topic, you should look for clear, factual evidence that links specific causes to specific effects. Using trustworthy sources will lead you to the best information.

While doing her research, Christina avoided sources that took a distorted or overly biased stance on her topic. Here are some examples of information that distorts cause-effect logic:

- **Broad Generalization:** An assertion that is based on too little evidence or allows no exceptions

  > Video games are the reason that today's youth have a shorter attention span. *(The claim disregards the possibility of other reasons.)*

- **Straw Man:** A claim that exaggerates or misrepresents an opponent's position

  > If you cause deforestation, you hate the planet.

- **False Cause:** A claim that confuses sequence with causation (If A comes before B, A must have caused B.)

  > Since that new skate park opened, vandalism among young people has increased. The skate park should never have been built. *(The two factors may have no real connection.)*

Speaking & Listening

Listen to a political debate or watch a political attack ad. See if you can detect any of these distortions in cause-effect logic. What does the distortion do to the speaker's credibility?

Forming a Cause-Effect Topic Sentence

Christina used the following formula to write the topic sentence for her cause-effect paragraph. Using your topic and research from page 154, write your own topic sentence below.

Topic		Cause-Effect Relationship		Topic Sentence
U.S. Airways Flight 1549	**+**	struck a flock of geese, causing the plane to lose power in both its engines	**=**	In January 2009, U.S. Airways Flight 1549 struck a flock of geese, causing the plane to lose power in both its engines.

Topic

Answers will vary.

Cause-Effect Relationship: _____

_____

_____

Topic Sentence: _____

_____

_____

_____

LO3 Writing: Creating a First Draft

In the paragraph below, Christina wrote about a remarkable airplane landing. The paragraph uses an effect-based approach, beginning with the main cause of the event and then focusing on three specific effects.

Read/React Read Christina's paragraph, paying attention to the way she organizes the causes and effects. Afterward, answer the questions about the paragraph.

Emergency Landing

Topic Sentence

In January 2009, U.S. Airways Flight 1549 struck a flock 1
of geese, causing the plane to lose power in both its engines. The
situation forced pilot Chesley "Sully" Sullenberger to perform an
emergency landing on the Hudson River outside of New York City.
Not only did he land safely, but all 150 passengers survived without 5
a single serious injury. The event had many meaningful effects.

Body Sentences

Massive media coverage of the landing made "Sully" a household
name. Many hailed him as an American hero. Meanwhile, the
passengers on the flight, though safe, suffered emotional trauma
from the landing. Many refuse to step back onto a plane. Maybe the 10
greatest effect, however, was the impact on the airline industry. The
result of the landing led to a greater awareness of the dangers of
bird populations near airways. Government agencies have gone so

Closing Sentence

far as to **eradicate** geese populations in the proximity of airports. For
this reason, Sully's remarkable landing may make air travel safer for 15
generations to come.

1. What is the topic sentence in the paragraph? (Underline it.) What does the sentence tell us about the paragraph?

   It introduces the topic and tells about a specific cause.

2. What three specific effects does the author focus on?

   1) "Sully" became a household name. 2) Passengers suffered emotional

   trauma. 3) It created greater awareness of birds near airways.

3. What two things do you especially like in the paragraph? (Consider words, sentences, or ideas.)

   Answers will vary.

ArchMan, 2010/used under license
from www.shutterstock.com

Write Create a first draft of your paragraph using the ideas and details from your cause-effect chart on page 154. Follow the paragraph outline below and use the cause-effect transition words to the right as you write your paragraph.

Paragraph Outline

Topic Sentence: Begin with the topic sentence you wrote on page 155.

Body Sentences: Write body sentences that describe specific causes and effects related to your topic.

Closing Sentence: Write a closing sentence that sums up the main point.

Traits

Transitions that show cause-effect relationships: accordingly / as a result / because / consequently / for this purpose / for this reason / hence / just as / since / so / such as / therefore / thus / to illustrate / whereas

Speaking & Listening

Have your partner read your paragraph aloud. Then complete the response sheet together.

LO4 Revising: Improving the Writing

Revising involves sharing your work with a peer and improving your writing by adding, cutting, reworking, or rearranging material.

Peer Review

Sharing your writing is especially important when you are revising a first draft. The feedback that you receive will help you improve your paragraph. To help you respond to a classmate's writing or receive help with your own writing, use a peer-response sheet.

Respond Complete this response sheet after reading a classmate's paragraph. Then share the sheet with the writer. (Keep your comments helpful and positive.)

Paragraph title: Answers will vary. _____

Writer: _____   Reviewer: _____

1. Which part seems to work best: topic sentence, middle, or closing sentence?

   Why? _____

   _____

   _____

2. Which part needs some work? Why? _____

   _____

   _____

3. What are the causes and effects discussed in the paragraph?

   _____

   _____

   _____

4. Name two favorite details.

   a. _____

   b. _____

5. Identify a phrase or two that shows the writer's level of interest.

   _____

   _____

   _____

Using an Academic Style

Cause-effect paragraphs require an academic style, which sounds knowledgeable and confident without being stuffy. Consider the quick tips below as you revise your paragraph.

Quick Tips for Academic Style

- **Avoid personal pronouns.** Unless your instructor tells you differently, avoid using personal pronouns such as *I, we,* and *you* in your cause-effect paragraph.
- **Define technical terms and jargon.** If your readers are not experts on your topic, make sure to define the specialized vocabulary or technical words you use.
- **Beware of unnecessary intensifiers.** Words such as *really, totally,* and *completely* "overqualify" your writing and create an informal style.

Revising in Action:

Read aloud the unrevised and then the revised version of the following excerpt. Note how the changes improved the excerpt's academic style.

> Maybe the greatest effect, however, was the impact on the airline industry. ~~I think the greatest effect was the impact on aviation.~~ The result of the landing led
>
> to a ~~completely and totally~~ greater awareness of the dangers of bird populations airways.
> near ~~air hubs. You see~~ government agencies have . . .

Revise Use the following checklist and your partner's comments on the response sheet to improve your writing. Continue working until you can check off each item in the list.

Ideas

☐ **1.** Does the topic sentence clearly introduce the cause-effect relationship?

☐ **2.** Are all major causes and effects addressed?

☐ **3.** Are all the links between the causes and effects clear and logical?

Organization

☐ **4.** Do I have a topic sentence, body sentences, and a closing sentence?

☐ **5.** Have I used transitions to show cause-effect relationships and connect my ideas?

Voice

☐ **6.** Have I used an academic voice?

Insight

Think of writing style in the same way that you think of clothing style. For a formal occasion, you would dress more formally than for an everyday event. In the same way, when you write an academic essay, you use more formal language.

LO5 Editing: Pronoun-Antecedent Agreement

A **pronoun** is a word that is used in place of noun.

Pronoun-Antecedent Agreement

A pronoun usually has an **antecedent**, which is a word that the pronoun refers to or replaces. Each pronoun must agree with its antecedent in three ways: in number, in person, and in gender. When a pronoun and an antecedent fail to agree in number, person, or gender, the sentence can be confusing for the reader.

Number

Somebody needs to bring **his or her** laptop to the meeting.

(The singular pronouns *his* or *her* agree with the antecedent *somebody*.)

Person

If **students** want to do better research, **they** should talk to a librarian.

(The third person pronoun *they* agrees with the antecedent *students*.)

Gender

Chris picked up **his** lawn mower from **his** parents' garage.

(The masculine pronoun *his* agrees with the antecedent *Chris*.)

Practice Read the sentences below. Correct the pronouns so that they agree with their antecedents in number, person, and gender.

1. The musicians strummed ~~his~~ *their* guitars.

2. After Shauna finished washing the dishes, ~~it~~ *they* sparkled.

3. If the waitress wants a better tip, ~~he~~ *she* should be more polite.

4. As the basketball players walked onto the court, ~~he~~ *they* waved to the crowd.

5. Mrs. Jackson started ~~their~~ *her* car.

6. Everyone can attend the extra study session if ~~they need~~ *he or she needs* help.

7. Eric poured root beer in ~~their~~ *his* favorite mug.

Apply Read your cause-effect paragraph, watching for agreement issues between pronouns and their antecedents. Correct any pronouns that fail to agree with their antecedents in person, number, or gender.

Case of Pronouns

The case of a pronoun tells what role it can play in a sentence. There are three cases: *nominative, possessive,* and *objective*. Examine the information below, which explains how pronouns of each case are correctly used.

The nominative case is used for subjects and predicate nouns.
I, you, he, she, it, we, they

> **She** walked to the bank.

The possessive case shows possession or ownership.
my, mine, our, ours, his, her, hers, their, theirs, its, your, yours

> The jacket is **his**. This jacket is **mine**. **Your** jacket is gone.

The objective case is used for direct or indirect objects and for objects of prepositions or infinitives.
me, us, you, him, her, it, them

> Reid told **her** that going to the movie was okay with **him**.

Insight

When it comes to understanding the case of pronouns, you may have an advantage over native English speakers, who may never have thought about case. Think about how case works in your heritage language and compare English use of case.

Practice In the sentences below, replace each incorrect pronoun with a pronoun of the correct case.

1. Frank said that ~~him~~ [he] needed someone to pick ~~his~~ [him] up.

2. I looked over ~~theirs~~ [their] expense report, and ~~them~~ [they] went way over budget.

3. ~~Her~~ [She] worked on ~~she~~ [her] new project.

4. The judge commended the competitor on ~~him~~ [his] speed and agility.

5. ~~Theirs~~ [Their] lawn service is better than ~~our~~ [ours].

6. It was ~~him~~ [he] who spotted the bird.

7. The CEO increased ~~she~~ [her] pay.

8. My brother and ~~me~~ [I] attended the film festival.

Apply Read your cause-effect paragraph, checking the pronouns you've used. Make sure each pronoun is in the correct case.

Marking a Paragraph

The model that follows has a number of errors.

Editing Practice Correct the following paragraph, using the marks to the left. One correction has been done for you.

Correction Marks

- ✄ delete
- d̲ capitalize
- ᴅ̸ lowercase
- ∧ insert
- ⌄ add comma
- ? ∧ add question mark
- word ∧ add word
- ⊙ add period
- ◯ spelling
- ∿ switch

Divided Parallel

Though the fighting ceased in 1953 the effects of the Korean War resonate today. The war began in 1950 when communist-occupied North Korea, Waged war with south Korea. In a larger context, the war was caused by the United States' desire to stop communism and the Soviet Union's desire to spread communism. The effects of the conflict were considerable. Both sides suffered massive casualties, while the battle sparked the start of the cold war between the United States and the Soviet Union. Today, Korea remain divided along the 38th parallel. North Korea maintains a heavy military presence and has suffered much poverty meanwhile, South Korea has thrived economically. Though the countries have taken smalls steps toward political piece, the war has not ended.

1

5

10

Insight

All English clauses (excluding imperatives in which the subject *you* is understood) must include subjects. In sentences with more than one clause, every clause needs a subject, even if a subject has already been established in one of the other clauses.

Incorrect: Though Jerry loves baseball, prefers to play soccer.

Correct: Though Jerry loves baseball, **he** prefers to play soccer.

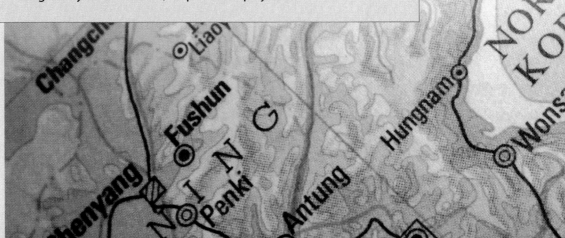

Correcting Your Paragraph

Now it's time to correct your own paragraph.

Apply Create a clean copy of your paragraph and use the following checklist to check for errors. When you can answer yes to a question, check it off. Continue working until all items are checked.

WAC

Use this checklist for editing writing assignments in all of your classes.

Editing Checklist

Words

☐ **1.** Have I used specific nouns and verbs? (See page 103.)

☐ **2.** Have I used more action verbs than "be" verbs? (See page 73.)

Sentences

☐ **3.** Have I varied the beginnings and lengths of sentences? (See pages 226–231.)

☐ **4.** Have I combined short choppy sentences? (See page 232.)

☐ **5.** Have I avoided shifts in sentences? (See page 278.)

☐ **6.** Have I avoided fragments and run-ons? (See pages 261–266, 270–271.)

Conventions

☐ **7.** Do I use correct verb forms *(he saw,* not *he seen)*? (See pages 320, 324.)

☐ **8.** Do my subjects and verbs agree *(she speaks,* not *she speak)*? (See pages 245–260.)

☐ **9.** Have I used the right words *(their, there, they're)*?

☐ **10.** Have I capitalized first words and proper nouns and adjectives? (See page 386.)

☐ **11.** Have I used commas after long introductory word groups? (See page 358.)

☐ **12.** Have I carefully checked my spelling?

Adding a Title

Make sure to add an effective title. Here are two strategies for creating one.

- **Grab the reader's attention:** Cutting Down the Atmosphere
- **Use an idea from the paragraph:** Emergency Landing

Insight

Have a classmate, friend, or family member read your work to catch any missed errors.

Sean Gladwell, 2010/used under license from www.shutterstock.com

LO6 Reviewing Cause-Effect Writing

Complete these activities as needed to help you better understand writing cause-effect paragraphs.

Cause/Effect Consider the photograph to the right. Think about potential causes and effects of forest fires. Fill in the following cause-effect chart with your ideas.

Topic: Forest Fire

1. **Cause:** Answers will vary.
   Dry conditions

1. **Effect:** Destroyed forests and homes

2. **Cause:** Human carelessness

2. **Effect:** Polluted skies

3. **Cause:** Lightning

3. **Effect:** New laws

Match In your own words, explain how to write in an academic style. (See page 159.)

Answers will vary.

Sort Circle transitions that show a *cause-effect relationship*: (See page 157.)

as a result   behind   soon   therefore   because   since

"He who establishes his argument by noise and command shows that his reason is weak."

—Michel de Montaigne

15

Argument Paragraph

Talk to enough people about any hot-button issue—whether it's health care, the economy, or the results of *American Idol*—and you are bound to get in an argument. And that's okay. Argumentation and debate make up the foundation of democracy. But an argument is only effective when it is supported by reason and logic rather than anger and fallacy.

In this chapter you will write an argument paragraph in which you take up a position on a debatable issue and give reasons to support it. Along the way you will learn how to make a compelling argument based on well-reasoned support.

Learning Outcomes

LO1 Understand argument paragraphs.

LO2 Plan an argument paragraph.

LO3 Write the first draft.

LO4 Revise the writing.

LO5 Edit the writing.

LO6 Reflect on the experience.

What do you think?

Why might a noisy argument be fueled by weak reasoning?

Answers will vary.

LO1 Reviewing a Paragraph

When you write to take a stand on a debatable issue, you are writing an argument. This chapter focuses on writing an argument paragraph. The paragraph that follows demonstrates this form.

Read/React Read the following paragraph. Then answer the questions below to identify your first impressions about it.

Support Wind Farm Energy

The **topic sentence** introduces the writer's stance on an issue.

The **body sentences** provide support for the writer's position.

The **closing sentence** reinforces the writer's position.

To counteract its dependence on fossil fuels, the United States must invest in wind farms for its energy needs. A wind farm is made up of a group of large wind turbines, which convert wind into energy. The benefits of wind farms are numerous. First, wind is a free and renewable source of energy. In comparison, fossil fuels like oil and coal are limited in supply and cost money to extract from the earth. Secondly, wind farms are a clean energy source. Unlike power plants, which emit dangerous pollutants, wind farms release no pollution into the air or water, meaning less smog, less acid rain, and fewer greenhouse emissions. And then there's this: the American Wind Energy Association reports that running a single wind turbine has the potential to displace 2,000 tons of carbon dioxide, or the equivalent of one square mile of forest trees. But despite being the fastest growing energy source in the U.S., wind energy only accounts for 1.5 percent of power supplied in the country. If the United States wants to limit carbon emissions and lessen its dependence on fossil fuels, it must act now and invest more money in wind farms. The answer is in the air.

1. Name two things you like about the paragraph.

   a. Answers will vary. _____

   _____

   b. _____

   _____

2. List two questions that you have about the paragraph. (Does the writer make a strong argument? Is more support needed?)

   a. Answers will vary. _____

   _____

   b. _____

   _____

A Closer Look

Clair's argument paragraph takes a **defensible position** on the issue of renewable energy. Her position on wind farms is debatable, but it is supported by the details in her paragraph.

Vocabulary

defensible position
a claim that is neither a fact nor an unsupportable opinion

claim
an assertion that something is true or factual

Identify Clair's position on wind farms is supported by two main **claims** regarding the benefits of wind farms. In the chart below, identify the two claims and the evidence (facts, statistics) used to support them.

Position: The U.S. should invest in wind farm technology.

■ Claim 1: Wind is a free and renewable source of energy.

Supporting evidence:

Fossil fuels are limited and cost money to extract from the earth.

■ Claim 2: Wind farms are a clean energy source.

Supporting evidence:

Wind farms release no dangerous pollutants or greenhouse emissions. A single wind turbine can displace 2,000 tons of carbon dioxide

Explain In your opinion, which claim is backed by the strongest evidence? Why?

Answers will vary.

LO2 Prewriting: Planning

In your own paragraph, you will take a position on a debatable issue. Choose an issue that you care about and a position you believe in.

Selecting a Topic

Will began his topic search by browsing newspapers, magazines, and the Internet for current issues that people have strong feelings about.

Select In the space below, list three or four debatable issues you could write about in an argument paragraph. Circle your favorite topic.

Answers will vary.

Selecting a Position

Once you decide on a topic, state a preliminary position about it. In one sentence, write a defensible **position statement** using the formula below.

Topic			Position		Position Statement
Text messaging while driving	+	*would, should, must, ought to, needs*	be banned in all states	=	Text messaging while driving should be banned in all states.

Create Write a position statement by providing the topic, selecting a verb, and indicating your position.

Topic: Answers will vary. + *would, should, must, ought to, needs* +

Position: _____

Position Statement: _____

Refining a Position

With your initial position written, use the following strategies to develop and refine your opinion on the issue:

- **Research** all possible positions on the issue. Who supports each position and why? Who opposes it and why?

- **Gather** solid evidence regarding your issue. Does the most compelling evidence support or oppose your position?

- **Refine** your position. At this point, you may have new convictions about your position, or you may have changed your mind about it. Before you are ready to write, clarify your position statement.

WAC

In any discipline, the ability to make a strong argument is important. In the sciences, you might need to argue for a specific theory or practice. In business, you might need to convince colleagues or clients of a specific solution.

Gathering Details

When you take a stand on an issue, you must gather convincing support to defend your position. Will gathered four different types of details to support his position: **facts**, **statistics**, **testimonials**, and **predictions**.

Support Chart

Fact
Nineteen states and the District of Columbia have passed laws against text messaging while driving.

Statistic
According to the U.S. Department of Transportation, mobile devices contribute to 6,000 deaths per year.

Testimony
In the words of U.S. Secretary of Transportation Ray LaHood, "This is an important safety step, and we will be taking more to eliminate the threat of distracted driving."

Prediction
Roads will be a safer place when text messaging while driving is banned in all states.

Gather Fill in the support chart below with the research you have gathered about your issue. If you have not found supporting details for each category, consider doing additional research.

Facts	Answers will vary.
Statistics	
Testimonials	
Predictions	

Traits

Gathering different types of details will strengthen your ability to argue your point.

Vocabulary

facts
details that offer statements or claims of verified information

statistics
details that offer concrete numbers about a topic

testimonials
details that offer insight from an authority on the topic

predictions
details that offer insights into possible outcomes or consequences by forecasting what might happen under certain conditions

LO3 Writing: Creating a First Draft

Provided below is Will's paragraph, arguing for a nationwide ban on text messaging while driving. Will used a variety of supporting details to build his argument.

Read/React Carefully read Will's argument paragraph. Then answer the questions that follow.

Text Messaging and Driving Don't Mix

Position
      Text messaging while driving should be banned in all states 1 because the practice is making U.S. roadways dangerous. Car crashes rank among the leading causes of death in the United States, but many blame the frequency of drinking and driving and ignore the dangers of **texting** and driving. Studies by the National 5 Highway Traffic Safety Administration show that text messaging while driving is about six times more likely to result in an accident than drunk driving. And according to the U.S. Department of Transportation, mobile devices contribute to almost 6,000 deaths

Support
per year. The major danger associated with texting is the distraction 10 it causes to the driver. When a driver's eyes are concentrating on a phone instead of the road, he or she is more likely to get in an accident. Some critics say teenage drivers are the problem, but 20 percent of adults in a recent AAA study admitted regularly sending text messages while driving. At least nineteen states and 15 the District of Columbia understand the aforementioned dangers and have passed bans on texting while driving. Let's make all of

Call to Action
our roads a safer place; the time has come to make text messaging while driving illegal in every state.

1. What is the position statement in the paragraph? (Underline it.) What does it tell you about the paragraph?

   It introduces the topic and explains why it is important.

2. What types of supporting details are included in the paragraph? Give examples.

   Fact: 19 states and the District of Columbia banned texting while driving;

   Stat: Mobile devices contribute to 6,000 deaths per year.

3. Do you think Will makes a reasonable argument? Why or why not?

   Answers will vary.

Khromov Alexey ,2010 / Used under license from Shutterstock.com

Write Using the information you gathered during prewriting, create a first draft of your argument paragraph. Connect your thoughts with appropriate transitions, and follow the paragraph outline below.

Transition words that show importance:

first of all / to begin / secondly / another reason / the best reason / also / in addition / more importantly / most importantly / finally

Paragraph Outline

Topic Sentence: Start your paragraph with a statement that introduces the topic and gives your position on the issue.

Body Sentences: Clarify and support your position statement, using logical and reliable support.

Closing Sentence: Reaffirm your position and, if appropriate, encourage the reader to adopt it.

Speaking & Listening

Have your partner read your paragraph aloud. Then complete the response sheet together.

LO4 Revising: Improving the Writing

Revising involves sharing your work with a peer and improving your writing by adding, cutting, reworking, or rearranging material.

Peer Review

Sharing your writing is especially important when you are revising a first draft. The feedback that you receive will help you improve your paragraph. To help you respond to a classmate's writing or receive help with your own, use a peer-response sheet.

Respond Complete this response sheet after reading the first draft of a classmate's paragraph. Then share the sheet with the writer. (Keep your comments helpful and positive.)

Paragraph title: _Answers will vary._

Writer: _____ Reviewer: _____

1. Which part seems to work best: topic sentence, middle, or closing sentence?

   Why? _____

   _____

   _____

2. Which part needs some work? Why? _____

   _____

   _____

3. What are two types of support used in the paragraph?

   _____

   _____

   _____

4. Identify a portion of the paragraph that illustrates the writer's passion for the subject.

   _____

   _____

   _____

Ustyujanin, 2010/used under license from www.shutterstock.com

Five Common Logical Fallacies

A **logical fallacy** is a false assertion that weakens an argument by distorting an issue, drawing faulty conclusions, misusing evidence, or misusing language. Below are five common logical fallacies that should be removed from your writing.

Logical Fallacies

1. A **bare assertion** denies that an issue is debatable, claiming, "That's just how it is."

   > Withdrawal of troops is our only option for peace.
   > *(The claim discourages discussion of other ways to promote peace.)*

2. A **threat** is a simple way to sabotage an argument, claiming, "If you don't agree with me, you'll regret it."

   > If you don't accept alternative fuel sources, get ready to move back to the Stone Age.

3. A **slippery slope** fallacy argues that a single step will start an unstoppable chain of events. While such a slide may occur, the prediction lacks hard evidence.

   > If we build a skate park, vandalism is going to run rampant in our city.

4. An **unreliable testimonial** is a statement made by a biased or unqualified source. A testimonial only has force if it is made by an authority qualified in the proper field.

5. A **half-truth** contains part of but not the whole truth.

   > Three out of five doctors recommend ibuprofen, according to a recent study. *(This may be true in this one study but not universally.)*

Revise Improve your writing using the following checklist and your partner's comments on the response sheet. Continue working until you can check off each item in the list.

Ideas
- [ ] **1.** Does my topic sentence identify an issue and my position?
- [ ] **2.** Do I include a variety of supporting details?
- [ ] **3.** Do I avoid errors in logic?

Organization
- [ ] **4.** Do I have a topic sentence, body sentences, and a closing sentence?
- [ ] **5.** Have I used transitions to connect my ideas?

Voice
- [ ] **6.** Do I sound knowledgeable and passionate about the issue?

Speaking & Listening

Listen to a political debate or watch a political attack ad. See if you can detect any of these distortions in logic. What does the distortion do to the speaker's credibility?

Vocabulary

logical fallacy
a false assertion that may distort an issue, sabotage an argument, draw faulty conclusions, misuse evidence, or misuse language

LO5 Editing: Mechanics

"Mechanics" refers to the standards of presenting written language; capitalization and number use are two of the mechanics issues writers encounter.

Capitalization Errors

Capitalizing proper nouns and proper adjectives (adjectives derived from proper nouns) is a basic rule of capitalization. There are times, however, when certain words are capitalized in one instance but not in another. The quick guide below refers to a number of these special cases. (Also see pages 385–394.).

Capitalize	Do Not Capitalize
American	un-American
January, May	winter, spring
The South is quite conservative	Turn south at the stop sign.
Duluth City College	a Duluth college
Chancellor John Bohm	John Bohm, our chancellor
President Obama	the president of the United States
Earth (planet name)	the earth
Internet	electronic communications network

Proofreading Practice In each sentence below, indicate which words should be capitalized, using the correction mark (≡).

1. with november around the corner, it's only so long until winter engulfs minnesota.

2. Flag burning is the definition of an un-american activity.

3. I caught up with chancellor Greg Williams of the university of pittsburgh.

4. I used the internet to find out that Missouri is nicknamed the show-me state.

5. My favorite french restaurant rests in a quiet neighborhood off college avenue.

6. The west coast is known for its laid-back lifestyle.

7. Does the winter sports season begin before or after december?

8. The president of the united states lives in the white house.

Apply As you edit your paragraph, be careful to discern common nouns from proper nouns. Remember: **Do not** capitalize common nouns and titles that appear near, but are not part of, a proper noun.

Using Numbers

When a paragraph includes numbers or statistics, you will have to know whether to write them as words or as numerals. Below are three basic rules to follow.

Numerals or Words

Numbers from one to one hundred are usually written as words; numbers 101 and greater are usually written as numerals.

two	seven	twenty-five	103	1,489

Numerals Only

Use numerals for the following forms: decimals, percentages, pages, chapters, addresses, dates, telephone numbers, identification numbers, and statistics.

13.1	20 percent	Highway 41	chapter 6
February 12, 2010	(273) 289-2288	2.4 feet	

Words Only

Use words to express numbers that begin a sentence.

Thirteen players suffered from food poisoning.

WAC

When writing in a specific subject area such as mathematics or science, use the number conventions of that discipline.

Proofreading Practice In each sentence below, cross out any incorrect numbers and write the correct form above.

1. My 2 (two) cousins, Braden and Candace, live 4 (four) miles apart on Highway ~~Eleven~~ (11).

2. ~~300~~ (Three hundred) raffle tickets were bought at the gates.

3. The results showed ~~twenty-five~~ (25) percent of participants were born before January ~~first~~ (1), 1985.

4. Please review chapter ~~seventeen~~ (17) for the test on Monday.

5. The coastal reef is ~~two point eight~~ (2.8) knots away.

6. ~~15~~ (Fifteen) of us are hoping to complete the ~~three point one~~ (3.1)-mile race.

Apply Read your argument paragraph, paying special attention to sentences that include numbers and statistics. Present numbers in the correct way: either as numerals or as words.

Marking a Paragraph

Editing Practice Correct the following paragraph, using the marks to the left. One correction has been done for you.

Correction Marks

- ℑ delete
- d̲ capitalize
- ∅ lowercase
- ∧ insert
- ⌃ add comma
- ? add question
- ∧ mark
- word ∧ add word
- ⊙ add period
- ◯ spelling
- ∿ switch

A Super Blow to Roscoe

For the good of the local economy⌃ the Roscoe City Council must vote down a   1

proposal to build a SuperMart store on Highway ⌃Thirty-One⌃ The discount chain

(31)

may slash prices,⌃ it will slash local businesses in the process. ⌃a University of

(but)

Iowa study showed a group of small towns lost up to 47 percent of ◯they're◯ retail

trade after ten years of a SuperMart moving in nearby. Grocery stores and retail   5

businesses were hit the hardest. If a SuperMart comes to Roscoe⌃ local grocers

like Troyer's will have to lower wages or risk ◯clozing◯ A 2007 study showed how a

SuperMart caused a ⌃one point five⌃ percent reduction in earnings for local grocery

(1.5)

stores. Proponents of a SuperMart expansion ⌃says⌃ the store will bring new jobs,

(say)

more sales taxes, and great bargains. But all SuperMart will accomplish is   10

reallocating where existing income is spent. The Roscoe City Council should look

for alternatives to jump-start the community's economy⌃ vote no for SuperMart.

Insight

On the previous page, you learned some basic rules for using numbers in your writing. Here is another useful guideline:

- Use numerals when the time of day is expressed with an abbreviation; spell out the number when time is expressed in words.

  6:00 p.m. or **six o'clock** (not *6 o'clock*)

  the **2:15** p.m. train (not *two-fifteen p.m. train*)

  an **eleven o'clock** wake-up call (not *an 11 o'clock wake-up call*)

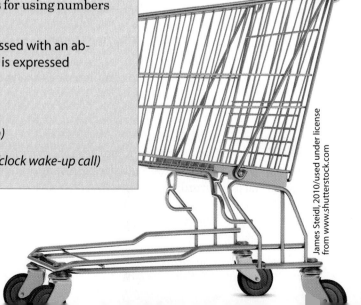

James Steidl, 2010/used under license from www.shutterstock.com

Correcting Your Paragraph

WAC

Use this checklist for editing writing assignments in all of your classes.

Now it's time to correct your own paragraph.

Apply Create a clean copy of your paragraph and use the following checklist to check for errors. When you can answer yes to a question, check it off. Continue working until all items are checked.

Words

☐ **1.** Have I used specific nouns and verbs? (See page 103.)

☐ **2.** Have I used more action verbs than "be" verbs? (See page 73.)

Sentences

☐ **3.** Have I varied the beginnings and lengths of sentences? (See pages 226–231.)

☐ **4.** Have I combined short choppy sentences? (See page 232.)

☐ **5.** Have I avoided shifts in sentences? (See page 278.)

☐ **6.** Have I avoided fragments and run-ons? (See pages 261–266, 270–271.)

Conventions

☐ **7.** Do I use correct verb forms (*he saw,* not *he seen*)? (See pages 320, 324.)

☐ **8.** Do my subjects and verbs agree (*she speaks,* not *she speak*)? (See pages 245–260.)

☐ **9.** Have I used the right words (*their, there, they're*)?

☐ **10.** Have I capitalized first words and proper nouns and adjectives? (See page 386.)

☐ **11.** Have I used commas after long introductory word groups? (See page 358.)

☐ **12.** Have I carefully checked my spelling?

Adding a Title

Make sure to add an attention-getting title. Here are three simple strategies for creating one.

- **Create a slogan:** Support Wind Farm Energy
- **Sum up your argument:** Texting and Driving Don't Mix
- **Use a play on words:** A Super Blow to Roscoe

Insight

Have a classmate, friend, or family member read your work to catch any missed errors.

Create Prepare a clean final copy of your paragraph and proofread it.

LO6 Reviewing Argument Writing

Complete these activities as needed to help you better understand writing argument paragraphs.

Explain In three or four sentences, respond to the following prompt:

> In an argument paragraph, a writer's argument succeeds or fails based on its support.

What does this statement mean? What kinds of support can make a claim more convincing? (See page 169.)

Answers will vary.

Match Draw a line to connect each logical fallacy with the claim that best demonstrates that fallacy.

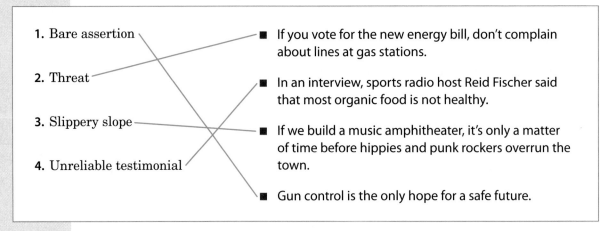

1. Bare assertion

2. Threat

3. Slippery slope

4. Unreliable testimonial

- If you vote for the new energy bill, don't complain about lines at gas stations.

- In an interview, sports radio host Reid Fischer said that most organic food is not healthy.

- If we build a music amphitheater, it's only a matter of time before hippies and punk rockers overrun the town.

- Gun control is the only hope for a safe future.

Sort Circle the words that should be capitalized (See page 174.)

e-mail   winter   (internet)   (american)

(president obama)   earthmover   (earth (planet name))   (july)

Ilja Mašík, 2010/used under license from www.shutterstock.com

> "Prose is architecture, not interior decoration."
> —Ernest Hemingway

16 Writing Essays

Architecture is the art or science of building. Using steel, glass, stone, concrete, and other composites, the architect creates unified forms or structures that can stand up to the elements

Writing, too, is the art or science of building. Using sentences and paragraphs, not steel and concrete, the writer creates strong writing forms that can stand up to repeated readings.

This chapter addresses the essay, the academic form most commonly assigned in the college classroom. As you learn about the essay-writing process, you yourself will develop an essay of definition.

Learning Outcomes

LO1 Review an academic essay.

LO2 Plan an essay.

LO3 Draft an essay.

LO4 Revise an essay.

LO5 Edit an essay.

LO6 Prepare the final copy for publishing.

What do you think?

Why does Hemingway connect writing with architecture but not with interior decoration?

Answers will vary.

LO1 Reviewing an Academic Essay

An **essay** is a piece of academic writing containing multiple paragraphs. Because it is a longer piece of writing, you can go into more depth in an essay than you can in a single paragraph. The following essay of definition by student writer Martina Lincoln explores the concept of tact from a number of different angles.

Read Carefully read the following essay and side notes.

Break It to Them Gently

Beginning
The first paragraph gains the reader's attention and states the thesis.

A few years ago, there was a new student in one of my high school classes. (I'll call him Bill.) Bill suffered from unbearably yellow teeth that grossed everyone out. One loudmouthed boor suggested that Bill "Ajax" his teeth. Of course, Bill turned every shade of red and just wanted to disappear. Had the boor any sense of empathy, he would have realized that there were far more tactful ways to address the new student. Tact is the sensitive handling of situations, even those that are potentially hurtful.

Middle
Each middle paragraph addresses an important element of tact.

Sensitivity is a major component of tact. If a person isn't sensitive to another person's feelings, there is no way that he or she can be tactful. Young people are especially vulnerable and must be handled sensitively. My five-year-old nephew proudly announced that he had cleaned the screen on the family television. Unfortunately, he used a furniture polish that left an oily film on the screen. My sister thanked him for his efforts—and then showed him how to clean the screen properly. Her sensitivity enabled my nephew to keep his self-respect. But sensitivity by itself is not enough.

Truthfulness is another important component of tact. A tactful person expresses herself sensitively and truthfully. Doctors, for example, must be truthful when conversing with patients. If a patient is seriously ill, a tactful doctor will truthfully explain the situation but do so with as much sensitivity as possible. Part of the discussion will certainly focus on the best ways to deal with the illness. An understanding doctor will use tact with the patient's relatives as well. Instead of bluntly stating the patient's condition, she might say, "I'm sorry to report that . . . ." and/or "The good news is that . . . ." These are tactful ways of dealing with uncomfortable truths.

Tact should not be confused with deceit or cleverness. Deceit occurs when a credit card company fails to clearly explain the penalties for missed or late payments. It occurs in the courtroom when a lawyer phrases his questions in such a way that a witness says something he or she never meant to say. An admiring listener might say, "How tactful he is, this lawyer!" Crafty he may be, but tactful he is not. Being tactful requires speaking sincerely, not talking around or avoiding an issue.

Closing
The last paragraph summarizes the essay's main points and stresses the importance of tact.

Sensitivity, truthfulness, and sincerity are all connected to tactfulness. They all must be utilized, especially in touchy situations when people's feelings are an issue. Tactful people are individuals that we should admire and respect. They should be our role models, showing by example how to deal with our peers, our family members, and our fellow citizens. Thinking of the opposite, living in a society that condones insensitivity and deceit, reveals the importance of tact in our lives.

React Answer the following questions about the essay on page 180.

1. What sentence in the first paragraph states the focus of the essay? Write it here.

   Tact is the sensitive handling of situations, even those that are potentially hurtful.

2. What is the topic sentence of the second paragraph?

   Sensitivity is a major component of tact.

3. How does the writer support or develop this topic sentence?

   The writer uses a personal anecdote to support the idea of the topic sentence.

4. What is the topic sentence of the third paragraph?

   Truthfulness is another important component of tact.

5. How does the writer support or develop this topic sentence?

   The writer describes how truthfulness is used in a professional setting (doctor's office) as a form of tact.

6. What is the topic sentence of the fourth paragraph?

   Tact should not be confused with deceit or cleverness.

7. How does this paragraph differ from the other middle paragraphs?

   It offers examples of situations that are confused as tactful, but are actually the opposite of tactful.

8. What is the topic sentence of the closing paragraph?

   Sensitivity, truthfulness, and sincerity are all connected to tactfulness.

9. What is the writer attempting to accomplish in this paragraph?

   The writer wants to commend the actions of tactful people and explain how important they are in a sometimes not-so-tactful society.

"When I wear high heels, I have a great vocabulary and I speak in paragraphs. I'm most **eloquent**. I plan to wear them more often."

—Meg Ryan

Vocabulary

eloquent
effective or powerful in speech

WAC

Often, instructors will assign essays to help you deepen your thinking about a topic and share what you know about it.

LO2 Prewriting: Planning

On the following pages, you will learn about the essay-writing process, and at the same time, you will develop an essay of definition, much like the one you read and reacted to on pages 180–181. Refer to that essay as needed while you write your own essay.

Selecting a Topic

In the sample essay, Martina defined the **abstract** term *tact*. A list of other abstract ideas follows. Consider these terms as possible topics for your own essay. (Use a dictionary to look up any words that are unfamiliar.)

| courage | empathy | honesty | humility | joy | envy | competitiveness |

Create List four or five more abstract terms of your own choosing. Then circle the one idea (above or below) that you want to write about in a definition essay.

Answers will vary. _____ _____ _____ _____

Gathering Your Own Thoughts

Once you select an essay topic, explore your thoughts and feelings about it. This will help you discover what you already know about the topic and what you still need to find out about it.

Explore In the space provided below, write freely about your topic. Consider why you selected it, what you already know about it, when and where you have seen it in action, and so on. (Use your own paper if you need more space.)

Answers will vary.

Collecting Additional Information

For most types of academic essays, you will need to find out more information than you already know about a topic. Martina, for example, found a definition of her term and used it in the first paragraph of her essay. Then, in her middle paragraphs, she identified the idea's essential parts and also determined what her topic isn't.

Collect Complete the gathering grid below to collect information about your topic.

Gathering Grid

Dictionary definition	Answers will vary.
One component or part of the topic	
Another component or part of the topic	
A third component (optional)	
What your topic is not (consider a key antonym or two)	

Focusing Your Efforts

Once you understand your topic well, you are ready to write a thesis statement that explains the focus of your essay.

Create Write a thesis statement for your essay of definition following this formula:

Topic		Thought or Feeling		Thesis Statement
Tact	**+**	the sensitive handling of situations, even those that are potentially hurtful	**=**	Tact is the sensitive handling of situations, even those that are potentially hurtful.

Thesis Statement:

Answers will vary.

Organizing Your Ideas for Writing

To complete your planning, decide which main points to include (*ideas that support your thesis*) and how to arrange them.

Arrange Number the main points in your gathering grid above to put them in the best order for your essay.

LO3 Writing: Creating a First Draft

An essay consists of the opening, the middle, and the closing parts, just as a paragraph has a topic sentence, body sentences, and a closing sentence.

- The topic sentence becomes the opening paragraph.
- The body sentences become the middle paragraphs.
- The closing sentence becomes the closing paragraph.

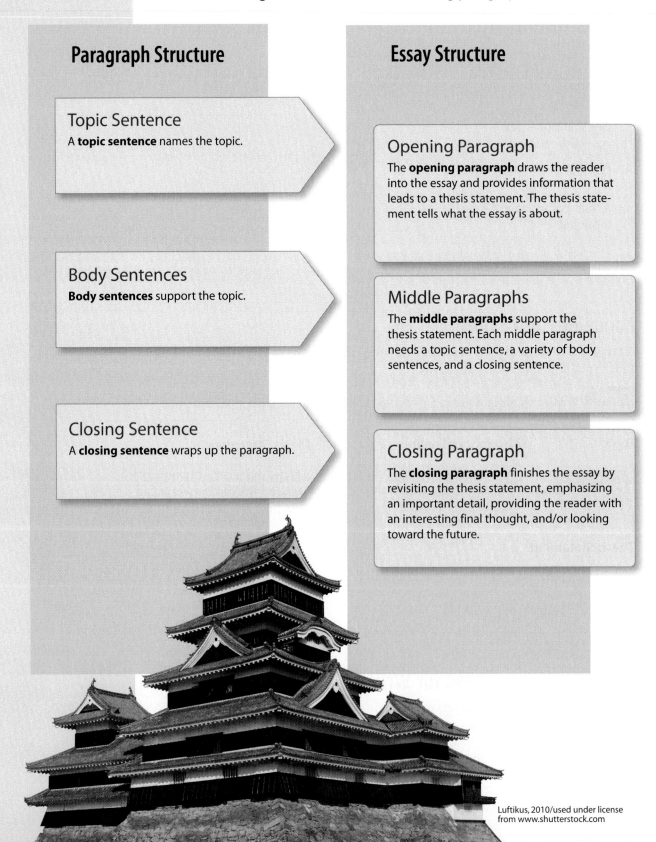

Paragraph Structure

Topic Sentence
A **topic sentence** names the topic.

Body Sentences
Body sentences support the topic.

Closing Sentence
A **closing sentence** wraps up the paragraph.

Essay Structure

Opening Paragraph
The **opening paragraph** draws the reader into the essay and provides information that leads to a thesis statement. The thesis statement tells what the essay is about.

Middle Paragraphs
The **middle paragraphs** support the thesis statement. Each middle paragraph needs a topic sentence, a variety of body sentences, and a closing sentence.

Closing Paragraph
The **closing paragraph** finishes the essay by revisiting the thesis statement, emphasizing an important detail, providing the reader with an interesting final thought, and/or looking toward the future.

Luftikus, 2010/used under license from www.shutterstock.com

Writing the Opening Paragraph

The thesis statement is the most important part of the opening paragraph. But of course, there is more to an opening than this one statement. The writer must get the reader's attention with (1) a surprising statement, (2) an appropriate quotation, (3) a thought-provoking question, or (4) an anecdote (interesting story). Martina opens her essay with an anecdote and then states her thesis.

Create On your own paper, develop the opening paragraph for your definition essay. Begin by getting your reader's attention using one of the strategies above, then provide any necessary background information, and, finally, state your thesis.

Developing the Middle Part

The middle paragraphs in an essay support or explain the thesis. In most cases, each middle paragraph develops one main supporting point. Here is the thesis statement and the topic sentences for each of the middle paragraphs in Martina's essay.

> ### Thesis Statement
> *Tact is the sensitive handling of situations, even those that are potentially hurtful.*
>
> ### Topic Sentences:
> ■ *Sensitivity is a major component of tact.*
> ■ *Truthfulness is another important component of tact.*
> ■ *Tact should not be confused with deceit or cleverness.*

Traits

To support each topic sentence in your middle paragraphs, provide examples as Martina does in her paragraphs.

Write Continue your essay by writing the middle paragraphs. Be sure that each middle paragraph focuses on one main supporting point. Refer to your list of main points on page 183.

Ending the Essay

The closing paragraph brings an essay to a logical stopping point. An effective closing will often do one or more of these things: (1) restate the thesis, (2) review the main supporting points, (3) stress a key point, and/or (4) provide a final thought for the reader to consider.

In the sample essay, Martina reviews her main points and provides the reader with a few final key thoughts.

Create Complete your essay with a closing paragraph. Use at least two of the strategies listed above. Be sure to share important thoughts and ideas since they will create the final image of your topic for the reader.

Lev Olkha, 2010/used under license from www.shutterstock.com

Traits

Revising deals with improving the ideas and organization in your writing; it does not deal with correcting a few surface errors. That comes later.

LO4 Revising: Improving the Essay

During revising, you review your first draft to determine what parts work and what parts need to be improved. *Remember:* All first drafts require changes before they read clearly and logically. Your basic revising moves include adding, deleting, rewriting, and/or rearranging information.

Having a Peer Review Your Work

Always ask at least one of your writing peers to review your first draft. The feedback you receive will help you identify changes that you need to make. Use a peer-response sheet like the one below.

Respond Exchange first drafts with a classmate and complete this response sheet for each other's writing. (Keep your comments helpful and positive.)

Essay title: _Answers will vary._ _____

Writer: _____ Reviewer: _____

1. What is the thesis of the essay? _____
   _____
   _____

2. List the main points that support the thesis. (There should be three or more.) _____
   _____
   _____

3. Does the closing paragraph bring the essay to an effective stopping point? If so, how?
   _____
   _____

4. What do you like most about the essay? _____
   _____
   _____
   _____

5. What could the writer do to improve the essay? _____
   _____
   _____
   _____

Building Coherence

To make sure that your essay is coherent, connect your ideas by repeating key words and adding transitions. Martina repeated key words and used a transition in the first and last sentences of her paragraphs to build coherence into her essay.

Coherence in Martina's Essay

- **Thesis statement:** Tact is the sensitive handling of situations, even those that are potentially hurtful.

- **First middle paragraph:** Sensitivity is a major component of tact.... But sensitivity by itself is not enough.

- **Second middle paragraph:** Truthfulness is another important component of tact.... These are tactful ways of dealing with uncomfortable truths.

- **Third middle paragraph:** Tact should not be confused with deceit and cleverness.... Being tactful requires speaking sincerely, not talking around or avoiding an issue.

- **Closing paragraph:** Sensitivity, truthfulness, and sincerity are all connected to tactfulness.

Revise Use your classmate's comments and the following checklist to improve the first draft of your essay. Add, cut, rewrite, and rearrange information as needed. Continue revising until you can check off each item in the list.

Ideas

- ☐ **1.** Does my essay draw the reader in and include a clear thesis statement?
- ☐ **2.** Do I support my thesis with at least three main ideas developed in separate paragraphs?
- ☐ **3.** Do I include enough details and examples in each paragraph?
- ☐ **4.** Does my closing paragraph bring the essay to an effective end?

Organization

- ☐ **5.** Does my essay include opening, middle, and closing paragraphs?
- ☐ **6.** Are my middle paragraphs in the best order?
- ☐ **7.** Are all of my details organized in the best way?
- ☐ **8.** Is my essay coherent, with key words or transitions linking paragraphs?

Voice

- ☐ **9.** Do I sound knowledgeable about and interested in my topic?

Vocabulary

coherent
logically ordered and connected

LO5 Editing: Modifiers

When you edit your essay, you check it for style and correctness. Editing for style means making sure that you have used the best words and that your sentences read smoothly. Editing for correctness means making sure that you have followed the rules for punctuation, capitalization, usage, grammar, and spelling.

Dangling Modifiers

Test Taking

Some tests require you to correct errors with modifiers. For more practice, see pages 276–277.

Dangling modifiers are a type of sentence error that can confuse the reader. They are modifiers that describe a word that isn't in the sentence.

> **Dangling modifier:**
>
> After finishing her routine, the judge rated the performance.
> *(It sounds as if the judge finished the routine.)*
>
> **Corrected:**
>
> After Juanita finished her routine, the judge rated the performance.

Editing Practice Correct any dangling modifiers below by rewriting the sentences. If a sentence contains no modifying error, write a C on the line. (The first one has been done for you.)

1. Using a computer to diagnose the engine problem, my car was repaired. _____

   Using a computer to diagnose the engine problem, the mechanic repaired

   my car.

2. While playing the piano, our dog began to howl. While I played the piano, our

   dog began to howl.

3. Scanning the horizon, a faint plume of smoke appeared. When we scanned the

   horizon, a faint plume of smoke appeared.

4. After standing in line all morning, the ticket seller said all tickets were sold out.

   After I stood in line all morning, the ticket seller said all tickets were sold out.

5. After finishing the main course, the server wheeled out the dessert tray. _____

   After we finished the main course, the server wheeled out the dessert tray.

Apply Read through your essay, looking for dangling modifiers. Correct any that you find by rewriting the sentence so that the modifier clearly modifies the correct word.

Misplaced Modifiers

Misplaced modifiers are similar to dangling modifiers in that they create a confusing or illogical idea. They occur when a modifier seems to modify the wrong word in a sentence.

> **Misplaced modifier:**
>
> Ms. Jones fixed several snacks for the kids with healthful ingredients.
> *(It sounds as if the kids contain the healthful ingredients.)*
>
> **Corrected:**
>
> Ms. Jones fixed several snacks with healthful ingredients for the kids.

Editing Practice Underline the misplaced modifier in each of the following sentences. Then correct the error by rewriting the sentence. (The first one has been done for you.)

1. That painting is my favorite piece in the entire gallery <u>with the brilliant colors</u>.

   That painting with the brilliant colors is my favorite piece in the entire gallery.

2. Athletes must train rigorously to prepare for the Olympics <u>without any letup</u>.

   Athletes must train rigorously without any letup to prepare for the Olympics.

3. When women rode bicycles, they were told it was not feminine <u>in the 1890s</u>.

   When women rode bicycles in the 1890s, they were told it was not feminine.

4. I am visiting two apartments that I will consider renting <u>over the weekend</u>.

   Over the weekend, I am visiting two apartments that I will consider renting.

5. Please review the résumé describing my qualifications and experience <u>enclosed</u>.

   Please review the enclosed résumé describing my qualifications

   and experience.

Apply Read through your essay, checking for misplaced modifiers. Correct any that you find by rewriting the sentence so that the modifier is placed next to the appropriate word.

Speaking & Listening

When editing, always read the writing out loud, at least once. Hearing the words will help you catch some errors that are easily missed during silent readings.

Correction Marks

 delete

d̲ capitalize

D̸ lowercase

∧ insert

∧̂ add comma

? ∧ add question mark

word ∧ add a word

⊙ add period

⬭ spelling

⏝ switch

Using the Editing Symbols

When editing for correctness, use the correction marks on the left side of this page to mark errors and show how you would correct them.

Editing Practice Correct the following paragraphs from a student's definition essay, using the editing symbols.

Different Shades of Equality

Webster's collegiate Dictionary defines feminism as "the theory of   1
political, economic, and social equality of the sexes." However, feminism
is a movement that has significantly affected all women with varied
interpretations. Ultimately, it defines itself according to the situation and the
people involved.   5

Some feminists expect to be treated like men, while others want
freedoms more closely associated with their there own sex. Some feminists find
nudity degrading, while others see it as an expression of art. Some feminists
still appreciate **chivalry**, while others find it offensive⊙

Some critics of the movement believe that some feminists have gone   10
too ∧ to far. Individuals that question the movement believe that some feminists
equate equality with the freedom to do whatever they want. **skeptics** also
say that radical feminists begrudge men their sexual difference∧ That true
equality should negate the facts of life.

A more moderate approach to feminism focuses on issues such as sharing   15
with men the right to justice, the right to be treated with respect∧and the right
to make important lifestyle choices. A moderate feminist wants the freedom to
decide whether to focus on a career, on motherhood, or on a combination of the
two. What a moderate feminist doesn't want is to be accused of surrendering
to male dominance. If she, for example, chooses to be a stay-at-home mom, at   20
least for part of her life.

Some women don't want to be associated with feminism. They don't
want to get a job because they are the token woman, they are not interested in
recieving any other special favors. They are is quite satisfied with being a woman,
but in a world where the capabilities and interests of the individual are what   25
really matters.

Vocabulary

chivalry
acting like a gentleman, with honesty, courtesy, and bravery

skeptics
people who doubt or question accepted beliefs

Correcting Your Essay

When editing your paragraphs and essays, it helps to use a basic checklist as a guide. You may also want to keep a personal list of errors as a handy reference.

Apply Create a clean copy of your essay; then use the following checklist to edit it for errors. When you can answer yes to a question, check it off. Continue editing until all of the items are checked.

Editing Checklist

Words

- ☐ **1.** Have I used specific nouns and verbs? (See page 103.)

- ☐ **2.** Have I used more action verbs than "be" verbs? (See page 73.)

Sentences

- ☐ **3.** Have I varied the beginnings and lengths of sentences? (See pages 226–231.)

- ☐ **4.** Have I combined short choppy sentences? (See page 232.)

- ☐ **5.** Have I avoided shifts in sentences? (See page 278.)

- ☐ **6.** Have I avoided fragments and run-ons? (See pages 261–266, 270–271.)

Conventions

- ☐ **7.** Do I use correct verb forms (*he saw*, not *he seen*)? (See pages 320, 324.)

- ☐ **8.** Do my subjects and verbs agree (*she speaks*, not *she speak*)? (See pages 245–260.)

- ☐ **9.** Have I used the right words (*their, there, they're*)?

- ☐ **10.** Have I capitalized first words and proper nouns and adjectives? (See page 386.)

- ☐ **11.** Have I used commas after long introductory word groups? (See page 358.)

- ☐ **12.** Have I punctuated dialogue correctly? (See pages 104–105.)

- ☐ **13.** Have I carefully checked my spelling?

Adding a Title

Be sure to add an appropriate title to your essay. Here are three simple strategies for creating one.

- **Pick up on a key phrase:** A Movement Gone Too Far?
- **Focus on an important element:** Different Shades of Equality
- **Use strong, colorful words from the paragraph:** A Defining Movement

Create Prepare a clean final copy of your essay and proofread it.

> **Insight**
>
> Remember to have a classmate or writing tutor check your writing for errors. You are too close to your writing to catch everything.

WAC

The most immediate form of publishing is submitting your writing to your instructor. Other forms of publishing include sharing your work with your writing peers or posting it on a class wiki or your own blog for comments.

LO6 Preparing Your Final Copy

After revising and editing your essay, you're ready to prepare the final copy for publishing. The guide that follows will help you complete this important final step in the writing process.

Preparation Guide

Be sure that you have . . .

- made all of the necessary revising and editing changes.
- responded to peer reviews of your work.
- saved all of your drafts for handy reference.
- developed a neat final copy of your work.
- **proofread** this copy for errors.
- adhered to the design guidelines provided by your instructor.

Effective Design in Action

Maintain a uniform margin.

Double-space throughout.

Use an easy-to-read typeface.

Indent first words of paragraphs.

> Martina Lincoln
>
> Dr. Meyer
>
> Composition 101
>
> October 15, 2011
>
> Break It to Them Gently
>
> A few years ago, there was a new student in one of my high school classes. *1* (I'll call him Bill.) Bill suffered from unbearably yellow teeth that grossed everyone out. One loudmouthed boor suggested that Bill "Ajax" his teeth. Of course, Bill turned every shade of red and just wanted to disappear. Had the boor any sense of empathy, he would have realized that there were far more *5* tactful ways to address the new student. Tact is the sensitive handling of situations, even those that are potentially hurtful.
>
> Sensitivity is a major component of tact. If a person isn't sensitive to another person's feelings, there is no way that he or she can be tactful. Young people are especially vulnerable and must be handled sensitively. . . . *10*

Prepare Complete the final copy of your definition essay, using the information on this page as a guide. Be sure to proofread this copy before you submit it.

Reinforcement

Complete these activities as needed to help you better understand the essay-writing process.

Paragraph vs. Essay Explain below the basic differences between a paragraph and an essay. (See pages 54–55.)

A paragraph is complete when it includes a topic sentence, details sentences, and a closing sentence. A complete essay includes an opening paragraph (including a thesis statement), a number of supporting paragraphs, and a closing paragraph.

Collecting Information Once you select a specific topic for an essay, what first step should you take to gather information, and why is the step important? (See page 182.)

Gather your own thoughts. Exploring your thoughts will help you discover what you already know about the topic and what you still need to find out.

Thesis Statement What formula can you use to write a thesis statement? (See page 183.)

topic + thought or feeling = thesis statement

Drafting an Essay An essay must have opening, middle, and closing parts. What type of information should you include in each part? (See page 184.)

Opening: Information that draws readers into the essay and information that leads to a thesis statement

Middle: Information that supports the thesis statement

Closing: Information that restates the thesis, emphasizes an important detail, and provides the reader with a final thought or call to action

"Grasp the subject; the words will follow."
—Cato the Elder

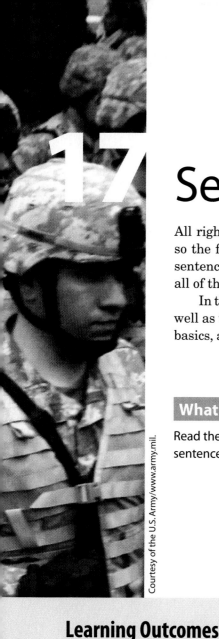

17 Sentence Basics

All right, soldiers, fall in for basic training. Of course, you've studied all of this before, so the following pages will be a review. And the basics of sentences really *are* basic. A sentence is the connection between a noun and a verb (or a subject and a predicate), with all of the other words modifying those two parts.

In the pages that follow, you will explore the ins and outs of subjects and predicates, as well as the words, phrases, and clauses that describe them. Fear not. These are sentence basics, and we'll make sure they are easy to understand.

What do you think?

Read the quotation from Cato the Elder on the facing page. How does grasping the subject of a sentence (or of a longer piece of writing) help you write the rest of the words?

Answers will vary.

Learning Outcomes

LO1 Understand subjects and predicates.

LO2 Work with special subjects.

LO3 Work with special predicates.

LO4 Understand adjectives.

LO5 Understand adverbs.

LO6 Use prepositional phrases.

LO7 Use clauses.

LO8 Apply sentence basics in a real-world context.

Volodymyr Krasyuk, 2010/used under license from www.shutterstock.com

LO1 Subjects and Verbs (Predicates)

The subject of a sentence tells what the sentence is about. The verb (predicate) of a sentence tells what the subject does or is.

> Parrots talk.
>
> └ Subject: what the sentence is about   └ Predicate: what the subject does

Simple Subject and Simple Predicate

The **simple subject** is the subject without any modifiers, and the **simple predicate** is the predicate without modifiers or objects.

> The red and black parrot sang the song all day.
>   simple subject   simple predicate

Complete Subject and Complete Predicate

The **complete subject** is the subject with modifiers, and the **complete predicate** is the predicate with modifiers and objects.

> The red and black parrot sang the song all day.
>   complete subject   complete predicate

Implied Subject

In commands, the subject *you* is implied. Commands are the only type of sentence in English that can have an **implied subject**.

> (You)   Stop singing!
> implied subject   complete predicate

Inverted Order

Most often in English, the subject comes before the predicate. However, in questions and sentences that begin with *here* or *there*, the subject comes after the predicate.

>   subject   subject
> Why are you so loud?   Here is a cracker.
>   predicate   predicate

Vocabulary

simple subject
the subject without any modifiers

simple predicate
the predicate without modifiers or objects

complete subject
the subject with modifiers

complete predicate
the predicate with modifiers and objects

implied subject
the word *you* implied in command sentences

Creating Subjects and Verbs (Predicates)

Identify/Write For each sentence below, underline and label the simple subject (SS) and simple predicate (SP). Then write a similar sentence of your own and identify the simple subject and simple predicate in the same way.

1. In the wild, <u>parrots</u> <u>gather</u> in large groups.
   SS   SP

   Answers will vary.

2. In a person's home, a <u>parrot</u> <u>needs</u> constant companionship.
   SS   SP

3. Without enough attention, some <u>parrots</u> <u>pluck</u> their feathers.
   SS   SP

4. A caring pet <u>owner</u> <u>understands</u> the parrot's need for attention.
   SS   SP

Identify/Write For each sentence below, underline and label the complete subject (CS) and complete predicate (CP). Then write a similar sentence of your own and identify the complete subject and complete predicate in the same way.

1. <u>A typical pet parrot</u> <u>can live to be eighty years old.</u>
   CS   CP

2. <u>A baby parrot bought by a forty-year-old</u> <u>could outlive the person.</u>
   CS   CP

3. <u>Parrot owners</u> <u>often place their parrots in their wills.</u>
   CS   CP

4. <u>Why do</u> <u>parrots</u> <u>live so long?</u>
   CP   CS   CP

5. <u>There must be</u> <u>an explanation.</u>
   CP   CS

LO2 Special Types of Subjects

As you work with subjects, watch for these special types.

Compound Subjects

A **compound subject** is two or more subjects connected by *and* or *or*.

> My brother and sister swim well. Dajohn, Larinda, and I love to dive.
>   compound subject   compound subject

"To" Words (Infinitives) as Subjects

An **infinitive** can function as a subject. An infinitive is a verbal form that begins with *to* and may be followed by objects or modifiers.

> To complete a one-and-a-half flip is my goal.
>   infinitive subject

"Ing" Words (Gerunds) as Subjects

A **gerund** can function as a subject. A gerund is a verb form that ends in *ing* and may be followed by objects or modifiers.

> Swimming is his favorite sport. Handing him the goggles would be nice.
> gerund subject   gerund subject

Noun Clause as Subject

A **noun clause** can function as a subject. The clause itself has a subject and a verb but cannot stand alone as a sentence. Noun clauses are introduced by words like *what, that, when, why, how, whatever,* or *whichever.*

> Whoever wants to go swimming must remember to bring a swimsuit.
>   noun clause subject

> Whatever remains of the afternoon will be spent at the pool.
>   noun clause subject

Say It

Pair up with a partner and read each sentence aloud. Take turns identifying the type of subject—compound subject, infinitive subject, gerund subject, or noun-clause subject. Discuss your answers.

1. Swimming across the pool underwater is challenging.

2. To get a lifesaving certificate is hard work.

3. Whoever gets a certificate can be a lifeguard.

4. You and I should go swimming sometime.

Creating Special Subjects

Identify/Write For each sentence below, underline and label the complete subject: compound subject (CS), infinitive (I), gerund (G), or noun clause (NC). Then write a similar sentence of your own and identify the complete subject in the same way.

1. <u>To clean the car thoroughly</u> requires a vacuum.
   I

   Answers will vary.

2. <u>Wishing for better weather</u> won't stop the rain.
   G

3. <u>The river and the lake</u> are flooding into the streets.
   CS

4. <u>Whoever needs to set the table</u> should get started now.
   NC

5. <u>Shoes, shirts, and pants</u> are required in this restaurant.
   CS

6. <u>Reading us the riot act</u> is not the best way to win us over.
   G

7. <u>To reassure your boss about the expenditures</u> is your first priority.
   I

8. <u>Whatever you plan</u> needs to be simple and affordable.
   NC

9. Are <u>Jason, Micah, and Eli</u> in the play?
   CS

10. <u>Helping us change the tire</u> will speed everything along.
   G

LO3 Special Verbs (Predicates)

As you work with predicates, watch for these special types.

Aaron Amat, 2010/used under license from www.shutterstock.com

Compound Predicates

A **compound predicate** consists of two or more predicates joined by *and* or *or*.

I sang and danced. The audience laughed, clapped, and sang along.
  └── compound predicate   └── compound predicate

Predicates with Direct Objects

A **direct object** follows a transitive verb and tells what or who receives the action of the verb.

I sang a song. I danced a few dances. I told a joke or two.
      └ direct object   └ direct object   └ direct objects

Predicates with Indirect Objects

An **indirect object** comes between a transitive verb and a direct object and tells to whom or for whom an action was done.

I sang Jim his favorite song. I told Ellen her favorite joke.
      └ indirect object   └ indirect object

Passive Predicates

When a predicate is **passive**, the subject of the sentence is being acted upon rather than acting. Often, the actor is the object of the preposition in a phrase that starts with *by*. Using that object as the subject, the sentence can be rewritten to be **active**.

Passive

Teri was serenaded by Josh.
subject   passive verb   object of the preposition

Active

Josh serenaded Teri.
subject   active verb   direct object

Say It

Pair up with a partner and read each sentence aloud. Take turns identifying the sentence as active or passive. If the sentence is passive, speak the active version out loud.

1. I threw out my back.

2. My friends were warned by the bouncer.

3. A camera crew was escorted to the exit by the guard.

4. I plan to go.

Creating Special Predicates

Identify/Write For each sentence below, underline and label any compound predicate (CP), direct object (DO), and indirect object (IO). Then write a similar sentence of your own and identify the compound predicate and direct or indirect object in the same way.

1. Everyone at the party <u>danced and sang</u>.

CP

2. The DJ played dance <u>music</u>.

DO

3. I gave <u>him</u> a <u>request</u>.

IO   DO

4. The crowd <u>twisted and shouted</u>.

CP

5. I gave my <u>date</u> a <u>kiss</u>.

IO   DO

6. The music <u>rattled and boomed</u>.

CP

7. The DJ provided <u>everyone</u> some awesome <u>entertainment</u>.

IO   DO

Identify/Write For each passive sentence below, underline and label the simple subject (SS), the simple predicate (SP), and the object of the preposition *by* (O). Then rewrite each sentence, making it active. (See "Passive Predicates" on the previous page.)

1. Many <u>songs</u> <u>were played</u> by the <u>DJ</u>.

SS   SP   O

   The DJ played many songs.

2. A good <u>time</u> <u>was had</u> by the <u>partygoers</u>.

SS   SP   O

   The partygoers had a good time.

3. My <u>friend</u> <u>was asked</u> by <u>Sarah</u> to the next party.

SS   SP   O

   Sarah asked my friend to the next party.

LO4 Adjectives

To modify a noun, use an adjective or a phrase or clause acting as an adjective.

Adjectives

Adjectives answer these basic questions: *which, what kind of, how many, how much.*

To modify the noun **books,** ask ...

Which books? ⟶ hardbound books

What kind of books? ⟶ old books

How many books? ⟶ five books

> five old hardbound **books**

Adjective Phrases and Clauses

Phrases and clauses can also act as adjectives to modify nouns.

To modify the noun **books,** ask ...

What kind of books? ⟶ books about women's issues

⟶ books showing their age

Which books? ⟶ books that my mother gave me

> Showing their age, **the books** that my mother gave me about women's issues **rest on the top shelf.**

Insight

It's less important to know the name of a phrase or clause than to know how it functions. If a group of words answers one of the adjective questions, the words are probably functioning as an adjective.

Say It

Pair up with a classmate to find adjectives—words, phrases, or clauses—that modify the nouns below. Take turns asking the questions while the other person answers.

1. **Cars**
   Which cars?
   What kind of cars?
   How many cars?

2. **Trees**
   Which trees?
   What kind of trees?
   How many trees?

Use Adjectives

Answer/Write For each noun, answer the questions using adjectives—words, phrases, or clauses. (See page 202 for help.) Then write a sentence using two or more of your answers.

1. **Dogs**   Answers will vary.

   Which dogs? _Labrador dogs_____

   What kind of dogs? _black dogs_____

   How many dogs? _two dogs_____

   Sentence: _Two black Labrador dogs played in the yard._____

   _____

   _____

   _____

2. **Classes**   Answers will vary.

   Which classes? _business classes_____

   What kind of classes? _core classes_____

   How many classes? _three classes_____

   Sentence: _I took three core business classes during my freshman year._

   _____

   _____

   _____

3. **Ideas**   Answers will vary.

   Which ideas? _Jason's idea_____

   What kind of ideas? _practical ideas_____

   How many ideas? _one idea_____

   Sentence: _Jason's one practical idea helped us get out of a jam._

   _____

   _____

   _____

LO5 Adverbs

To modify a verb, use an adverb or a phrase or clause acting as an adverb.

Adverbs

Adverbs answer these basic questions: *how, when, where, why, how long,* and *how often.*

To modify the verb **jumped,** ask . . .

How did they jump? ⟶ jumped exuberantly

When did they jump? ⟶ jumped today

Where did they jump? ⟶ jumped there

How often did they jump? ⟶ jumped often

> The children jumped exuberantly and often today, there on the pile of old mattresses.

Adverb Phrases and Clauses

Phrases and clauses can also act as adverbs to modify verbs.

To modify the verb **jumped,** ask . . .

How did they jump? ⟶ jumped with great enthusiasm

When did they jump? ⟶ jumped before lunchtime

Where did they jump? ⟶ jumped on the trampoline

Why did they jump? ⟶ jumped to get some exercise

⟶ jumped because it's fun

How long did they jump? ⟶ jumped for an hour

> To get some exercise before lunchtime, the children jumped on the trampoline with great enthusiasm. I think, though, that they jumped for an hour just because it's fun!

Jacek Chabraszewski 2010/used under license from www.shutterstock.com

Using Adverbs

Answer/Write For each verb, answer the questions using adverbs—words, phrases, or clauses. (See page 204 for help.) Then write a sentence using three or more of your answers.

1. **Sang**   Answers will vary.

   How did they sing? _sang beautifully_

   When did they sing? _sang last night_

   Where did they sing? _sang here_

   Why did they sing? _sang to provide entertainment_

   How long did they sing? _sang for 15 minutes_

   How often did they sing? _sang often_

   Sentence: _Kristie sang beautifully here last night._

2. **Ate**   Answers will vary.

   How did they eat? _ate sloppily_

   When did they eat? _ate two hours ago_

   Where did they eat? _ate at Rick's BBQ_

   Why did they eat? _ate to fulfill a craving_

   How long did they eat? _ate for hours_

   How often did they eat? _ate every Friday_

   Sentence: _Every Friday JT and Alex ate at Rick's BBQ to fulfill a craving._

LO6 Prepositional Phrases

One of the simplest and most versatile types of phrases in English is the prepositional phrase. A prepositional phrase can function as an adjective or an adverb.

Building Prepositional Phrases

A prepositional phrase is a preposition followed by an object (a noun or pronoun) and any modifiers.

Preposition	+	Object	=	Prepositional Phrase
at		noon		at noon
in		an hour		in an hour
beside		the green clock		beside the green clock
in front of		my aunt's vinyl purse		in front of my aunt's vinyl purse

As you can see, a propositional phrase can be just two words long, or many words long. As you can also see, some prepositions are themselves made up of more than one word. Here is a list of common prepositions.

Prepositions

aboard	back of	except for	near to	round
about	because of	excepting	notwithstanding	save
above	before	for	of	since
according to	behind	from	off	subsequent to
across	below	from among	on	through
across from	beneath	from between	on account of	throughout
after	beside	from under	on behalf of	'til
against	besides	in	onto	to
along	between	in addition to	on top of	together with
alongside	beyond	in behalf of	opposite	toward
alongside of	but	in front of	out	under
along with	by	in place of	out of	underneath
amid	by means of	in regard to	outside	until
among	concerning	inside	outside of	unto
apart from	considering	inside of	over	up
around	despite	in spite of	over to	upon
as far as	down	instead of	owing to	up to
aside from	down from	into	past	with
at	during	like	prior to	within
away from	except	near	regarding	without

Using Phrases

Create For each item below, create a prepositional phrase by writing a preposition in the first box and an object (and any modifiers) in the second box. Then write a sentence using the prepositional phrase.

1. | Preposition
   Answers will vary. | **+** | Object (and any modifiers)
   Answers will vary. |

   Sentence: Answers will vary.

2. | Preposition | **+** | Object (and any modifiers) |

   Sentence:

3. | Preposition | **+** | Object (and any modifiers) |

   Sentence:

4. | Preposition | **+** | Object (and any modifiers) |

   Sentence:

5. | Preposition | **+** | Object (and any modifiers) |

   Sentence:

LO7 Clauses

A clause is a group of words with a subject and a predicate. If a clause can stand on its own as a sentence, it is an **independent clause**, but if it cannot, it is a **dependent clause**.

Independent Clause

An independent clause has a subject and a predicate and expresses a complete thought. It is the same as a simple sentence.

> I have nineteen pets.

Dependent Clause

A dependent clause has a subject and a predicate but does not express a complete thought. Instead, it is used as an **adverb clause**, an **adjective clause**, or a **noun clause**.

An adverb clause begins with a subordinating conjunction (see below) and functions as an adverb, so it must be connected to an independent clause to be complete.

after	before	since	when
although	even though	so that	whenever
as	given that	that	where
as if	if	though	whereas
as long as	in order that	unless	while
because	provided that	until	

> Because I have nineteen pets, I have a big pet-food bill.

An adjective clause begins with a relative pronoun (*which, that, who*) and functions as an adjective, so it must be connected to an independent clause to be complete.

> My oldest pet is a cat that thinks he is a person.

A noun clause begins with words like those below and functions as a noun. It is used as a subject or an object in a sentence.

how	what	whoever	whomever
that	whatever	whom	why

> My cat doesn't care about what I think.

Using Clauses

Identify/Write For each sentence below, underline and label any adverb clauses (ADVC), adjective clauses (ADJC), or noun clauses (NC). Then write a similar sentence of your own and identify the clauses.

1. I know a woman <u>who has fifteen cats.</u>
   ADJC
   Answers will vary.

2. The number is so high <u>because she takes care of shelter kittens.</u>
   ADVC

3. <u>When a pregnant cat is dropped at the shelter,</u> this woman takes her home.
   ADVC

4. She provides <u>what the mother and the kittens need.</u>
   NC

5. <u>Whatever cat comes to her</u> receives good care.
   NC

6. People <u>who are cruel to animals</u> should not have pets.
   ADJC

7. <u>When I visit my friend,</u> I see plenty of kittens.
   ADVC

8. All are safe <u>provided that they don't escape.</u>
   ADVC

9. My friend has a shirt <u>that has the words "Cat Lady" printed on it.</u>
   ADJC

10. <u>Though others might scoff,</u> my friend is proud of what she does.
    ADVC

LO8 Real-World Application

Identify In the e-mail below, underline simple subjects once and simple predicates twice. Circle dependent clauses.

| Send | Attach | Fonts | Colors | Save As Draft |

To: Robert Pastorelli

Subject: Meeting to Discuss Benefits and Policies

Dear Robert:

I am pleased to hear that you have accepted the Production Manager position 1
at Rankin Technologies. I believe that you'll find many opportunities for
professional growth with us.

Our Human Resources Department is here to help you grow. To that end,
I would like to discuss Rankin's benefit package, policies, and procedures. 5
Specifically, I'd like to share the following information:

- Profit-sharing plan
- Medical-plan benefits for you and your family
- Procedures for submitting dental and optometry receipts
- Counseling services   10
- Continuing-education programs
- Advancement policies and procedures
- Workplace policies

On Friday, I'll call to set up a convenient time for your orientation meeting. I
look forward to spending time with you reviewing this useful information. In 15
the meantime, if you have questions, please contact me at extension 3925 or
simply reply to this message.

Sincerely,
Julia

Expand Answer the adjective and adverb questions below. Then expand the sentence using some of the words, phrases, and clauses you have created.

The manager spoke.

Which manager? _Answers will vary._____

What kind of manager? _____

Spoke *how*? _____

Spoke *when*? _____

Sentence: _____

> "A complex system that works is invariably found to have evolved from a simple system that works."
>
> —John Gaule

Ocean/Corbis

18 Simple, Compound, and Complex Sentences

A two-by-four is a simple thing—a board with standard dimensions. But two-by-fours can be used to create everything from a shed to a mansion. It's the way that the boards are connected and combined that determines the proportions of the final structure.

A sentence can be a simple thing as well, just a subject and a verb. But sentences can also be connected to become compound or complex sentences. The way in which writers use simple, compound, and complex sentences determines the maturity of their writing.

What do you think?

If you could build anything out of two-by-fours, what would you build? If you could build anything out of sentences, what would you build? Why?

Answers will vary.

Learning Outcomes

LO1 Create simple sentences.

LO2 Create simple sentences with compound subjects.

LO3 Create simple sentences with compound verbs (predicates).

LO4 Create compound sentences.

LO5 Create complex sentences.

LO6 Create complex sentences with relative clauses.

LO7 Apply simple, compound, and complex sentences in a real-world context.

LO1 Simple Sentences

A **simple sentence** consists of a subject and a verb. The subject is a noun or pronoun that names what the sentence is about. The verb tells what the subject does or is.

<u>Terrance</u> <u>played</u>.
  subject   verb

Modifiers

Other words can modify the subject. Words and phrases that modify the subject answer the adjective questions: *which, what kind of, how many, how much.*

> **My longtime friend** Terrance played.
> (The phrase tells *which Terrance.*)

Other words can also modify the verb. These words and phrases answer the adverb questions: *how, when, where, why, how long,* and *how often.*

> Terrance played **all afternoon and into the evening**.
> (The phrases tell *when Terrance played.*)

Direct and Indirect Objects

The verb may also be followed by a **direct object**, a noun or pronoun that receives the action of the verb. The direct object answers the question *what* or *whom.*

> Terrance played **basketball**.
> (*Basketball* tells *what Terrance played.*)

A noun or pronoun that comes between the verb and its direct object is called an **indirect object**. The indirect object answers the question *to whom* or *for whom* an action is done.

> Terrance passed **me** the basketball.
> (*Me* tells *to whom Terrance passed the basketball.*)

Vocabulary

simple sentence
a subject and a verb that together form a complete thought

direct object
a noun or pronoun that follows a verb and receives its action

indirect object
a noun or pronoun that comes between a verb and a direct object, telling *to whom* or *for whom* an action is done

Insight

In item 1, you are adding modifiers to the verb, and in item 2, you are adding modifiers to the subject. In item 3, you are adding a direct object, and in item 4, you are adding an indirect object.

> **Say It**
>
> Team up with a partner and follow these steps: One of you speaks the sentence aloud, and the other asks the question in italics. Then the first person says the sentence again, inserting an answer.
>
> 1. We played basketball. *(Where did you play basketball?)*
> 2. The team won. *(Which team won?)*
> 3. Terrance passed. *(What did Terrance pass?)*
> 4. We gave a trophy. *(We gave a trophy to whom?)*

Jacek Naira, 2010 / Used under license from Shutterstock.com

Create Simple Sentences

Create For each item below, create a simple sentence by writing a subject in the first box and a verb in the second. Then write the sentence, including modifiers that answer the question in parentheses.

1. | **Subject** | **Verb** |
   Answers will vary. | Answers will vary.

   (Which?)

   Simple sentence: Answers will vary.

2. | **Subject** | **Verb** |

   (What kind of?)

   Simple sentence: _____

3. | **Subject** | **Verb** |

   (When?)

   Simple sentence: _____

4. | **Subject** | **Verb** |

   (Where?)

   Simple sentence: _____

5. | **Subject** | **Verb** |

   (How?)

   Simple sentence: _____

LO2 Simple Sentences with Compound Subjects

A simple sentence can have a **compound subject** (two or more subjects).

A Simple Sentence with Two Subjects

Traits

Using a compound subject in a simple sentence does not make the sentence compound. As long as the subjects connect to the same verb, the sentence is still considered simple.

To write a simple sentence with two subjects, join them using *and* or *or*.

> **One Subject:** **Chan** collected donations for the animal shelter.
> **Two Subjects:** **Chan and Lynn** collected donations for the animal shelter.
> **Chan or Lynn** collected the most donations.
>
> **One Subject:** The **president** of the shelter gave Lynn an award.
> **Two Subjects:** The **president and vice president** of the shelter gave Lynn an award.
> The **president or** the **vice president** of the shelter thanked her for her hard work.

A Simple Sentence with Three or More Subjects

To write a simple sentence with three or more subjects, create a series, using *and* or *or* before the last one.

> **Three Subjects: Chan, Lynn, and I** went out to celebrate.
> **Five Subjects: Chan, Lynn,** the **president,** the **vice president, and I** were interviewed by a reporter.

Note: When a compound subject is joined by *and*, the subject is plural and requires a plural verb. When a compound subject is joined by *or*, the verb should match the last subject.

> **Chan and Lynn plan** to help out again next year.
> **Chan or Lynn plans** to help out again next year.

> ## Say It
>
> Speak each of the following sentences out loud.
>
> 1. Chan *volunteers* regularly.
> 2. Chan *and* Lynn *volunteer* regularly.
> 3. Chan *or* Lynn *volunteers* once a month.
> 4. Chan, Lynn, *and* Dave *help* at the shelter each week.
> 5. Chan, Lynn, *or* Dave *helps* at the shelter each week.

214

Using Compound Subjects

Create For each item below, write subjects in the boxes provided. Then connect the subjects using *and* or *or* and use the compound subject in a simple sentence.

1. | Subject
Answers will vary. | Subject
Answers will vary. |

   Simple sentence: Answers will vary. _____

   _____

2. | Subject | Subject |

   Simple sentence: _____

   _____

3. | Subject | Subject | Subject |

   Simple sentence: _____

   _____

4. | Subject | Subject | Subject |

   Simple sentence: _____

   _____

5. | Subject | Subject | Subject | Subject |

   Simple sentence: _____

   _____

6. | Subject | Subject | Subject | Subject |

   Simple sentence: _____

   _____

LO3 Simple Sentences with Compound Verbs

A simple sentence can have a **compound verb** (two or more verbs).

A Simple Sentence with Two Verbs

To write a simple sentence with two verbs, join them using *and* or *or*.

> **One Verb:** The tornado **roared**.
> **Two Verbs:** The tornado **roared and twisted**.

Remember that the predicate often includes words that modify or complete the verbs.

> **One Verb:** A tornado **tore** through our town.
> **Two Verbs:** A tornado **tore** through our town **and damaged** buildings.

A Simple Sentence with Three or More Verbs

To write a simple sentence with three or more verbs, create a series, using *and* or *or* before the last one.

> **Three Verbs:** The tornado **roared, twisted, and shuddered**.
> **Five Verbs:** People **shouted, ran, gathered, hid, and waited**.

Each verb in a series can also include modifiers or completing words (direct and indirect objects).

> The tornado **tore** apart a warehouse, **ripped** the roofs from homes, **and flattened** trailers in a local park.

Jacek Don Hammond/Design Pics/Corbis

Using Compound Verbs

Create For each subject below, write verbs, along with modifiers or completing words, in the boxes provided. (See page 216.) Then create a compound verb using *and* or *or* and write the complete simple sentence on the lines.

1. The hailstorm

Verb
Answers will vary.

Verb
Answers will vary.

   Simple sentence: _Answers will vary._ _____

   _____

2. Driving rain

Verb

Verb

   Simple sentence: _____

   _____

3. A news crew

Verb

Verb

   Simple sentence: _____

   _____

4. Many homes

Verb

Verb

Verb

   Simple sentence: _____

   _____

   _____

LO4 Compound Sentences

A **compound sentence** is made out of simple sentences joined by a coordinating conjunction: *and, but, or, nor, for, so,* or *yet.*

Compound of Two Sentences

Insight

The word *and* indicates that the second clause provides additional information. The words *but, or, nor,* and *yet* create a contrast. The words *for* and *so* indicate that the idea shared in one clause is the cause of the other.

Most compound sentences connect two simple sentences, or independent clauses. Connect the sentences by placing a comma and a coordinating conjunction between them.

> **Two Sentences:** We drove all night. The sun rose behind us.
> **Compound Sentence:** We drove all night, **and** the sun rose behind us.

You can also join two sentences with a semicolon.

> **Compound Sentence:** We drove all night; the sun rose behind us.

Compound of Three or More Sentences

Sometimes, you may want to join three or more short sentences to form a compound sentence.

> **Three Sentences:** I drove. Janice navigated. Paulo slept.
> **Compound Sentence:** I drove, Janice navigated, **and** Paulo slept.

You can also join the sentences with semicolons. This approach works well for sharing a long, involved process or a flurry of activity.

> I took the shift from Williamsburg to Monticello; Janice drove from Monticello to Louisville; Paulo brought us from Louisville to Indianapolis.

Note: Remember that a compound sentence is made of two or more simple sentences, each containing its own subject and verb.

Image Source/Corbis

Create Compound Sentences

Write Write a simple sentence for each prompt; then combine them into a compound sentence.

1. What did you do on a road trip? _Answers will vary._

   What did a different person do? _Answers will vary._

   Compound sentence: _Answers will vary._

   _____

2. What do you like to eat? _____

   What does a friend like to eat? _____

   Compound sentence: _____

   _____

3. What did you do last weekend? _____

   What did a friend do? _____

   What did a relative do? _____

   Compound sentence: _____

   _____

4. Where do you want to go? _____

   Where does a friend want to go? _____

   Where does a relative want to go? _____

   Compound sentence: _____

   _____

   _____

5. What is your favorite place? _____

   What is a friend's favorite place? _____

   What is a relative's favorite place? _____

   Compound sentence: _____

   _____

   _____

LO5 Complex Sentences

A **complex sentence** shows a special relationship between two ideas. Instead of connecting two sentences as equal ideas (as in a compound sentence), a complex sentence shows that one idea depends on the other.

Using a Subordinating Conjunction

You can create a complex sentence by placing a subordinating conjunction before the sentence that is less important. Here are common subordinating conjunctions:

after	before	so that	when
although	even though	that	where
as	if	though	whereas
as if	in order that	till	while
as long as	provided that	'til	
because	since	until	

The subordinating conjunction shows that the one sentence depends on the other and cannot stand on its own.

Two Sentences: We searched the package. We found no instructions.

Complex Sentence: **Though** we searched the package, we found no instructions.

We found no instructions **though** we searched the package.

Note: The subordinating conjunction begins the dependent clause, but the two clauses can be in either order. When the dependent clause comes second, it is usually not separated by a comma.

Compound-Complex

You can also create a **compound-complex sentence** by placing a subordinating conjunction before a simple sentence and connecting it to a compound sentence.

Simple Sentence: I wouldn't give up.

Compound Sentence: Jan went to watch TV, and Bill joined her.

Compound-Complex: **Although I wouldn't give up,** Jan went to watch TV, and Bill joined her.

Speaking & Listening

Read the example complex and compound-complex sentences aloud. Despite their daunting names, these sentences aren't that complicated and are used often in speech. Experiment with them in your writing.

Create Complex Sentences

Write Write a simple sentence for each prompt. Then select a subordinating conjunction from the facing page, place it at the beginning of one sentence, and combine the two sentences into a single complex sentence.

1. What did you look for? _Answers will vary._

   What did you find? _Answers will vary._

   Complex sentence: _Answers will vary._

2. Who helped you? _____

   Who did not help? _____

   Complex sentence: _____

3. What do you need? _____

   What did you get? _____

   Complex sentence: _____

4. What did you see? _____

   What did a friend see? _____

   Complex sentence: _____

5. Whom did you meet? _____

   Whom did you avoid? _____

   Complex sentence: _____

6. What did you win? _____

   What did you lose? _____

   Complex sentence: _____

In a complex sentence, one idea depends on the other. You've seen how a dependent clause can start with a subordinating conjunction. Another type of dependent clause starts with a relative pronoun.

Relative Clauses

A **relative clause** is a group of words that begins with a **relative pronoun** (*that, which, who, whom*) and includes a verb and any words that modify or complete it.

> **Relative Clauses:** that celebrates my promotion
> which is very generous
> who comes to the party
> whom I contacted yesterday

Each relative clause above has a subject and a verb, but none of the clauses is a complete sentence. All need to be connected to independent clauses to complete their meaning.

> **Complex Sentences:** I hope you come to the party that celebrates my promotion.
> My boss gave me an office, which is very generous.
> I'll have a gift for everyone who comes to the party.
> I hope to see Lavonne, whom I contacted yesterday.

That and *Which*

The pronoun *that* signals information that is necessary to the meaning of the sentence. The pronoun *which* signals information that is not necessary, so the clause is set off with a comma.

> ***That:*** Please reserve the room **that** we will use. (The clause beginning with *that* defines the room.)
> ***Which:*** We'll have cheesecake, **which** I love. (The clause beginning with *which* just adds information about the cake.)

Who and *Whom*

The pronoun *who* is the subject of the relative clause that it introduces. The pronoun *whom* is a direct object in the clause it introduces.

> ***Who:*** I spoke to the woman **who** baked the cake. (*Who* is the subject.)
> ***Whom:*** I greeted the Joneses, **whom** I invited. (*Whom* is the direct object.)

Create Complex Sentences with Relative Clauses

Write For each item, write a relative clause beginning with the pronoun provided. Then write a complex sentence that includes the relative clause. (If you need a topic idea, consider writing about a party, concert, or family gathering you attended.)

1. Relative clause: __that__

   Complex sentence: _Answers will vary._

2. Relative clause: __who__

   Complex sentence: _____

3. Relative clause: __which__

   Complex sentence: _____

4. Relative clause: __whom__

   Complex sentence: _____

5. Relative clause: __that__

   Complex sentence: _____

6. Relative clause: __which__

   Complex sentence: _____

Learning Outcome

Apply simple, compound, and complex sentences in a real-world context.

LO7 Real-World Application

Rewrite Read the following invitation to a party. Note how every sentence is a simple sentence. Rewrite the invitation, combining some sentences into compound or complex sentences to improve the flow.

Workplace

Using a variety of sentences in workplace writing will improve the flow of ideas and give the organization a polished, capable image.

Dear Ms. Jamison:

You are invited to a party. The party celebrates my promotion to store manager. I've been working toward this promotion all year. The store owner notified me yesterday. This is a big step for me. I want to share my day with you.

The party takes place Tuesday, July 13, at 8:00 p.m. at the Lucky Star restaurant. I've invited my colleagues and friends. Don't bring a gift. Just bring an appetite and a party spirit. I will provide beverages and cake. You've been a great support. I hope to see you there.

Dear Ms. Jamison:

Answers will vary.

Dear Ms. Jamison:

You are invited to a party that celebrates my promotion to store manager. I've been working toward this promotion all year, and the store owner notified me yesterday. This is a big step for me, and I want to share my day with you.

The party takes place Tuesday, July 13, at 8:00 p.m. at Lucky Star restaurant. I've invited my colleagues and friends. Don't bring a gift; just bring an appetite and a party spirit, because I will provide beverages and cake. You've been a great support, and I hope to see you there.

Jacek Ewan Burns/Fancy/Corbis

19

Sentence Style

Your style of clothing speaks volumes about how you want to be perceived. The young men above have selected every article of clothing very carefully. These guys are dressed to exude "cool skater dude." But the same people in suits and ties would look like congressional pages.

Your sentence style also speaks volumes about who you are and how you want to be perceived. Different sentences have different effects. Short sentences punctuate important thoughts. Long sentences create elaborate relationships.

This chapter focuses on ways to improve and perfect your sentence style. Through varying, combining, expanding, and modeling sentences, you'll hone the look and feel of your writing.

Learning Outcomes

LO1 Vary sentence lengths.

LO2 Vary sentence beginnings.

LO3 Combine with coordination.

LO4 Combine with subordination.

LO5 Combine by moving parts.

LO6 Combine by deleting.

LO7 Expand sentences.

LO8 Model professional sentences.

LO9 Revise a real-world document for sentence style.

What do you think?

What style of clothing fits you best? How could your writing style reflect your clothing style?

Answers will vary.

LO1 Varying Sentence Lengths

To create a smooth flow of thought, use a variety of sentence lengths.

Short Sentences

Short sentences are powerful. They make a point. In dramatic circumstances, a series of short sentences can create a staccato effect:

> I came. I saw. I conquered.
>
> —Julius Caesar

For less dramatic situations, a series of short sentences may start to sound choppy. So remember to use short sentences in combination with longer sentences.

Medium Sentences

Medium-length sentences do most of the work in everyday writing. They are not overly punchy or overly complicated, and so they communicate well.

> If you want to know what God thinks of money, just look at the people he gave it to.
>
> —Dorothy Parker

Long Sentences

Long sentences express complex ideas and create an expansive feeling. The long sentence may be the hardest type to pull off because it needs to have a clear sense of direction. Otherwise, it may begin to ramble.

> The history of our race and each individual's experience are sown thick with evidence that a truth is not hard to kill and that a lie told well is immortal.
>
> —Mark Twain

Varying Lengths

The most effective paragraphs include sentences of different lengths. Read the following famous paragraph from the Gettysburg Address and note the different sentence lengths and their effect.

> Now we are engaged in a great civil war, testing whether that nation, or any nation so conceived and so dedicated, can long endure. We are met on a great battlefield of that war. We have come to dedicate a portion of that field, as a final resting place for those who here gave their lives that that nation might live. It is altogether fitting and proper that we should do this.
>
> —Abraham Lincoln

WAC

Read an article or a speech in your major, noting the lengths of the sentences. Count the words in each. What effect does the variety of sentences (or lack of variety) have on readability?

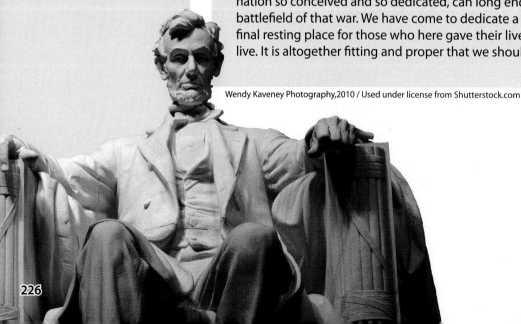

226

Varying Sentence Lengths

Create Write the types of sentences requested below.

> Answers will vary.
> 1. Write a short sentence naming your favorite type of music.
>
> _____
>
> 2. Write a medium sentence describing that kind of music.
>
> _____
>
> _____
>
> 3. Write a long sentence indicating why you like that kind of music.
>
> _____
>
> _____
>
> _____
>
> 4. Write a medium sentence providing a final thought about the kind of music.
>
> _____
>
> _____

Create Write the types of sentences requested below.

> Answers will vary.
> 1. Write a short sentence naming your favorite actor or writer.
>
> _____
>
> 2. Write a medium sentence describing the actor or writer.
>
> _____
>
> _____
>
> 3. Write a long sentence indicating why you like this actor or writer.
>
> _____
>
> _____
>
> _____
>
> 4. Write a medium sentence providing a final thought about the actor or writer.
>
> _____
>
> _____

LO2 New Beginnings 1

If every sentence begins with the subject, writing can become monotonous. Vary sentence beginnings by starting in these different ways.

Prepositional Phrase

A **prepositional phrase** is formed from a preposition (*in, at, through*) followed by an object (a noun and any modifiers). (For more prepositions, see page 350.)

PR = Preposition
O = Object

After the game . . .	For that matter . . .	With a renewed interest . . .
PR O	PR O	PR O

A prepositional phrase functions as an adjective or an adverb. That means that a prepositional phrase can answer any of the adjective or adverb questions:

Adjective Questions	Adverb Questions
Which?	How?
What kind of?	When?
How many?	Where?
How much?	Why?
	How often?
	How long?

Infinitive Phrase

An **infinitive phrase** is formed from the word *to* followed by a verb and any objects and modifiers.

V = Verb
O = Object

To prove my point . . .	To complete the comparison . . .	To do this . . .
V O	V O	V O

An infinitive phrase functions as a noun, an adjective, or an adverb. It can answer any of the adjective and adverb questions above, but it can also serve as the subject of the sentence:

To complete my degree is my goal.

(*To complete my degree* functions as the subject of the sentence.)

Varying with Prepositional and Infinitive Phrases

Vary For each sentence below, add the requested type of beginning.

Answers will vary.

1. (Prepositional phrase):

For that matter,

a high-calorie diet can lead to weight gain.

2. (Infinitive phrase):

To get in better shape,

you should exercise and reduce calorie intake.

3. (Prepositional phrase):

In most cases,

lifestyle changes require time to become habits.

4. (Infinitive phrase):

To achieve a healthy lifestyle,

a balanced diet is the most healthful choice.

Create Write the types of sentences requested below.

Answers will vary.

1. Write a short sentence about exercise. (Begin with a prepositional phrase.)

2. Write a medium sentence about exercise. (Begin with an infinitive phrase.)

3. Write a long sentence about exercise. (Begin with a prepositional phrase.)

4. Write a medium sentence about exercise. (Begin with an infinitive phrase.)

LO2 New Beginnings 2

If sentences still sound repetitive, you can start with two other constructions—participial phrases and adverb clauses.

Participial Phrase

Insight

Participial phrases and
gerund phrases both can
start with the *ing* form
of a verb, but participial
phrases function as
adjectives, and gerund
phrases function as
nouns. For a closer look
at these phrases, see
page 326.

A **participial phrase** is formed from a participle (verb ending in *ing* or *ed*) and any objects and modifiers.

PA = Participle
O = Object

Expecting the best . . .	Considering the source . . .	Concerning the plan . . .
PA O	PA O	PA O

A participial phrase functions as an adjective. That means that the phrase answers one of the adjective questions.

Adjective Questions	
Which?	How many?
What kind of?	How much?

Adverb Clause

An **adverb clause** is formed from a subordinating conjunction (see page 208) followed by a noun (or pronoun) and verb (and any objects and modifiers).

SC = Subordinating Conjunction   N = Noun   V = Verb

When Bill arrived . . .	Because Jan climbed so high . . .	While Ted watched . . .
SC N V	SC N V	SC N V

Subordinating Conjunctions			
after	before	since	when
although	even though	so that	whenever
as	given that	that	where
as if	if	though	whereas
as long as	in order that	unless	while
because	provided that	until	

An adverb clause functions as an adverb, answering one of the adverb questions.

Adverb Questions	
How?	Why?
When?	How often?
Where?	How long?

Vocabulary

participial phrase
a phrase beginning with a
participle (*ing* or *ed* form
of verb) plus objects and
modifiers; used as an adjective

adverb clause
a clause beginning with a
subordinating conjunction
and functioning as an adverb

Varying with Participial Phrases and Adverb Clauses

Vary For each sentence below, add the requested type of beginning.

Answers will vary.

1. (Participial phrase):

Taking in the scenery,

we hiked up the trail toward Bear Lake.

2. (Adverb clause):

While we hiked,

we spotted a couple of porcupines waddling across the road.

3. (Participial phrase):

Sensing our presence,

the porcupines preceded us across a footbridge.

4. (Adverb clause):

After we crossed paths,

I realized it was better to encounter porcupines than bears.

Create Write the types of sentences requested below.

Answers will vary.

1. Write a short sentence about hiking. (Begin with a participial phrase.)

2. Write a medium sentence about hiking. (Begin with an adverb clause.)

3. Write a long sentence about hiking. (Begin with an adverb clause.)

4. Write a medium sentence about hiking. (Begin with a participial phrase.)

LO3 Using Coordination

When you have too many short sentences, writing begins to sound choppy. Look for sentences that have related ideas and combine them.

Coordination

Traits

The word *coordinate* means "to place together." A *coordinating conjunction*, then, is a word that places ideas of equal importance together.

If two sentences express ideas of equal importance, you can combine the sentences by connecting them with a **coordinating conjunction**. (See the following list.)

Coordinating Conjunctions						
and	but	or	nor	for	so	yet

Choppy: Arthur Marx played the harp. He got the nickname Harpo.

Combined: Arthur Marx played the harp, **so** he got the nickname Harpo.

Note: Remember to place a comma before the conjunction.

The different coordinating conjunctions make different connections between ideas:

Comparison → and
Contrast → but, yet
Options → or, nor
Cause → so, for

Julius Marx was a grump, **so** he got the nickname Groucho.
Another brother was nicknamed Chico, **for** he was a lady's man.
Zeppo was in the Marxes' first films, **but** he left show business.

Mike Flippo, 2010 / Used under license
from Shutterstock.com

Combining Using Coordination

Coordinate Mark the sentences below to show which coordinating conjunction you would insert to combine them. Use the correction marks as needed to add words and change punctuation and capitalization.

Correction Marks

⌐	delete
d	capitalize
∅	lowercase
∧	insert
∧	add comma
?	add question mark
word ∧	add word
⊙	add period
◯	spelling
⌐⌐	switch

Answers will vary.

1. The Marx Brothers began in vaudeville. Their mother managed them. *and*

2. Their father was a bad tailor. He was a great cook. *but*

3. The Marxes grew up in New York. They moved to Chicago. *but*

4. The boys had a singing act. Once Groucho ad-libbed a couple of jokes. *and*

5. Increasingly, they added jokes. The act soon was a comedy routine. *so*

6. The boys had a script. An ad-lib from one would get all off topic. *yet*

7. Minnie feared they would be fired. She yelled their mortgage holder's name. *so*

8. Each of the boys had a persona. Their characters suited them. *and*

9. Groucho was a wisecracker. Chico was an Italian huckster. *and*

10. Harpo was a mute tramp. His top hat and shock wig became iconic. *and*

11. The Marx brothers signed with Paramount. *The Cocoanuts* was their first film. *and*

12. *Horse Feathers* made fun of college. A crazy football game ended the show. *and*

13. In *Duck Soup,* they satirized war. This was seven years before WWII. *but*

14. The film featured the fake country Freedonia. The real village Fredonia was unhappy. *but*

15. They said the film hurt their image. Groucho said the town hurt their film. *but*

16. The Marxes moved to MGM. They made *A Night at the Opera.* *and*

17. *The Big Store* was supposed to be their last film. They made two more. *yet*

18. The Marx Brothers retired from movies. Groucho had a TV show. *but*

LO4 Using Subordination

If sentences sound choppy, you can combine them using subordination.

Subordination

Insight

The word *subordinate* means "to place below." A *subordinating conjunction*, then, is a word that makes one idea less important than (or dependent on) another idea.

If one sentence is more important than the other, you can combine the sentences by connecting them with a **subordinating conjunction**. (See the list below.) Place the conjunction before the less important sentence.

Subordinating Conjunctions			
after	before	since	when
although	even though	so that	whenever
as	given that	that	where
as if	if	though	whereas
as long as	in order that	unless	while
because	provided that	until	

Choppy: Facebook and Twitter both connect people. They do so in different ways.

Combined: **Though** Facebook and Twitter both connect people, they do so in different ways.

Choppy: Facebook connects friends. Twitter connects strangers.

Combined: Facebook connects friends **while** Twitter connects strangers.

Note: If the subordinate clause comes first, put a comma between the clauses.

Different subordinating conjunctions show different kinds of connections:

Time → after, as, as long as, before, since, until, when, whenever, while

Cause → because, given that, if, in order that, provided that, since, so that

Contrast → although, as if, even though, though, unless, whereas, while

Alex Mit,2010 / Used under license from Shutterstock.com

Vocabulary

subordinating conjunction a word or phrase that begins a subordinate (adverb) clause, showing that the ideas in the clause are dependent on those in the main clause

Combining Using Subordination

Subordinate Mark the sentences below to show which subordinating conjunction you would use to combine them. Use the correction marks as needed to add words and change punctuation and capitalization.

Correction Marks

ℐ	delete
d	capitalize
ℓ	lowercase
∧	insert
⌃	add comma
?	add question mark
word ∧	add word
⊙	add period
⌒	spelling
⌓	switch

Answers will vary.

while
1. Facebook began in 2004. Twitter got started in 2006.

because
2. Both applications are social media. They connect people.

as
3. Facebook helps friends communicate. People share pictures, videos, and thoughts.

since
4. Twitter is called microblogging. Users send messages of 140 characters.

given that
5. The two platforms connect to each other. They take feeds from each other.

While
6. Some people are Facebook based. Others use Twitter primarily.

so that
7. Each application thrives on links. They connect to anything on the Internet.

Because
8. Social media are changing ideas of privacy. They encourage sharing.

while
9. Older Americans want privacy. Younger Americans fear obscurity.

though
10. Everyone gets 15 minutes of fame. Some get it 140 characters at a time.

Write For each prompt, write a simple sentence with a subject and predicate. Then combine the sentences using subordination.

1. What social media do you use? _Answers will vary._____

   What do your friends use? _____

   Combine: _____

   _____

2. What do you share online? _Answers will vary._____

   What do your friends share? _____

   Combine: _____

   _____

LO5 Combining by Moving Parts

Sometimes sentences need to be combined because they cover the same material. The way to combine such sentences is to move one part of one sentence into the other sentence.

Moving a Word

Before: Every Fourth of July has fireworks. ~~They are~~ (beautiful).

After: Every Fourth of July has beautiful fireworks.

Moving a Phrase

Before: Fireworks were invented in the seventh century. ~~They were invented~~ (in China).

After: Fireworks were invented in the seventh century in China.

Before: A peony , which is the most common type of firework. ~~A peony~~ looks like a flower.

After: A peony, which looks like a flower, is the most common type of firework.

Reworking Sentences

Before: ~~Some~~ fireworks that propel themselves. ~~They~~ are called skyrockets.

After: Fireworks that propel themselves are called skyrockets.

Before: ~~Some~~ fireworks are launched from mortars. ~~They~~ are called aerial shells.

After: Fireworks launched from mortars are called aerial shells.

Speaking & Listening

On the facing page, read each of the sentence pairs out loud. Then ask yourself how you could say the same thing in one sentence. Say it aloud before writing it down. In this way, your conversational skills can help you improve your writing skills.

Combining by Moving Parts

Combine Combine each pair of sentences below by moving a word or phrase or by reworking the sentences.

Answers will vary.

1. Many fireworks are named after plants. They look like the named plants.

   Many fireworks look like the plants they are named after.

2. A willow firework trails long streamers. It looks like a fiery willow tree.

   A willow firework, which trails long streamers, looks like a fiery willow tree.

3. A palm firework has a short lateral burst. The burst looks like fronds.

   A palm firework has a short lateral burst that looks like fronds.

4. Other fireworks have object names. Other fireworks have animal names.

   Other fireworks have object and animal names.

5. The ring firework creates a bright circle. It resembles a ring of stars.

   The ring firework, which resembles a ring of stars, creates a bright circle.

6. A diadem is a type of peony. The diadem has a crown in the center.

   A diadem, which is a type of peony, has a crown in the center.

7. Some little bursts "swim" away. Those little bursts are called "fish."

   Little firework bursts called "fish" "swim" away.

8. A spider shell sends out long lines. They look like a spider's legs.

   A spider shell that looks like a spider's legs sends out long lines.

9. One type is called a kamuro. Kamuro is Japanese for "boy's haircut."

   A kamuro firework means "boy's haircut" in Japanese.

10. Another type leaves a long streamer. It is called a horsetail or waterfall.

    A horsetail or waterfall firework leaves a long streamer.

LO6 Combining by Deleting

When writing is wordy or repetitious, the best way to combine sentences is by finding the key pieces of information, deleting the rest, and writing new sentences from what is left.

Finding the Key Pieces

Read the following paragraph, noting how wordy and repetitious it is. Afterward, consider the important ideas that the writer underlined.

> When people go to a city that they haven't ever been to before [1] or a foreign place that is new to them, they often decide that what they have to do is to figure out how to use the mass-transit system. They will try to use a subway or the buses or trains in order to get all around a major city like Paris or London. Another way to tour the [5] capital of another country is to take a walking tour through all of its tourist spots and also many other spots along the way. A walking tour allows the person to get a feel for where everything is in a city and also provides opportunities for the person to meet and greet the people who live and work in the city and go about their daily lives there. Often [10] on a walking tour of a city, a person discovers that all of the many tourist attractions that she or he wants to see are not as interesting or memorable as the unexpected experiences that happen along the way.

Rewriting and Combining

Now read the much shorter and more effective paragraph that the writer wrote using the main ideas.

> When people go to a city, they often use mass-transit systems, but [1] another option is to take a walking tour. A walking tour lets the person get a feel for the city's layout and meet the people who live there. Often, tourist attractions turn out to be less memorable than the unexpected experiences along the way. [5]

Aurelie and Morgan David de Lossy/cultura/Corbis

Combining by Deleting

Underline Read the following wordy, repetitive paragraph. Afterward, reread the paragraph, looking for important details. Underline them.

What people seem to forget is that <u>most major cities</u> in the world such as New York, London, *1*

Paris, Rome, Athens, and other major cities <u>were originally designed</u> not for traveling through in

motorized vehicles like cars, buses, and trains, but <u>for going around on foot</u>. In fact, <u>one of the</u>

<u>biggest problems for</u> all of these cities has been having to deal with the headaches of <u>motorized</u>

<u>transportation</u>, including the inconvenience and expense of such things as finding and affording *5*

<u>a parking place</u> or <u>paying tolls</u> for different bridges or tunnels, not to mention the frustration of

<u>fighting through traffic</u>. These <u>problems are solved by</u> taking to the sidewalks for a <u>walking tour</u>

rather than by always needing to pay money for taxis or subway rides or having to figure out bus

schedules and so forth. <u>With a simple map</u>, whether one printed on paper or one available on a cell

phone or through some kind of other digital device like a GPS, <u>the walker can find wherever he or</u> *10*

<u>she is currently</u>. If the map does not do the job, <u>then the person can always ask for help and direction</u>

from someone who lives locally in the city, who usually will be more than happy to help someone

who is lost.

Combine Rewrite the paragraph above by deleting the unimportant details and combining the important ones into new sentences. Make the new paragraph concise and smooth.

> Answers will vary.
>
> Most major cities were designed for foot transportation instead of motor vehicles.
>
> Walking is a great alternative to having to deal with parking rates, toll booths, and clogged
>
> traffic. All you need is a map to get you where you need to go. And if you get lost, ask a local
>
> for directions.

LO7 Sentence Expanding

Sometimes a sentence does not say enough, or it is too general. When that happens, the sentence needs to be expanded. Sentence expanding simply means adding details. The best way to expand a sentence is to answer the 5 W's about the topic.

Original Sentence: ___My friend is odd.___

Who is odd? ___my friend Jacob___

What is odd about him? ___He has a collection of___ ___bottle caps.___

Where are his bottle caps? ___in a set of boxes in his___ ___basement___

When did he start collecting? ___about five years ago___

Why did he start? ___He had a Guinness in Dublin and___ ___saved the cap.___

Expanded Sentence: ___My friend Jacob is odd___ ___because he has a collection of bottle caps in a___ ___set of boxes in his basement.___

Note: The expanded sentence does not use all of the answers to the 5 W's, but a second sentence could cover the other details.

He started the collection five years ago when he bought a Guinness in Dublin and saved the cap.

Listening & Speaking

Imagine each sentence-expanding activity on the facing page as a conversation you are having with a friend. Read the short sentence aloud and have a friend ask you the questions that follow. Then roll some of your answers into a single more informative sentence.

Expanding Sentences

Expand Expand the sentences below by answering the questions provided.

1. **Short Sentence:** My friend has a hobby.

    a. Who is your friend? Answers will vary.

    b. What hobby does your friend have?

    c. Where does your friend do the hobby?

    d. When did your friend start?

    e. Why does your friend like it?

    Expanded Sentence:

2. **Short Sentence:** My friend has a job.

    a. Who is your friend? Answers will vary.

    b. What job does your friend have?

    c. Where does your friend do the job?

    d. When did your friend start the job?

    e. Why does your friend do this job?

    Expanded Sentence:

LO8 Sentence Modeling

Sentence modeling helps you see new ways to put sentences together. Modeling involves reading a well-written sentence and then writing a similar sentence by substituting words. Below are two example original sentences and the sentences modeled after them.

Original Sentence: We slid the boxcar door wide open at dawn to see a vast prairie, pale gold in the east, dark in the west.

—"On Running Away," John Keats

Modeled Sentence: I propped the tree-house hatch up at noon to see a small boy, pale in the corner, dark in the eyes.

Note: The new sentence doesn't *exactly* match the model. The writer made adjustments to make the sentence work.

Original Sentence: As the warm spring day lengthened, the young man grew increasingly restless, grumbling because there was not enough to eat, cursing the broken promises of the white men at Medicine Lodge.

—*Bury My Heart at Wounded Knee,* Dee Brown

Modeled Sentence: When the early October day ended, the old woman grew gradually more content, laughing because there was no more raking to do, recalling the easy grace of her young daughter at the ballet.

Note: In the sentence above, the writer chose words that had an opposite feeling from the ones in the original and created a passage with a very different impact. Notice, however, that the sentence still works and makes sense.

Modeling Sentences

Model Create sentences that model the ones below.

Answers will vary.

1. Their greasy uncolored hair hung down, uncombed, with a grim finality.
   —*I Know Why the Caged Bird Sings,* Maya Angelou

_____

_____

2. He stretched, looking straight up at the sun for a second.
   —*Tiger, Tiger, Burning Bright,* Ron Koertge

_____

_____

3. The monster jigged and joggled, nodding its head, flopping all its prickles and plates.
   —*The Moon's Revenge,* Joan Aiken

_____

_____

4. A thrifty homemaker, wife, mother of three, she also did all of her own cooking.
   —"The Little Store," Eudora Welty

_____

_____

5. They'll honk nonstop for 10 minutes at a time, until the horns get tired and out of breath.
   —"Canal Street," Ian Frazier

_____

_____

6. The hotel lobby was a dark, derelict room, narrow as a corridor, and seemingly without air.
   —"Total Eclipse," Annie Dillard

_____

_____

7. My fingers a-tremble, I complied, smelling the fresh leather and finding an official-looking document inside.
   —*Invisible Man,* Ralph Ellison

_____

_____

LO9 Real-World Application

Expand Read the following cover letter, written to present a résumé for a job. Note how the writer uses a lot of short, say-nothing sentences that could refer to anyone. Then rewrite the letter below, expanding the sentences with details from your own life. Make the letter interesting, informative, and engaging by improving the sentence style and enriching the content.

Workplace

As you can see from this exercise, bland sentences can cost you a job, and great sentences can land you one.

Dear Mr. Dawson:

Do you need a good worker? I need a good employer. My education is good. I have work experience.

Many traits make me a good worker. I do well with many things.

Do you need a good worker? If so, please contact me.

I look forward to hearing from you.

Sincerely,

Dear Mr. Dawson:

Answers will vary.

"Men keep agreements when it is to the advantage of neither to break them."

—Solon

© Jamie Kingham/cultura/Corbis

20
Agreement

When people come to an agreement, they can begin to work together. Until an agreement is reached, the people most often work against each other, or perhaps have no working relationship at all.

The same goes for subjects and verbs. If the verb does not agree with the subject in number, both being either singular or plural, these two crucial sentence parts cannot work together. They fight each other, or even disconnect. And the same happens when pronouns and antecedents don't agree. Sentences break down.

This chapter helps you recognize and correct agreement errors. It also focuses on a few other pronoun problems. After you review the information and complete the exercises, you will be prepared to write well-connected sentences that work.

What do you think?

What would happen if all agreements that have been made were suddenly broken?

Answers will vary.

Learning Outcomes

LO1 Make subjects and verbs agree.

LO2 Make two subjects agree with verbs.

LO3 Practice agreement with *I* and *you*.

LO4 Practice agreement with indefinite pronouns.

LO5 Practice pronoun-antecedent agreement.

LO6 Correct other pronoun problems.

LO7 Check agreement in a real-world context.

LO1 Subject-Verb Agreement

A verb must **agree in number** with the subject of the sentence. If the subject is singular, the verb must be singular. If the subject is plural, the verb must be plural.

singular subject	+	singular verb	= agreement		plural subject	+	plural verb	= agreement

The truck needs a tune-up.   The trucks need tune-ups.

Note how plural subjects often end in *s*, but plural verbs usually do not. Also note that only present-tense verbs and certain *be* verbs have separate singular and plural forms.

Present:	**singular**	**plural**		**Past:**	**singular**	**plural**
	walks	walk			walked	walked
	sees	see			saw	saw
	eats	eat			ate	ate
	is/am	are			was	were

To make most verbs singular, add just an *s*.

    run—runs   write—writes   stay—stays

The verbs *do* and *go* are made singular by adding an *es*.

    do—does   go—goes

When a verb ends in *ch, sh, x,* or *z,* make it singular by adding *es:*

    latch—latches   wish—wishes   fix—fixes   buzz—buzzes

When a verb ends in a consonant followed by a *y,* change the *y* to *i* and add *es.*

    try—tries   fly—flies   cry—cries   quantify—quantifies

Insight

The "Say It" activity below will help you become familiar with the subject-verb agreement patterns in English. Practice it aloud, and for added practice, write the sentences as well.

> **Say It**
>
> Read the following sentences aloud, emphasizing the words in *italics*.
>
> 1. The alarm *rings*. The alarms *ring*. The dog *barks*. The dogs *bark*.
> 2. The man *is*. The men *are*. The woman *is*. The women *are*.
> 3. She *sits*. They *sit*. He *walks*. They *walk*.
> 4. The woman *tries*. The women *try*. The man *does*. The men *do*.
> 5. The door *latches*. The doors *latch*. The bee *buzzes*. The bees *buzz*.

Correcting Basic Subject-Verb Agreement

Write In each sentence below, write the correct form of the verb in parentheses.

1. The people at the help desk _____are_____ knowledgeable. (is)

2. They _____know_____ more about computers than most. (know)

3. Any question _____receives_____ a quick, helpful answer. (receive)

4. One student _____asks_____ about the "any" key. (ask)

5. The instructions _____say_____ to press the "any" key. (say)

6. One tech helper _____tapes_____ the word "any" to space bars. (tape)

7. That sign _____does_____ prevent many questions. (do)

8. The tech also _____fixes_____ any computer that breaks down. (fix)

9. Or at least the tech _____tries_____ to fix any problems. (try)

10. Most users _____are_____ glad they don't have to fix the computers. (is)

Correct Read the following paragraph. Correct any agreement errors you find by crossing out the incorrect verb and writing the correct verb above.

Those who study computer science ~~has~~ *have* a challenging career. Since computer   1
technology ~~change~~ *changes* so quickly, the things students ~~learns~~ *learn* when they ~~is~~ *are* starting out
will probably be outdated by the time they ~~graduates~~ *graduate*. Memory capacity ~~double~~ *doubles*
every few years, and high-speed connections ~~creates~~ *create* new possibilities. Innovations
on the Web and in handheld devices ~~drives~~ *drive* change in all areas. One computer-   5
science major ~~confess~~ *confesses*, "Students ~~doesn't~~ *don't* have the luxury of being amazed by new
technology. As soon as they ~~hears~~ *hear* about a new software or hardware development,
they ~~has~~ *have* to check it out and get on board—or they ~~gets~~ *get* left behind."

Write For each plural verb below, write one sentence using the verb in its singular form.

Answers will vary.

1. do _(does)_ _____

2. go _(goes)_ _____

3. wash _(washes)_ _____

4. scratch _(scratches)_ _____

5. tax _(taxes)_ _____

6. dry _(dries)_ _____

LO2 Agreement with Two Subjects

Sentences with **compound subjects** have special rules to make sure that they agree.

Two or More Subjects

When a sentence has two or more subjects joined by *and,* the verb should be plural.

plural **+** plural **=** agreement
subject   verb

Bill and Sue try new hairstyles.

When a sentence has two or more subjects joined by *or, nor,* or *but also,* the verb should agree with the last subject.

singular **+** singular **=** agreement
subject   verb

Either Bill or Sue tries a new hairstyle.

Not only Bill but also Sue looks cool.

or

© Rubberball/Corbis

Test Taking

For more practice with compound subjects, see pages 214–215.

> ### Say It
>
> Read the following sentences aloud, emphasizing the words in *italics*.
>
> 1. The woman *and* man *talk*. The woman *or* man *talks*.
> 2. A mouse *and* gerbil *run*. A mouse *or* a gerbil *runs*.
> 3. Either Sarah *or* Steve *phones*. Neither Sarah *nor* Steve *phones*.
> 4. Not only Jim *but also* Patty *responds*.
> 5. A man, woman, *and* child *arrive*. A man, a woman, *or* a child *arrives*.

Vocabulary

compound subject
two or more subjects that share the same verb or verbs

Fixing Agreement with Two Subjects

Write In each sentence below, write the correct form of the verb in parentheses.

1. The office manager and secretary _____have_____ to multitask. (has)

2. The secretary or manager _____acts_____ as receptionist. (act)

3. Calls and faxes _____arrive_____ every few minutes. (arrive)

4. Customer service and satisfaction _____are_____ the keys to their jobs. (is)

5. Neither the secretary nor the manager _____minds_____ the rush. (mind)

6. Not only excitement but also challenge _____comes_____ with each call. (come)

7. Either the manager or the secretary _____greets_____ visitors as well. (greet)

8. A friendly smile and a polite word _____smooth_____ the conversations. (smooth)

9. Praise or complaints _____receive_____ the same professional reply. (receive)

10. Not only the manager but also the secretary _____was_____ voted employee of the month. (was)

Correct Read the following paragraph. Correct any agreement errors you find by crossing out the incorrect verb and writing the correct verb above.

     Multitasking is the ability to do more than two things at a time. Talking *1*
on the phone and cooking dinner ~~makes~~ *make* a person focus on both tasks at once.
Multitaskers and nonmultitaskers ~~disagrees~~ *disagree* about the value of doing more than
one thing. Cooking, cleaning, and taking care of children ~~is~~ *are* daily tasks for stay-
at-home parents. Office workers and blue collar workers often ~~focuses~~ *focus* on one *5*
task at a time. Who gets more done? Multitaskers and nonmultitaskers ~~sees~~ *see* it
differently. Dinner, a clean house, and happy kids ~~is~~ *are* the results of a multitasker's
labor at home. A job done right and another job underway ~~is~~ *are* the product of a
nonmultitasker's attention at work. Both approaches ~~succeeds~~ *succeed*. Not only the
multitasker but also the nonmultitasker ~~work~~ *works* efficiently and ~~complete~~ *completes* the task. *10*
The difference is perhaps not in the person but in the work.

Write Write a sentence with a compound subject joined by *and*. Write a sentence with a compound subject joined by *or*. Check subject-verb agreement.

Answers will vary.

LO3 Agreement with *I* and *You*

The pronouns *I* and *you* usually take plural verbs, even though they are singular.

plural verb

Correct: I sit here and think. You talk to me.

singular verb

Incorrect: I sits here and thinks. You talks to me.

> **Note:** The pronoun *I* takes the singular verbs *am* and *was*. **Do not** use *I* with *be* or *is*.

Correct: I am glad. I was hoping to go. I am excited to see the show.

Incorrect: I are glad. I were hoping to go. I is excited to see the show.

Insight

The word *am* exists for one reason only, to go along with the word *I*. There is no other subject for the verb *am*. In academic or formal writing, *I* should never be used with *be* or *is*. Think of René Descartes saying, "I think, therefore I am."

Quick Guide

Using *am, is, are, was,* and *were*

	Singular	Plural
Present Tense	I *am* you *are* he *is* she *is* it *is*	we *are* you *are* they *are*
Past Tense	I *was* you *were* he *was* she *was* it *was*	we *were* you *were* they *were*

Say It

Read the following word groups aloud, emphasizing the words in *italics*.

1. I *walk* / You *walk* / She *walks* / They *walk*

2. I *drive* / You *drive* / He *drives* / They *drive*

3. I *do* / You *do* / He *does* / They *do*

4. I *am* / You *are* / She *is* / They *are*

5. I *was* / You *were* / He *was* / They *were*

Correcting Agreement with *I* and *You*

Speaking & Listening

After completing the sentences in the first exercise, say them aloud, emphasizing the underlined verbs.

Write In each sentence below, write the correct forms of the verb in parentheses. (Do not change the tense.)

1. I ____work____ as hard as he ____works____ . (work)

2. You ____sing____ as beautifully as she ____sings____ . (sing)

3. The group ____decides____ together, or you ____decide____ alone. (decide)

4. My brother ____plays____ guitar while I ____play____ piano. (play)

5. I ____forgive____ you if you ____forgive____ me. (forgive)

6. I ____applaud____ just as loudly as she ____applauds____ . (applaud)

7. I ____am____ tired, but he ____is____ tired, too. (is)

8. You ____are____ full of energy, and she ____is____ also. (is)

9. Yesterday, I ____was____ late, but you ____were____ late, too. (was)

10. You ____are____ my friend; I hope I ____am____ yours. (is)

Correct Read the following paragraphs. Correct any agreement errors you find by crossing out the incorrect verb and writing the correct verb above.

> I ~~wants~~ *want* to thank you for such a wonderful day yesterday. I ~~is~~ *am* still smiling   *1*
> to think about the art exhibit. You ~~knows~~ *know* so much about the history of art, and
> you ~~shares~~ *share* what you ~~knows~~ *know* so willingly. You ~~am~~ *are* my new favorite tour guide. I ~~be~~ *am*
> happy to go back to the art institute any time you ~~wants~~ *want*.
>
> What were my favorite paintings? I ~~were~~ *was* thrilled by the Impressionist   *5*
> paintings, especially the Monets and Manets. I ~~weren't~~ *wasn't* even sure there was
> a difference before yesterday. You ~~was~~ *were* very gentle to point out they ~~was~~ *were* two
> different people. I ~~be~~ *am* glad to know that now.
>
> Thank you again for the guided tour. You ~~is~~ *are* generous with your time, and I
> ~~is~~ *am* always interested to hear what you ~~says~~ *say* about each artwork. Next time you   *10*
> ~~is~~ *are* going, give me a call!

Write Write two sentences using "I" as the subject. Then write two more using "you" as the subject. Check your subject-verb agreement.

Answers will vary.

_____

_____

_____

_____

LO4 Agreement with Singular Indefinite Pronouns

An **indefinite pronoun** is intentionally vague. Instead of referring to a specific person, place, or thing, it refers to something general or unknown.

Singular Indefinite Pronouns

Singular indefinite pronouns take singular verbs:

Someone donates $10 a week.
No one knows who it is.
Everyone appreciates the generosity.

Note that indefinite pronouns that end in *one, body,* or *thing* are singular, just as these words themselves are singular. Just as you would write, "That thing is missing," so you would write "Something is missing." The words *one, each, either,* and *neither* can be tricky because they are often followed by a prepositional phrase that contains a plural noun. The verb should still be singular.

One of our roommates is generous.
Each of us wants to know who it is.

Remember that a compound subject joined with *and* needs a plural verb, and a compound subject joined with *or* needs a verb that matches the last subject.

Everybody and everything need to stay out of my way.
Something or someone prevents us from succeeding.

Singular
someone
somebody
something
anyone
anybody
anything
no one
nobody
nothing
everyone
everybody
everything
one
each
either
neither

> "Everybody needs somebody to love."
> —Solomon Burke

Say It

Read the following word groups aloud, emphasizing the words in *italics.*

1. Someone *is* / Somebody *has* / Something *does*

2. Anyone *is* / Anybody *has* / Anything *does*

3. One of the books *is* / Each of the books *has* / Either of the books *does*

© Tetra Images/Corbis

DONATIONS

Vocabulary

indefinite pronoun
a special type of pronoun that does not refer to a specific person or thing

Correcting Indefinite Pronoun Agreement I

Write In each sentence below, write the correct form of the verb in parentheses. (Do not change the tense.)

1. Someone _____ needs _____ a new muffler. (need)

2. Each of the cars _____ needs _____ repair. (need)

3. Something _____ rattles _____ when I turn the ignition. (rattle)

4. Either of the garages _____ does _____ good work. (do)

5. Neither of the options _____ is _____ very affordable. (is)

6. Somebody _____ has _____ to fix the tailgate. (have)

7. Nobody _____ wants _____ to drive a broken-down car. (want)

8. Nobody and nothing _____ deter _____ me from fixing the car. (deters)

9. Either of the repair jobs _____ costs _____ a fortune. (cost)

10. One of my paychecks _____ vanishes _____ each time I get repairs. (vanish)

Write Write sentences using each indefinite pronoun as a subject. Choose present-tense verbs and check subject-verb agreement.

1. Everyone _____ Answers will vary. _____

2. Each _____

3. No one _____

4. Anything _____

5. One _____

6. Either _____

Agreement with Other Indefinite Pronouns

Other indefinite pronouns are always plural, or have a singular or plural form, depending on how they are used.

Plural Indefinite Pronouns

Plural

both
few
many
several

Plural indefinite pronouns take plural verbs:

Both of us match the donation.
Many are wishing they did.

Singular or Plural Indefinite Pronouns

Singular or Plural

all
any
half
part
most
none
some

Some indefinite pronouns or quantity words are singular or plural. If the object of the preposition in the phrase following the pronoun is singular, the pronoun takes a singular verb; if the object is plural, the pronoun takes a plural verb.

All of the pizza is gone.
All of the pizzas are gone.

Notice the shift in meaning, depending on the prepositional phrase. "All of the pizza" means every last bit of a pizza is gone. "All of the pizzas" means each of the multiple pizzas is gone. Here is another startling difference:

Half of the mortgage is paid off.
Half of the mortgages are paid off.

In the first example, one mortgage is half paid off. In the second, out of a group of mortgages, half of them are fully paid off. What a difference one *s* can make!

Speaking & Listening

The "Say It" activity below will help you become familiar with subject-verb agreement patterns with indefinite pronouns.

Say It

Read the following word groups aloud, emphasizing the words in *italics*.

1. Both *are* / Few *have* / Many *do* / Several *were*

2. All of the budget *is* / Any of the budgets *are* / Half of the budget *does*

3. Part of the pie *is* / Most of the pies *are* / None of the foods *are* / Some of the food *is*

Correcting Indefinite Pronoun Agreement II

Speaking & Listening

After completing the sentences in the first exercise, say them aloud, emphasizing the underlined verbs.

Write In each sentence below, write the correct forms of the verb in parentheses. (Do not change the tense.)

1. Someone ___provides___ for others, but both of us ___provide___ for ourselves. (provide)

2. All of the book ___was___ scary, but all of the scares ___were___ fun. (was)

3. Some of my friends ___have___ Facebook pages, and part of my Facebook page ___has___ photos of friends. (have)

4. Everyone ___wants___ to be famous, but few ___want___ to be followed day and night. (want)

5. One of my friends ___broadcasts___ a Webcast show; several episodes ___broadcast___ in a row. (broadcast)

6. Either ___is___ a valuable idea, and neither ___is___ expensive. (is)

7. Few ___have___ thought about the final exam, though all of the students ___have___ reason to study. (has)

8. Of the competing bids, several ___are___ desirable, but none of them ___are___ affordable. (is)

9. Most of us ___watch___ the lions pace, though some of the lions ___watch___ us. (watch)

10. Half of the car ___was___ submerged, and half of the spectators ___were___ gasping. (was)

Write Write sentences using each indefinite pronoun as a subject. Choose present-tense verbs and check subject-verb agreement.

1. Several ___Answers will vary.___ _____

   _____

2. Few _____

   _____

3. All _____

   _____

4. Most _____

   _____

5. Part _____

   _____

6. Both _____

   _____

LO5 Pronoun-Antecedent Agreement

A pronoun must agree in **person**, **number**, and **gender** with its **antecedent**. (The antecedent is the word the pronoun replaces.)

The man went to lunch but forgot his lunch box.

antecedent **+** pronoun **=** agreement
(third person (third person
singular singular
masculine) masculine)

Quick Guide

	Singular	Plural
First Person:	I, me (my, mine)	we, us (our, ours)
Second Person:	you (your, yours)	you (your, yours)
Third Person:		
masculine	he, him (his)	they, them (their, theirs)
feminine	she, her (her, hers)	they, them (their, theirs)
neuter	it (its)	they, them (their, theirs)

Two or More Antecedents

When two or more antecedents are joined by *and*, the pronoun should be plural.

Juan and Maria will do their dance.

When two or more singular antecedents are joined by *or, nor,* or *but also,* the pronoun or pronouns should be singular.

Juan or Maria will do his or her dance.

Not only Juan but also Maria presses his or her own costume.

Note: Avoid sexism when choosing pronouns that agree in number.

Sexist: Each student should bring his project.

Correct: Each student should bring her or his project.

Correct: Students should bring their projects.

Vocabulary

person
the person speaking (first person—*I, we*), the person being spoken to (second person—*you*), or the person being spoken about (third person—*he, she, it, they*)

number
singular or plural

gender
masculine, feminine, neuter, or indefinite

antecedent
the noun (or pronoun) that a pronoun refers to or replaces

Correcting Pronoun-Antecedent Agreement

Insight

Different languages treat gender differently. For example, Romance languages have masculine and feminine forms for nonliving things. In English, gender is reserved for people and animals.

Write In each sentence below, write the pronoun that agrees with the underlined word.

1. The <u>cha-cha-cha</u> began in Cuba, and _____it_____ got its name from the shuffling sound of the dancers' feet.

2. In the 1950s, <u>Monsieur Pierre</u> traveled to Cuba, where _____he_____ studied dance styles and from them created the ballroom rumba.

3. <u>Pepe Sanchez</u> is the father of the Cuban bolero, even though _____he_____ was untrained as a musician and dancer.

4. The *paso doble* came from bullfight music, so _____it_____ depicts the lead dancer as the bullfighter and the follower as the cape.

5. In the early twentieth century, <u>Brazilians</u> created the samba, and _____they_____ danced three steps for each two-count measure.

6. The <u>tango</u> had _____its_____ start in Argentina and Uruguay.

7. Stiff and stylized, the tango is performed with the <u>man</u> holding _____his_____ arms in a rigid frame and the <u>woman</u> matching _____her_____ steps to her partner's.

8. Salsa dancing combines other <u>styles</u> and blends _____them_____ together like the ingredients in hot sauce.

9. Most of these styles require hip <u>movements</u> from side to side; _____they_____ reflect a sensuous nature.

10. Northern European dancing, however, calls for straight hips and leaping, hopping <u>movements</u>; _____they_____ may help the dancers stay warm.

Revise Rewrite each of the following sentences to avoid sexism.

1. Every dancer should put on his shoes.

   Every dancer should put on her or his shoes.

2. Each dancer must keep track of her equipment.

   Each dancer must keep track of his or her equipment.

3. One of the applicants will have his application accepted.

   One of the applicants will have her or his application accepted.

Insight

Use *my* before the thing possessed and use *mine* afterward: *my cat,* but *that cat is mine.* Do the same with *our/ours, your/ yours,* and *her/hers.*

LO6 Other Pronoun Problems

Missing Antecedent

If no clear antecedent is provided, the reader doesn't know what or whom the pronoun refers to.

Confusing: In Wisconsin, they produce many types of cheese.

(Who does "they" refer to?)

Clear: In Wisconsin, cheese makers produce many types of cheese.

Vague Pronoun

If the pronoun could refer to two or more words, the passage is **ambiguous**.

Indefinite: Ben told his son to use his new surfboard.

(To whom does the pronoun "his" refer, Ben or Ben's son?)

Clumsy: Ben told his son to use Ben's new surfboard.

Clear: Ben lent his new surfboard to his son.

Double Subject

If a pronoun is used right after the subject, an error called a double subject occurs.

Incorrect: My grandmother, she is a great baker.

Correct: My grandmother is a great baker.

Incorrect Case

Personal pronouns can function as subjects, objects, or possessives. If the wrong case is used, an error occurs.

Incorrect: Them are the wrong size.

Correct: They are the wrong size.

The list below tells you which pronouns to use in each case.

Subject	Object	Possessive
I	me	my, mine
we	us	our, ours
you	you	your, yours
he	him	his
she	her	her, hers
it	it	its
they	them	their, theirs

Vocabulary

ambiguous
unclear, confusing

258

Correcting Other Pronoun Problems

Write In each blank below, write the correct pronoun from the choices in parentheses.

1. _____I_____ want to give ___you___ some advice.
   (I, me, my, mine)   (you, your, yours)

2. ___You___ should watch ___him___ and learn what ___he___ does.
   (you, your, yours)   (he, him, his)   (he, him, his)

3. ___She___ agreed to lend ___me___ that book of ___hers___ .
   (she, her, hers)   (I, me, my, mine)   (she, her, hers)

4. _____I_____ grant ___my___ permission for ___her___ to go.
   (I, me, my, mine)   (I, me, my, mine)   (she, her, hers)

5. ___We___ watched ___our___ dog do tricks for ___us___ .
   (we, us, our, ours)   (we, us, our, ours)   (we, us, our, ours)

Revise Rewrite each sentence below, correcting the pronoun problems.

Answers will vary.

1. David and Jerry took his car to the shop.

   David and Jerry took their car to the shop.

2. Clare needed to work with Linda, but she had no time.

   Clare needed to work with Linda, but Linda had no time.

3. After driving all the way, it gave out.

   After driving all the way, the engine gave out.

4. When are they going to make an effective vaccine?

   When is the World Health Organization going to make an
   effective vaccine?

5. Bill and Sarah, they went to the movies.

   Bill and Sarah went to the movies.

6. Steve told Dave to bring his book.

   Steve told Dave to bring Dave's book.

LO7 Real-World Application

Correct In the letter below, correct the agreement errors. Use the correction marks to the left.

Correction Marks

✂ delete

d̲ capitalize

∅ lowercase

∧ insert

⅄ add comma

? add question
∧ mark

word add word
∧

⊙ add period

⬭ spelling

⏝ switch

Hope Services Child Development Center

2141 South Fifth Place, Seattle, WA 90761
414-555-1400 www.hopeserv.org

May 17, 2010
Mr. Donald Keebler
Keebler Electronics
466 Hanover Boulevard
Penticton, BC V2A 5S1

Dear Mr. Keebler:

Everyone at Hope Services want to thank you for helping us choose a sound   *1*
system that fits both our needs and our budget. I is especially thankful for the
way you worked around our schedule during installation.

We found that the system meets all their needs. Being able to adjust sound input
and output for different uses in different rooms has been wonderful. The system   *5*
help staff in the family room with play-based assessment, and team members
are tuning in to different conversations as if they were in the room himself. As a
result, children who might feel overwhelmed with too many people in the room
relaxes and plays naturally. In addition, parents use the sound system to listen
in on sessions in the therapy room as therapists model constructive one-on-one   *10*
communication methods with children.

You does excellent work, Donald. I are happy to recommend your services to
anyone needing sound equipment.

Yours friend,

Barbara Talbot

Barbara Talbot
Executive Director

> "The verb is the heartthrob of the sentence. Without a verb, a group of words can never hope to be anything more than a fragment, a hopelessly incomplete sentence . . ."
>
> —Karen Elizabeth Gordon

Yellow Dog Productions/Taxi/Getty Images

21 Sentence Fragments

What is a heartthrob? The meaning is literally there in the word. A heartthrob is something that makes one's heart throb—pound in desire and hope and love. The ancient philosopher Plato suggested that human beings were once connected and complete, but the gods became jealous and split people up. Afterward, we all sought our "better halves," and our hearts throbbed to be complete again.

A sentence fragment is in a similar position. By itself, the fragment is incomplete. It needs to be part of a whole sentence.

This chapter shows you how to make fragments into complete sentences. It's all about supplying what the fragment lacks.

Learning Outcomes

LO1 Correct common fragments.

LO2 Correct tricky fragments.

LO3 Check for fragments in a real-world context.

What do you think?

Explain how the verb could be "the heartthrob of the sentence."

Answers will vary.

Learning Outcome

Correct common fragments.

Insight

In English, command sentences have an understood subject—*you.*

(*You*) Take my car.

Command sentences are not fragments because the subject is understood.

LO1 Common Fragments

In spoken conversation and informal writing, fragments occasionally occur and are understood. In formal writing however, fragments should be avoided.

Missing Parts

A sentence requires a subject and a predicate. If one or the other or both are missing, the sentence is a **fragment**. Such fragments can be fixed by supplying the missing part.

Fragment:	Went to the concert.
Fragment + Subject:	We went to the concert.
Fragment:	Everyone from Westville Community College.
Fragment + Predicate:	Everyone from Westville Community College may participate.
Fragment:	For the sake of student safety.
Fragment + Subject and Predicate:	The president set up a curfew for the sake of student safety.

Incomplete Thoughts

A sentence also must express a complete thought. Some fragments have a subject and a verb but do not express a complete thought. These fragments can be corrected by providing words that complete the thought.

Fragment:	The concert will include.
Completing Thought:	The concert will include an amazing light show.
Fragment:	If we arrive in time.
Completing Thought:	If we arrive in time, we'll get front-row seats.
Fragment:	That opened the concert.
Completing Thought:	I liked the band that opened the concert.

Say It

Read these fragments aloud. Then read each one again, but this time supply the necessary words to form a complete thought.

1. The student union building.
2. Where you can buy used books.
3. Walked to class every morning.
4. When the instructor is sick.
5. The cop was.

Vocabulary

fragment
a group of words that is missing a subject or a predicate (or both) or that does not express a complete thought

Fixing Common Fragments

Practice A Add words to correct each fragment below. Write the complete sentence on the lines provided.

1. Groceries for our special meal. _Answers will vary._

2. While I made the pasta, Maya prepared. _____

3. Finished everything within forty-five minutes. _____

4. Easily, the best meal ever. _____

5. Not everyone likes. _____

Practice B The following paragraph contains numerous fragments. Either add what is missing or combine fragments with other sentences to make them complete. Use the correction marks to the right.

Correction Marks

ℐ	delete
d	capitalize
∅	lowercase
∧	insert
⌃	add comma
? ∧	add question mark
word ∧	add word
⊙	add period
◯	spelling
∿	switch

Answers will vary.

The kitchen truly needs a new coat of paint. Everyone who uses the kitchen. Should help out. We Need lots of help. If you have next Saturday afternoon to spare, plan to paint. Ben and I will provide the supplies. We'll try to pick a color that goes with the cabinets. When we are finished. The kitchen will be more pleasant for everyone to use. However, we won't guarantee that the food will taste any better.

Practice C On your own paper or orally, correct the following fragments by supplying the missing part.

1. The front hall of the dorm. Answers will vary.

2. When I arrived.

3. Was filled with new students.

4. Worked hard all morning.

5. Which was more than most people had done.

LO2 Tricky Fragments

Some fragments are more difficult to find and correct. They creep into our writing because they are often part of the way we talk.

Absolute Phrases

An **absolute phrase** looks like a sentence that is missing its helping verb. An absolute phrase can be made into a sentence by adding the helping verb or by connecting the phrase to a complete sentence.

Absolute Phrase (Fragment):	Our legs trembling from the hike.
Absolute Phrase + Helping Verb:	Our legs were trembling from the hike.
Absolute Phrase + Complete Sentence:	We collapsed on the couch, our legs trembling from the hike.

Informal Fragments

Fragments that are commonly used in speech should be eliminated from formal writing. Avoid the following types of fragments unless you are writing dialogue.

Interjections:	Hey! Yeah!
Exclamations:	What a nuisance! How fun!
Greetings:	Hi, everybody. Good afternoon.
Questions:	How come? Why not? What?
Answers:	About three or four. As soon as possible.

Note: Sentences that begin with *Here* or *There* have a **delayed subject**, which appears after the verb. Other sentences (commands) have an **implied subject** (*you*). Such sentences are not fragments.

Delayed Subject:	Here are some crazy fans wearing wild hats.
Implied Subject:	Tackle him! Bring him down!

Insight

Some situations are
formal—like a dress-up
dance. Other situations
are informal, like walking
around the mall. English
works the same way.
When writing a formal
assignment, you should
use formal language.
When writing to friends
on the Internet, you may
use informal language.
(See page 5.)

Vocabulary

absolute phrase
a group of words with a
noun and a participle (a
word ending in *ing* or *ed*)
and the words that modify
them

delayed subject
a subject that appears
after the verb, as in a
sentence that begins with
here or *there* or a sentence
that asks a question

implied subject
the word *you*, assumed
to begin command
sentences

> ### Say It
>
> Read these fragments aloud. Then read each one again, but this time supply the necessary words to form a complete thought.
>
> **1.** Are three types of laptop computers.
>
> **2.** Our instructor explaining the assignment.
>
> **3.** About three in the morning.
>
> **4.** Is my favorite Web site.
>
> **5.** My friend working at a half-priced disk shop.

Fixing Tricky Fragments

Practice A Rewrite each tricky fragment below, making it a sentence.

1. Their hearts melting at the sight of the orphaned pets.

   Their hearts melted at the sight of the orphaned pets.

2. The dogs yelping hellos and wagging their tails.

   The dogs were yelping hellos and wagging their tails.

3. Our cats and dogs chasing each other and playing together.

   Our cats and dogs are chasing each other and playing together.

4. Are many benefits to pet ownership.

   There are many benefits to pet ownership.

5. The vet's office teeming with a variety of pets.

   The vet's office is teaming with a variety of pets.

Practice B The following paragraph contains a number of informal fragments. Identify and delete them. Reread the paragraphs and listen for the difference.

Both dogs and cats have long been companions to humans. ~~Awesome!~~ Dogs started off as wolves at the end of the last Ice Age. ~~What then?~~ Human hunters killed off wolves that tried to take their food, but a wolf that was neither afraid of humans nor aggressive toward them might be spared. Living alongside people meant wolves were beginning to be domesticated, or comfortable in a human environment.

Cats, however, came a bit later, when humans had become farmers. ~~Yeah.~~ Ancient "barn cats" were probably the first kind. They loved to eat the mice and rats that fed on stored grains, and farmers let them. ~~Perfect!~~ If kittens are handled by humans, they become tame. If they are not, they stay wild.

That's why dogs like walks and cats like to stay home. Dogs joined us when we were walking everywhere, and cats arrived when we were staying put. ~~Yessir.~~

LO3 Real-World Application

Correct Correct any sentence fragments in this cover letter for a job application. Either add what is missing or combine the fragment with another sentence.

3041 45th Avenue
Lake City, WI 53000
November 14, 2010

Ms. Colleen Turner
Human Resource Director
Western Printing Company
100 Mound Avenue
Racine, WI 53001

Dear Ms. Turner:

In response to your advertisement in the *Racine Standard Press* on November 12, I am *1* writing to apply for the position of Graphic Designer. I Have worked as a designer for Alpha Publications in Brookfield, Wisconsin, for the past three years.

I worked with a team of talented designers to create business handbooks and workbooks, including the award-winning handbook *Write for Business*. Our team creates *5* each product from early design ideas to preparation of the final disk. My special skills include coloring illustrations and incorporating graphics in page design.

My experience with design software packages includes: Adobe InDesign, Photoshop, and Illustrator. I also have basic knowledge of black-and-white photographic processes and digital print processes. *10*

Enclosed is my résumé. it Gives more information about my qualifications and training. I look forward to hearing from you and can be reached at (200) 555-6655 or at aposada@atz.com. Thank you for your consideration.

Sincerely,

Anna Posada

Anna Posada

Encl. résumé

Workplace

A cover letter filled with sentence fragments makes a bad impression on employers. To get the job, get help to make sure your letter is correct.

Grant V. Faint/Photodisc/gettyimages

22

Comma Splices, Run-Ons, and Ramblers

Let's face it: Some sentences cause problems. Don't worry, though; this chapter offers solutions. You'll not only learn to recognize comma splices, run-ons, and ramblers, but you also learn a number of strategies for fixing them. Once sentences are solid, your ideas come pouring out of them.

What do you think?

Do your sentences tend to ramble, or are they short and sweet? How do your sentences reflect who you are?

Answers will vary.

Learning Outcomes

LO1 Correct comma splices.

LO2 Correct run-on sentences.

LO3 Fix rambling sentences.

LO4 Correct comma splices and run-ons in a real-world context.

LO1 Comma Splices

Comma splices occur when two sentences are connected with only a comma. A comma splice can be fixed by adding a coordinating conjunction (*and, but, or, nor, for, so, yet*) or a subordinating conjunction (*while, after, when,* and so on). The two sentences could also be joined by a semicolon (;) or separated by a period.

Comma Splice: The winners were announced, we were not mentioned.

Corrected by adding a coordinating conjunction:	The winners were announced, but we were not mentioned.
Corrected by adding a subordinating conjunction:	When the winners were announced, we were not mentioned.
Corrected by replacing the comma with a semicolon:	The winners were announced; we were not mentioned.

Comma Splice: Our instructor praised our efforts, he thought we deserved an award.

Corrected by adding a coordinating conjunction:	Our instructor praised our efforts, and he thought we deserved an award.
Corrected by adding a subordinating conjunction:	Our instructor praised our efforts because he thought we deserved an award.
Corrected by replacing the comma with a period:	Our instructor praised our efforts. He thought we deserved an award.

Say It

Read the following comma splices aloud. Then tell a classmate how you would correct each one.

1. Everyone owns at least one pair of tennis shoes, some people own many pairs of them.

2. Tennis shoes are also called sneakers, they are lightweight with rubber soles.

3. Tennis shoes are not used just for playing tennis, people use them for walking and for playing other sports.

4. Tennis shoes are very comfortable to wear, cheap ones wear out rather quickly.

5. Designer tennis shoes are quite fashionable, they are also very expensive.

Correcting Comma Splices

Practice A Correct the following comma splices by adding a coordinating conjunction (*and, but, or, nor, for, so, yet*), a subordinating conjunction (*when, while, because,* and so on), or replacing the comma with a semicolon or period. Use the approach that makes the sentence read most smoothly. (The first one has been done for you.)

1. Contests are set up to have many participants ^*but* very few actually win.

2. Businesses run contests to stir up buzz, ^*for* they are trying to advertise.

3. The business gives away a few prizes, ^*but* it brings in many names and addresses.

4. Most people enter a contest for one reason, they want the prize, of course.

5. A business should follow up with entrants, ^*because* they provide a marketing opportunity.

6. Both Bill and I entered the contest, ^*but* we both were disappointed.

7. Then we received discount coupons, ^*and* we were happy to get them.

8. Winning is a long shot, ^*yet* there are other benefits to entering.

9. We each used our coupons, ^*because* the discount was significant.

10. We're on the lookout for another contest, maybe we'll have better luck in the future.

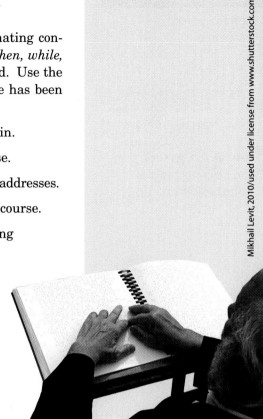

Practice B Rewrite the following paragraph, correcting any comma splices that you find.

    Braille is a system of communication used by the blind. It was developed by Louis Braille in 1824. The system uses combinations of small raised dots to create an alphabet, the dots are imprinted on paper and can be felt. A blind person reads the page by running his or her fingers across the dots. The basic unit is called a cell, a cell is two dots wide and three dots high. Numbers, punctuation marks, and written music can be expressed with this system. Braille has allowed the blind to read, it is truly a great invention.

> Braille is a system of communication used by the blind. It was developed by Louis Braille in 1824. The system uses combinations of small raised dots to create an alphabet, and the dots are imprinted on paper and can be felt. A blind person reads the page by running his or her fingers across the dots. The basic unit is called a cell, which is two dots wide and three dots high. Numbers, punctuation marks, and written music can be expressed with this system. Braille has allowed the blind to read, and it is truly a great invention.

LO2 Run-On Sentences

A **run-on sentence** occurs when two sentences are joined without punctuation or a connecting word. A run-on can be fixed by adding a comma and a conjunction or by inserting a semicolon or period between the two sentences.

Insight

As you can see, run-ons
and comma splices are
very similar. As such, they
can be corrected in the
same basic ways.

Run-On: I was feeling lucky I was totally wrong.

Corrected by adding a comma and coordinating conjunction:	I was feeling lucky, but I was totally wrong.
Corrected by adding a subordinating conjunction and comma:	Although I was feeling lucky, I was totally wrong.
Corrected by inserting a semicolon:	I was feeling lucky; I was totally wrong.

Run-On: I signed up for the contest I had to write a story about **robotic** life.

Corrected by adding a comma and a coordinating conjunction:	I signed up for the contest, so I had to write a story about robotic life.
Corrected by adding a subordinating conjunction and a comma:	When I signed up for the contest, I had to write a story about robotic life.
Corrected by inserting a period:	I signed up for the contest. I had to write a story about robotic life.

Traits

Here's an additional
way to correct a run-on
sentence. Turn one of the
sentences into a phrase
and combine it with the
other one. Number two
could be combined in this
way: *Robots are artificial
helpers, doing jobs
unsuited for humans.*

Say It

Read the following run-ons aloud. Then be prepared to tell a classmate how you would correct each one.

1. The word robot was introduced in a play in 1920 the next use of the word was in 1941.

2. Robots are artificial helpers they do jobs unsuited for humans.

3. Robots are used in manufacturing they work cheaply and accurately.

4. Many robots are battery powered others run on compressed gases.

5. Scientists have developed SmartHand it works like a real hand.

Vocabulary

run-on sentence
a sentence error that occurs
when two sentences are
joined without punctuation
or a connecting word

robotic
related to robots

Correcting Run-On Sentences

Correct Correct the following run-on sentences. Use the approach that makes the sentence read most smoothly.

Penelope Berger 2010/used under license from Shutterstock.com

Answers will vary.

1. John McCarthy coined the term artificial intelligence ⊙= this field deals with the intelligence of machines. _____

2. Thinking machines first appeared in Greek myths ∧and∧ they have been a common feature in fiction since the 1800s. _____

3. True artificial intelligence could become a reality ∧if∧ an electronic brain could be produced. _____

4. ∧When∧ Scientists had computers solving algebra word problems ∧ people knew these machines could do incredible things. _____

5. Reports criticized the artificial intelligence movement ∧so∧ funding for research stopped. _____

6. Funding is again very strong today ∧and∧ artificial intelligence plays an important role in the technology industry. _____

7. Computers solve problems in one way ∧,∧ human beings solve them in other ways. _____

8. ∧Although∧ People acquire a great deal of basic knowledge ∧ it would not be so easy to build this knowledge into machines. _____

Extend

Compare your answers with a classmate's. Did you both correct each sentence in the same way?

Rewrite Rewrite the following paragraph on your own paper, correcting any run-on sentences that you find. Answers will vary.

Smart Cars look like little water bugs on the road. They are only about eight feet long they are less than five feet wide. You can fit two or three smart cars in a typical parking space. Smart Cars have been quite popular in Europe it remains to be seen how they will be received in the United States. By the way, the two co-stars in *Da Vinci Code* raced around Rome in one of these cars. Some versions of the Smart Car run on a three-cylinder engine they still can go from zero to 60 in about 15 seconds. They can get about 33 miles per gallon in the city and 41 miles per gallon on the highway.

LO3 Rambling Sentences

A **rambling sentence** occurs when many ideas are strung together by linking words such as *and* or *but*. The result is an unfocused unit of writing that goes on and on. To correct a rambling sentence, break it into smaller units adding and cutting words as needed.

Rambling: When we first signed up for the contest, I had no thought that we would win, but then my brother started talking about how he would spend the money and he asked me if he could have my share of it, so we were counting on winning even though we really had no chance and as it turned out we of course didn't win.

Corrected: When we first signed up for the contest, I had no thought that we would win. Then my brother started talking about how he would spend the money. He even asked for my share. Soon, we were counting on winning even though we had no chance. As it turned out, we didn't win.

Say It

Read each following rambling sentence aloud. Afterward, circle all of the connecting words (*and, but, so*), and be prepared to suggest different ways to break each rambling idea into more manageable units.

1. I enjoyed touring the hospital and I would enjoy joining the nursing staff and I believe that my prior work experience will be an asset but I also know that I have a lot more to learn.

2. The electronics store claims to offer "one-stop shopping" and they can take care of all of a customer's computer needs and they have a fully trained staff to answer questions and solve problems so there is really no need to go anywhere else.

webphotographeer/istockphoto.com

Vocabulary

rambling sentence
a sentence error that occurs
when a long series of separate
ideas are connected by one
and, but, or *so* after another

Correct Correct the following rambling sentences by dividing some of the ideas into separate sentences.

1. The cat entered silently through the window and next he jumped onto a chair and darted behind the curtain so he could hide from everyone and then he curled up and relaxed for awhile.

   The cat entered silently through the window. Next he jumped onto a

   chair, darted behind the curtain, and hid from everyone. Then he curled

   up and relaxed for a while.

2. I went to the dentist yesterday and when I got there, I had to wait forever to see him and when he finally examined my teeth, he found two cavities and now I have to go back next week to get fillings and I don't want to go.

   I went to the dentist yesterday. When I got there, I had to wait forever to

   see him. When he finally examined my teeth, he found two cavities. Now

   I have to go back next week to get fillings, and I don't want to go.

3. We use trampolines for entertainment but they were used for other purposes a long time ago and Eskimos once used a form of a trampoline made from skins to watch for whales and seals and I think that is a much better use of a trampoline than to just jump up and down on it so I wonder what practical way we can use them today.

   We use trampolines for entertainment, but they were used for other

   purposes a long time ago. Eskimos once used a form of a trampoline

   made from skins to watch for whales and seals. I think that is a much

   better use of a trampoline than to just jump up and down on it. I

   wonder what practical way we can use them today.

Correct In the space provided below, write a rambling sentence or idea about a topic of your own choosing. Afterward, exchange your work with a classmate, and correct each other's rambling idea.

   Answers will vary.

Extend

Share your corrections with a classmate. Did you change each rambling sentence in the same way?

Learning Outcome

Correct comma splices
and run-ons in a real-
world context.

LO4 Real-World Application

Correct Correct any comma splices or run-on sentences in the following sales letter.

Dale's Garden Center
405 Cherry Lane
Flower City, IL 53185

February 1, 2011

Dear Gateway College Student:

Did one of your science instructors ever tell you that plants can talk? Well, they can⊙ *1*
Dale's flowers speak the language of romance.

With Valentine's Day just two weeks away, let Dale's flowers give you the words to share
with your sweetheart. Red roses share your love in the traditional way, ^while^ a Southern
Charm Bouquet says the same thing with a little more class. Or send "poetry" by *5*
choosing our Valentine Special in a porcelain vase!

Check out the enclosed selection guide ⊙ then place your order by phoning 1-800-555-LEAF.
If you call by February 13, we promise delivery of fresh flowers on Valentine's Day.

Let Dale's flowers help you start a conversation that could last a lifetime!

Sincerely,
10

Dale Brown

P.S. Long-distance romances are not a problem, ^for^ we deliver flowers anywhere in the
world.

Extend Correct each of the following comma splices or run-on sentences by changing one of the sentences into an *-ing* or *-ed* phrase and connecting it to the other
sentence. The first one has been done for you.

1. Carnations are a very popular flower they show love and wonder.

    Carnations are a very popular flower, showing love and wonder.

2. The iris is an elegant flower, it is distinguished by its special blue color.

    Distinguished by its special blue color, the iris is an elegant flower.

3. Orchids are tropical flowers they suggest delicate beauty.

    Orchids are tropical flowers, suggesting delicate beauty.

4. Sunflowers follow the sun, they turn to face it as the day goes on.

    Sunflowers follow the sun, turning to face it as the day goes on.

> "Another way to look at sentences is to see them as carriers of 'news.'"
>
> —Scott Rice

23

Additional Sentence Problems

Mathematics is full of problems. The whole point of math is to puzzle out a solution. And for each problem, there should be only one or, occasionally, a small set of right answers.

Writing is different. Sentences should not be full of problems. If a reader has to puzzle out the meaning of a sentence, the sentence *is* a problem. Sometimes a shift has occurred in person, tense, or voice. At other times, a modifier is misplaced or dangling. The result can be a sentence that confuses instead of communicates.

This chapter focuses on correcting these additional sentence problems. You'll find exercises for each type of problem as well as a real-world application.

Learning Outcomes

LO1 Correct misplaced and dangling modifiers.

LO2 Correct shifts in sentence construction.

LO3 Correct sentence problems in a real-world context.

What do you think?

How do sentence problems impact the sentence's ability to be a carrier of news?

Answers will vary.

Dangling Modifiers

A modifier is a word, phrase, or clause that functions as an adjective or adverb. When the modifier does not clearly modify another word in the sentence, it is called a **dangling modifier**. This error can be corrected by inserting the missing word and/or rewriting the sentence.

Dangling Modifier: After buckling the fancy red collar around his neck, my dog pranced proudly down the street. *(The dog could buckle his own collar?)*

Corrected: After I buckled the fancy red collar around his neck, my dog pranced proudly down the street.

Dangling Modifier: Trying desperately to chase a rabbit, I was pulled toward the bushes. *(The person was chasing the rabbit?)*

Corrected: Trying desperately to chase a rabbit, my dog pulled me toward the bushes.

Misplaced Modifiers

When a modifier is placed beside a word that it does not modify, the modifier is misplaced and often results in an amusing or **illogical** statement. A **misplaced modifier** can be corrected by moving it next to the word that it modifies.

Misplaced Modifier: The dog was diagnosed by the vet with mange. *(The vet has mange?)*

Corrected: The vet diagnosed the dog with mange.

Misplaced Modifier: The vet's assistant gave a chewable pill to the dog tasting like liver. *(The dog tastes like liver?)*

Corrected: The vet's assistant gave a chewable pill tasting like liver to the dog.

> **Say It**

Read the following sentences aloud, noting the dangling or misplaced modifier in each one. Then tell a classmate how you would correct each error.

1. The new dog park makes good use of vacant property called Dog Heaven.

2. You will usually find an old basset hound running around the park with extremely stubby legs.

3. Though only five months old, my mother taught Marley to heel.

4. After running around for half an hour, I signaled Marley to stop.

5. One dog owner has worked with his golden lab to teach him to roll over for four weeks.

Correcting Dangling and Misplaced Modifiers

Rewrite Rewrite each of the sentences below, correcting the misplaced and dangling modifiers.

Insight

When a modifier comes at the beginning of the sentence or the end of the sentence, make sure it modifies the word or phrase closest to it. Ask yourself, "Who or what is being described?"

1. We saw a buck and a doe on the way to marriage counseling.

   We saw a buck and a doe on our way to marriage counseling.

2. The car was reported stolen by the police.

   The police reported the car stolen.

3. We have new phones for hard-of-hearing people with loud ring tones.

   We have new phones with loud ring tones for hard-of-hearing people.

4. Please present the proposal that is attached to Mr. Brumbly.

   Please present the attached proposal to Mr. Brumbly.

5. I drove with Jennie to the place where we live in a Buick.

   I drove with Jennie in a Buick to the place where we live.

6. I found some moldy cheese in the fridge that doesn't belong to me.

   In the fridge, I found some moldy cheese that doesn't belong to me.

7. I bought a parrot for my brother named Squawky.

   I bought a parrot named Squawky for my brother.

8. The doctor diagnosed me and referred me to a counselor with severe depression.

   The doctor diagnosed me with severe depression and referred me to a counselor.

9. I gave the cashier my ID that works in the cafeteria.

   I gave my ID to the cashier that works in the cafeteria.

10. I couldn't believe my sister would buy a cat who is allergic to fur.

    I couldn't believe my sister who is allergic to fur would buy a cat.

Correct For each sentence, correct the placement of the adverb.

1. Provide promptly the form to Human Resources.

   Promptly provide the form to Human Resources.

2. We will initiate immediately your new insurance.

   We will immediately initiate your new insurance.

3. Please fill carefully out the form.

   Please carefully fill out the form.

Katrina Brown, 2010/used under license from www.shutterstock.com

LO2 Shifts in Sentences

Shift in Person

A **shift in person** is an error that occurs when first, second, and/or third person are improperly mixed in a sentence.

Shift in person: Once you feel better, you can do everything an individual loves to do. (The sentence improperly shifts from second person—*you*—to third person—*individual*.)

Corrected: Once you feel better, you can do everything you love to do.

Shift in Tense

A **shift in tense** is an error that occurs when more than one verb tense is improperly used in a sentence. (See pages 318–325 for more about tense.)

Shift in tense: I searched everywhere before I find my essay. (The sentence improperly shifts from past tense—*searched*—to present tense—*find*.)

Corrected: I searched everywhere before I found my essay.

Shift in Voice

A **shift in voice** is an error that occurs when active voice and passive voice are mixed in a sentence.

Shift in voice: As you search for your essay, your keys may also be found. (The sentence improperly shifts from active voice—*search*—to passive voice—*may be found*.)

Corrected: As you search for your essay, you may also find your keys.

Say It

Read the following sentences aloud, paying careful attention to the improper shift each one contains. Then tell a classmate how you would correct each error.

1. Margo drinks plenty of fluids and got plenty of rest.
2. Landon is running again and many new routes are being discovered by him.
3. When you are ready to work, a person can search for jobs online.
4. Charley served as a tutor in the writing lab and helps English language learners with their writing.
5. My mechanic replaced the front tires on my car and the radiator was flushed by him.

Correcting Improper Shifts in Sentences

Rewrite Rewrite each sentence below, correcting any improper shifts in construction.

1. I jogged along the wooded path until I feel exhausted.

I jogged along the wooded path until I felt exhausted.

2. As we drove to the movie theater, favorite comedies had been discussed by us.

As we drove to the movie theater, we discussed our favorite comedies.

3. When you drop off my toolbox, can he or she also return my grill?

When you drop off my toolbox, can you also return my grill?

4. Cordero works for the city during the day, and school has been attended by him at night.

Cordero works for the city during the day and attends school at night.

5. You should dress professionally for a person's job interview.

You should dress professionally for your job interview.

Correct Correct the improper shifts in person, tense, or voice in the following paragraph. Use the correction marks to the right when you make your changes.

When you think about today's technology, the first word that comes ₁
to mind ~~was~~ is convenience. For instance, if you traveled before the creation
of the Internet, printed maps ~~were used by you~~ you used. And if you were traveling
out of state, ~~a person~~ you needed to purchase other state maps from a gas
station or convenience store. You would unfold each map and plan the best ₅
possible route ~~was planned by you~~. Now you have access to digital maps,
personal navigation systems, and Web sites to find your way. You probably
enjoy the ease and speed of the new technology and ~~thought~~ think the old
methods are tiresome. ₉

Correction Marks

℘	delete
d̲	capitalize
∅	lowercase
∧	insert
⁄∧	add comma
? ∧	add question mark
word ∧	add word
⊙	add period
◯	spelling
⌐⌐	switch

LO3 Real-World Application

Correct Correct any dangling modifiers, misplaced modifiers, or shifts in construction in the following message. (Only one sentence is free of errors.) Use the correction marks to the left.

Home Builders

1650 Northwest Boulevard • St. Louis, MO 63124
314-555-9800 • FAX 314-555-9810 • www.homebuilders-stl.org

February 15, 2010

Philip Tranberg
1000 Ivy Street
St. Louis, MO 63450

Dear Philip:

You show a strong interest in Home Builders and the desire to provide people with affordable housing is expressed by you.   *1*

First review the enclosed list in Missouri of Home Builders affiliates. Each affiliate handles your own assignments and work groups. Then check the enclosed brochure for additional affiliates on Home Builders campus chapters. This brochure shows   *5* you how to join or start a campus chapter and explained service learning for academic credit. Ben Abramson, the Campus Outreach Coordinator, would love to talk with you, and can be contacted by you at the address printed on the brochure.

Again, thank you for your interest in providing affordable housing with Home Builders.   *10*

Sincerely,

Matthew Osgoode

Matthew Osgoode

Enclosures

Rewrite The sentences that follow come from *The Suspended Sentence* by Roscoe C. Born. Born found these sentences in newspaper and magazine articles, and each one contains a misplaced modifier. (Yes, even the professionals sometime make mistakes.) Working with a partner, rewrite each sentence to correct the error.

1. The Pistons' general manager wants a big guy who can bang in Tuesday's National Basketball Association draft.

   In Tuesday's National Basketball Association draft, the Pistons' general

   manager wants a big guy who can bang.

2. Fiekens is to make a final decision on how the contractors, Vista and Michigan Disposal, Inc., can continue to haul Detroit sludge in a meeting next Monday with their lawyers.

   In a meeting next Monday with the contractors' lawyers, Fiekens is

   to make a final decision on how the contractors, Vista and Michigan

   Disposal, Inc., can continue to haul Detroit sludge.

3. Jessica W., 28, and Abernathy A., 26, both of Detroit, were charged with delivery of cocaine after the raid.

   After the raid, Jessica W., 28, and Abernathy A., 26, both of Detroit, were

   charged with delivery of cocaine.

4. In 1935 he joined the embryonic [Count] Basie group and remained with what many consider the greatest jazz organization of all time until 1948.

   In 1935 he joined the embryonic [Count] Basie group, what many

   consider the greatest jazz organization, and remained in the group

   until 1948.

Write Write the first draft of a personal narrative (true story) in which you share a time when you misplaced or lost something important to you or to someone else. Here are some tips for adding interest to your story:

- Start right in the middle of the action.
- Build suspense to keep the reader's interest.
- Use dialogue.
- Use sensory details (what you heard, saw, felt, and so on).

Afterward, exchange your writing with a classmate. Read each other's narrative first for enjoyment and a second time to check it for the sentence errors discussed in this chapter.

Part 5 Word Workshops

"Mathematics, rightly viewed, possesses not only truth, but supreme beauty—a beauty cold and austere, like that of sculpture."
—Bertrand Russell

24 Noun

Boykov, 2010/used under license from www.shutterstock.com

You have probably heard that a noun names a person, place, or thing. For example, the words *man* and *woman* are nouns. The words *Millennium Park* and *lakefront* also are nouns. And the words *sculpture* and *bean* are nouns as well.

But you may not know that nouns can also name ideas. The word *beauty* is a noun, for example, as are *artistry, mathematics,* and *awe.* You can't see these things, but they are real, and they change the world. At one point, this sculpture was only an idea in the mind of Anish Kapoor, who wanted to create a polished drop of mercury hovering above the ground. Years and $26 million dollars later, the "Cloud Gate" has become a real things—one of the most popular attractions along the Chicago lakefront.

This chapter helps you find the right nouns to name people, places, things, and ideas. You'll learn about the different classes of nouns, singular and plural nouns, count and noncount nouns, and noun markers. Last, you'll get to apply what you have learned in a real-world document.

What do you think?

Which do you most like to work with—people, places, things, or ideas? Why?

Answers will vary.

Learning Outcomes

LO1 Understand classes of nouns.

LO2 Use singular and plural nouns.

LO3 Form tricky plurals.

LO4 Use count and noncount nouns.

LO5 Use articles.

LO6 Use other noun markers.

LO7 Use nouns correctly in a real-world context.

LO1 Classes of Nouns

All nouns are either *common* or *proper*. They can also be *individual* or *collective*, *concrete* or *abstract*.

Common or Proper Nouns

Common nouns name a general person, place, thing, or idea. They are not capitalized as names. Proper nouns name a specific person, place, thing, or idea, and they are capitalized as names.

	Common Nouns	**Proper Nouns**
Person:	rapper	P. Diddy
Place:	memorial	Vietnam Veterans Memorial
Thing:	car	Ford
Idea:	religion	Islam

Individual or Collective Nouns

Most nouns are individual: They refer to one person or thing. Other nouns are collective, referring most commonly to a group of people or animals.

	Individual Nouns	**Collective Nouns**
Person:	chairperson	committee
	quarterback	team
	tourist	crowd
	son	family
Animal:	bird	flock
	gnat	swarm
	lion	pride
	whale	pod
	fish	school

Concrete or Abstract

If a noun refers to something that can be seen, heard, smelled, tasted, or touched, it is a concrete noun. If a noun refers to something that can't be sensed, it is an abstract noun. Abstract nouns name ideas, conditions, or feelings.

Concrete Nouns	**Abstract Nouns**
sanctuary	Christianity
heart	love
skin	health

Vocabulary

common noun
noun referring to a general person, place, thing, or idea; not capitalized as a name

proper noun
noun referring to a specific person, place, thing, or idea; capitalized as a name

individual noun
noun referring to one person or thing

collective noun
noun referring to a group of people or animals

concrete noun
noun referring to something that can be sensed

abstract noun
noun referring to an idea, a condition, or a feeling—something that cannot be sensed

Using Different Classes of Nouns

Identify In each sentence below, identify the underlined nouns as common (C) or proper (P).

1. <u>Waterfalls</u> capture the <u>imagination</u>.
       C   C

2. <u>Niagara Falls</u> is the most powerful <u>set</u> of <u>falls</u> in <u>North America</u>.
       P   C   C   P

3. <u>Niagara Falls</u> is nearly 4,400 feet wide, but <u>Victoria Falls</u> is well over 5,500 feet wide.
       P   P

4. Every second, 85,000 <u>gallons</u> of <u>water</u> rush over <u>Niagara Falls</u>.
       C   C   P

Identify In each sentence below, identify the underlined nouns as individual (I) or collective (CL).

1. The tallest <u>cascade</u> is Angel Falls in <u>Venezuela</u> at 3,212 <u>feet</u>.
       I   I   I

2. A <u>team</u> of <u>explorers</u> led by <u>Ruth Robertson</u> measured the <u>height</u> of Angel Falls in 1949.
     CL   CL   I   I

3. In <u>1937</u>, <u>Jimmie Angel</u> crash-landed on the falls; a <u>crew</u> had to bring the plane down.
     I   I   CL

4. The <u>company</u> that made *Up* drew <u>inspiration</u> for Paradise Falls from Angel Falls.
     CL   I   I

Identify In each sentence below, identify the underlined nouns as concrete (CT) or abstract (A).

1. Iguazu Falls is at the <u>border</u> of <u>Argentina</u> and <u>Brazil</u>.
     CT   CT   CT   CT

2. <u>Tourists</u> gaze with <u>wonder</u> and <u>amazement</u> at 275 <u>falls</u> spread over 1.9 <u>miles</u>.
     CT   A   A   CT   CT

3. The largest <u>fall</u>, <u>Devil's Throat</u>, roars like a <u>devil</u> full of <u>rage</u>.
     CT   CT   A   A

4. When <u>Eleanor Roosevelt</u> saw them, she said in <u>awe</u>, "Poor <u>Niagara</u>!"
       CT   A   CT

LO2 Singular or Plural

The **number** of a noun indicates whether it is singular or plural. A **singular** noun refers to one person, place, thing, or idea. A **plural** noun refers to more than one person, place, thing or idea. For most words, the plural is formed by adding *s*. For nouns ending in *ch, s, sh, x,* or *z*, add an *es*.

	Most Nouns Add *s*		Nouns Ending in *ch, s, sh, x,* or *z* Add *es*	
	Singular	**Plural**	**Singular**	**Plural**
Person:	sister	sisters	coach	coaches
Place:	park	parks	church	churches
Thing:	spoon	spoons	kiss	kisses
Idea:	solution	solutions	wish	wishes

Same in Both Forms or Usually Plural

Some nouns are the same in both forms, and others are usually plural:

Same in Both Forms		Usually Plural	
Singular	**Plural**	**Plural**	
deer	deer	clothes	series
fish	fish	glasses	shears
moose	moose	pants	shorts
salmon	salmon	proceeds	species
sheep	sheep	savings	tongs
swine	swine	scissors	trousers

Irregular Plurals

Irregular plurals are formed by changing the words themselves. That is because the plural form comes from Old English or Latin.

From Old English		From Latin	
Singular	**Plural**	**Singular**	**Plural**
child	children	alumnus	alumni
foot	feet	axis	axes
goose	geese	crisis	crises
man	men	datum	data
mouse	mice	millennium	millennia
person	people	medium	media
tooth	teeth	nucleus	nuclei
woman	women	phenomenon	phenomena

Using Singular and Plural Nouns

Identify For each word, fill in the blank with either the singular or plural form, whichever is missing. If the word usually uses the plural form or is the same in both forms, write an X on the line.

1. boy   boys
2. girl   girls
3. child   children
4. man   men
5. woman   women
6. deer   X
7. X   clothes
8. X   species
9. swine   X
10. axis   axes
11. tooth   teeth
12. millennium   millennia
13. automobile   automobiles
14. tree   trees
15. X   pants
16. X   moose
17. phenomenon   phenomena
18. crisis   crises
19. mouse   mice
20. X   savings
21. datum   data
22. alumnus   alumni
23. goose   geese
24. fish   X
25. X   shears

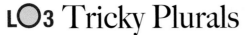

Learning Outcome

Form tricky plurals.

LO3 Tricky Plurals

Some plural nouns are more challenging to form. Words ending in *y, f,* or *fe* and certain compound nouns require special consideration.

Nouns Ending in *y*

If a common noun ends in *y* after a consonant, change the *y* to *i* and add *es.* If the noun ends in *y* after a vowel, leave the *y* and add *s.*

Jim Vallee, 2010/used under license from www.shutterstock.com

y After a Consonant		*y* After a Vowel	
Singular	**Plural**	**Singular**	**Plural**
fly	flies	bay	bays
lady	ladies	key	keys
penny	pennies	toy	toys
story	stories	tray	trays

Nouns Ending in *f* or *fe*

If a common noun ends in *f* or *fe,* change the *f* or *fe* to a *v* and add *es*—unless the *f* sound remains in the plural form. Then just add an *s.*

v Sound in Plural		*f* Sound in Plural	
Singular	**Plural**	**Singular**	**Plural**
calf	calves	belief	beliefs
life	lives	chef	chefs
self	selves	proof	proofs
shelf	shelves	safe	safes

Compound Nouns

A **compound noun** is made up of two or more words that function together as a single noun. Whether the compound is hyphenated or not, make it plural by placing the *s* or *es* on the most important word in the compound.

Important Word First		Important Word Last	
Singular	**Plural**	**Singular**	**Plural**
editor in chief	editors in chief	bird-watcher	bird-watchers
mother-in-law	mothers-in-law	human being	human beings
professor emeritus	professors emeritus	test tube	test tubes
secretary of state	secretaries of state	well-wisher	well-wishers

Vocabulary

compound noun
noun made up of two or more words

288

Forming Tricky Plurals

Form Plurals For each word below, create the correct plural form.

1. ray __rays__
2. elf __elves__
3. high school __high schools__
4. bunny __bunnies__
5. boy __boys__
6. leaf __leaves__
7. reef __reefs__
8. calf __calves__
9. guy __guys__
10. credit card __credit cards__

11. brother-in-law __brothers-in-law__
12. day __days__
13. patty __patties__
14. café __cafés__
15. sister-in-law __sisters-in-law__
16. fife __fifes__
17. rear guard __rear guards__
18. jury __juries__
19. power of attorney __powers of attorney__
20. poppy __poppies__

Form Plurals In the sentences below, correct the plural errors by circling them and writing the correct forms above.

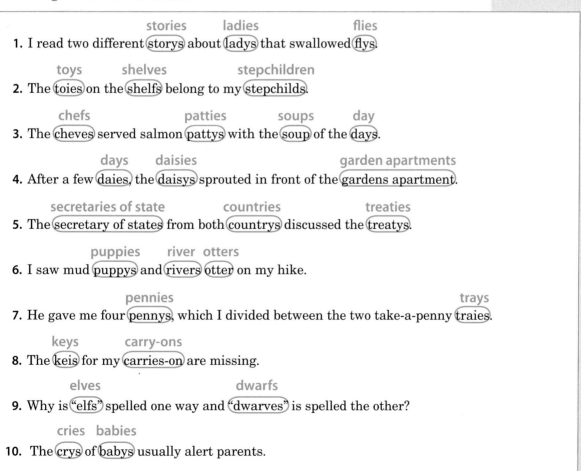

1. I read two different ⟨storys⟩ about ⟨ladys⟩ that swallowed ⟨flys⟩.
   stories   ladies   flies

2. The ⟨toies⟩ on the ⟨shelfs⟩ belong to my ⟨stepchilds⟩.
   toys   shelves   stepchildren

3. The ⟨cheves⟩ served salmon ⟨pattys⟩ with the ⟨soup⟩ of the ⟨days⟩.
   chefs   patties   soups   day

4. After a few ⟨daies⟩, the ⟨daisys⟩ sprouted in front of the ⟨gardens apartment⟩.
   days   daisies   garden apartments

5. The ⟨secretary of states⟩ from both ⟨countrys⟩ discussed the ⟨treatys⟩.
   secretaries of state   countries   treaties

6. I saw mud ⟨puppys⟩ and ⟨rivers⟩ ⟨otter⟩ on my hike.
   puppies   river otters

7. He gave me four ⟨pennys⟩, which I divided between the two take-a-penny ⟨traies⟩.
   pennies   trays

8. The ⟨keis⟩ for my ⟨carries-on⟩ are missing.
   keys   carry-ons

9. Why is "⟨elfs⟩" spelled one way and "⟨dwarves⟩" is spelled the other?
   elves   dwarfs

10. The ⟨crys⟩ of ⟨babys⟩ usually alert parents.
    cries   babies

LO4 Count and Noncount Nouns

Some nouns name things that can be counted, and other nouns name things that cannot. Different rules apply to each type.

Count Nouns

Count nouns name things that can be counted—*pens, people, votes, cats,* and so forth. They can be singular or plural, and they can be preceded by numbers or articles (*a, an,* or *the*).

Singular	Plural
grape	grapes
dog	dogs
car	cars
idea	ideas

Sirko Hartmann 2010/used under license from www.shutterstock.com

Noncount Nouns

Noncount nouns name things that cannot be counted. They are used in singular form, and they can be preceded by *the,* but not by *a* or *an.*

> This semester, I'm taking **mathematics** and **biology** as well as **Spanish**.

Substances	Foods	Activities	Science	Languages	Abstractions
wood	water	reading	oxygen	Spanish	experience
cloth	milk	boating	weather	English	harm
ice	wine	smoking	heat	Mandarin	publicity
plastic	sugar	dancing	sunshine	Farsi	advice
wool	rice	swimming	electricity	Greek	happiness
steel	meat	soccer	lightning	Latin	health
aluminum	cheese	hockey	biology	French	joy
metal	flour	photography	history	Japanese	love
leather	pasta	writing	mathematics	Afrikaans	anger
porcelain	gravy	homework	economics	German	fame

Two-Way Nouns

Two-way nouns can function as count or noncount nouns, depending on their context.

> Please set a **glass** in front of each place mat. (count noun)

> The display case was made of tempered **glass**. (noncount noun)

Using Count and Noncount Nouns

Sort Read the list of nouns below and sort the words into columns of count and noncount nouns.

door	wool	vacation	happiness	sunshine
heat	tablecloth	wagon	photography	flour
swimming	cherry	French	ruler	tablespoon

Count Nouns	Noncount Nouns
door	heat
tablecloth	swimming
cherry	wool
vacation	French
wagon	happiness
ruler	photography
tablespoon	sunshine
	flour

Correct Read the following paragraph and correct the noun errors. Remember to delete articles or numbers in front of noncount nouns and to change verbs as needed. The first sentence has been corrected for you.

There are different activities for ~~four~~ different weather~~s~~. For days with ~~sunshines,~~ ^sunshine outdoor activities are best. Some people enjoy swimming~~s~~, others like boating~~s~~, and even more play soccer~~s~~. For days in the spring or fall, quieter activities work well. Writing ~~poetries~~ ^poetry or enjoying ~~photographies~~ ^photography are good pastimes, as well as dancing~~s~~. During the winter, there ~~are~~ ^is reading~~s~~ and homework~~s~~ to do. The key to ~~happinesses~~ ^happiness is to enjoy whatever you are doing.

Correction Marks

⌐	delete
d̲	capitalize
Ø	lowercase
∧	insert
⌄	add comma
?	add question mark
word ∧	add word
⊙	add period
◯	spelling
∿	switch

Granite, 2010/used under license from www.shutterstock.com

LO5 Articles

Articles help you to know if a noun refers to a specific thing or to a general thing. There are two basic types of articles—definite and indefinite.

Definite Article

The **definite article** is the word *the*. It signals that the noun refers to one specific person, place, thing, or idea.

> Get off the laptop.
> (Get off a specific laptop.)
>
> > **Note:** *The* can be used with most nouns, but usually not with proper nouns.
>
> **Incorrect:** The Fluffy got off the laptop.
> **Correct:** Fluffy got off the laptop.

Indefinite Articles

The **indefinite articles** are the words *a* and *an*. They signal that the noun refers to a general person, place, thing, or idea. The word *a* is used before nouns that begin with consonant sounds, and the word *an* is used before nouns that begin with vowel sounds.

> Chan needs a laptop.
> (He'll take any laptop.)
>
> > **Note:** Don't use *a* or *an* with plural count nouns or noncount nouns.
>
> **Incorrect:** Pass me a cheese.
> **Correct:** Pass me the cheese.
>
> > **Note:** If a word begins with an *h* that is pronounced, use *a*. If the *h* is silent, use *an*.
>
> **Incorrect:** It is a honor.
> **Correct:** It is an honor.

Using Articles

Identify Add the appropriate indefinite article (*a* or *an*) to each of the words below. The first one has been done for you.

1. _____*an*_____ anthill
2. _____ pear
3. _____ hog
4. _____ hour
5. _____ apple
6. _____ ad
7. _____ heap
8. _____ honor
9. _____ dolphin
10. _____ egg
11. _____ euro
12. _____ honest man
13. _____ idea
14. _____ exaggeration
15. _____ handshake

Correct Either delete or replace any articles that are incorrectly used in the following paragraph. The first sentence has been done for you.

Scientists wonder whether a planet Neptune collided with the "super-Earth" when a solar system was forming. The Neptune emits much more radiation than the Uranus, though they are otherwise twins in a solar system. An extra radiation may be left over from this collision with the planet twice the size of an Earth. The Neptune's large moon, the Triton, rotates in an opposite direction to a planet's spin. That fact shows that a Triton was probably a moon of the super-Earth and was captured. If scientists are right, the Neptune holds another planet inside its gassy belly.

Correction Marks

- ﹂ delete
- d̲ capitalize
- Ð lowercase
- ∧ insert
- ⌄ add comma
- ? add question
- ∧ mark
- word∧ add word
- ⊙ add period
- ◯ spelling
- ∿ switch

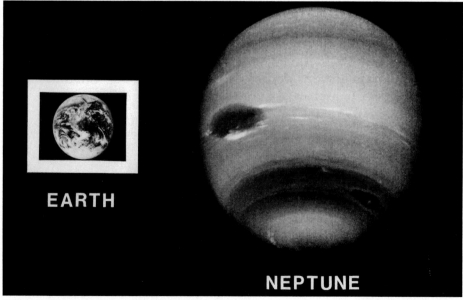

EARTH

NEPTUNE

Courtesy S. Meszaros and Lunar and Planetary Institute.

LO6 Other Noun Markers

Other words help provide information about nouns.

Possessive Adjective

A **possessive adjective** is the possessive form of a noun or pronoun. Possessive adjectives can be formed by adding *'s* to singular nouns and *'* to plural nouns.

Traits

These noun markers show if a noun is owned, if it is very general, if it is very specific, or if it is numerous or plentiful.

Dave's e-mail came back, but **Ellen's** didn't.

Milwaukee's harbor is usually calm.

The **Smiths'** house needs painting.

That is **my** car. That car is **mine**.

It's **your** book. The book is **yours**.

Possessive Pronouns

	Singular		Plural	
	Before	After	Before	After
First Person	my	mine	our	ours
Second Person	your	yours	your	yours
Third Person	his	his	their	theirs
	her	hers	their	theirs
	its	its	their	theirs

Note: One form of a possessive pronoun is used before the noun, and a different form is used after.

Indefinite Adjectives

An **indefinite adjective** signals that the noun it marks refers to a general person, place, thing, or idea. Some indefinite adjectives mark count nouns and others mark noncount nouns.

All people are welcome to join. **Much** celebrating will be done.

With Count Nouns			With Noncount Nouns	With Count or Noncount		
each	either	every	much	all	any	more
few	many	neither		most	some	
several						

Demonstrative Adjectives

A **demonstrative adjective** marks a specific noun. The words *this* and *that* (singular) or *these* and *those* (plural) demonstrate exactly which one is meant.

These songs are by **that** artist.   **This** song includes **those** lyrics.

Quantifiers

A **quantifier** tells *how many* or *how much* there is of something.

Vocabulary

possessive adjective
the possessive form of a noun or pronoun, showing ownership of another noun

indefinite adjective
an indefinite pronoun (*many, much, some*) used as an adjective to mark a nonspecific noun

demonstrative adjective
a demonstrative pronoun (*this, that, those*) used as an adjective to mark a specific noun

quantifier
a modifier that tells *how many* or *how much*

With Count Nouns		With Noncount Nouns		With Count or Noncount		
each	a couple of	a bag of	a little	no	a lot of	most
several	every	a bowl of	much	not any	lots of	all
a number of	many	a piece of	a great deal of	some	plenty of	
both	a few					
nine						

Using Noun Markers

Identify Circle the appropriate noun marker in parentheses for each sentence.

1. Please leave (*your,* *yours*) phone number after the beep.

2. Is this phone number (*your,* *yours*)?

3. How (*many,* *much*) students are allowed in the class?

4. The professor did not give us (*any,* *each*) homework.

5. I want to buy (*this,* *these*) shirts.

6. The resident assistant didn't like (*that,* *those*) idea.

7. After making the dough, we had (*several,* *a little*) flour left.

8. I liked (*a number of,* *much*) the suggestions.

9. The proposal was originally (*her,* *hers*).

10. Let's make sure to return (*their,* *theirs*) pillows.

Correct Delete and replace any incorrectly used noun markers in the following paragraph. The first two have been done for you.

What is ~~yours~~ *your* major? You probably have heard that ~~much~~ *many* times. But *1* taking a ~~little~~ *few* courses in one area does not mean it is ~~yours~~ *your* major. ~~Much~~ *Many* students don't choose a major until ~~theirs~~ *their* junior year. ~~This~~ *These* students have to explore ~~theirs~~ *their* options before making up ~~theirs~~ *their* minds. ~~Those~~ *That* delay isn't a problem. ~~Those~~ *This* exploration is the point of undergraduate study. Until *5* you know for sure a major is ~~your~~ *yours,* you should taste-test ~~much~~ *many* fields. In ~~mine~~ *my* junior year, I was told I would not graduate unless I picked ~~mine~~ *my* major. I added up ~~mine~~ *my* hours, and that total showed I was closest to English. Two weeks later, the head of the English Department called and said, "I thought we should meet since you are one of ~~mine~~ *my* majors." *10*

Correction Marks

✄	delete
d̲	capitalize
Đ	lowercase
∧	insert
⌄	add comma
? ∧	add question mark
word ∧	add word
⊙	add period
◯	spelling
∿	switch

LO7 Real-World Application

Correct In the letter that follows, correct any errors with nouns, articles, or other noun markers. Use the correction marks to the left.

Correction Marks

~~9~~ delete

d̲ capitalize

∅ lowercase

∧ insert

⌃ add comma

? add question
∧ mark

word
∧ add word

⊙ add period

◯ spelling

∿ switch

Dale's Garden Center
405 Cherry Lane
Flower City, IL 53185

DALE'S
Garden
Center

February 1, 2010

Dear Student:

Did one of ~~yours~~ *your* science professors ever tell you that plants can talk? Well, they   1
can. ~~Dale~~ *Dale's* flowers speak a language of love to the ~~womans~~ *women* or ~~mans~~ *men* in your life.

If you're at ~~an~~ *a* loss for words with valentine's day just two weeks away, let Dale's
flowers give you the words. Red roses share ~~yours~~ *your* love in the language of Romance.
A Southern charm bouquet says it with class and ~~a~~ *an* added touch of Magnolias. Or   5
send ~~poetries~~ *poetry* by choosing our Valentine's Day special in a porcelain vase!

Come browse our ~~shelfs~~ *shelves*. Or check out the enclosed catalog and place ~~yours~~ *your* order
by phoning 1-800-555-LEAF. If you call by february 13, we guarantee delivery of
fresh flowers on Valentine's Day. Order by ~~Februaries~~ *February* 10, and you'll receive ~~an~~ *a* 20
percent discount.   10

Let Dales flowers help you start a conversation that could last a lifetime!

Sincerely,

Jerilynn Bostwick

Jerilynn Bostwick
Sales Manager

P.S. Is ~~your~~ *yours* a long-distance romance? Remember, we deliver flowers anywhere in
the world through the telefloral network.

Workplace

Note how the errors in nouns and noun markers make this letter less persuasive. Readers notice errors instead of hearing the persuasive pitch.

> "The personal pronoun in English has three cases, the dominative, the objectionable, and the oppressive."
>
> —Ambrose Bierce

Photo by Jay Bergesen

25 Pronoun

Mannequins are everywhere—trying to sell this dress or that shirt, trying to show you a suit or a pair of shorts. The reason mannequins are everywhere is that it would be too expensive and boring for real people to stand around all day showing off clothing.

Pronouns are like mannequins—they are stand-ins for nouns. Writing that has no pronouns quickly becomes overloaded with nouns, repetitive and hard to read. So a pronoun can take the noun's place.

This chapter will show you how to make sure your pronoun stand-ins work well.

What do you think?

Have you ever confused a mannequin for a real person? What was the result?

Answers will vary.

Learning Outcomes

LO1 Understand personal pronouns.

LO2 Create pronoun-antecedent agreement.

LO3 Correct other pronoun problems.

LO4 Create agreement with indefinite pronouns.

LO5 Use relative pronouns.

LO6 Use other pronouns.

LO7 Use pronouns correctly in a real-world context.

297

LO1 Personal Pronouns

A **pronoun** is a word that takes the place of a noun or another pronoun. The most common type of pronoun is the **personal pronoun**. Personal pronouns indicate whether the person is speaking, is being spoken to, or is being spoken about.

	Singular			Plural		
Person	**Nom.**	**Obj.**	**Poss.**	**Nom.**	**Obj.**	**Poss.**
First (speaking)	I	me	my/mine	we	us	our/ours
Second (spoken to)	you	you	your/yours	you	you	your/yours
Third (spoken about) masculine	he	him	his	they	them	their/theirs
feminine	she	her	her/hers	they	them	their/theirs
neuter	it	it	its	they	them	their/theirs

Nom.=nominative case / **Obj**=objective case / **Poss.**=possessive case

Case of Pronouns

The **case** of a personal pronoun indicates how it can be used.

- **Nominative** pronouns are used as the subjects of sentences or as subject complements (following the linking verbs *am, is, are, was, were, be, being,* or *been*).

  > **I** was nominated, but the person selected was **she**.

- **Objective** pronouns are used as direct objects, indirect objects, or objects of prepositions.

  > The professor lectured **them** about **it**.

- **Possessive** pronouns show ownership and function as adjectives.

  > **My** notebook has fewer notes than **hers**.

Gender

Pronouns can be **masculine**, **feminine**, or **neuter**.

> **She** helped **him** with **it**.

> ### Say It
>
> Read the following aloud.
>
> 1. *I* am / *You* are / *He* is / *She* is / *It* is / *We* are / *They* are
>
> 2. Help *me* / Help *you* / Help *him* / Help *her* / Help *it* / Help *us* / Help *them*
>
> 3. *My* book / *Your* book / *His* book / *Her* book / *Their* book
>
> 4. The book is *mine*. / The book is *yours*. / The book is *his*. / The book is *hers*. / The book is *theirs*.

Vocabulary

pronoun
a word that takes the place of a noun or other pronoun

personal pronoun
a pronoun that indicates whether the person is speaking, is spoken to, or is spoken about

case
whether a pronoun is used as a subject, an object, or a possessive

nominative
used as a subject or subject complement

objective
used as a direct object, an indirect object, or an object of a preposition

possessive
used to show ownership

masculine
male

feminine
female

neuter
neither male nor female

Using Personal Pronouns

Select For each sentence below, circle the correct personal pronoun in parentheses.

1. The dorm cafeteria is where *(I, me, my)* friends gather.

2. *(We, Us, Our)* talk about classes and also about each other.

3. I told Emily that I would help *(she, her, hers)* with her homework.

4. I have a heavy schedule, but not as heavy as *(she, her, hers)* is.

5. *(I, Me, My, Mine)* 18 credits require less work than *(she, her, hers)* 20.

6. Emily told *(I, me, my, mine)* that *(she, her, hers)* is free on Friday.

7. Kim and Jamie wanted to join *(we, us, our, ours)*.

8. Emily and *(I, me, my, mine)* told *(they, them, their, theirs)* to come.

9. Of course, Kim and Jamie need to bring *(they, them, their, theirs)* books.

10. We'll never forget *(we, us, our, ours)* afternoons in the cafeteria.

Correct In the following paragraph, correct the pronouns by crossing out the incorrect forms and writing the correct forms above.

I asked ~~me~~ [my] sons if ~~them~~ [they] would like to take a walk around Lake Geneva. ~~Them~~ [They] asked

how ~~us~~ [we] could walk around the lake. I told ~~they~~ [them] that a path goes all the way around

the lake, and ~~its~~ [it] is open to the public. My sons said that ~~them~~ [they] wanted to go, but ~~them~~ [they]

wondered how far the walk was. ~~Me~~ [I] told ~~they~~ [them] that it was about 30 miles. ~~They~~ [Their] mouths

dropped open. ~~Them~~ [They] couldn't figure out what to say to ~~I~~ [me]. My sons and ~~me~~ [I] looked at each

other. Then I said ~~them~~ [they] needed to get ~~theirs~~ [their] backpacks and shoes. They told me that I

should get a life. But I convinced ~~they~~ [them], and ~~us~~ [we] hiked all the way around Lake Geneva.

When it was over, I wished I had listened to ~~they~~ [them]. My legs hurt so much!

LO2 Pronoun-Antecedent Agreement

The **antecedent** is the word that a pronoun refers to or replaces. A pronoun must have the same person, number, and gender as the antecedent, which is called **pronoun-antecedent agreement**.

> **third-person**   **singular feminine**
>
> **Linda** asked to borrow a pen but then found **hers**.

Agreement in Person

A pronoun needs to match its antecedent in **person** (first, second, or third).

> **third person   second person**
>
> Incorrect: If **people** look hard, **you** might find some good deals.
> Correct: If **you** look hard, **you** might find some good deals.
> Correct: If **people** look hard, **they** might find some good deals.

Agreement in Number

A pronoun needs to match its antecedent in **number** (singular or plural).

> **singular   plural**
>
> Incorrect: Each **student** should bring **their** assignment.
> Correct: **Students** should bring **their** assignments.
> Correct: Each **student** should bring **her** or **his** assignment.

Agreement in Gender

A pronoun needs to match its antecedent in **gender** (masculine, feminine, or neuter).

> **feminine   masculine**
>
> Incorrect: **Janae** will share **his** project.
> Correct: **Janae** will share **her** project.

> **Say It**
>
> Speak the following words aloud.
>
> 1. First person: *I, me, my, mine; we, us, our, ours*
> 2. Second person: *you, your, yours*
> 3. Third person feminine: *she, her, hers; they, them, their, theirs*
> 4. Third person masculine: *he, him, his; they, them, their, theirs*
> 5. Third person neuter: *it, its; they, them, their, theirs*

Correcting Agreement Errors

Correct Person Rewrite each sentence to correct the person error.

1. If both of you go to the job fair, they will probably find job opportunities.

   If both of you go to the job fair, **you** will probably find job opportunities.

2. We went to the fair last year, and they landed some good jobs.

   We went to the fair last year, and **we** landed some good jobs.

3. If the graduates fill out applications, you may find jobs.

   If the graduates fill out applications, **they** may find good jobs.

4. One considers the future when you attend the fair.

   One considers the future when **one** attends the fair.

Correct Number Rewrite each sentence to correct the number error.

5. Each applicant should put down their name.

   Applicants should put down their **names**.

6. An employee will greet you, and they will interview you.

   An employee will greet you, and **she or he** will interview you.

7. Applicants should supply his contact information.

   Applicants should supply **their** contact information.

8. Answer the interviewer unless they ask unfair questions.

   Answer the interviewer unless **she or he asks** unfair questions.

Correct Gender Rewrite each sentence to correct the gender error.

9. If Lionel goes, she can drive others.

   If Lionel goes, **he** can drive others

10. Tawny said he was going.

    Tawny said **she** was going.

11. Ask David if she is planning to attend.

    Ask David if **he** is planning to attend.

12. The hall is big, and she sits at a major intersection.

    The hall is big, and **it** sits at a major intersection.

LO3 Other Pronoun Problems

Pronouns are very useful parts of speech, but if they are mishandled, they can cause problems.

Vague Pronoun

Do not use a pronoun that could refer to more than one antecedent.

> **Unclear:** Lupe spoke to her roommate and **her** sister.
> **Clear:** Lupe spoke to her roommate and **her roommate's** sister.

Missing Antecedent

Avoid using *it* or *they* without clear antecedents.

> **Unclear:** **It** says in the tabloid that a donkey-boy was born.
> **Clear:** The **tabloid** says that a donkey-boy was born.
>
> **Unclear:** **They** have found one of the causes of arthritis.
> **Clear:** **Scientists** have found one of the causes of arthritis.

Double Subjects

Do not place a pronoun right after the subject. Doing so creates an error called a **double subject**, which is not a standard construction.

> **Nonstandard:** Kyle and Jules, **they** went to the movies.
> **Standard:** Kyle and Jules went to the movies.

Usage Errors *(They're, You're, It's)*

Do not confuse possessive pronouns *(your, their, its)* with contractions *(you're, they're, it's)*. Remember that the contractions use apostrophes in place of missing letters.

> **Incorrect:** Please place **you're** plastic bottles in **they're** recycling bin.
> **Correct:** Please place **your** plastic bottles in **their** recycling bin.

Ieva Geneviciene, 2010/used under license from www.shutterstock.com

Correcting Other Pronoun Problems

Rewrite Rewrite each sentence to correct the pronoun-reference problems.

1. Raul asked his father and his friend to help him move.

   (AWV) Raul asked his father and his father's friend to help him move.

2. It says in the article that three people are trapped.

   The article says that three people are trapped.

3. They are proposing an amendment to the Constitution.

   (AWV) Congress is proposing an amendment to the Constitution.

4. Shakira wants her sister and her friend to help.

   (AWV) Shakira wants her sister and her sister's friend to help.

5. It says in the news report that stocks are down.

   The news report says that stocks are down.

6. They have a new cure for baldness.

   (AWV) Scientists have a new cure for baldness.

Correct In the following paragraph, correct the pronoun errors. Use the correction marks to the right.

An article on   says
~~It says on~~ the Internet that many major companies have pulled April Fool's

Google
Day pranks. ~~They~~ replaced the name "Google" with the name "Topeka," for one.

The article   a skeksis
~~It~~ says also that a rare baby skeksis was born in a zoo, but ~~it~~ exists only in the

film *The Dark Crystal*. One classical music station, ~~it~~ claimed that a British

                                                        The spaceship's
billionaire was sending a violinist to the moon in a special spaceship. ~~It's~~ console

                                                        The station
had a button to make the ship's cockpit sound like the Royal Albert Hall. ~~They~~

        their
had a lot of fun with ~~they're~~ gags, but gullible people kept getting tripped up all

The article
day. ~~It~~ also claims that in the UK, Australia, and South Africa, the gags stop at

        their
noon, but ~~they're~~ citizens, ~~they~~ still get pranked by Americans all day.

LO4 Indefinite Pronouns

An **indefinite pronoun** does not have an antecedent, and it does not refer to a specific person, place, thing, or idea. These pronouns pose unique issues with subject-verb and pronoun-antecedent agreement.

Singular Indefinite Pronouns

Some indefinite pronouns are singular. When they are used as subjects, they require a singular verb. As antecedents, they must be matched to singular pronouns.

each	anyone	anybody	anything
either	someone	somebody	something
neither	everyone	everybody	everything
another	no one	nobody	nothing
one			

> **Someone is** supposed to empty the dishwasher.
> **No one** has said **he** will do it.

Insight

For more practice with indefinite pronouns, see pages 252–255.

Plural Indefinite Pronouns

Some indefinite pronouns are plural. As subjects, they require a plural verb, and as antecedents, they require a plural pronoun.

both	few	several	many

> **A few** of the housemates **leave** dirty dishes everywhere.
> **Several** of their friends said **they** are fed up.

Singular or Plural Indefinite Pronouns

Some indefinite pronouns can be singular or plural, depending on the object of the preposition in the phrase that follows them.

all	any	most	none	some

> **All** of the **pies were** eaten.
> **All** of the **pie was** eaten.

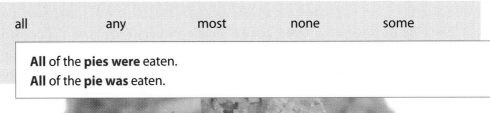

Vocabulary

indefinite pronoun
a pronoun that does not refer to a specific person, place, thing, or idea

Correcting Agreement

Correct Rewrite each sentence to correct the agreement errors. (Hint: the sentences are about a group of male roommates.)

1. Everyone needs to wash their own dishes.

   Everyone needs to wash his own dishes.

2. No one are exempt.

   No one is exempt.

3. Anyone not washing their dishes must wash everyone else's.

   Anyone not washing his dishes must wash everyone else's.

4. Nothing short of illness are an excuse.

   Nothing short of illness is an excuse.

5. Few is arguing with the new policy.

   Few are arguing with the new policy.

6. Several says it is about time.

   Several say it is about time.

7. Many expresses their appreciation.

   Many express their appreciation.

8. For a week, all of the dishes has been washed.

   For a week, all of the dishes have been washed.

9. Ted made sure all of his plates was washed and put away.

   Ted made sure all of his plates were washed and put away.

10. Most of the roommates agrees that this works.

    Most of the roommates agree that this works.

11. Most of the morning are spent cleaning up.

    Most of the morning is spent cleaning up.

12. None of the dishes is left lying about.

    None of the dishes are left lying about.

13. None of the food are left to eat either, since everybody have forgotten to go shopping.

    None of the food is left to eat either, since everybody has forgotten to go shopping.

LO5 Relative Pronouns

A **relative pronoun** introduces a dependent clause and relates it to the rest of the sentence.

who	whom	which	whose
whoever	whomever	that	

relative clause

I would like to meet the man **who** invented the World Wide Web.

Who/Whoever and Whom/Whomever

Who, whoever, whom, and *whomever* refer to people. *Who* or *whoever* functions as the subject of the relative clause, while *whom* or *whomever* functions as the object of the clause.

relative clause

I would like to thank **whoever** chose the playlist for this party.
The person **whom** I thanked had terrific taste in music.

relative clause

Note: In the second **relative clause**, *whom* introduces the clause even though it is the direct object, not the subject (I thanked whom).

That and Which

That and *which* usually refer to things. When *that* introduces the clause, the clause **is not** set off with commas. When *which* introduces the clause, the clause **is** set off with commas.

relative clause

I read the book **that** told of Teddy Roosevelt's journey down the Amazon.
I enjoyed *The River of Doubt,* **which** was a $29 hardback.

relative clause

Note: In the first example, the *that* clause is restrictive, or essential to the meaning of the sentence. In the second example, the *which* clause is nonrestrictive, or unnecessary to the meaning of the sentence.

Whose

Whose shows ownership or connection.

relative clause

The mechanic **whose** hand got cut was fixing our car.

Note: Do not confuse *whose* with the contraction *who's* (who is).

Insight

For more practice with relative pronouns, see pages 222–223.

Vocabulary

relative pronoun
a pronoun that begins a relative clause, connecting it to a sentence

relative clause
a type of dependent clause that begins with a relative pronoun that is either the subject or the direct object of the clause

Using Relative Pronouns

Select For each sentence, circle the correct relative pronoun.

1. Theo Jansen is an engineer and artist *(who, whom)* is creating new life.

2. He builds sculptures *(that, which)* harness the wind to walk.

3. Theo refers to his sculptures as animals, *(that, which)* is unusual for an engineer.

4. These animals are built of plastic pipe, *(that, which)* is inexpensive and strong.

5. Another engineer and artist *(who, whom)* Jansen admires is Leonardo da Vinci.

6. Theo's creations are on display for *(whoever, whomever)* is on the beach.

7. His most famous creation is the Strandbeest, *(that, which)* has wings on top.

8. The wings pump air into plastic bottles, *(that, which)* store it up.

9. The air powers "muscles" *(that, which)* are made of sliding tubes.

10. Muscles open taps that activate other muscles, *(that, which)* makes the beest walk.

11. Theo Jansen, *(who, whose)* creations are spellbinding, hopes these "animals" will roam on their own one day.

12. Theo feels that the boundary between art and engineering is only in our minds, *(that, which)* allows him to create such creatures.

Fabio Bruna from Flickr

Write On your own paper, write a relative clause for each of these relative pronouns:

1. who **3.** whom **5.** which **7.** whose

2. whoever **4.** whomever **6.** that

Write a sentence including one of your clauses.

Answers will vary.

LO6 Other Pronoun Types

Other types of pronouns have specific uses in your writing: asking questions, pointing to specific things, reflecting back on a noun (or pronoun), or intensifying a noun (or pronoun).

Interrogative Pronoun

An **interrogative pronoun** asks a question—*who, whose, whom, which, what.*

> **Who** will help me make the salads? **What** is your favorite dressing?

Demonstrative Pronoun

A **demonstrative pronoun** points to a specific thing—*this, that, these, those.*

> **This** is the best of times! **These** are wonderful days!

Reflexive Pronoun

A **reflexive pronoun** reflects back to the subject of a sentence or clause—*myself, ourselves, yourself, yourselves, himself, herself, itself, themselves.*

> I e-mailed **myself** the file. You can send **yourself** the vacation photos.

Intensive Pronoun

An **intensive pronoun** emphasizes the noun or pronoun it refers to—*myself, ourselves, yourself, yourselves, himself, herself, itself, themselves.*

> I **myself** will be there. You **yourself** will see me.

Reciprocal Pronoun

A **reciprocal pronoun** refers to two things in an equal way—*each other, one another.*

> We should apologize to **each other**. We should love **one another**.

> **Say It**
>
> Speak the following words aloud.
> 1. Interrogative: *Who* is? / *Whose* is? / *Which* is? / *What* is? / *Whom* do you see?
> 2. Demonstrative: *This* is / *That* is / *These* are / *Those* are
> 3. Reflexive: I helped *myself.* / You helped *yourself.* / They helped *themselves*
> 4. Intensive: *I myself* / *You yourself* / *She herself* / *He himself* / *They themselves*
> 5. Reciprocal: *We helped each other.* / *We helped one another.*

Using Other Types of Pronouns

Identify Indicate the type of each underlined pronoun: *interrogative, demonstrative, reflexive, intensive,* or *reciprocal.*

1. That is the reason we should fill the tank. ___demonstrative___

2. What should we use to pay for gas? ___interrogative___

3. I myself expected you to bring money. ___intensive___

4. You should pat yourself on the back. ___reflexive___

5. That is all the money you have? ___demonstrative___

6. The change itself won't be enough. ___intensive___

7. Who gets $1.73 worth of gas? ___interrogative___

8. That won't get us far. ___demonstrative___

9. This is ridiculous. ___demonstrative___

10. What should we do? ___interrogative___

11. I myself am prepared to push. ___intensive___

12. We should be ashamed of ourselves. ___reflexive___

13. We shouldn't blame each other. ___reciprocal___

14. Let's help one another move this car. ___reciprocal___

15. Then let's get ourselves a soda. ___reflexive___

Write Create a sentence using *myself* as a reflexive pronoun, and a second using *myself* as an intensive pronoun.

1. ___Answers will vary.___

2. ___Answers will vary.___

LO7 Real-World Application

Correct In the letter that follows, correct any pronoun errors. Use the correction marks to the left.

Correction Marks

ℐ delete

d̲ capitalize

ᴅ̸ lowercase

∧ insert

∧̓ add comma

? add question
∧ mark

word
∧ add word

⊙ add period

◯ spelling

∩ switch

⬛ Rankin Technologies

401 South Manheim Road, Albany, NY 12236 ▪ Ph: 708.555.1980 ▪ Fax: 708.555.0056

April 28, 2010

Mr. Henry Danburn
Construction Manager
Titan Industrial Construction, Inc.
P.O. Box 2112
Phoenix, AZ 85009-3887

Dear Mr. Danburn:

Thank you for meeting with ~~I~~ me last week at the National Convention in Las Vegas.   *1*
I want to follow up on ~~ours~~ our discussion of ways ~~which~~ that Rankin Technologies could
work with Titan Industrial Construction.

Enclosed is the information that ~~your~~ you requested. I believe this material
demonstrates ~~what~~ why Rankin Technologies would be a solid match for ~~yours~~ your projects   *5*
in western Illinois.

You ~~yourselves~~ yourself are the construction manager for the Arrow Mills renovation
project in California. Rankin did the electrical installation on that project initially,
and ~~us~~ we would be very interested in working with you on the renovation. Someone
~~whom~~ who is familiar with our work at Arrow Mills is Mike Knowlan. ~~She~~ He is the plant   *10*
manager and can be reached at 606-555-6328.

~~Us~~ We are excited about working with ~~yous~~ you on any future projects, and on the Arrow
Mills project in particular. Please call ~~I~~ me with any questions (708-555-1980).

Sincerely,

James Gabriel

James Gabriel
Vice President
Enclosures 5

Workplace

In workplace documents, correct grammar is critical to creating a strong impression.

26

Verb

Of course, we call ourselves human beings, but a few people have suggested we should think of ourselves as human doings. They would argue that our actions define us more than who we are.

Whether you are a human being or a human doing, you are thinking of yourself as a verb. Verbs express states of being and actions (doing). They give a sentence energy, movement, and meaning. This chapter provides practice working with these amazing words.

Learning Outcomes

LO1 Understand and use verb classes.

LO2 Work with number and person.

LO3 Work with voice.

LO4 Form basic verb tenses.

LO5 Form progressive tense.

LO6 Form perfect tense.

LO7 Understand verbals.

LO8 Use verbals as objects.

LO9 Apply learning to real-world examples.

What do you think?

Are you a human being or a human doing? Why?

Answers will vary.

LO1 Verb Classes

Verbs show action or states of being. Different classes of verbs do these jobs.

Action Verbs

Verbs that show action are called **action verbs**. Some action verbs are **transitive**, which means that they transfer action to a direct object.

> Bill **clutches** the pillow.
> (The verb *clutches* transfers action to the direct object *pillow*.)

Others are **intransitive**: They don't transfer action to a direct object.

> Bill **sleeps**.
> (The verb *sleeps* does not transfer action to a direct object.)

Linking Verbs

WAC

If you are mathematically minded, think of a linking verb as an equal sign. It indicates that the subject equals (or is similar to) what is in the predicate.

Verbs that link the subject to a noun, a pronoun, or an adjective are **linking verbs**. Predicates with linking verbs express a state of being.

> Bill **is** a heavy sleeper.
> (The linking verb *is* connects *Bill* to the noun *sleeper*.)

> He **seems** weary.
> (The linking verb *seems* connects *He* to the adjective *weary*.)

Linking Verbs

is	am	are	was	were	be	being	been	become
grow	feel	seem	look	smell	taste	sound	appear	remain

Note: The bottom-row words are linking verbs if they don't show action.

Helping Verbs

Vocabulary

action verb
word that expresses action

transitive verb
action verb that transfers action to a direct object

intransitive verb
action verb that does not transfer action to a direct object

linking verb
verb that connects the subject with a noun, a pronoun, or an adjective in the predicate

helping (auxiliary) verb
verb that works with a main verb to form some tenses, mood, and voice

A verb that works with an action or linking verb is a **helping** (or auxiliary) verb. A helping verb helps the main verb form tense, mood, and voice.

> Bill **has** slept till noon before, and today he **will be** sleeping even longer.
> (The helping verb *has* works with the main verb *slept*; the helping verbs *will be* work with *sleeping*. Both form special tenses.)

Note: Helping verbs work with verbs ending in *ing* or in past tense form.

Helping Verbs

am	been	could	does	have	might	should	will
are	being	did	had	is	must	was	would
be	can	do	has	may	shall	were	

Using Verb Classes

Identify/Write For each sentence below, identify the underlined verbs as transitive action verbs (T), intransitive action verbs (I), linking verbs (L), or helping verbs (H). Then write your own sentence using the same class of verb.

1. I **need** eight hours of sleep per night, but I often **get** only six.

Answers will vary.

2. This weekend, I **will be** getting even less sleep.

3. One of my favorite bands is **playing** in town.

4. They **rock**, and whenever I **see** a concert of theirs, I hardly **sleep**.

5. I **am** eager, but after the weekend, I **will** be worn out.

6. The problem with having too much fun on the weekend **is** the week after.

7. Maybe I **should** go to bed earlier so that I **can** store up sleep.

8. I **feel** awake now, but next week I will **look** weary.

Corbis Images by: Radius Images/Corbis

LO2 Number and Person of Verb

Verbs reflect number (singular or plural) and person (first person, second person, or third person).

Number

The **number** of the verb indicates whether the subject is singular or plural. Note that most present tense singular verbs end in *s*, while most present tense plural verbs do not.

Singular: The Gettysburg Address **speaks** of those who "gave the last full measure of devotion."

Plural: Many historians **speak** of it as the greatest American speech.

Person

The **person** of the verb indicates whether the subject is speaking, being spoken to, or being spoken about.

	Singular	**Plural**
First Person:	(I) am	(we) are
Second Person:	(you) are	(you) are
Third Person:	(she) is	(they) are

Note that the pronoun *I* takes a special form of the *be* verb—*am*.

Correct: I am excited about going to Gettysburg.
Incorrect: I is excited about going to Gettysburg.

The pronoun *I* also is paired with plural present tense verbs.

Correct: I want to go with you.
Incorrect: I wants to go with you.

In a similar way, the singular pronoun *you* takes the plural form of the *be* verb—*are, were*.

Correct: You are going to the Gettysburg National Military Park.
Incorrect: You is going to the Gettysburg National Military Park.

Correct: You were my first choice.
Incorrect: You was my first choice.

Vocabulary

number
singular or plural

person
whether the subject is speaking *(I, we)*, is being spoken to *(you)*, or is being spoken about *(he, she, it, they)*

Using Number and Person

Provide For each sentence below, provide the correct person and number of present tense *be* verb (*is, am, are*).

1. We ____are____ interested in going to Gettysburg.

2. It ____is____ a town in Pennsylvania where a great battle took place.

3. You ____are____ welcome to come on the trip with us.

4. Little Round Top ____is____ a hill where the fighting focused.

5. The Union troops ____are____ memorialized in statues on the hill.

6. You ____are____ standing on a piece of American history.

7. Pickett's Charge ____is____ considered General Lee's greatest mistake.

8. Troops from both sides ____are____ buried in the cemetery.

9. I ____am____ eager to see where Lincoln gave the Gettysburg Address.

10. We ____are____ hoping to spend two days in Gettysburg.

Rewrite Rewrite each sentence below to fix the errors in the number and person of the verb.

1. I listens as the tour guide describe the last day of battle.

   I listen as the tour guide describes the last day of battle.

2. Rifle shots hails down on the Confederate soldiers.

   Rifle shots hail down on the Confederate soldiers.

3. General Pickett order them to charge Little Round Top.

   General Pickett orders them to charge Little Round Top.

4. Flying lead kill many Southern soldiers.

   Flying lead kills many Southern soldiers.

5. The Union troops repels the charge and wins the day.

   The Union troops repel the charge and win the day.

6. President Lincoln deliver the Gettysburg Address.

   President Lincoln delivers the Gettysburg Address.

LO3 Voice of the Verb

The **voice** of the verb indicates whether the subject is acting or being acted upon.

Voice

An **active voice** means that the subject is acting. A **passive voice** means that the subject is acted on.

Active: The usher **led** us to our seats.

Passive: We **were led** by the usher to our seats.

	Active Voice		Passive Voice	
	Singular	**Plural**	**Singular**	**Plural**
Present Tense	I see you see he/she/it sees	we see you see they see	I am seen you are seen he/she/it is seen	we are seen you are seen they are seen
Past Tense	I saw you saw he saw	we saw you saw they saw	I was seen you were seen it was seen	we were seen you were seen they were seen
Future Tense	I will see you will see he will see	we will see you will see they will see	I will be seen you will be seen it will be seen	we will be seen you will be seen they will be seen
Present Perfect Tense	I have seen you have seen he has seen	we have seen you have seen they have seen	I have been seen you have been seen it has been seen	we have been seen you have been seen they have been seen
Past Perfect Tense	I had seen you had seen he had seen	we had seen you had seen they had seen	I had been seen you had been seen it had been seen	we had been seen you had been seen they had been seen
Future Perfect Tense	I will have seen you will have seen he will have seen	we will have seen you will have seen they will have seen	I will have been seen you will have been seen it will have been seen	we will have been seen you will have been seen they will have been seen

Active voice is preferred for most writing because it is direct and energetic.

Active: We gave the band a standing ovation.

Passive: The band was given a standing ovation by us.

Passive voice is preferred when the focus is on the receiver of the action or when the subject is unknown.

Passive: A rose was thrown onstage.

Active: Someone threw a rose onstage.

Workplace

In workplace writing, use active voice for most messages. Use passive voice to deliver bad news.

Vocabulary

voice
active or passive

active voice
voice created when the subject is performing the action of the verb

passive voice
voice created when the subject is receiving the action of the verb

Using Voice of a Verb

Rewrite Read each passive sentence below and rewrite it to be active. Think about who or what is performing the action and make that the subject. The first one is done for you.

1. The concert was attended by 3,000 fans.

   Three thousand fans attended the concert.

2. A good time was had by everyone.

   Everyone had a good time.

3. The ten greatest hits of the band were played by them.

   The band played their ten greatest hits.

4. Three concert T-shirts were bought by my friends and me.

   My friends and I bought three concert T-shirts.

5. The opening acts were tolerated by the crowd.

   The crowd tolerated the opening acts.

6. The air was electrified by the appearance of the main act.

   The appearance of the main act electrified the air.

7. I was not disappointed by their performance.

   Their performance did not disappoint me.

8. My short friend's view was blocked by a tall guy.

   A tall guy blocked my short friend's view.

9. The guy was asked by my friend to switch seats.

   My friend asked the guy to switch seats.

10. Every new song was cheered by the crowd.

    The crowd cheered for every new song.

Write Using the chart on the facing page, write a sentence for each situation below.

1. (a present tense singular active sentence) ___Answers will vary.___

2. (a past tense plural passive sentence) ___

LO4 Present and Future Tense Verbs

Basic verb tenses tell whether action happens in the past, in the present, or in the future.

Present Tense

Present tense verbs indicate that action is happening right now.

> A cruise ship **arrives** in Cabo San Lucas, Mexico.

Present tense verbs also can indicate that action happens routinely or continually.

> Every day, ships **drop** anchor outside of the harbor.

Present Tense in Academic Writing

Use present tense verbs to describe current conditions.

> Cabo San Lucas **makes** most of its income through tourism.

Use present tense verbs also to discuss the ideas in literature or to use historical quotations in a modern context. This use is called the "historical present," which allows writers to continue speaking.

> Some **say** that those who see Cabo do not truly see Mexico, or as G. K. Chesterton **writes**, "The traveler sees what he sees; the tourist sees what he has come to see."

Note: It is important to write a paragraph or an essay in one tense. Avoid shifting needlessly from tense to tense as you write. (See also page 278.)

Future Tense

Future tense verbs indicate that action will happen later on.

> Cruise ships **will visit** Cabo San Lucas for many years to come.

WAC

Look at writing in your field of study. Is most writing done in present tense or past tense? When writing in your field, use the tense that is most expected.

Vocabulary

present tense
verb tense indicating that action is happening now

future tense
verb tense indicating that action will happen later

gary718,2010 / Used under license from Shutterstock.com

Using Present and Future Verb Tenses

Write For each sentence below, fill in the blank with the present tense form of the verb indicated in parentheses.

1. Many visitors _____ snorkel _____ in Cabo's warm waters. (snorkeled)

2. White, sandy beaches _____ attract _____ many swimmers. (attracted)

3. Parasailors _____ fly _____ overhead from parachutes. (flew)

4. Waves _____ pick up _____ if winds are strong. (picked up)

5. Boats _____ run _____ people from cruise ships to shore. (ran)

Change Cross out and replace the verbs in the following paragraph, making them all present tense.

        We ~~went~~ go to Lover's Beach in Cabo San Lucas. The beach ~~was~~ is very busy. About a third of the people ~~sunbathed~~ sunbathe, a third ~~scuba dived~~ scuba dive, and a third just ~~splashed~~ splash in the waves. The waves ~~were~~ are large because the wind ~~was~~ is strong. We ~~swam~~ swim all afternoon until the water taxi ~~returned~~ returns for us. The day we ~~spent~~ spend in Cabo San Lucas ~~was~~ is one of our favorite days of the trip.

Write Write a sentence of your own, using each word below in the form indicated in parentheses.

1. enjoy (present) _Answers will vary._

2. swim (future) _____

3. realize (present) _____

4. complete (future) _____

Past Tense Verbs

Past tense verbs indicate that action happened in the past.

> When referring to his campaign in England, Julius Caesar **reported**, "I **came**. I **saw**. I **conquered**."

Forming Past Tense

Most verbs form the past tense by adding *ed*. If the word ends in a silent *e*, drop the *e* before adding *ed*.

help ➔ help**ed**	love ➔ lov**ed**
look ➔ look**ed**	hope ➔ hop**ed**

If the word ends in a consonant preceded by a single vowel and the last syllable is stressed, double the final consonant before adding *ed*.

stop ➔ stop**ped**	occur ➔ occur**red**
plan ➔ plan**ned**	refer ➔ refer**red**

If the word ends in a *y* preceded by a consonant, change the *y* to *i* before adding *ed*.

study ➔ stud**ied**	hurry ➔ hurr**ied**
worry ➔ worr**ied**	carry ➔ carr**ied**

Irregular Verbs

Some of the most commonly used verbs form the past tense by changing the verb itself. See the chart below:

Present	Past	Present	Past	Present	Past
am	was, were	fly	flew	see	saw
become	became	forget	forgot	shake	shook
begin	began	freeze	froze	shine	shone
blow	blew	get	got	show	showed
break	broke	give	gave	shrink	shrank
bring	brought	go	went	sing	sang
buy	bought	grow	grew	sink	sank
catch	caught	hang	hung	sit	sat
choose	chose	have	had	sleep	slept
come	came	hear	heard	speak	spoke
dig	dug	hide	hid	stand	stood
do	did	keep	kept	steal	stole
draw	drew	know	knew	swim	swam
drink	drank	lead	led	swing	swung
drive	drove	pay	paid	take	took
eat	ate	prove	proved	teach	taught
fall	fell	ride	rode	tear	tore
feel	felt	ring	rang	throw	threw
fight	fought	rise	rose	wear	wore
find	found	run	ran	write	wrote

Insight

Note that the irregular verbs at the bottom of the page are some of the oldest verbs in the English language. That's why they are irregular. Even so, they are used quite often because they describe the everyday tasks that English speakers have been doing for more than a thousand years.

Vocabulary

past tense
verb tense indicating that action happened previously

Using Past Tense Verbs

Write For each verb, write the correct past tense form.

1. give — gave
2. shop — shopped
3. trick — tricked
4. type — typed
5. teach — taught
6. cry — cried
7. sing — sang
8. soap — soaped
9. cap — capped
10. cope — coped

11. try — tried
12. fly — flew
13. think — thought
14. grip — gripped
15. gripe — griped
16. pour — poured
17. swing — swung
18. slip — slipped
19. reply — replied
20. tip — tipped

Edit Make changes to the following paragraph, converting it from present tense to past tense. Use the correction marks to the right.

During my junior year of high school, I ~~become~~ became a lifeguard at a campground pool. 1

I ~~think~~ thought it ~~is~~ was a cushy job, sitting poolside all summer. However, this pool ~~hosts~~ hosted many

day camps, meaning hundreds of little kids with little supervision. I quickly ~~discover~~ discovered

that the other guards and I ~~are~~ were the supervision. It ~~is~~ was hard to yell at kids all day, but it

~~is~~ was more dangerous to stay silent. They ~~run~~ ran on the deck or ~~dive~~ dove into shallow water or 5

~~jump~~ jumped into deep water when they ~~don't~~ didn't know how to swim. Worse yet, families ~~come~~ came,

and when their kids ~~do~~ did the same things and I ~~yell~~ yelled, parents ~~tell~~ told me their kids ~~can~~ could

run on deck if they ~~want~~ wanted. Facing down adults at sixteen ~~isn't~~ wasn't easy. Still, my brother's

summer job ~~is~~ was mowing lawns at the same campground. When he ~~walks~~ walked by, drenched

in sweat, my job sitting in my lifeguard chair suddenly ~~seems~~ seemed cushy. 10

Correction Marks

- ✄ delete
- d̲ capitalize
- ∅ lowercase
- ∧ insert
- ⌃ add comma
- ? add question mark
- ∧ word add word
- ⊙ add period
- ◡ spelling
- ∿ switch

LO5 Progressive Tense Verbs

The basic tenses of past, present, and future tell when action takes place. The progressive tense or aspect tells that action is ongoing.

Progressive Tense

Progressive tense indicates that action is ongoing. Progressive tense is formed by using a helping verb along with the *ing* form of the main verb.

Scientists **are studying** the growth of human populations.

There are past, present, and future progressive tenses. Each uses a helping verb in the appropriate tense.

In 1804, one billion people **were sharing** the globe.

Currently, about seven billion people **are living** on Earth.

In 2040, about nine billion people **will be calling** this planet home.

Forming Progressive Tenses

Past:	was/were	+	main verb	+	ing
Present:	am/is/are	+	main verb	+	ing
Future:	will be	+	main verb	+	ing

Insight

Avoid using progressive tense with the following:

- Verbs that express thoughts, attitudes, and desires: *know, understand, want, prefer*

- Verbs that describe appearances: *seem, resemble*

- Verbs that indicate possession: *belong, have, own, possess*

- Verbs that signify inclusion: *contain, hold*

  I **know** your name, not I **am knowing** your name.

Vocabulary

progressive tense
verb tense that expresses ongoing action

Using Progressive Tense

Form Rewrite each sentence three times, changing the tenses as requested in parentheses.

> Epidemics drop populations, but vaccination leads to upswings.

1. (present progressive) Epidemics are dropping populations, but vaccination is leading to upswings.

2. (past progressive) Epidemics were dropping populations, but vaccination was leading to upswings.

3. (future progressive) Epidemics will be dropping populations, but vaccination will be leading to upswings.

> Though food production grows by addition, population grows by multiplication.

4. (present progressive) Though food production is growing by addition, population is growing by multiplication.

5. (past progressive) Though food production was growing by addition, population was growing by multiplication.

6. (future progressive) Though food production will be growing by addition, population will be growing by multiplication.

> Improved public-health programs led to lower mortality rates.

7. (present progressive) Improved public-health programs are leading to lower mortality rates.

8. (past progressive) Improved public-health programs were leading to lower mortality rates.

9. (future progressive) Improved public-health programs will be leading to lower mortality rates.

LO6 Perfect Tense Verbs

The perfect tense tells that action is not ongoing, but is finished, whether in the past, present, or future.

Perfect Tense

Perfect tense indicates that action is completed. Perfect tense is formed by using a helping verb along with the past tense form of the main verb.

> An estimated 110 billion people **have lived** on earth.

There are past, present, and future perfect tenses. These tenses are formed by using helping verbs in past, present, and future tenses.

> By 1804, the world population **had reached** one billion.
> We **have added** another billion people in the last 13 years.
> In 13 more years, we **will have welcomed** another billion.

Forming Perfect Tense

Past:	had	+	past tense main verb
Present:	has/have	+	past tense main verb
Future:	will have	+	past tense main verb

Perfect Tense with Irregular Verbs

Insight

For the simple past tense form of these irregular verbs, see page 320.

To form perfect tense with irregular verbs, use the past participle form instead of the past tense form. Here are the past participles of common irregular verbs.

Present	Past Part.	Present	Past Part.	Present	Past Part.
am, be	been	fly	flown	see	seen
become	become	forget	forgotten	shake	shaken
begin	begun	freeze	frozen	shine	shone
blow	blown	get	gotten	show	shown
break	broken	give	given	shrink	shrunk
bring	brought	go	gone	sing	sung
buy	bought	grow	grown	sink	sunk
catch	caught	hang	hung	sit	sat
choose	chosen	have	had	sleep	slept
come	come	hear	heard	speak	spoken
dig	dug	hide	hidden	stand	stood
do	done	keep	kept	steal	stolen
draw	drawn	know	known	swim	swum
drink	drunk	lead	led	swing	swung
drive	driven	pay	paid	take	taken
eat	eaten	prove	proven	teach	taught
fall	fallen	ride	ridden	tear	torn
feel	felt	ring	rung	throw	thrown
fight	fought	rise	risen	wear	worn
find	found	run	run	write	written

Using Perfect Tense

Form Rewrite each sentence three times, changing the tenses as requested in parentheses.

> According to scientists, the earth circles the sun over 4.5 billion times.

1. (past perfect) _According to scientists, the earth had circled the sun over 4.5 billion times._

2. (present perfect) _According to scientists, the earth has circled the sun over 4.5 billion times._

3. (future perfect) _According to scientists, the earth will have circled the sun over 4.5 billion times._

> The sun lives half of its lifetime.

4. (past perfect) _The sun had lived half of its lifetime._

5. (present perfect) _The sun has lived half of its lifetime._

6. (future perfect) _The sun will have lived half of its lifetime._

> Two stars within our galaxy go supernova.

7. (past perfect) _Two stars within our galaxy had gone supernova._

8. (present perfect) _Two stars within our galaxy have gone supernova._

9. (future perfect) _Two stars within our galaxy will have gone supernova._

LO7 Verbals

A **verbal** is formed from a verb but functions as a noun, an adjective, or an adverb. Each type of verbal—gerund, participle, and infinitive—can appear alone or can begin a **verbal phrase**.

Gerund

A **gerund** is formed from a verb ending in *ing,* and it functions as a noun.

> **Swimming** is my favorite pastime. (subject)
>
> I love **swimming.** (direct object)

A **gerund phrase** begins with the gerund and includes any objects and modifiers.

> **Swimming laps at the pool** builds endurance. (subject)
>
> I prefer **swimming laps in pools rather than in lakes**. (direct object)

Participle

A **participle** is formed from a verb ending in *ing* or *ed,* and it functions as an adjective.

> **Excited**, I received my lifesaving certification! (*excited* modifies *I*)
>
> What an **exciting** day! (*exciting* modifies *day*)

A **participial phrase** begins with the participle and includes any objects and modifiers.

> **Exciting the crowd of young swimmers**, I said we were diving today.

Infinitive

An **infinitive** is formed from *to* and a present-tense verb, and it functions as a noun, an adjective, or an adverb.

> **To teach** is a noble profession. (noun)
>
> This is an important point **to remember**. (adjective)
>
> Students must pay attention **to understand**. (adverb)

An **infinitive phrase** begins with an infinitive and includes any objects or modifiers.

> I plan lessons **to teach an easy progression of swimming skills**.

Vocabulary

verbal
gerund, participle, or infinitive; a construction formed from a verb but functioning as a noun, an adjective, or an adverb

verbal phrase
phrase beginning with a gerund, a participle, or an infinitive

gerund
verbal ending in *ing* and functioning as a noun

gerund phrase
phrase beginning with a gerund and including objects and modifiers

participle
verbal ending in *ing* or *ed* and functioning as an adjective

participial phrase
phrase beginning with a participle and including objects and modifiers

infinitive
verbal beginning with *to* and functioning as a noun, an adjective, or an adverb

infinitive phrase
phrase beginning with an infinitive and including objects and modifiers

Using Verbals

Identify Identify each underlined verbal by circling the correct choice in parentheses. (gerund, participle, infinitive).

1. <u>Jogging</u> is another excellent exercise. ((gerund), participle, infinitive)

2. You should plan <u>to jog</u> three times a week. (gerund, participle, (infinitive))

3. <u>Jogging</u> with friends, you can also be social. (gerund, (participle), infinitive)

4. Try <u>to wear</u> good shoes. (gerund, participle, (infinitive))

5. <u>Avoiding</u> joint injury is important. ((gerund), participle, infinitive)

6. <u>Toned</u> through exercise, your body will look better. (gerund, (participle), infinitive)

Form Complete each sentence below by supplying the type of verbal requested in parentheses.

1. The exercise I would choose is _Answers will vary._____. (gerund)

2. _____, I would lose weight. (participle)

3. _____ is a good toning exercise. (infinitive)

4. I would also like to try _____. (gerund)

5. When exercising, remember _____. (infinitive)

6. _____, I'll be in great shape. (participle)

Write For each verbal phrase below, write a sentence that correctly uses it.

1. to lift weights _Answers will vary._____

_____

2. preparing myself for a marathon _____

_____

3. filled with anticipation _____

_____

LO8 Verbals as Objects

Though both infinitives and gerunds can function as nouns, they can't be used interchangeably as direct objects. Some verbs take infinitives and not gerunds. Other verbs take only gerunds and not infinitives.

Gerunds as Objects

Verbs that express facts are followed by **gerunds**.

admit	deny	enjoy	miss	recommend
avoid	discuss	finish	quit	regret
consider	dislike	imagine	recall	

I enjoy **playing** cards.
not I enjoy to play cards.

I imagine **winning** a poker tournament.
not I imagine to win a poker tournament.

Infinitives as Objects

Verbs that express intention, hopes, and desires are followed by **infinitives**.

agree	demand	hope	prepare	volunteer
appear	deserve	intend	promise	want
attempt	endeavor	need	refuse	wish
consent	fail	offer	seem	
decide	hesitate	plan	tend	

I attempt **to win** every hand.
not I attempt winning every hand.

I need **to get** a better poker face.
not I need getting a better poker face.

Gerunds or Infinitives as Objects

Some verbs can be followed by either a gerund or an infinitive.

begin	hate	love	remember	stop
continue	like	prefer	start	try

I love **to play** poker.
or I love **playing** poker.

Using Verbals as Objects

Select For each sentence below, circle the appropriate verbal in parentheses.

1. I enjoy (to play, **playing**) canasta.

2. We should promise (**to play**, playing) canasta this weekend.

3. In canasta, you need (**to get**, getting) seven-card melds.

4. You and a partner endeavor (**to meld**, melding) suits.

5. You and your partner can discuss (to go, **going**) out.

6. The rules demand (to keep, **keeping**) other table talk down.

7. I recall (to win, **winning**) three hands in a row.

8. If you lose a hand, you'll regret (to have, **having**) wild cards.

9. If you fail (**to use**, using) a wild card, it costs.

10. You'll dislike (to get, **getting**) penalized 50 points.

Write For each verb below, write your own sentence using the verb and following it with a gerund or an infinitive, as appropriate.

1. deny _Answers will vary._ _____

_____

2. promise _____

_____

3. refuse _____

_____

4. consider _____

_____

5. recommend _____

_____

6. avoid _____

_____

LO9 Real-World Application

Revise Rewrite the following paragraph, changing passive verbs to active verbs. (See page 316.)

Your request to send all the sales reps to the Adobe training seminar in Cincinnati was reviewed by me. Your idea that this training would help your staff is agreed to by me. Our training budget was reviewed by me to see if the seminar could be afforded by us.

I reviewed your request to send all the sales reps to the Adobe training seminar in

Cincinnati. I agree with your idea that this training would help your staff. I reviewed our

training budget to see if we could afford the seminar.

Revise In the following paragraph, change future perfect verbs into past perfect verbs by crossing out helping verbs and writing new helping verbs. (See page 312.)

We ~~will have~~ **had** used a large portion of our budget to upgrade design software for the engineering staff. In addition, we ~~will have~~ **had** made prior commitments to train office staff in August. As a result, we ~~will not have~~ **had not** reserved enough money to send all sales reps to Cincinnati.

Revise In the following paragraph, correct misused verbals by crossing out the gerund or infinitive and replacing it with the correct verbal form. (See page 328.)

I want ~~exploring~~ **to explore** other solutions with you. Do you recommend ~~to send~~ **sending** two reps who then could train others? I recall ~~to do~~ **doing** that in previous situations. I admit ~~to agree~~ **agreeing** that this isn't the optimal course, but I hope ~~doing~~ **to do** something.

> "We do our best that we know how at the moment,
> and if it doesn't turn out, we modify it."
>
> —Franklin Delano Roosevelt

Photo by Jenny Solecki

27
Adjective and Adverb

All right, so you have a car. Lots of people have cars. It's a vintage Volkswagen beetle? Nice. And it's decked out with custom paint, toys, barrettes, and words like "smile," "laugh," and "let flow"? You call it your "crazy, lovey, hippy, dippy, vintage buggy"? Wow, do *you* have a car!

The owner of the car above has totally modified it and then has used strings of modifying words and phrases to describe it. That's what adjectives and adverbs do. They add color, texture, shape, size, and many more vivid details to each picture. Remember, though, that too many modifiers can overload a sentence—much as bric-a-brac can overwhelm a car.

Learning Outcomes

LO1 Understand adjective basics.

LO2 Put adjectives in order.

LO3 Use adjectivals.

LO4 Understand adverb basics.

LO5 Place adverbs well.

LO6 Use adverbials.

LO7 Apply adjectives and adverbs in real-world contexts.

What do you think?

How would you describe a car you wish you had?

Answers will vary.

LO1 Adjective Basics

An **adjective** is a word that modifies a noun or pronoun. Even **articles** such as *a, an,* and *the* are adjectives, because they indicate whether you mean a general or specific thing. Adjectives answer these basic questions: *which, what kind of, how many / how much?*

Speaking & Listening

Read the first example sentence aloud. Then read it without the adjectives. Note how adjectives add spice to the description. Like spice, though, adjectives should be used sparingly, to "season" nouns, not to overwhelm them.

Adjectives often appear before the word they modify.

> You have **a cute, fluffy** dog.

A **predicate adjective** appears after the noun it modifies and is linked to the word by a linking verb.

> Your dog is **cute** and **fluffy**.

Proper adjectives come from proper nouns and are capitalized.

> He is a **Yorkshire** terrier.

Forms of Adjectives

Adjectives come in three forms: positive, comparative, and superlative.

- **Positive adjectives** describe one thing without making any comparisons.

> Keats is a **friendly** dog.

- **Comparative adjectives** compare the thing to something else.

> Keats is **friendlier** than our cat, Yeats.

- **Superlative adjectives** compare the thing to two or more other things

> He is the **friendliest** dog you will ever meet.

Note: For one- and two-syllable words, create the comparative form by adding *er,* and create the superlative form by added *est.* For words of three syllables or more, use *more* (or *less*) for comparatives and *most* (or *least*) for superlatives. Also note that *good* and *bad* have special superlative forms:

Positive	Comparative	Superlative
good	better	best
bad	worse	worst
big	bigger	biggest
happy	happier	happiest
wonderful	more wonderful	most wonderful

Vocabulary

adjective
word that modifies a noun or pronoun

articles
the adjectives *a, an,* and *the*

predicate adjective
adjective that appears after a linking verb and describes the subject

positive adjective
word that modifies a noun or pronoun without comparing it

comparative adjective
word that modifies a noun or pronoun by comparing it to something else

superlative adjective
word that modifies a noun or pronoun by comparing it to two or more things

Using the Forms of Adjectives

Identify/Write In each sentence below, identify the underlined adjectives as positive (P), comparative (C), or superlative (S). Then write a new sentence about a different topic, but use the same adjectives.

1. We once had a <u>beautiful</u> collie with a <u>long</u>, <u>shiny</u> coat.
                P   P   P

   Answers will vary.

2. She was <u>smarter</u> than our last dog, perhaps the <u>smartest</u> pet we've ever owned.
            C   S

3. She thought she was the <u>alpha</u> female and my wife was the <u>beta</u> female.
                     P   P

4. My wife became even <u>more unhappy</u> when the dog tore up her <u>best</u> couch.
                     C   S

5. My wife was <u>happiest</u> on the day we gave the dog to a farmer.
            S

Correct Read the paragraph below and correct adjective errors, using the correction marks to the right. The first one has been done for you.

Did you know there is an ~~I~~ntelligence test for dogs? It includes ~~V~~arious tasks *1*

to check the dog's ~~A~~daptive intelligence or problem-solving ability. The ~~most~~

smartest dogs can quickly find a treat under one of three buckets, get a treat from

under a piece of furniture, find its ~~F~~avorite spot after a room is rearranged, and

get
∧ ~~gets~~ a towel off its head. In tests, border collies, poodles, and german shepherds *5*

have tested as the ~~most~~ smartest, and afghan hounds, british bulldogs, and chow

              lowest   most intelligent
chows tested at the ~~most low~~ end. Even if they aren't the ~~intelligentest~~, these dogs

might still be the ~~most~~ cuddliest.

Correction Marks

✄	delete
d̲	capitalize
ⅅ	lowercase
∧	insert
⌃̦	add comma
? ∧	add question mark
word ∧	add word
⊙	add period
◯	spelling
∿	switch

LO2 Adjective Order

Adjectives aren't all created equally. Native English speakers use a specific order when putting multiple adjectives before a noun, and all speakers of English can benefit from understanding this order.

Begin with . . .

1.	articles	a, an, the
	demonstrative adjectives	that, this, these, those
	possessives	my, our, her, their, Kayla's

Then position adjectives that tell . . .

2.	time	first, second, next, last
3.	how many	three, few, some, many
4.	value	important, prized, fine
5.	size	giant, puny, hulking
6.	shape	spiky, blocky, square
7.	condition	clean, tattered, repaired
8.	age	old, new, classic
9.	color	blue, scarlet, salmon
10.	nationality	French, Chinese, Cuban
11.	religion	Baptist, Buddhist, Hindu
12.	material	cloth, stone, wood, bronze

Finally place . . .

| 13. | nouns used as adjectives | baby [seat], frog [legs] |

Example:

that gorgeous old French shrimp boat

(1 + 7 + 8 + 10 + 13 + **noun**)

Note: Avoid using too many adjectives before a noun. An article and one or two adjectives are usually enough. More adjectives may overload the noun.

| **Too many:** | my last three spiky old blue Cuban coral souvenirs |
| **Effective:** | my last three coral souvenirs |

As the introduction indicates, native English speakers use this order unconsciously because it sounds right to them. If you put adjectives in a different order, a native English speaker might say, "That's not how anybody says it." One way to avoid this issue is to avoid stacking multiple adjectives before nouns.

Placing Adjectives in Order

Order Rearrange each set of adjectives and articles so that they are in the correct order. The first one has been done for you.

1. purple   rectangular   this

   this rectangular purple   carton

2. your   Mexican   beautiful

   your beautiful Mexican   guitar

3. wooden   worn-out   many

   many worn-out wooden   blocks

4. precious   the   Islamic

   the precious Islamic   mosaic

5. traditional   several   Russian

   several traditional Russian   dolls

6. stone   chess   Doug's

   doug's stone chess   pieces

7. pen   French   my

   my French pen   pal

8. broken-down   that   old

   that broken-down old   sedan

9. felt   his   pin-striped

   his pin-striped felt   fedora

10. old   the   mossy

    the mossy old   temple

11. original   three   piano

    three original piano   pieces

12. first   real   our

    our first real   vacation

LO3 Adjective Questions and Adjectivals

Adjectives answer four basic questions: *which, what kind of, how many / how much?*

Photo by McKay Savage

	Children
Which?	those children
What kind of?	smiling Indian children
How many/how much?	many children

those many smiling Indian children

Adjectivals

A single word that answers one of these questions is called an adjective. If a phrase or clause answers one of these questions, it is an **adjectival** phrase or clause.

	Children
Which?	children who were waiting to vote
What kind of?	children wanting to get photographed

Wanting to get photographed, the children **who were waiting to vote** crowded my camera.

The following types of phrases and clauses can be adjectivals:

Prepositional phrase:	from the school
Participial phrase:	standing in a line
Adjective clause:	who greeted me warmly

Say It

Partner with a classmate. One of you should say the noun, and the other should ask the adjective questions. Then the first person should answer each question with adjectives or adjectivals.

1. **mini-vans**

   Which mini-vans?

   What kind of mini-vans?

   How many mini-vans?

2. **shampoo**

   Which shampoo?

   What kind of shampoo?

   How much shampoo

Using Adjectives and Adjectivals

Answer/Write For each word, answer the adjective questions using adjectives and adjectivals. Then write a sentence using two or more of your answers.

1. **Cats**

   Which cats? _Answers will vary._____

   What kind of cats? _____

   How many cats? _____

   Sentence: _____

   _____

   _____

   _____

2. **Hobbies**

   Which hobbies? _____

   What kind of hobbies? _____

   How many hobbies? _____

   Sentence: _____

   _____

   _____

   _____

3. **Plans**

   Which plans? _____

   What kind of plans? _____

   How many plans? _____

   Sentence: _____

   _____

   _____

   _____

LO4 Adverb Basics

An **adverb** modifies a verb, a **verbal**, an adjective, an adverb, or a whole sentence. An adverb answers five basic questions: *how, when, where, why, to what degree, how often / how long.*

AYAKOVLEV.COM shutterstock

> He danced **boldly**.
> (*Boldly* modifies the verb *danced.*)
>
> He leaped **very high.**
> (*Very* modifies the adverb *high,* which modifies *leaped.*)
>
> **Apparently,** he has had dance training.
> (*Apparently* modifies the whole sentence.)

Note: Most adverbs end in *ly.* Some can be written with or without the *ly,* but when in doubt, use the *ly* form.

loud ⟶ loud**ly**   tight ⟶ tight**ly**   deep ⟶ deep**ly**

Insight

In the United States, intensifying adverbs such as *very* and *really* are used sparingly. Also, in academic writing, it is considered better to find a precise, vivid verb than to prop up an imprecise verb with an adverb.

Forms of Adverbs

Adverbs have three forms: positive, comparative, and superlative.

- **Positive adverbs** describe without comparing.

> He danced **skillfully**.

- **Comparative adverbs** (*er, more,* or *less*) describe by comparing with one other action.

> He danced **more skillfully** than his brother.

- **Superlative adverbs** (*est, most,* or *least*) describe by comparing with more than one action.

> He danced **most skillfully** of any of those trying out.

Note: Some adjectives change form to create comparative or superlative forms.

well ⟶ better ⟶ best   badly ⟶ worse ⟶ worst

Vocabulary

adverb
word that modifies a verb, a verbal, an adjective, an adverb, or a whole sentence

verbal
word formed from a verb but functioning as a noun, an adjective, or an adverb

positive adverb
adverb that modifies without comparing

comparative adverb
adverb that modifies by comparing with one other thing

superlative adverb
adverb that modifies by comparing to two or more things

Using the Forms of Adverbs

Provide In each sentence below, provide the correct form of the adverb in parentheses—positive, comparative, or superlative.

1. I like to dance _____fast_____ (fast).

2. I dance _____faster_____ (fast) than any of my friends.

3. My moves are the _____fastest_____ (fast) of anyone on the floor.

4. My brother moves _____well_____ (well) for an older guy.

5. He certainly dances _____better_____ (well) than my father.

6. But I dance _____best_____ (well) in my family.

7. I ask the band to play the song _____quickly_____ (quickly).

8. They sometimes play it _____more quickly_____ (quickly) than I intended.

9. A thrash band played _____most quickly_____ (quickly) of any band I've heard.

10. That's when I danced _____worst_____ (badly) in my whole life.

Choose In each sentence, circle the correct word in parentheses. If the word modifies a noun or pronoun, choose the adjective form (*good, bad*). If the word modifies a verb, a verbal, an adjective, or an adverb, choose the adverb form (*well, badly.*)

1. I hope this turns out to be a (**good**, well) movie.

2. Even if the actors do (good, **well**), the plot might not be (**good**, well).

3. I don't want to spend (**good**, well) money on a (**bad**, badly) movie.

4. I wanted to see this movie (bad, **badly**).

5. Every time Richard comes along, he behaves (bad, **badly**).

6. If I tell him to straighten up, he takes it (bad, **badly**).

7. That guy has a (**bad**, badly) attitude.

8. I have done (good, **well**) not to invite him.

9. The movie was (good, **well**) acted.

10. Its plot was (**good**, well).

LO5 Placement of Adverbs

Adverbs should be placed in different places in sentences, depending on their use.

How Adverbs

Adverbs that tell *how* can appear anywhere except between a verb and a direct object.

> **Furiously** we paddled the raft.
> We **furiously** paddled the raft.
> We paddled the raft **furiously**.
> **not** We paddled furiously the raft.

When Adverbs

Adverbs that tell *when* should go at the beginning or end of the sentence.

> We ran the white water **yesterday**. **Today** we'll tackle the course again.

Where Adverbs

Adverbs that tell where should follow the verb they modify, but should not come between the verb and the direct object. (**Note:** Prepositional phrases often function as *where* adverbs.)

> The raft shot **downstream** and plunged **over a waterfall**.
> Our guide shouted instructions **from the back of the boat**.
> **not** Our guide shouted from the back of the boat instructions.

To What Degree Adverbs

Adverbs that tell *to what degree* go right before the adverb they modify.

> I learned **very** quickly to hang on tight.

How Often Adverbs

Adverbs that tell *how often* should go right before an action verb, even if the verb has a helping verb.

> I **often** dreamed about going white-water rafting.
> Before that trip, I had **never** gotten to go.

> "The road to hell is paved with adverbs."
> —Stephen King

Placing Adverbs Well

Place   For each sentence below, insert the adverb (in parentheses) in the most appropriate position. The first one has been done for you.

1. The instructor ^often^ reminded us to stay alert. (often)

2. He began our training by ^thoroughly^ explaining the equipment. (thoroughly)

3. ^Next^ We got our paddles and helmets. (next)

4. The instructor was ^very^ careful about safety. (very)

5. We took our positions ^in the raft^. (in the raft)

6. ^Soon^ The rapids chattered all around us. (soon)

7. We ^often^ went over challenging rapids. (often)

8. ^Fortunately^ No one fell out. (fortunately)

9. I would ^highly^ recommend that guide. (highly)

10. I hope to go rafting again ^someday^. (someday)

Revise   In the paragraph below, use the transpose mark (⁀) to move adverbs that incorrectly come between a verb and a direct object.

Adrenaline junkies ⌐seek⌐ ⌐often⌐ thrills by putting themselves in danger. Dangerous situations ⌐trigger⌐ ⌐usually⌐ the release of adrenaline. Adrenaline is a hormone that ⌐causes⌐ ⌐typically⌐ the heart rate to increase. It ⌐triggers⌐ ⌐also⌐ the fight-or-flight response. Adrenaline junkies ⌐enjoy⌐ ⌐very much⌐ this feeling and ⌐seek⌐ ⌐often⌐ it out through high-risk activities. They ⌐try⌐ ⌐frequently⌐ skydiving or bungee jumping. Some ⌐use⌐ ⌐repeatedly⌐ white-water rafting to get their thrills.   5

1

LO6 Adverb Questions and Adverbials

Adverbs answer six basic questions: *how, when, where, why, to what degree,* and *how often.*

Photo by Kevin Tostado

	They bounced.
How?	bounced joyously
When?	bounced yesterday
Where?	bounced around
Why?	bounced spontaneously
To what degree?	extremely joyously
How often?	bounced repeatedly

Yesterday, they **repeatedly, spontaneously,** and **extremely joyously** bounced **around.**

Note: Avoid this sort of adverb overload in your sentences.

Adverbials

Often, the adverb questions are answered by **adverbial** phrases and clauses, which answer the same six questions.

	They bounced.
How?	bounced doing the splits
When?	bounced during the Fun Day Festival
Where?	bounced in the inflatable castle
Why?	bounced because they had been studying too much
To what degree?	bounced until they got sick
How often?	bounced throughout the afternoon

Because they had been studying too much, they bounced **in the inflatable castle throughout the afternoon until they got sick.**

Note: Again, avoid this sort of adverbial overload in your sentences.

The following types of phrases and clauses can be adverbials:

Prepositional phrase:	in the inflatable castle
Participial phrase:	doing the splits
Dependent clause:	because they had been studying too much

Using Adverbials

Answer/Write For each sentence, answer the adverb questions using adverbs and adverbials. Then write a sentence using three or more of your answers.

1. **They ran.**

   How did they run? _Answers will vary._____

   When did they run? _____

   Where did they run? _____

   Why did they run? _____

   To what degree did they run? _____

   How often did they run? _____

   Sentence: _____

   _____

   _____

   _____

2. **They laughed.**

   How did they laugh? _Answers will vary._____

   When did they laugh? _____

   Where did they laugh? _____

   Why did they laugh? _____

   To what degree did they laugh? _____

   How often did they laugh? _____

   Sentence: _____

   _____

   _____

   _____

LO7 Real-World Application

Correct In the following document, correct the use of adjectives and adverbs. Use the correction marks to the left.

Correction Marks

⌦ delete

d̲ capitalize

∅ lowercase

∧ insert

⌄ add comma

? add question
∧ mark

word add word
∧

⊙ add period

⬭ spelling

∿ switch

Verdant Landscaping

1500 West Ridge Avenue
Tacoma, WA 98466

January 6, 2011

Ms. Karen Bledsoe
Blixen Furniture
1430 North Bel Air Drive
Tacoma, WA 98466-6970

Dear Ms. Bledsoe:

We miss you! Verdant Landscaping has been scheduled ~~not~~ **not** to care for your grounds   *1*
since fall 2008. You were a valued customer. Did our service fall short in some
way? Whatever prompted you to make a change, we would like to discuss ways we
could serve you ~~gooder~~ **better**.

During the past year, Verdant has added ~~important these new three services~~ **these three important new services**: A full-   *5*
time landscape architect helps happily you improve your grounds with flower beds,
hardy shrubs, and blooming trees. A tree surgeon can give at a moment's notice
you help with diseased or damaged trees. And our lawn crews offer now mulching
services. We provide the ~~most good~~ **best** service and value at the ~~most good~~ **best** price!

I'd like to call next week you to discuss whatever concerns you may have, and to   *10*
offer you a 10 percent discount on a lawn-service new agreement. I can answer at
that time any questions you may have about our new services as they are described
in the enclosed brochure.

Sincerely,
~~Sincere,~~

Stephen Bates

Stephen Bates   *15*
Customer Service

Enclosure

Workplace

Note the effect of adjectives and adverbs on voice. Errors make the writer sound odd, but careful use can create energy and interest.

Anthony Harris, 2010/used under license from www.shutterstock.com

28

Conjunction and Preposition

Every relationship is different. A boyfriend and girlfriend will probably be equals, but a mother and daughter probably won't be. In fact, the daughter may be legally classified as a dependent.

Ideas have relationships, too. Sometimes ideas are equal—you can tell by the conjunction that connects them. At other times, one idea depends on another. There are conjunctions for that situation, too. And when words form a special relationship, prepositions are there to connect them.

Conjunctions and prepositions make connections in your writing and help your ideas relate to each other. This chapter shows how.

Learning Outcomes

LO1 Use coordinating and correlative conjunctions.

LO2 Use subordinating conjunctions.

LO3 Understand common prepositions.

LO4 Use *by*, *at*, *on*, and *in*.

LO5 Use conjunctions and prepositions in real-world documents.

What do you think?

What kind of relationship does the photo suggest?

Answers will vary.

345

LO1 Coordinating and Correlative Conjunctions

A **conjunction** is a word or word group that joins parts of a sentence—words, phrases, or clauses.

Coordinating Conjunctions

A **coordinating conjunction** joins grammatically equal parts—a word to a word, a phrase to a phrase, or a clause to a clause. (A clause is basically a sentence.)

Andresr, 2010/used under license from www.shutterstock.com

Coordinating Conjunctions

and	but	or	nor	for	so	yet

Equal importance: A coordinating conjunction shows that the two things joined are of equal importance.

> Ted and Jana like rhythm and blues.
> (*And* joins words in an equal way.)
>
> I have R&B songs on my iPod and on CDs.
> (*And* joins the phrases *on my iPod* and *on CDs*.)
>
> I want to download more, but I lost my USB cord.
> (*But* joins the two clauses, with a comma after the first.)

Items in a series: A coordinating conjunction can also join more than two equal things in a series.

> Ted, Jana, and I are planning to attend an R&B festival.
> (*And* joins *Ted, Jana,* and *I*. A comma follows each word except the last.)
>
> We will drive to the fest, check out the acts, and buy our tickets.
> (*And* joins three parts of a compound verb.)

Correlative Conjunctions

Correlative conjunctions consist of a coordinating conjunction paired with another word. They also join equal grammatical parts: word to word, phrase to phrase, or clause to clause.

Correlative Conjunctions

either/or	neither/nor	whether/or	both/and	not only/but also

Stressing equality: Correlative conjunctions stress the equality of parts.

> I like not only rock but also classical.
> (*Not only / but also* stresses the equality of *rock* and *classical*.)
>
> Either I will become a musician, or I will be a recording technician.
> (*Either / or* joins the two clauses, with a comma after the first.)

Vocabulary

conjunction
word or word group that joins parts of a sentence

coordinating conjunction
conjunction that joins grammatically equal components

correlative conjunction
pair of conjunctions that stress the equality of the parts that are joined

Using Coordinating and Correlative Conjunctions

Traits

When two ideas correlate, they work together. They co-relate. Thinking in this way can help you remember the term *correlative conjunctions*.

Correct In each sentence below, circle the best coordinating conjunction in parentheses.

1. I should buy an MP3 player (but, for, **or**) an iPod.

2. Kelly, Eli, (**and**, nor, yet) I sometimes share music.

3. We have different tastes, (or, **so**, yet) we get to hear a variety.

4. Kelly likes hip hop, (nor, **but**, for) I like Latin music.

5. Eli likes classic rock, (but, yet, **so**) he shares '70s bands.

6. Each week, Kelly, Eli, (**and**, but, or) I meet to talk about music.

7. We want to broaden our tastes, (and, or, **yet**) we don't like everything we hear.

8. I like rhythm, Kelly likes words, (**and**, nor, so) Eli likes melodies.

9. Ask us for recommendations, (and, **for**, so) we are committed fans.

10. We'll tell you what we like, (**but**, nor, for) you have to choose for yourself.

Write Create sentences of your own, using a coordinating conjunction (*and, but, or, nor, for, so, yet*) as requested in each.

1. joining two words: Answers will vary. _____

_____

2. joining two phrases: _____

_____

3. creating a series: _____

_____

4. joining two clauses (place a comma after the first clause, before the conjunction): _____

_____

_____

_____

Write Create a sentence using a pair of correlative conjunctions:

Answers will vary.

_____

_____

LO2 Subordinating Conjunctions

A **subordinating conjunction** is a word or word group that connects two clauses of different importance. (A clause is basically a sentence.)

Subordinating Conjunctions

after	as long as	if	so that	till	whenever
although	because	in order that	than	unless	where
as	before	provided that	that	until	whereas
as if	even though	since	though	when	while

Subordinate clause: The subordinating conjunction comes at the beginning of the less-important clause, making it subordinate (it can't stand on its own). The subordinate clause can come before or after the more important clause (the independent clause).

I go out to eat. I like to order Mexican food.
(two clauses)

Whenever I go out to eat, I like to order Mexican food.
(*Whenever* introduces the subordinate clause, which is followed by a comma.)

I like to order Mexican food whenever I go out to eat.
(If the subordinate clause comes second, a comma usually isn't needed.)

Special relationship: A subordinating conjunction shows a special relationship between ideas. Here are the relationships that subordinating conjunctions show:

Time	after, as, before, since, till, until, when, whenever, while
Cause	as, as long as, because, before, if, in order that, provided that, since, so that, that, till, until, when, whenever
Contrast	although, as if, even though, though, unless, whereas

Whenever Mexican food is on the menu, I will order it.
(time)

I order it extra spicy because I love to feel the burn.
(cause)

Even though I ask for extra heat, I often still have to add hot sauce.
(contrast)

Traits

In the military, a *subordinate* is someone who takes orders from a superior. Think of a subordinate clause as one that takes orders from the main clause.

Vocabulary

subordinating conjunction
word or word group that connects clauses of different importance

subordinate clause
word group that begins with a subordinating conjunction and has a subject and verb but can't stand alone as a sentence

independent clause
group of words with a subject and verb and that expresses a complete thought; it can stand alone as a sentence

Using Subordinating Conjunctions

Write Fill in the blank in each sentence with an appropriate subordinating conjunction. Then circle what type of relationship it shows.

1. _____Answers will vary._____ we washed the car, I got sprayed many times.
   (time, cause, contrast)

2. Car washing is work _____ it feels like play.
   (time, cause, contrast)

3. _____ the hoses go on, a splash fight is inevitable.
   (time, cause, contrast)

4. I usually don't start the fight _____ I'm willing to join in.
   (time, cause, contrast)

5. _____ people can't resist sudsy buckets, the fight begins.
   (time, cause, contrast)

6. The car may not get clean _____ the people do.
   (time, cause, contrast)

7. _____ I first get sprayed, I yell in shock.
   (time, cause, contrast)

8. _____ I get used to it, all bets are off.
   (time, cause, contrast)

9. I can be pretty ruthless _____ I have a hose in hand.
   (time, cause, contrast)

10. _____ people have such fun, not much washing gets done.
    (time, cause, contrast)

Write Create three of your own sentences, one for each type of relationship.

1. time: _Answers will vary._ _____

   _____

   _____

2. cause: _____

   _____

   _____

3. contrast: _____

   _____

   _____

LO3 Common Prepositions

A **preposition** is a word or word group that shows a relationship between a noun or pronoun and another word. Here are common prepositions:

Prepositions

aboard	back of	except for	near to	round
about	because of	excepting	notwithstanding	save
above	before	for	of	since
according to	behind	from	off	subsequent to
across	below	from among	on	through
across from	beneath	from between	on account of	throughout
after	beside	from under	on behalf of	'til
against	besides	in	onto	to
along	between	in addition to	on top of	together with
alongside	beyond	in behalf of	opposite	toward
alongside of	but	in front of	out	under
along with	by	in place of	out of	underneath
amid	by means of	in regard to	outside	until
among	concerning	inside	outside of	unto
apart from	considering	inside of	over	up
around	despite	in spite of	over to	upon
as far as	down	instead of	owing to	up to
aside from	down from	into	past	with
at	during	like	prior to	within
away from	except	near	regarding	without

Prepositional Phrases

A **prepositional phrase** starts with a preposition and includes an object of the preposition (a noun or pronoun) and any modifiers. A prepositional phrase functions as an adjective or adverb.

> The store at the corner advertises in the newspaper.
> (*At the corner* modifies *store*, and *in the newspaper* modifies *advertises*.)
>
> Hand me the keys on the rack by the side of the door.
> (*On the rack* modifies *keys; by the side* modifies *rack; of the door* modifies *side*.)

Using Common Prepositions

Create In each sentence, fill in the blanks with prepositional phrases. Create them from the prepositions on page 350 and nouns or pronouns of your own choosing. Be creative!

1. This morning, I drove _Answers will vary._____.

2. Another driver _____ honked loudly.

3. I was so startled, I swerved _____.

4. The other driver swerved _____.

5. We both had looks of shock _____.

6. I accelerated _____.

7. My car shot _____.

8. Next thing I knew, I was _____.

9. The incident _____ was a lesson.

10. The lesson was never to drive _____.

Model Read each sentence below and write another sentence modeled on it. Note how the writer uses prepositional phrases to create specific effects.

1. The boat went through the rapids, down a bowl, into the air, and over the falls.

   _Answers will vary._____

   _____

2. I don't want to talk at you, but to you—but with you.

   _____

   _____

3. After days of arguing and hours of negotiation, the Senate compromised.

   _____

   _____

4. Go through the back door, up the stairs, past the security guard, and into the party.

   _____

   _____

LO4 *By, At, On,* and *In*

Prepositions often show the physical position of things—above, below, beside, around, and so on. Four specific prepositions show position but also get a lot of other use in English.

Uses for *By, At, On,* and *In*

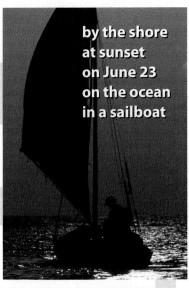

by the shore
at sunset
on June 23
on the ocean
in a sailboat

Photo by Lauri Väin

By means "beside" or "up to a certain place or time."

> by the shed, by the road
>
> by midnight, by April 15

At refers to a specific place or time.

> at the corner, at the station
>
> at 4:35 p.m., at noon

On refers to a surface, a day or date, or an electronic medium.

> on the desk, on the cover
>
> on June 9, on Tuesday
>
> on the disk, on TV, on the computer

In refers to an enclosed space; a geographical location; an hour, month, or year; or a print medium.

> in the drawer, in the room
>
> in Seattle, in Britain
>
> in an hour, in May, in 2012
>
> in the book, in the newspaper

> **Say It**
>
> Team up with a partner. Have the first person read one of the words below, and have the second person use it in a prepositional phrase beginning with *by, at, on,* or *in.* The first person should check if the form is correct. (Some have more than one correct answer.) Then you should switch roles.
>
> 1. the living room
> 2. October 9
> 3. 11:15 a.m.
> 4. the cell phone
> 5. the edge
> 6. Chicago
> 7. the table
> 8. the restaurant
> 9. sunrise
> 10. the magazine

Using *By, At, On,* and *In*

Provide In each sentence, circle the correct preposition in parentheses.

1. Please arrive (**by**, on, in) 11:55 p.m. because we will leave promptly (**at**, on, in) noon.

2. Make sure your carry-on fits (by, at, on, **in**) the overhead compartment or (by, at, on, **in**) the foot well in front of you.

3. I looked for a science article (by, at, on, **in**) the journal but could find only one (by, at, **on**, in) the Internet.

4. Though we sat (by, at, on, **in**) the waiting room, we weren't called (**by**, on, in) 3:15 p.m. for our appointment.

5. Four people standing (by, **at**, in) the corner reported a fire (at, on, **in**) a nearby garbage can.

6. (By, At, **On**, In) July 20, 1969, Neil Armstrong stepped (by, at, **on**, in) the surface of the moon.

7. I will meet you (by, **at**, on) the restaurant for our dinner reservation (by, **at**, on, in) 8:00 p.m.

8. Please place your check (by, at, on, **in**) the envelope, seal it, and write the following address (by, at, **on**, in) the envelope.

9. A parrot sat (by, at, **on**, in) the pirate's shoulder and looked me (by, at, on, **in**) the eye.

10. The song goes, "Under the boardwalk, down (**by**, at, on, in) the sea, (by, at, **on**, in) a blanket with my baby is where I'll be."

Write Write a sentence that uses all four of these prepositions in phrases: *by, at, on, in.*

Answers will vary.

LO7 Real-World Application

Revise Read the following e-mail, noting how choppy it sounds because all of the sentences are short. Connect some of the sentences using a coordinating conjunction and a comma, and connect others using a subordinating conjunction. You can also change other words as needed. (Use the correction symbols to the left.) Reread the e-mail to make sure it sounds smooth.

Coordinating Conjunctions

and	but	or	nor
for	so	yet	

Subordinating Conjunctions

after	as long as	if	so that	till	whenever
although	because	in order that	than	unless	where
as	before	provided that	that	until	whereas
as if	even though	since	though	when	while

Correction Marks

✄	delete
d̲̲	capitalize
℘	lowercase
∧	insert
⌃	add comma
? ∧	add question mark
word ∧	add word
⊙	add period
◯	spelling
∿	switch

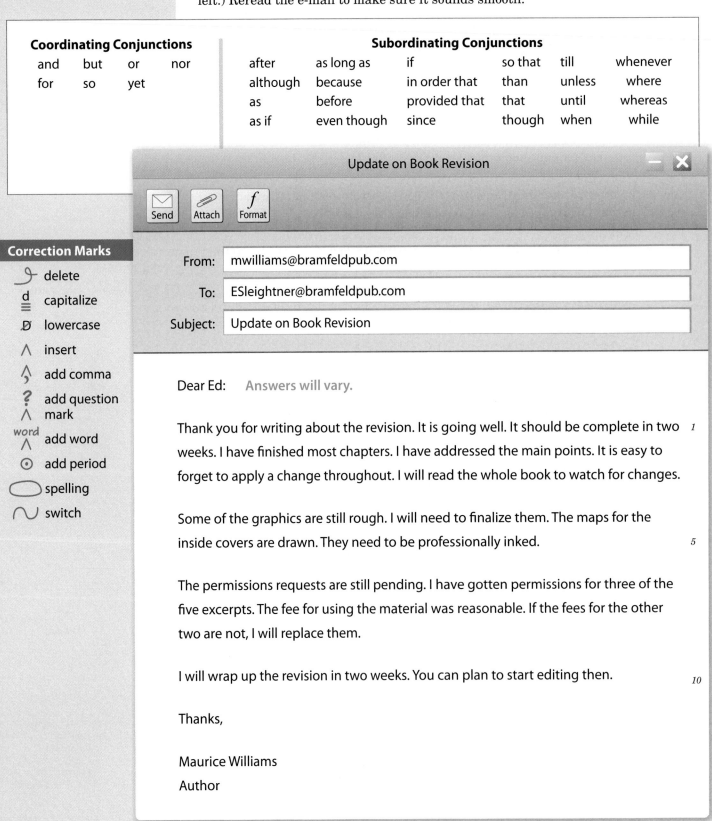

Update on Book Revision

Send   Attach   Format

From: mwilliams@bramfeldpub.com

To: ESleightner@bramfeldpub.com

Subject: Update on Book Revision

Dear Ed: Answers will vary.

Thank you for writing about the revision. It is going well. It should be complete in two   1
weeks. I have finished most chapters. I have addressed the main points. It is easy to
forget to apply a change throughout. I will read the whole book to watch for changes.

Some of the graphics are still rough. I will need to finalize them. The maps for the
inside covers are drawn. They need to be professionally inked.   5

The permissions requests are still pending. I have gotten permissions for three of the
five excerpts. The fee for using the material was reasonable. If the fees for the other
two are not, I will replace them.

I will wrap up the revision in two weeks. You can plan to start editing then.   10

Thanks,

Maurice Williams
Author

Rankin Technology Annual Picnic

| Send | Attach | *f* Format |

From: Josiah Warren

To: Rankin Staff

Subject: Rankin Technology Annual Picnic

Dear Staff:

It's time for the Rankin Technology Annual Picnic! *1*

  Who? All employees and their families

  What? Should come have fun, eat corn ^on^ by the cob, and burgers cooked ^on^ in the grill!

Where? ^At^ On Lakeside Park, ^in^ on the main pavilion.

  When? ^On^ At Wednesday, July 18, starting ^at^ on noon and finishing ^at^ in 6 p.m. *5*

  Why? We're celebrating another year ^at^ on Rankin Technologies!

The day is full of fun, including a watermelon-seed-spitting contest ^at^ in 1:00 p.m., a water-balloon toss ^at^ on 2:00 p.m., and a karaoke sing-along ^in^ on the main pavilion ^at^ in 3:00 p.m. Of course, there will be plenty of burgers and hot dogs ^on^ in every plate, and lots of soda ^in^ on every glass. *10*

Please RSVP ^by^ at July 12 to let us know how many people from your family will be ^at^ on the park for the picnic.

We look forward to having fun with everyone ^on^ in Wednesday, July 18.

Sincerely,

Josiah Warren *15*

Human Resources

Part 6 Punctuation and Mechanics Workshops

"The writer who neglects punctuation, or mispunctuates, is liable to be misunderstood"
—Edgar Allan Poe

29

Comma

Commas divide sentences into smaller sections so that they may be read more easily and more precisely. Of all the punctuation marks, commas are used most frequently—and oftentimes incorrectly.

This chapter will guide you in the conventional use of commas. Understanding correct comma usage is an important step in becoming a college-level writer.

bikeriderlondon, 2010/used under license from www.shutterstock.com

What do you think?

Commas are said to be the most important form of punctuation. Why do you think this might be true? Explain.

Answers will vary.

Learning Outcomes

LO1 Use commas in compound sentences.

LO2 Use commas with introductory words and equal adjectives.

LO3 Use commas between items in a series.

LO4 Use commas with appositives and nonrestrictive modifiers.

LO5 Use commas in real-world writing.

LO1 In Compound Sentences and After Introductory Clauses

The following principles will guide the conventional use of commas in your writing.

In Compound Sentences

Use a comma before the coordinating conjunction *(and, but, or, nor, for, yet, so)* in a compound sentence.

> Heath Ledger completed his brilliant portrayal as the Joker in *The Dark Knight,* **but** he died before the film was released.

Note: Do not confuse a compound verb with a compound sentence.

> Ledger's Joker became instantly iconic and won him the Oscar for best supporting actor. (compound verb)
>
> His death resulted from the abuse of prescription drugs**,** but it was ruled an accident. (compound sentence)

After Introductory Clauses

Use a comma after most introductory clauses.

> **Although Charlemagne was a great patron of learning,** he never learned to write properly. (adverb dependent clause)

When the clause follows the independent clause and is not essential to the meaning of the sentence, use a comma. This comma use generally applies to clauses beginning with *even though, although, while,* or some other conjunction expressing a contrast.

> Charlemagne never learned to write properly, **even though he continued to practice**.

Note: A comma is *not* used if the dependent clause following the independent clause is needed.

Correcting Comma Errors

Correct For each sentence below, add a comma ($\wedge$) before the coordinating conjunction *(and, but, or, nor, for, so, yet)* if the clause on each side could stand alone as a sentence. Write "correct" if the conjunction separates word groups that can't stand alone.

---

1. I was sick of sitting around on the couch, so I drove over to the driving range. _____

2. Her cell phone rang, but she decided against answering it. _____

3. Maria downloaded some new music and imported it on her iPod. <u>correct</u>

4. I wanted to finish my assignment, but I couldn't turn away from the *House* marathon. _____

5. Should I put a down payment on a new car, or should I save my money for a new apartment? _____

6. Kelly is studying frog populations in the rain forest, and she hopes to publish her work. _____

7. Ryan wanted to make a new style of chili, but he lost the recipe. _____

8. Trisha was looking forward to the baseball game, but it got rained out. _____

Correct For each sentence below, add a comma after any introductory clauses. If no comma is needed, write "correct" next to the sentence.

---

1. While Becca prefers grilled salmon, Mia's favorite food is sushi. _____

2. Although the water conditions were perfect, I couldn't catch a wave to save my life. _____

3. Perhaps I should rethink my major because I don't enjoy the classes. <u>correct</u>

4. Even though the Cubs haven't won a World Series since 1901, I still cheer for them. _____

5. While *American Idol* is popular in America, *Britain's Got Talent* is the craze in England. _____

LO2 With Introductory Words and Equal Adjectives

After Introductory Phrases

Use a comma after introductory phrases.

> **In spite of his friend's prodding,** Jared decided to stay home and study.

A comma is usually omitted if the phrase follows an independent clause.

> Jared decided to stay home and study **in spite of his friend's prodding.**

You may omit a comma after a short (four or fewer words) introductory phrase unless it is needed to ensure clarity.

> **At 10:30 p.m.** he would quit and go to sleep.

To Separate Adjectives

Use commas to separate adjectives that equally modify the same noun. Notice in the examples below that no comma separates the last adjective from the noun.

> You should exercise regularly and follow a **sensible, healthful** diet.
>
> A good diet is one that includes lots of **high-protein, low-fat** foods.

To Determine Equal Modifiers

To determine whether adjectives modify a noun equally, use these two tests.

1. Reverse the order of the adjectives; if the sentence is clear, the adjectives modify equally. (In the example below, *hot* and *crowded* can be reversed, but *and* does not make sense between *short* and *coffee*.)

   > Matt was tired of working in the **hot, crowded** lab and decided to take a **short coffee** break.

2. Insert *and* between the adjectives; if the sentence reads well, use a comma when *and* is omitted. (The word *and* can be inserted between *hot* and *crowded*, but *and* does not make sense between *short* and *coffee*.)

Brian K., 2010/used under license from www.shutterstock.com

Correcting Comma Errors

Correct For each sentence below, insert a comma after the introductory phrase if it is needed. If no comma is needed, write "correct" next to the sentence.

1. Before you can receive your diploma‸you will need to pay your unpaid parking tickets. _____

2. At Central Perk Ross, Rachel, and the gang sipped coffee and exchanged barbs. *correct*

3. In accordance with state law‸Hanna decided against sending a text message while driving on the interstate. _____

4. On the other hand pursuing the wrong type of adrenaline high can be destructive. *correct*

5. After handing in her paper‸Eva felt a great wave of relief. _____

6. Eva felt a great wave of relief after handing in her paper. *correct*

7. Based on his primary research‸Andy came up with a preliminary hypothesis. _____

8. To save a few dollars‸Stephanie rode her bike to work. _____

Correct For each sentence below, determine whether or not a comma is needed to separate the adjectives that modify the same noun. Add any needed commas (‸). Write "no" next to the sentence if a comma is not needed.

1. The **long‸difficult** exam took a lot out of me. _____

2. Last night I went to a **fun graduation** party. *no*

3. A good concert includes many **memorable‸hair-raising** moments. _____

4. A **thoughtful‸considerate** friend goes an extra mile to make you smile. _____

5. I could really use a **relaxing back** massage. *no*

6. When dressing for skiing, consider wearing a **thick‸well-insulated** jacket. _____

LO3 Between Items in a Series and Other Uses

Between Items in Series

Use commas to separate individual words, phrases, or clauses in a series. (A series contains at least three items.)

> Many college students must balance studying with **taking care of a family, working a job, getting exercise, and finding time to relax**.

Do not use commas when all the items in a series are connected with *or, nor,* or *and.*

> Hmm . . . should I study **or** do laundry **or** go out?

To Set Off Transitional Expressions

Use a comma to set off conjunctive adverbs and transitional phrases.

> Handwriting is not, **as a matter of fact,** easy to improve upon later in life; **however,** it can be done if you are determined enough.

If a transitional expression blends smoothly with the rest of the sentence, it does not need to be set off.

> If you are **in fact** coming, I'll see you there.

To Set Off Dialogue

Use commas to set off the words of the speaker from the rest of the sentence.

> **"Never be afraid to ask for help,"** advised Ms. Kane

> **"With the evidence that we now have,"** Professor Thom said, **"many scientists believe there could be life on Mars."**

To Enclose Explanatory Words

Use commas to enclose an explanatory word or phrase.

> Time management, **according to many professionals,** is an important skill that should be taught in college.

Correcting Comma Errors

Correct Indicate where commas are needed in the following sentences.

1. I'm looking forward to graduation, summer vacation, and moving into a new apartment.

2. A new strain of virus, according to biologists, could cause future outbreaks of poultry disease.

3. "To confine our attention to terrestrial matters would be to limit the human spirit," said Stephen Hawking.

4. I need you to pick up two jars of peanut butter, a half-gallon of skim milk, and snacks for the party.

5. I enjoy live music; however, I don't like big crowds.

6. "With all the advancements in technology," Sara said, "you'd think we would have invented a quicker toaster by now."

7. Eighty percent of states, as a matter of fact, are in financial trouble.

8. We can meet up at either the library, the student union, or memorial hall.

9. The difference between perseverance and obstinacy, according to Henry Ward Beecher, is that one comes from strong will, and the other from a strong won't.

10. Chicago, Detroit, and Indianapolis are the most-populated cities in the Midwest.

Correct Indicate where commas are needed in the following paragraph.

The Erie Canal is a man-made waterway that connects the Atlantic Ocean to Lake Erie. It 1
was the first transportation system to connect the eastern seaboard and the Great Lakes, was
faster than carts pulled by animals, and significantly cut transportation time. "The opening of the
Erie Canal to New York in 1825 stimulated other cities on the Atlantic seaboard to put themselves
into closer commercial touch with the West," said John Moody. Since the 1990s the canal is mostly 5
home to recreational traffic; however, some cargo is still transported down the waterway.

LO4 With Appositives and Other Word Groups

To Set Off Some Appositives

A specific kind of explanatory word or phrase called an **appositive** identifies or renames a preceding noun or pronoun.

> Albert Einstein**, the famous mathematician and physicist,** developed the theory of relativity.

Do not use commas if the appositive is important to the basic meaning of the sentence.

> The famous physicist **Albert Einstein** developed the theory of relativity.

Traits

Do not use commas to set off necessary clauses and phrases, which add information that the reader needs to understand the sentence.

Example: Only the professors **who run at noon** use the locker rooms in Swain Hall to shower. (necessary clause)

With Some Clauses and Phrases

Use commas to enclose phrases or clauses that add information that is not necessary to the basic meaning of the sentence. For example, if the clause or phrase (in **boldface**) were left out of the two examples below, the meaning of the sentences would remain clear. Therefore, commas are used to set off the information.

> The locker rooms in Swain Hall, **which were painted and updated last summer,** give professors a place to shower. (nonrestrictive clause)
>
> Work-study programs, **offered on many campuses,** give students the opportunity to earn tuition money. (nonrestrictive phrase)

Using "That" or "Which"

Use *that* to introduce necessary clauses; use *which* to introduce unnecessary clauses.

> Campus jobs **that are funded by the university** are awarded to students only. (necessary)
>
> The cafeteria, **which is run by an independent contractor,** can hire nonstudents. (unnecessary)

Correcting Comma Errors

Correct Indicate where commas are needed in the following sentences. If no commas are needed, write "correct" next to the sentence.

1. John D. Rockefeller, the famous American philanthropist and oil executive, is sometimes referred to as the richest person in history. _____

2. The new library, which is scheduled to open in July, will include three different computer labs. _____

3. The renowned trumpeter Louis Armstrong sang the song "What a Wonderful World." _____correct_____

4. Kansas City, along with Memphis, Tennessee, is known for its delicious barbecue. _____

5. Judge Sonya Sotomayer, the first Hispanic Supreme Court justice, was confirmed into office in 2009. _____

6. The book *The Notebook*, which was later adapted into a movie, was written by Nicolas Sparks. _____

Write The following sentences contain clauses using *that*. Rewrite the sentences with clauses using *which*, and insert commas correctly. You may need to reword some parts.

1. The road construction that delayed traffic yesterday should be completed by the end of the week.
   The road construction, which delayed traffic yesterday, should be completed by the
   end of the week.

2. The homework that Dr. Grant assigned yesterday will consume the next two weeks of my life.
   The homework, which Dr. Grant assigned yesterday, will consume the next two weeks
   of my life.

3. The earplugs that we bought before the race made the deafening noise more bearable.
   The earplugs, which we bought before the race, made the deafening noise more bearable.

   _____

LO5 Real-World Application

Correct Indicate where commas are needed in the following e-mail message.

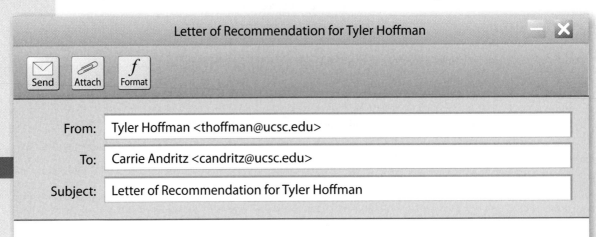

Letter of Recommendation for Tyler Hoffman

| Send | Attach | Format |

From: Tyler Hoffman <thoffman@ucsc.edu>

To: Carrie Andritz <candritz@ucsc.edu>

Subject: Letter of Recommendation for Tyler Hoffman

Dear Professor Andritz:

I enjoyed meeting with you today to discuss my letter of recommendation. You know the quality of my academic work my qualities as a person and my potential for working in the marketing industry.   *1*

As my professor for Marketing 303 and Economics 401 you have witnessed my hardworking nature. As my adviser you know my career plans and should   *5* have a good sense of whether I have the qualities needed to succeed in the fast-paced competitive marketing industry.

Please send your letter to Craig Emmons human resources director at FastTech by April 14. If you have any questions please call me at (324) 472-3489.

Sincerely,   *10*

Tyler Hoffman

Correction Marks

ℐ	delete
d̲̲	capitalize
⌿	lowercase
∧	insert
⌄	add comma
? ∧	add question mark
word ∧	add word
⊙	add period
◯	spelling
∿	switch

Workplace

Correct comma use is critical for clear business communication.

"If the English language made any sense, a catastrophe
would be an apostrophe with fur."
—Doug Larson

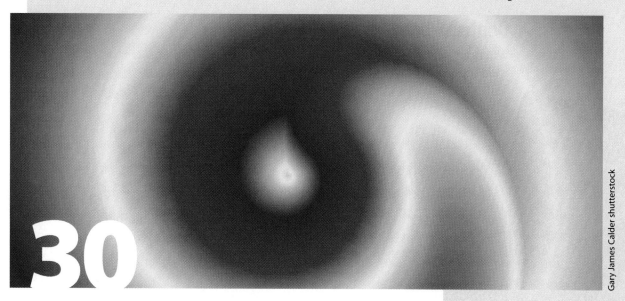

Gary James Calder shutterstock

30

Apostrophe

You may be surprised to discover that the words *catastrophe* and *apostrophe* have something in common. Both come from the Greek word for "turn." An apostrophe simply turns *away*, but a catastrophe *over*turns.

Sometimes the use of apostrophes becomes a catastrophe. Apostrophes shouldn't be used to form plurals of words. Their main use is to form possessives and contractions. The rules and activities in this chapter will help you understand their usage and avoid an apostrophe catastrophe.

Learning Outcomes

LO1 Use apostrophes for contractions and possessives.

LO2 Apply apostrophes in real-world documents.

What do you think?

Why do you think *apostrophe* comes from the word "to turn away?"

Answers will vary.

LO1 Contractions and Possessives

Apostrophes are used primarily to show that a letter or number has been left out, or that a noun is possessive.

Contractions

When one or more letters is left out of a word, use an apostrophe to form the **contraction**.

don't	he'd	would've
(*o* is left out)	(*woul* is left out)	(*ha* is left out)

Missing Characters

Use an apostrophe to signal when one or more characters are left out.

class of '16	rock 'n' roll	good mornin'
(*20* is left out)	(*a* and *d* are left out)	(*g* is left out)

Possessives

Form possessives of singular nouns by adding an apostrophe and an *s*.

Sharla's pen	the man's coat	*The Pilgrim's Progress*

Singular Noun Ending In *s* (One Syllable)

Form the possessive by adding an apostrophe and an *s*.

the boss's idea	the lass's purse	the bass's teeth

Singular Noun Ending In *s* (Two Or More Syllables)

Form the possessive by adding an apostrophe and an *s*—or by adding just an apostrophe.

Kansas's plains	*or*	Kansas' plains

Plural Noun Ending In *s*

Form the possessive by adding just an apostrophe.

the bosses' preference	the Smiths' home

Note: The word before the apostrophe is the owner.

the girl's ball	the girls' ball
(*girl* is the owner)	(*girls* are the owners)

Plural Noun Not Ending In *s*

Form the possessive by adding an apostrophe and an *s*.

the children's toys	the women's room

Insight

Pronoun possessives *do not use* apostrophes: *its, whose, hers, his, ours*

Vocabulary

contraction
word formed by joining two words, leaving out one or more letters (indicated by an apostrophe)

Forming Contractions and Possessives

Write For each contraction below, write the words that formed the contraction. For each set of words, write the contraction that would be formed.

1. they're ___they are___
2. you've ___you have___
3. Charlie is ___Charlie's___
4. wouldn't ___would not___
5. we have ___we've___

6. have not ___haven't___
7. I would ___I'd___
8. I had ___I'd___
9. won't ___will not___
10. will not ___won't___

Rewrite Rework the following sentences, replacing the "of" phrases with possessives using apostrophes.

1. The idea of my friend is a good one.

   My friend's idea is a good one.

2. I found the flyer of the orchestra.

   I found the orchestra's flyer.

3. The foundation of the government is democracy.

   The government's foundation is democracy.

4. He washed the jerseys of the team.

   He washed the team's jerseys.

5. I went to the house of the Kings.

   I went to the Kings' house.

6. The plan of the managers worked well.

   The managers' plan worked well.

7. I like the classic albums of Kiss.

   I like Kiss's classic albums.

8. I graded the assignment of Ross.

   I graded Ross's assignment.

9. The pastries of the chef were delicious.

   The chef's pastries were delicious.

10. The books of the children covered the floor.

    The children's books covered the floor.

LO2 Real-World Application

Correct The following letter sounds too informal because it contains too many contractions. Cross out contractions and replace them with full forms of the words. Also, correct any errors with apostrophes. Use the correction marks to the left.

Correction Marks

- ꝺ delete
- <u>d</u> capitalize
- Ð lowercase
- ∧ insert
- ⩔ add comma
- ? add question
  ∧ mark
- word add word
  ∧
- ⊙ add period
- ⟝⟞ spelling
- ∿ switch

Hanford Building
Supply Company, Inc.

5821 North Fairheights Road
Milsap, CA 94218
Ph: 567-555-1908

June 1, 2011

Account: 4879003

Mr. Robert Burnside, Controller
Circuit Electronic's Company
4900 Gorham Road
Mountain View, CA 94040-1093

Dear Mr. Burnside:

This ~~letter's~~ *letter is* a reminder that your ~~account's~~ *account is* past due (presently 60 days). 1

As of today, we ~~haven't~~ *have not* yet received your payment of $1,806.00, originally due March 31. ~~I've~~ *I have* enclosed the March 1 invoice. ~~It's~~ *It is* for the mitered flange's that you ordered January 10 and that we shipped January 28.

~~You've~~ *You have* been a valued customer, Mr. Burnside, and Hanford appreciate's your 5
business. ~~We've~~ *We have* enclosed a postage-paid envelope for your convenience.

If ~~there's~~ *there is* a problem, please call (567-555-1908, ext. 227) or e-mail me
(marta@hanford.comm). As always, we look forward to serving you.

Sincerely,

Marta Ramones 10

Marta Ramones'
Billing Department

Enclosures 2

Olga Utlyakova, 2010/used under license from www.shutterstock.com

> "The right word may be effective, but no word was ever as effective as a rightly timed pause."
>
> —Mark Twain

Alexander Nikitin 2010/used under license from www.shutterstock.com

31

Semicolon, Colon, Hyphen, Dash

Music notation contains notes and rests. The notes carry the melody and harmony. The rests punctuate sound with silence, giving rhythm. Whole, half, quarter, eighth, dotted eighth—there are different lengths of rest for different effects.

You can think of punctuation as rests in writing. They come in different lengths, from the period (sometimes called a full stop), through semicolons, colons, hyphens, and dashes. These marks help readers know which pieces of information belong together and which should be separated by pauses. In so doing, they help create rhythm in writing. This chapter shows how.

Learning Outcomes

LO1 Use semicolons and colons correctly.

LO2 Understand hyphen use.

LO3 Use dashes well.

LO4 Apply punctuation in real-world documents.

What do you think?

What would music sound like without rests? How about words without punctuation?

Answers will vary.

LO1 Semicolons and Colons

Semicolons and colons have specific uses in writing.

Semicolon

A **semicolon** is a sort of soft period. Use the semicolon to join two sentences that are closely related.

> The job market is improving; it's time to apply again.

Before a Conjunctive Adverb

Often, the second sentence will begin with a conjunctive adverb *(also, besides, however, instead, then, therefore)*, which signals the relationship between the sentences. Place a semicolon before the conjunctive adverb, and place a comma after it.

> I looked for work for two months; however, the market is better now.

With Series

Use a semicolon to separates items in a series if any of the items already include commas.

> I should check online ads, headhunting services, and position announcements; compile a list of job openings; create a résumé, an e-résumé, and a cover letter; and apply, requesting an interview.

Colon

The main use of a **colon** is to provide an example or a list. Write an introduction as a complete sentence, place the colon, and then provide the example or list.

> I've forgotten one other possibility: social networking.
>
> I'll plan to use the following: LinkedIn, Twitter, and Facebook.

After Salutations

In business documents, use a colon after **salutations** and in memo headings.

> Dear Mr. Ortez: To: Lynne Jones

Times and Ratios

Use a colon to separate hours, minutes, and seconds. Also use a colon between the numbers in a ratio.

> 7:35 p.m.   6:15 a.m.   The student-teacher ratio is 30:1

WAC

In addition to the colon uses listed below, a colon is often used in academic writing to separate the main title of a paper from its subtitle.

Vocabulary

semicolon
punctuation mark (;) that connects sentences and separates items in some series

colon
punctuation mark (:) that introduces an example or a list and has other special uses

salutation
the formal greeting in a letter; the line starting with "Dear"

Using Semicolons and Colons

Correct Add semicolons (⌃;) and commas (⌃,) as needed in the sentences below.

1. Searching for a job is nerve-wracking; however, it's also about possibilities.

2. Don't think about rejections; think about where you could be working.

3. Each résumé you send is a fishing line; then you wait for a nibble.

4. Put out dozens of lines; also give yourself time.

5. Make sure that you have a strong résumé, e-résumé, and cover letter; that you consult social networks, local newspapers, and friends; and that you keep your spirits up.

6. It doesn't cost much to send out résumés; therefore, send out many.

7. Job searching can feel lonely and frustrating; rely on friends and family to help you through.

8. Ask people if you can use them as references; don't provide the list of references until requested.

9. When you interview, wear professional clothing; show up at the right place, at the right time, and armed with any information you need; and be confident.

10. Try to enjoy the process; it is the gateway to your future.

Correct Add colons (⌃:) where needed in the sentences below.

1. Use your social resources: contacts, references, and organizations.

2. Call for an appointment between 9:00 a.m. and 4:00 p.m.

3. Remember a response rate of 1:10 is good for résumés submitted.

4. Politely start your cover letter with a salutation: "Dear Mrs. Baker."

5. For an interview, remember these three keys: Be punctual, be polite, and be professional.

6. Here's one last piece of advice: Be yourself.

L○2 Hyphens

A **hyphen** joins words to each other or to numbers or letters.

Compound Nouns

Use hyphens to create **compound nouns**:

| city-state | fail-safe | fact-check | one-liner | mother-in-law |

Compound Adjectives

Use hyphens to create **compound adjectives** that appear before the noun. If the adjective appears after, it usually is not hyphenated:

peer-reviewed article   an article that was peer reviewed

ready-made solution   a solution that is ready made

Note: Don't hyphenate a compound made up with an *-ly* adverb and an adjective or one that ends with a single letter.

newly acquired songs (*-ly* adverb) grade B plywood (ending with a letter)

Compound Numbers

Use hyphens for **compound numbers** from twenty-one to ninety-nine. Also use hyphens for numbers in a fraction and other number compounds.

| twenty-two | fifty-fifty | three-quarters | seven thirty-seconds |

With Letters

Use a hyphen to join a letter to a word that follows it.

| L-bracket | U-shaped | T-shirt | O-ring | G-rated | x-ray |

With Common Elements

Use hyphens to show word parts that are shared by two or more words.

We offer low-, middle-, and high-coverage plans.

WAC

The directions below for dividing words at the ends of lines date back to the time of typewriters, when it was difficult to guess whether a word would fit on a line. Now, in most disciplines, it is best to disable hyphenation in your word-processing program.

Vocabulary

hyphen
short, horizontal line (-) that joins words to words, numbers, or letters

compound noun
noun made of two or more words, often hyphenated or spelled closed

compound adjective
adjective made of two or more words, hyphenated before the noun but not afterward

compound numbers
two-word numbers from twenty-one to ninety-nine

To Divide Words at the Ends of Lines:

1. Divide a compound word between its basic units: *attorney-at-law*, not *at-tor-ney-at-law*.
2. When a vowel is a syllable by itself, divide the word after the vowel: *ori-gin*, not *or-igin*.
3. Divide at the prefix or suffix: *bi-lateral*, not *bilat-eral*.

Do Not Divide:

1. Never divide a word so that it is difficult to recognize.
2. Never divide a one-syllable word: *filed, trains, rough*.

3. Avoid dividing a word of five letters or fewer: *final, today, radar*.
4. Never leave a single letter at the end of a line: *omit-ted*, not *o-mitted*.
5. Never divide contractions or abbreviations: *couldn't*, not *could-n't*.
6. Avoid dividing a number written as a figure: *42,300,000*, not *42,300-000*.
7. Avoid dividing the last word in a paragraph.
8. Avoid ending two consecutive lines with a hyphen.

Using Hyphens

Correct Add hyphens ($\stackrel{-}{\wedge}$) to the following sentences as needed.

1. The secretary⌃treasurer recorded the vote as four⌃five.

2. We had to x⌃ray twenty⌃one people today.

3. Cut each board at seven⌃and⌃three⌃sixteenths inches.

4. The statistics on low⌃, middle⌃, and high⌃income households are ready.

5. A double⌃insulated wire should be used for high⌃voltage applications.

6. This application is high⌃voltage so the wire should be double⌃insulated.

7. The x⌃axis shows months and the y⌃axis shows dollar amounts.

8. The tax⌃rate table shows I should pay twenty⌃eight cents.

9. My mother⌃in⌃law thinks I am quite a fine son⌃in⌃law.

10. The L⌃bracket measured eleven⌃sixteenths by twenty⌃seven thirty⌃seconds.

Divide Use the guidelines for word division to decide where each word can be broken. (Write the word with hyphen at possible breaks.) If a word cannot be broken, write "NB" for "no break."

1. operate ___oper-ate___

2. anticipate ___antici-pate___

3. newsstand ___news-stand___

4. sister-in-law ___sister-in-law___

5. billed ___NB___

6. avoid ___NB___

7. helpfully ___help-fully___

8. bilateral ___bi-lateral___

9. staple ___NB___

10. 5,345,000 ___NB___

LO3 Dashes

Unlike the hyphen, the **dash** does more to separate words than to join them together. A dash is indicated by two hyphens with no spacing before or after. Most word-processing programs convert two hyphens into a dash.

For Emphasis

Use a dash instead of a colon if you want to emphasize a word, phrase, clause, or series.

> Ice cream—it's what life is about.
>
> I love two things about ice cream—making it and eating it.
>
> Ice cream is my favorite dessert—cold, sweet, and flavorful.

To Set Off a Series

Use a dash to set off a series of items.

> Rocky road, moose tracks, and chocolate-chip cookie dough—these are my favorite flavors.
>
> Neapolitan ice cream—chocolate, strawberry, and vanilla—is my sister's favorite.

With Nonessential Elements

Use a dash to set off explanations, examples, and definitions, especially when these elements already include commas.

> Ice milk—which, as you might guess, is made of milk instead of cream—provides a light alternative.

To Show Interrupted Speech

Use a dash to show that a speaker has been interrupted or has started and stopped while speaking.

> "Could you help me crank this—"
>
> "I've got to get more salt before—"
>
> "It'll freeze up if you don't—Just give me a hand, please."

Photo by Ivan Ahlert

Using Dashes

Correct In the sentences below, add a dash (⊼) where needed.

1. Which dessert would you prefer⁻brownies, apple pie, or ice cream?

2. I love the triple brownie surprise⁻a brownie with vanilla and chocolate ice cream covered in hot fudge.

3. Ice cream⁻it's what's for dinner.

4. "Could I have a taste of⁻" "You want to try some of⁻" "I want to try⁻um⁻could I try the pistachio?"

5. Bananas, ice cream, peanuts, and fudge⁻these are the ingredients of a banana-split sundae.

6. Making ice cream at home takes a long time⁻and a lot of muscle!

7. An electric ice-cream maker⁻which replaced arm power with a cranking motor⁻makes the job easier but less fun.

8. Nothing tastes better than the first taste of freshly made ice cream⁻nothing except perhaps the next taste.

9. Don't eat too quickly⁻brain-freeze.

10. A danger of ice cream⁻I'll risk it every time.

Correct Write your own sentence, correctly using dashes for each of the situations indicated below:

1. For emphasis: _Answers will vary._

2. To set off a series: _____

3. With nonessential elements: _____

Chapter 31 Semicolon, Colon, Hyphen, Dash

377

LO4 Real-World Application

Correct In the following e-mail message, insert semicolons (⋀), colons (⋀), hyphens (⋀), and dashes (⋀) where necessary. (Clearly distinguish short hyphens from long dashes.)

Ideas for Open House Displays ⬜ ✖

Send | Attach | Format

From: Jilliane Seaforth

To: Felton Engineering Staff

Subject: Ideas for Open House Displays

Hello, all:

September 1̄ that's the big open house we will celebrate our new location. To help visitors understand what Felton Engineering does, I plan to set up displays heater designs, product applications, and aerospace technology.   *1*

Please help me by doing the following looking for blueprints, sketches, small models, and prototypes that illustrate what we do identifying items that would interest visitors and setting them aside as you pack.   *5*

Then please respond to this e-mail with the following your name, the name of the product, the product number, and the type of display materials that you have.

Please respond no later than August 22. I will handle the other arrangements pick up your materials, set up the displays, and return the materials to you after the open house. Innovation̄ it's what drives Felton Engineering!   *10*

Thanks,

Jilliane Seaforth

"A fine quotation is a diamond on the finger of a man of wit,
and a pebble in the hand of a fool."

—Joseph Roux

Ken Lucas, Inc/Visuals Unlimited/Corbis

32
Quotation Marks and Italics

Much of the time, language flows from us as naturally as breathing. We think; we speak; someone hears and responds—all without consciously thinking about the words.

Sometimes, however, we have need to note a word as a word, to call attention to a phrase in a special sense, to use an apt or time-honored quotation from someone else, or to mark the title of a work. In such cases, quotation marks and italics allow us to indicate this special use of language.

What do you think?

Study the image and quotation. What makes the gemstones in the photo valuable? In what way does this relate to the Joseph Roux quotation?

Answers will vary.

Learning Outcomes

LO1 Understand the use of quotation marks.

LO2 Understand the use of italics.

LO3 Apply quotation marks and italics in a real-world document.

L◯1 Quotation Marks

To Punctuate Titles (Smaller Works)

Use quotation marks to enclose the titles of smaller works, including speeches, short stories, songs, poems, episodes of audio or video programs, chapters or sections of books, unpublished works, and articles from magazines, journals, newspapers, or encyclopedias. (For other titles, see page 382.)

Speech:	"The Cause Endures"
Song:	"Head Like a Hole"
Short Story:	"Dark They Were, and Golden Eyed"
Magazine Article:	"The Moral Life of Babies"
Chapter in a Book:	"Queen Mab"
Television Episode:	"The Girl Who Was Death"
Encyclopedia Article:	"Cetacean"

Placement of Periods and Commas

When quoted words end in a period or comma, always place that punctuation inside the quotation marks.

"If you want to catch the train," Grace said, "you must leave now."

Placement of Semicolons and Colons

When a quotation is followed by a semicolon or colon, always place that punctuation outside the quotation marks.

I finally read "Heart of Darkness"; it is amazingly well written!

Placement of Exclamation Points and Question Marks

If an exclamation point or a question mark is part of the quotation, place it inside the quotation marks. Otherwise, place it outside.

Marcello asked me, "Are you going to the Dodge Poetry Festival?" What could I reply except, "Yes, indeed"?

For Special Words

Quotation marks can be used (1) to show that a word is being referred to as the word itself; (2) to indicate that it is jargon, slang, or a coined term; or (3) to show that it is used in an ironic or sarcastic sense.

(1) Somehow, the term "cool" has survived decades.
(2) The band has a "wicked awesome" sound.
(3) I would describe the taste of this casserole as "swampy."

Insight

In British English, a single quotation mark is used instead of double quotation marks. Also, British English has different rules for using other punctuation with quotation marks. When writing in a U.S. setting, use the rules on this page.

Using Quotation Marks

Correct In the following sentences, insert quotation marks ("," ") where needed.

1. Kamala loves to listen to the song "I Take Time," over and over and over.

2. Ray Bradbury's short story "A Sound of Thunder" has been republished many times.

3. Fast Company published an article today called "How Google Wave Got Its Groove Back."

4. Angelo told Arlena, "I have a guy who can fix that fender."

5. Arlena asked, "How much will it cost me?"

6. Was she thinking, "This car is driving me into bankruptcy?"

7. This is the message of the article "Tracking the Science of Commitment": Couples that enhance one another have an easier time remaining committed.

8. I love the article "Tall Tales About Being Short"; it challenged my preconceptions about the effect of height on a person's life.

9. How many examples of the word "aardvark" can you find on this page?

10. Is anyone else here tired of hearing about his "bling bling?"

Write Write a sentence that indicates the actual meaning of each sentence below.

1. Hoyt's great Dane "skipped" across the floor and "settled" its bulk across his lap.

   (AWV) Hoyt's great Dane thundered across the floor and planted its bulk across his lap.

2. Our baked goods are always "fresh."

   Our baked goods are always stale.

3. And so began another "wonderful" day of marching through a "fairyland" of bugs.

   And so began another miserable day of marching through a swarm of bugs.

LO2 Italics

WAC

As you write research reports in different classes, find out which style your discipline uses for reporting titles of larger and smaller works.

To Punctuate Titles (Larger Works)

Use italics to indicate the titles of larger works, including newspapers, magazines, journals, pamphlets, books, plays, films, radio and television programs, movies, ballets, operas, long musical compositions, CD's, DVD's, software programs, and legal cases, as well as the names of ships, trains, aircraft, and spacecraft. (For other titles, see page 380.)

Magazine: *Wired*	Newspaper: *Washington Post*
Play: *Night of the Iguana*	Journal: *Journal of Sound & Vibration*
Film: *Bladerunner*	Software Program: *Paint Shop Pro*
Book: *Moby Dick*	Television Program: *The Prisoner*

For a Word, Letter, or Number Referred to as Itself

Use italics (or quotation marks—see page 380) to show that a word, letter, or number is being referred to as itself. If a definition follows a word used in this way, place that definition in quotation marks.

> The word *tornado* comes to English from the Spanish *tronar*, which means "to thunder."
>
> I can't read your writing; is this supposed to be a *P* or an *R*?

For Foreign Words

Use italics to indicate a word that is being borrowed from a foreign language.

> *Je ne sais pas* is a French phrase that many English speakers use as a fancy way of saying "I don't know what."

For Technical Terms

Use italics to introduce a technical term for the first time in a piece of writing. After that, the term may be used without italics.

> The heart's *sternocostal* surface—facing toward the joining of sternum and ribs—holds the heart's primary natural pacemaker. If this sternocostal node fails, a lower, secondary node can function in its place.

Note: If a technical term is being used within an organization or a field of study where it is common, it may be used without italics even the first time in a piece of writing.

Using Italics

Correct In the following sentences, underline words that should be in italics.

1. I almost couldn't finish Stephenie Meyer's second book, <u>New Moon</u>, because of its deep emotion.

2. What is your favorite part of the movie <u>Avatar</u>?

3. The Spanish say <u>duende</u> to describe a transcendent, creative passion.

4. Was the aircraft carrier <u>Enterprise</u> named after the vessel from the <u>Star Trek</u> series or the other way around?

5. You might use the term <u>bonhomie</u> to describe our relationship.

6. One thing I love about the <u>MS Word</u> program is its "Track Changes" feature.

7. In this course, we will use the term <u>noetics</u> as an indication of deep-felt self-awareness, beyond mere consciousness.

8. How am I supposed to compete at <u>Scrabble</u> when all I have is an <u>X</u> and a <u>7</u>.

9. Wait, that's not a <u>7</u>; it's an <u>L</u>.

10. That, ladies and gentleman, is what we in show business call a <u>finale</u>!

Write Write three sentences, each demonstrating your understanding of one or more rules for using italics.

1. Answers will vary.

2.

3.

LO3 Real-World Application

Practice In the following business letter, underline any words that should be italicized and add quotation marks ("") where needed.

Workplace

Note how improperly punctuated titles can lead to confusion in business writing. Correct punctuation makes for clear communication.

Brideshead Publishing
1012 Broadway
New York, New York 10011

May 13, 2010

Neva Konen
4004 W. Obleness Parkway
Hollenshead, New Hampshire 03305

Dear Neva Konen:

Thank you for your recent novel submission entitled A Time of Dimly 1
Perceived Wonders, which I read with great interest. The setting is richly
portrayed, and the main characters are at the same time both mysterious and
familiar, conveying a certain je ne sais quas about themselves. For example,
although his words land strangely on my ear, still I am overwhelmed with 5
feelings of kinship for Anibal when he cries out, "I could've et 'em up right
there 'n' then." Similarly, when at the end Kandis softly croons the words of
"Come One, Come All, to the Family Reunion," I feel I'm being called home
myself, although I've never actually seen the Appalachians.

While I greatly enjoyed the novel, and it would certainly receive an A in my 10
Creative Writing Seminar at Midtown College, I do have a few concerns.
For one thing, the title seems long and somewhat vague; I'd recommend
Foggy Mountain Memories, instead. Also, it seems unnecessary to print the
full text of Abraham Lincoln's "Gettysburg Address" and Martin Luther King,
Jr.'s "I Have a Dream" speech in the chapter entitled "A Few Words of Hope." 15
Modern readers are certainly familiar with both speeches. It should be
enough to merely include a few phrases, such as "Four score and seven years
ago" and "Let freedom ring from Lookout Mountain of Tennessee."

If you are willing to accept changes such as these, I believe we can work
together to make your novel a commercial success. Please review the 20
enclosed contract and return it to me at your earliest convenience.

Sincerely,

Christene Kaley

Christene Kaley
Assistant Editor
Brideshead Publishing

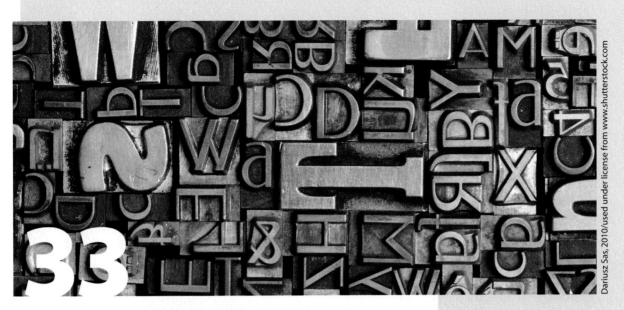

Dariusz Sas, 2010/used under license from www.shutterstock.com

Capitalization

By now you know writing requires correct capitalization. You know that every first word in a sentence should be capitalized and so should all proper nouns and proper adjectives. But what are the special uses of capitalization? And why are some nouns capitalized in one instance but not another?

This chapter will guide you in the conventional use of capital letters in writing. Throughout the section, examples demonstrate correct capitalization and serve as a handy reference during editing and proofreading.

Learning Outcomes

LO1 Understand basic capitalization rules.

LO2 Understand advanced capitalization rules.

LO3 Understand capitalization of titles, organizations, abbreviations, and letters.

LO4 Understand capitalization of names, courses, and Web terms.

LO5 Apply capitalization in real-world documents.

What do you think?

What does a word that is capitalized reveal to you? What does incorrect capitalization reveal about a writer?

Answers will vary.

LO1 Basic Capitalization

All first words, proper nouns, and proper adjectives must be capitalized. The following guidelines and examples will help explain these rules.

Proper Nouns and Adjectives

Capitalize all proper nouns and all proper adjectives (adjectives derived from proper nouns). The chart below provides a quick overview of capitalization.

Quick Guide: Capitalization at a Glance

Days of the week	Saturday, Sunday, Tuesday
Months	March, August, December
Holidays, holy days	Christmas, Hanukah, President's Day
Periods, events in history	the Renaissance, Middle Ages
Special events	Tate Memorial Dedication Ceremony
Political parties	Republican Party, Green Party
Official documents	Bill of Rights
Trade names	Frisbee disc, Heinz ketchup
Formal epithets	Alexander the Great
Official titles	Vice-President Al Gore, Senator Davis
Official state nicknames	the Garden State, the Beaver State
Planets, heavenly bodies	Earth, Mars, the Milky Way
Continents	Asia, Australia, Europe
Countries	France, Brazil, Japan, Pakistan
States, provinces	Montana, Nebraska, Alberta, Ontario
Cities, towns, villages	Portland, Brookfield, Broad Ripple
Streets, roads, highways	Rodeo Drive, Route 66, Interstate 55
Sections of the United States and the world	the West Coast, the Middle East
Landforms	Appalachian Mountains, Kalahari Desert
Bodies of water	Lake Erie, Tiber River, Atlantic Ocean
Public areas	Central Park, Rocky Mountain National Park

Insight

Different languages use capitalization differently. For example, German capitalizes not just proper nouns but all nouns. Compare and contrast capitalization styles between your heritage language and English.

First Words

Capitalize the first word in every sentence and the first word in a full-sentence direct quotation.

> **Preparing** for the final exam will help you get a good grade.
>
> Shawna asked, "**Does** anyone want to study with me at the coffee house?"

Correcting Capitalization

Practice A In each sentence below, place capitalization marks (≡) under any letters that should be capitalized.

1. Singer jack johnson finds musical inspiration in his hometown of oahu, hawaii.

2. Hawaii is the only state made up entirely of islands and is located in the pacific ocean.

3. Known as the aloha state, it's home to the hawaii volcanoes national park.

4. Another national park, the U.S.S. *arizona* memorial, is dedicated to the navy members who were lost during the attack on pearl harbor.

5. On december, 7, 1941, the United States naval base at pearl harbor, Hawaii, was attacked by japan.

6. The attack triggered the united states' entry in world war II.

7. President franklin d. roosevelt declared December 7 as "a day that will live in infamy."

8. Hawaii's beautiful beaches and tropical temperatures attract tourists from the midwest to the far east.

Practice B Read the following paragraph. Place capitalization marks (≡) under any letters that should be capitalized in proper nouns, adjectives, or first words.

My favorite holiday is thanksgiving. every november family members from illinois, 1

indiana, and Michigan travel to my parents' house to celebrate the best thursday of the

year. While Mom and my aunts work on the dressing and mashed potatoes, my cousins

and I watch football on the fox network. it has long been a tradition for the Detroit lions

to play a home game every thanksgiving. By the time the game is finished, the food 5

is ready and the feast is on. Turkey, gravy, and green-bean casserole—you can't beat

thanksgiving.

LO2 Advanced Capitalization

Sentences in Parentheses

Capitalize the first word in a sentence that is enclosed in parentheses if that sentence is not combined within another complete sentence.

> My favorite designer is hosting a fashion show for her new collection. (**Now** I just need a ticket.)

Note: Do *not* capitalize a sentence that is enclosed in parentheses and is located in the middle of another sentence.

> Rachel's cousin (his name is Carl) can't make it tonight.

Sentences Following Colons

Capitalize a complete sentence that follows a colon when that sentence is a formal statement, a quotation, or a sentence that you want to emphasize.

> I would like to paraphrase Patrick Henry: Give me chocolate or give me death.

Salutation and Complimentary Closing

In a letter, capitalize the first and all major words of the salutation. Capitalize only the first word of the complimentary closing.

> **Dear Dr. Howard**:   **Sincerely** yours,

Sections of the Country

Words that indicate sections of the country are proper nouns and should be capitalized; words that simply indicate directions are not proper nouns.

> I'm thinking about moving to the **West Coast**. *(section of country)*
>
> I'm thinking about driving **west** to California. *(direction)*

Insight

Do not capitalize words used to indicate direction or position.

Turn **south** at the stop sign. *(South refers to direction.)*

The **South** is known for its great Cajun food. *(South refers to a region of the country.)*

Languages, Ethnic Groups, Nationalities, and Religions

Capitalize languages, ethnic groups, nationalities, religions, Supreme Beings, and holy books.

> **African**   **Navajo**   **Islam**   **God**   **Allah**
>
> **Jehovah**   **the Koran**   **Exodus**   **the Bible**

Correcting Capitalization

Practice A In each sentence below, place capitalization marks (≡) under any letters that should be capitalized.

---

1. The midwest region of the United States is made up of 12 states.

2. The bible and the koran are considered holy books.

3. The navajo indians of the southwest have significant populations in an area known as the Four Corners (arizona, new mexico, utah, and Colorado).

4. Mark Twain once said this about adversity: "it's not the size of the dog in the fight; it's the size of the fight in the dog."

5. My brother Phil is starting college today. (my mom finally has the house to herself.)

6. I'm a proud member of the latino community in Miami.

7. In Quebec, Canada, many citizens speak both english and french.

Practice B Read the following paragraph. Place capitalization marks (≡) under any letters that should be capitalized.

I ate the best seafood of my life at a new england restaurant. The small, coastal restaurant in Massachusetts features fresh seafood from the atlantic ocean. I ordered the maine lobster, and I have one impression: it was awesome. If you have never tried fresh lobster before, I highly recommend it. You won't be disappointed. (now I need to figure out when I can go back.)

Practice C Place capitalization marks (≡) under any letters that should be capitalized.

---

tomorrow   hanukah   wednesday   bank   frisbee

u.s. bank   flying disc   russia   tree

LO3 Other Capitalization Rules I

Titles

Capitalize the first word of a title, the last word, and every word in between except articles *(a, an, the)*, short prepositions, *to* in an infinitive, and coordinating conjunctions. Follow this rule for titles of books, newspapers, magazines, poems, plays, songs, articles, films, works of art, and stories.

The Curious Case of Benjamin Button	*New York Times*
"Cry Me a River"	"Cashing in on Kids"
A Midsummer Night's Dream	*The Da Vinci Code*

Organizations

Capitalize the name of an organization or a team and its members.

American Indian Movement	Democratic Party
Lance Armstrong Foundation	Indiana Pacers
Susan G. Komen for the Cure	Boston Red Sox

Abbreviations

Capitalize abbreviations of titles and organizations.

M.D.	Ph.D.	NAACP	C.E.	B.C.E.	GPA

Letters

Capitalize letters used to indicate a form or shape.

U-turn	I-beam	V-shaped	T-shirt

WAC

Note that the American Psychological Association has a different style for capitalizing the titles of smaller works. Be sure you know the style required for a specific class.

Ramona Heim, 2010/used under license from www.shutterstock.com

Correcting Capitalization

Practice A In each sentence below, place capitalization marks (≡) under any letters that should be capitalized.

1. I'm stopping by the gas station to pick up the sunday *Chicago tribune*.

2. The Los Angeles lakers play in the staples center.

3. At the next stoplight, you will need to take a u-turn.

4. My favorite author is Malcolm Gladwell, who wrote the best-sellers *blink* and *The tipping point*.

5. How many times have you heard the song "I got a feeling" by the Black-eyed peas?

6. The American cancer society raises money for cancer research.

7. I was happy to improve my gpa from 3.1 to 3.4 last semester.

8. Where did you buy that Seattle mariners t-shirt?

9. The doctor charted the growth of the tumor using an s-curve.

10. The man read a copy of *gq* magazine in New York City's central park.

11. Jill was promoted to chief operating officer (ceo) this july.

Practice B Read the paragraph below, placing capitalization marks (≡) under letters that should be capitalized.

On our way to the Kansas city royals game, my friend Ted and I got in an argument *1* over our favorite music. He likes coldplay, while I prefer radiohead. His favorite song is "Vida la viva." My favorite is "Fake plastic trees." But as we argued about the merits of each band, we completely missed our exit to the stadium. Ted suggested we perform a u-turn. Instead, I used my gps to find a new route. Luckily, we made it to the ballpark in *5* time to grab a hot dog and coke before the opening pitch.

Chapter 33 Capitalization   391

LO4 Other Capitalization Rules II

Words Used as Names

Capitalize words like *father, mother, uncle, senator,* and *professor* only when they are parts of titles that include a personal name or when they are substitutes for proper nouns (especially in direct address).

> Hello, **Senator** Feingold. (*Senator* is part of the name.)
>
> It's good to meet you, **Senator.** (*Senator* is a substitute for the name.)
>
> Our **senator** is an environmentalist.
>
> Who was your chemistry **professor** last quarter?
>
> I had **Professor Williams** for Chemistry 101.
>
> Good morning, **Professor.**

Note: To test whether a word is being substituted for a proper noun, simply read the sentence with a proper noun in place of the word. If the proper noun fits in the sentence, the word being tested should be capitalized. Usually the word is not capitalized if it follows a possessive—*my, his, our, your,* and so on.

> Did **Dad** (Brad) pack the stereo in the trailer?
> (*Brad* works in the sentence.)
>
> Did your **dad** (Brad) pack the stereo in the trailer?
> (*Brad* does not work in the sentence; the word *dad* follows the *your.*)

Titles of Courses

Words such as *technology, history,* and *science* are proper nouns when they are included in the titles of specific courses; they are common nouns when they name a field of study.

> Who teaches **Art History 202**?
> (title of a specific course)
>
> Professor Bunker loves teaching **history**.
> (a field of study)

Internet and E-Mail

The words *Internet* and *World Wide Web* are capitalized because they are considered proper nouns. When your writing includes a Web address (URL), capitalize any letters that the site's owner does (on printed materials or on the site itself).

> When doing research on the **Internet**, be sure to record each site's **Web** address (URL) and each contact's **e-mail** address.

Correcting Capitalization

Practice A In each sentence below, place capitalization marks (≡) under any words that should be capitalized.

1. I met mayor Greg Ballard by chance today at the daily brew coffee shop.

2. When I was a freshman, I studied the history of roman art in art history 101.

3. Ever since I gained wireless access to the internet, I've spent hours each day on YouTube.

4. Let's hope dad can make it in time for our tee time.

5. In a speech to his constituents, congressman Paul Ryan called for fiscal responsibility.

6. My favorite class this semester is advanced forensics 332 with dr. Charles Wendell, a well-known professor.

7. My uncle Brad has no clue how to navigate the world wide web.

8. Elizabeth attended the Wayne State University senior Banquet.

9. In searching for exercise routines, Jack bookmarked a web address (url) for *men's health* magazine.

10. You will need to contact commissioner Sheffield for permission.

Practice B Read the paragraph below, placing capitalization marks (≡) under any words or letters that should be capitalized.

Before Steve Jobs became ceo of apple Inc. and the brainchild behind Macintosh, he attended high school in the San Francisco bay Area, a region that is famously known as silicon valley. Jobs enrolled at Reed College in portland, Oregon, but dropped out after the first semester to return home to co-create apple. At the same time, other tech innovators flooded the area to create companies such as Hewlett-packard and Intel. It is also here where internet giants google and Yahoo! were founded. Today Silicon valley remains a region of technological innovation.

LO5 Real-World Application

Correct In the following basic letter, place capitalization marks (≡) under letters that should be capitalized. If a letter is capitalized and shouldn't be put a lowercase editing mark (/) through the letter.

Workplace

Proper capitalization in a business document not only reflects well on the writer, but also shows respect for the names of readers and businesses.

Ball State university Volunteer Center
7711 S. Hampton drive
Muncie, IN 47302
July, 5 2010

Mr. Ryan Orlovich
Muncie parks Department
1800 Grant Street
Muncie, IN 47302

Dear superintendent Orlovich:

Last Saturday, the Ball State volunteer center committee met to discuss   1
new volunteer opportunities for the upcoming semester. We are interested
in putting together a service event at big oak park for the incoming
Freshmen.

We would like to get in contact with someone from your department to set   5
up a time and date for the event. We would prefer the event to take place
between thursday, August 23, and Sunday, August 26. Also, we hope to
design t-shirts for the volunteers and were wondering if your office knew
of any sponsors who might be interested in funding this expenditure.

When you have time, please contact me by phone at 317-555-3980 or   10
E-mail at ehenderson@bs23u.edu. (you may also e-mail the office at
bsuvolunteerism@bs23u.edu.)

Yours Truly,

Liz Henderson

Liz Henderson   15

BSU Volunteer President

Special Challenge Write a sentence that includes a colon followed by another sentence you want to emphasize. (See page 388).

LEARN YOUR WAY

We know that no two students are alike. **WRITE 1** was developed to help you improve your writing skills in a way that works for you.

Not only is the format fresh and contemporary, it's also concise and focused. **WRITE 1** is loaded with a variety of supplements like portable **In Review** cards, interactive online quizzes, vocabulary flashcards, videos, and more.

At **login.cengagebrain.com**, you'll find plenty of resources to help you become a more successful writer no matter what your learning style!

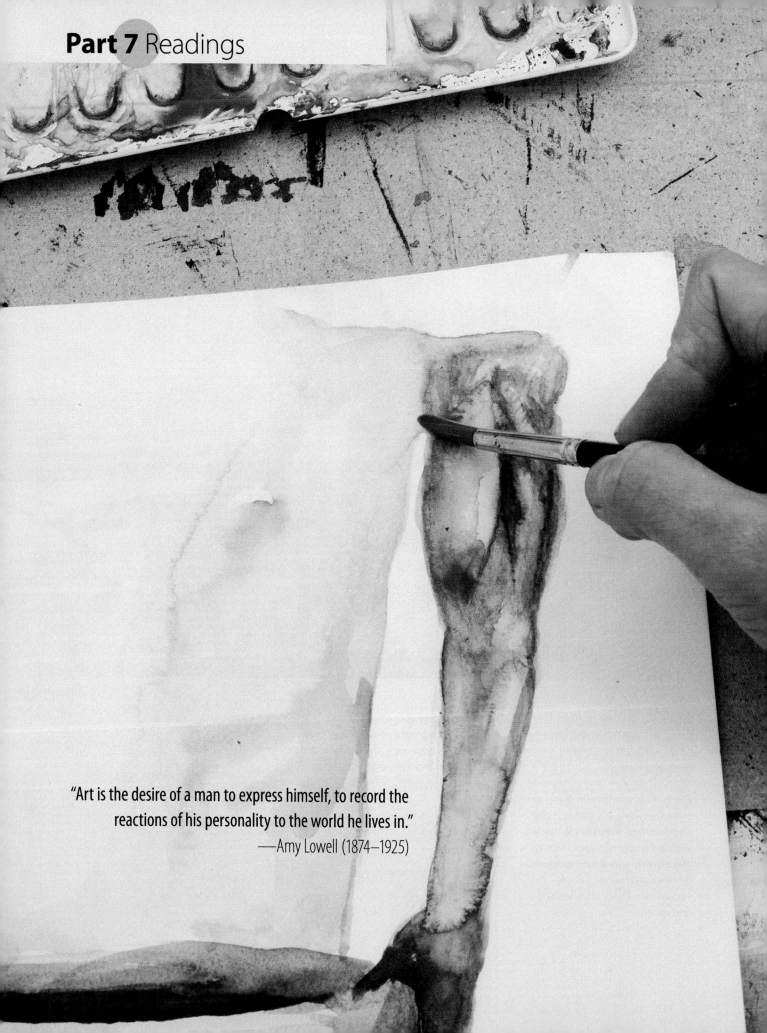

"Art is the desire of a man to express himself, to record the
reactions of his personality to the world he lives in."
—Amy Lowell (1874–1925)

34 Narrative Essays

When the American poet Amy Lowell (1874-1925) spoke of art in the quotation on the previous page, she certainly didn't mean only painting, drawing, and sculpture. Rather, she was referring to all the arts, including personal writing.

As the example essays in this chapter demonstrate, personal writing is a perfect opportunity to "record the reactions of [your] personality to the world [you live] in." In doing so, you not only communicate your thoughts to a reader; you also have an opportunity to better understand both yourself and the world around you.

What do you think?

How does your personality react to the world you live in? How could a personal essay record this reaction?

Answers will vary.

Learning Outcomes

LO1 Understand, read, and analyze narrative essays.

LO2 Write your own narrative essay.

LO1 Understanding Narrative Essays

This chapter contains three example personal essays, along with questions for analyzing each reading. You'll also find writing guidelines for creating a personal essay of your own.

SQ3R

When you read, become involved with the text by using the SQ3R approach.

Survey: Prepare by reading "About the Author," skimming the essay, and noting any vocabulary words.

Question: Ask yourself what the title and the author description might predict about the essay. List any questions that come to mind.

Read: Read the essay for effect, allowing the story to carry you along.

Recite: Read especially effective or enjoyable sections aloud to better understand and remember them.

Review: Scan the essay again, asking yourself what the author sought to accomplish and how successful you believe he or she was. Answer the questions provided to help you analyze the essay.

Traits

As you read these selections, focus first on ideas. Then reread the beginning and ending and skim the middle, noting organization. Afterward, think about the voice of the author, and how it reflects the writer's personality, subject, and purpose.

Essay List

A Brother's Murder:

Brent Staples poises his reader in a single moment, using it to reflect on the very different paths two brothers have taken.

My Body Is My Own Business:

Naheed Mustafa uses a collection of moments from her life to explain and defend a personal decision she has made. The topic of that choice may surprise you.

A Homemade Education:

As a boy, Malcolm X experienced the burning of his Milwaukee home by racists, the death of his father (a Baptist preacher) under mysterious circumstances, and the commitment of his mother to a mental hospital. As a rebellious young man, he was eventually sentenced to prison. Once there, he discovered a desire to educate himself but was unable to read the very books that held the knowledge he needed. The solution he devised would change his life forever.

About the Author

After receiving a Ph.D. from the University of Chicago, Brent Staples worked as an adjunct professor of psychology at colleges in Pennsylvania and Chicago, then as a reporter for the *Chicago Sun-Times*, and most recently as an editorial writer for the *New York Times*.

A Brother's Murder
by Brent Staples

1   It has been more than two years since my telephone rang with the news that my younger brother Blake—just 22 years old—had been murdered. The young man who killed him was only 24. Wearing a ski mask, he emerged from a car, fired six times at close range with a massive .44 Magnum, then fled. The two had
5   once been inseparable friends. A senseless rivalry—beginning, I think, with an argument over a girlfriend—escalated from posturing, to threats, to violence, to murder. . . .

   As I wept for Blake I felt wrenched backward into events and circumstances that had seemed **light-years** gone. Though a decade apart, we both were raised
10 in Chester, Pennsylvania, an angry, heavily black, heavily poor, industrial city southwest of Philadelphia. There, in the 1960s, I was introduced to mortality, not by the old and failing, but by beautiful young men who lay wrecked after sudden explosions of violence. . . .

   As I fled the past, so Blake embraced it. On Christmas of 1983, I traveled
15 from Chicago to a black section of Roanoke, Virginia, where he then lived. . . . One evening . . . standing in some Roanoke dive among drug dealers and grim, hair-trigger losers, I told him I feared for his life. He had **affected** the image of the tough he wanted to be. But behind the dark glasses and the swagger, I glimpsed the baby-faced toddler I'd once watched over. I nearly wept. I wanted desperately
20 for him to live. The young think themselves immortal, and a dangerous light shone in his eyes as he spoke laughingly of making fools of the policemen who had raided his apartment looking for drugs. He cried out as I took his right hand. A line of stitches lay between the thumb and index finger. Kickback from a shotgun, he explained, nothing serious. Gunplay had become part of his life.

25   I lacked the language simply to say: Thousands have lived this for you and died. I fought the urge to lift him bodily and shake him. This place and the way you are living smells of death to me, I said. Take some time away, I said. Let's go downtown tomorrow and buy a plane ticket anywhere, take a bus trip, anything to get away and cool things off.

Vocabulary

light-year
the distance light can travel in one year's time: about 6 trillion miles

affect
to adopt or pretend

He took my alarm casually. We arranged to meet the following night—an $_{30}$ appointment he would not keep. . . .

As I stood in my apartment in Chicago holding the receiver . . . I felt as though part of my soul had been cut away. I questioned myself then, and I still do.

Did I not reach back soon or **earnestly** enough for him? For weeks I awoke crying from a **recurrent** dream in which I chased him, urgently trying to get him $_{35}$ to read a document I had, as though reading it would protect him from what had happened in waking life.

His eyes shining like black diamonds, he smiled and danced just beyond my grasp. When I reached for him, I caught only the space where he had been. $_{39}$

Vocabulary

earnest
sincere

recurrent
repeating

Analyze This personal narrative is filled with thought details—sensations, emotions, and reflections. Review the essay and write at least three examples of each in the table below.

Sensations Think about sights, sounds, smells, tastes, feelings.	Emotions Think of feelings—happiness, loneliness, indifference.	Reflections Think of opinions and conclusions.
Ski mask and .44 Magnum, dark glasses and swagger, line of stitches on right hand, eyes like black diamonds	Devastation, Sadness, Regret	feared for his brother and his brother's lifestyle, questioned himself for not doing more

Think Critically Consider the opening paragraph and the last three paragraphs of this essay. In what obvious way are they related? What other stories, true or fictional, can you think of that are framed in a similar way?

(AWV) They both explain and reflect upon the news of the brother's death, in the past and in the present. The main way the paragraphs are related is through themes of regret, sadness, and futility.

About the Author

Naheed Mustafa is a Canadian-born Muslim woman and an award-winning independent journalist. In this essay, she uses several short examples of personal experience to make a larger point.

Naheed Mustafa, "My Body Is My Own Business," THE GLOBE AND MAIL, June 29, 1993, p. A26. Reprinted by permission of the author.

My Body Is My Own Business
by Naheed Mustafa

1   I often wonder whether people see me as a radical, **fundamentalist** Muslim terrorist packing an **AK-47** assault rifle inside my jean jacket. Or maybe they see me as the poster girl for oppressed womanhood everywhere. I'm not sure which it is.

5   I get the whole **gamut** of strange looks, stares, and covert glances. You see, I wear the hijab, a scarf that covers my head, neck, and throat. I do this because I am a Muslim woman who believes her body is her own private concern.

Young Muslim women are reclaiming the hijab, reinterpreting it in light of its original purpose to give back to women ultimate control of their own bodies.

10   The Qur'an teaches us that men and women are equal, that individuals should not be judged according to gender, beauty, wealth, or privilege. The only thing that makes one person better than another is her or his character.

Nonetheless, people have a difficult time relating to me. After all, I'm young, Canadian born and raised, university educated. Why would I do this to myself, 15   they ask.

Strangers speak to me in loud, slow English and often appear to be playing charades. They politely inquire how I like living in Canada and whether or not the cold bothers me. If I'm in the right mood, it can be very amusing.

But, why would I, a woman with all the advantages of a North American 20   upbringing, suddenly, at 21, want to cover myself so that with the hijab and the other clothes I choose to wear, only my face and hands show?

Because it gives me freedom.

Women are taught from early childhood that their worth is proportional to their attractiveness. We feel compelled to pursue abstract notions of beauty, half 25   realizing that such a pursuit is futile.

When women reject this form of oppression, they face ridicule and contempt. Whether it's women who refuse to wear makeup, or to shave their legs, or to expose their bodies, society, both men and women, have trouble dealing with them.

Vocabulary

fundamentalism
strict and literal adherence to a religious code

AK-47
a Russian-made military weapon, the most widespread in the world

gamut
an entire series or range of items

In the Western world, the hijab has come to symbolize either forced silence or radical, **unconscionable** militancy. Actually, it's neither. It is simply a woman's [30] assertion that judgment of her physical person is to play no role whatsoever in social interaction.

Wearing the hijab has given me freedom from constant attention to my physical self. Because my appearance is not subjected to public **scrutiny**, my beauty, or perhaps lack of it, has been removed from the realm of what can **legitimately** [35] be discussed.

No one knows whether my hair looks as if I just stepped out of a salon, whether or not I can **pinch an inch**, or even if I have unsightly stretch marks. And because no one knows, no one cares.

Feeling that one has to meet the impossible male standards of beauty is tiring [40] and often humiliating. I should know, I spent my entire teenage years trying to do it. I was a borderline **bulimic** and spent a lot of money I didn't have on potions and lotions in hopes of becoming the next **Cindy Crawford**.

The definition of beauty is ever-changing; waifish is good, **waifish** is bad, athletic is good—sorry, athletic is bad. Narrow hips? Great. Narrow hips? Too [45] bad.

Women are not going to achieve equality with the right to bare their breasts in public, as some people would like to have you believe. That would only make us party to our own **objectification**. True equality will be had only when women don't need to display themselves to get attention and won't need to defend their [50] decision to keep their bodies to themselves.

Think Critically In what ways does your own ethnic or social background affect other people's assumptions about you? What examples from your life can you use to illustrate those assumptions? How does your background affect your own assumptions about yourself?

Answers will vary.

Johner/Johner Images/gettyimages

A Homemade Education
by Malcolm X

1   It was because of my letters that I happened to stumble upon starting to acquire some kind of a homemade education.

I became increasingly frustrated at not being able to express what I wanted to convey in letters that I wrote, especially those to Mr. Elijah Muhammad. In 5 the street, I had been the most **articulate** hustler out there. I had commanded attention when I said something. But now, trying to write simple English, I not only wasn't articulate, I wasn't even functional. How would I sound writing in slang, the way I would say it, something such as, "Look, daddy, let me pull your coat about a cat, Elijah Muhammad—"

10   Many who today hear me somewhere in person, or on television, or those who read something I've said, will think I went to school far beyond the eighth grade. This impression is due entirely to my prison studies.

It had really begun back in the Charlestown Prison, when Bimbi first made me feel envy of his stock of knowledge. Bimbi had always taken charge of any 15 conversations he was in, and I had tried to **emulate** him. But every book I picked up had few sentences which didn't contain anywhere from one to nearly all of the words that might as well have been in Chinese. When I just skipped those words, of course, I really ended up with little idea of what the book said. So I had come to the Norfolk Prison Colony still going through only book-reading motions. Pretty 20 soon, I would have quit even these motions, unless I had received the motivation that I did.

I saw that the best thing I could do was get hold of a dictionary—to study, to learn some words. I was lucky enough to reason also that I should try to improve my penmanship. It was sad. I couldn't even write in a straight line. It was both 25 ideas together that moved me to request a dictionary along with some tablets and pencils from the Norfolk Prison Colony school.

I spent two days just **riffling** uncertainly through the dictionary's pages. I'd never realized so many words existed! I didn't know which words I needed to learn. Finally, just to start some kind of action, I began copying.

About the Author

Malcolm X (1925-1965) was a black Muslim minister, widely considered the U.S.'s second most influential civil rights figure, behind only Dr. Martin Luther King, Jr. While Dr. King preached pacifist resistance, Malcolm X argued for racial separation and justice by any means. Later, after traveling in the Middle East, he renounced racism and preached the universal family of humanity. He was assassinated three years before Dr. King.

"A Homemade Education" from THE AUTOBIOGRAPHY OF MALCOLM X. Copyright (c) 1987. Used by permission of Random House, Inc.

Vocabulary

articulate
able to speak effectively

emulate
to imitate or follow another person's model

riffle
to quickly thumb through or ruffle

In my slow, painstaking, ragged handwriting, I copied into my tablet 30 everything printed on that first page, down to the punctuation marks.

I believe it took me a day. Then, aloud, I read back, to myself, everything I'd written on the tablet. Over and over, aloud, to myself, I read my own handwriting.

I woke up the next morning, thinking about those words—immensely 35 proud to realize that not only had I written so much at one time, but I'd written words that I never knew were in the world. **Moreover**, with a little effort, I also could remember what many of these words meant. I reviewed the words whose meanings I didn't remember. Funny thing, from the dictionary's first page right now, that "aardvark" springs to my mind. The dictionary had a picture of it, a long- 40 tailed, long-eared, burrowing African mammal, which lives off termites caught by sticking out its tongue as an anteater does for ants.

I was so fascinated that I went on—I copied the dictionary's next page. And the same experience came when I studied that. With every succeeding page, I also learned of people and places and events from history. Actually the dictionary 45 is like a miniature encyclopedia. Finally the dictionary's A section had filled a whole tablet—and I went on into the B's. That was the way I started copying what eventually became the entire dictionary. It went a lot faster after so much practice helped me to pick up handwriting speed. Between what I wrote in my tablet, and writing letters, during the rest of my time in prison I would guess I 50 wrote a million words.

I suppose it was **inevitable** that as my word-base broadened, I could for the first time pick up a book and read and now begin to understand what the book was saying. Anyone who has read a great deal can imagine the new world that opened. Let me tell you something: from then until I left that prison, in every free moment 55 I had, if I was not reading in the library, I was reading on my bunk. You couldn't have gotten me out of books with a wedge. Between Mr. Muhammad's teachings, my **correspondence**, my visitors—usually Ella and Reginald—and my reading of books, months passed without my even thinking about being imprisoned. In fact, up to then, I never had been so truly free in my life. . . . 60

. . . I have often reflected upon the new **vistas** that reading opened to me. I knew right there in prison that reading had changed forever the course of my life. As I see it today, the ability to read awoke inside me some long **dormant** craving to be mentally alive. I certainly wasn't seeking any degree, the way a college confers a status symbol upon its students. My homemade education gave me, 65 with every additional book that I read, a little bit more sensitivity to the deafness, dumbness, and blindness that was **afflicting** the black race in America. Not long ago, an English writer telephoned me from London, asking questions. One was, "What's your alma mater?" I told him, "Books." You will never catch me with a free fifteen minutes in which I'm not studying something I feel might be able to help 70 the black man.

72 Yesterday I spoke in London, and both ways on the plane across the Atlantic I was studying a document about how the United Nations proposes to insure the human rights of the oppressed minorities of the world. The American black man

75 is the world's most shameful case of minority oppression. What makes the black man think of himself as only an internal United States issue is just a catchphrase, two words, "civil rights." How is the black man going to get "civil rights" before first he wins his human rights? If the American black man will start thinking about his human rights, and then start thinking of himself as part of one of the

80 world's great peoples, he will see he has a case for the United Nations.

I can't think of a better case! Four hundred years of black blood and sweat invested here in America, and the white man still has the black man begging for what every **immigrant** fresh off the ship can take for granted the minute he walks down the gangplank.

85 But I'm **digressing**. I told the Englishman that my alma mater was books, a good library. Every time I catch a plane, I have with me a book that I want to read—and that's a lot of books these days. If I weren't out here every day battling the white man, I could spend the rest of my life reading, just satisfying my curiosity—because you can hardly mention anything I'm not curious about. I

90 don't think anybody ever got more out of going to prison than I did. In fact, prison enabled me to study far more intensively than I would have if my life had gone differently and I had attended some college. I imagine that one of the biggest troubles with colleges is there are too many distractions, too much panty-raiding, **fraternities**, and **boola-boola** and all of that. Where else but in a prison could I

95 have attacked my ignorance by being able to study intensely sometimes as much as fifteen hours a day?

Write Describe your own best learning experience. How has it affected your life?

Answers will vary.

WAC

Find the full text of "A Homemade Education" online and consider what Malcolm X says he learned about human history. On what points do you agree or disagree with him? Explain why.

Vocabulary

immigrant
a person who has moved to a new country (as opposed to *emigrant*, a person who has moved from a previous country)

digress
to wander off topic

fraternity
literally "brotherhood," generally used to refer to an association of male students

"Boola Boola"
title of the Yale University football song

LO2 Writing a Narrative Essay

Prewrite To begin writing a narrative essay, you need to choose a memorable event from your life. One way to do this is to fill in a life map. At the beginning of the map, write the day you were born. At the end, write today's date. Then begin listing memorable events along the way.

Life Map

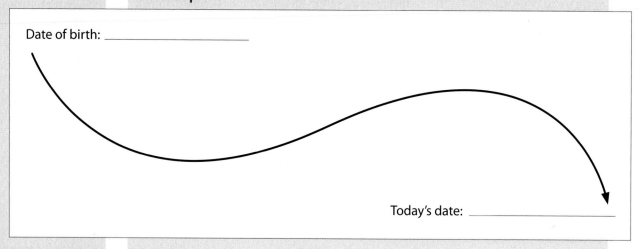

Date of birth: _____

Today's date: _____

Prewrite Next, you will need to choose one of the events and begin gathering details about it. Most stories occur in a linear fashion, from start to finish. To plan your essay, begin listing details on a time line. (Leave space between events to add new details as they occur to you.)

Time Line

Start:

Finish:

Draft Create a strong opening, middle, and closing for your essay. Use the supports below as you create each part.

Opening Paragraph

Capture your reader's attention in the first line of your personal essay. Use one of the following strategies:

- **Begin with action:** "Our car was halfway across the bridge when the driver passing us lost control of his vehicle."
- **Ask a question:** "Have you ever jumped off a cliff? That's basically what bungee jumping is all about."
- **Connect to the reader:** "We've all had a bad day from time to time. Oddly enough, my worst day ever started with a beautiful sunrise."

Once you have your reader's attention, lead up to your thesis statement. Here is a formula to use for writing a thesis statement.

Memorable Event		**Effect on Your Life**		**Thesis Statement**
Looking at my baby daughter for the first time	**+**	I felt a shock of recognition, like we had met before, and so the bond was set.	**=**	When I saw my baby daughter for the first time, I felt a shock of recognition, as if we had met before, and that is how the bond between us was set.

Memorable Event

Effect on My Life _____

_____

_____

Thesis Statement

_____

_____

Traits

As you draft your essay, focus on getting your ideas down, creating a three-part organizational structure. When you revise and edit, you will review these traits as well as voice, words, sentences, and conventions.

Middle Paragraphs

In your middle paragraphs, provide support for your thesis statement:

- Tell the story (review your time line for the most important facts).
- Draw the reader in with significant details, including sensory impressions.
- Explain the significance of what happened.

Closing Paragraph

The final paragraph of a personal essay should reflect back on the whole and, if possible, make a connection that was not visible at the beginning. At the very least, the closing paragraph should restate and reinforce the thesis of the essay. Review the closing paragraph of the readings in this chapter for examples of effective endings.

Revise Take a break from your writing. Then come back to it with fresh eyes. If possible, read your personal essay aloud to a friend or family member and ask if they are unclear about any of it. Then review your writing with the following checklist. Keep polishing until you can check off each item in the list.

Ideas

- [ ] **1.** Do I focus on one main event from my life?
- [ ] **2.** Do I include enough facts, details, and sensory impressions about the event?

Organization

- [ ] **3.** Does my opening grab the reader's attention and present a clear thesis?
- [ ] **4.** Do the middle paragraphs tell the story in chronological order and explain its significance?
- [ ] **5.** Do I use key words and transitions to effectively link my ideas?
- [ ] **6.** Does my closing reinforce the thesis of my essay?

Voice

- [ ] **7.** Do I tell the story in a way that keeps the reader interested to the end?

Edit Prepare a clean copy of your personal essay and use the following checklist to look for errors. Continue working until you can check off each item in the list.

Words

- [ ] **1.** Have I used specific nouns and verbs? (See page 103.)
- [ ] **2.** Have I used more action verbs than "be" verbs? (See page 73.)

Sentences

- [ ] **3.** Have I varied the beginnings and lengths of sentences? (See pages 226–231.)
- [ ] **4.** Have I combined short choppy sentences? (See page 232.)
- [ ] **5.** Have I avoided shifts in sentences? (See page 278.)
- [ ] **6.** Have I avoided fragments and run-ons? (See pages 261–266, 270–271.)

Conventions

- [ ] **7.** Do I use correct verb forms (*he saw,* not *he seen*)? (See pages 320, 324.)
- [ ] **8.** Do my subjects and verbs agree (*she speaks,* not *she speak*)? (See pages 245–260.)
- [ ] **9.** Have I used the right words (*their, there, they're*)?
- [ ] **10.** Have I capitalized first words and proper nouns and adjectives? (See page 386.)
- [ ] **11.** Have I used commas after long introductory word groups? (See page 358.)
- [ ] **12.** Have I carefully checked my spelling?

> "Writing became such a process of discovery that I couldn't wait to get to work in the morning: I wanted to know what I was going to say."
>
> —Sharon O'Brien

35

Process Essays

Isn't it odd? Someone asks you how to do something, and although you can easily do it yourself, explaining it to another person isn't so easy. Still, you do your best and, as a result, find that you yourself have developed a deeper understanding of the subject.

Explaining a process requires a special set of skills. First, you have to make certain you have all the details your reader will need. Then you have to organize those details in the most logical fashion. Finally, you have to express those details in terms your reader can easily understand.

Learning Outcomes

LO1 Understand, read, and analyze process essays.

LO2 Write your own process essay.

What do you think?

How would you describe your own process of discovery when it comes to writing?

Answers will vary.

LO1 Understanding Process Essays

This chapter contains three example process essays, along with questions for analyzing each reading. You'll also find writing guidelines for creating a process essay of your own.

SQ3R

When you read, become involved with the text by using the SQ3R approach.

> **Survey:** Prepare by reading "About the Author," skimming the essay, and noting any vocabulary words.
>
> **Question:** Make a list of questions you expect the essay to answer.
>
> **Read:** Read the essay, looking for each step in the process being described.
>
> **Recite:** Read through the steps aloud and in order to make sure you understand and remember them.
>
> **Review:** Scan the essay again, looking for details you may have missed and for answers to any questions that remain. Answer the questions provided to help you analyze the essay.

Essay List

From *The Undertaking*

In this essay from his book by the same name, Thomas Lynch casually lays out a process of preparing someone for burial. He uses this opportunity to treat the much larger process of grieving.

From "Flirting Fundamentals: A Glance, a Smile—So Sexy, So Subtle . . . So Scientific"

Reporter Geraldine Baum introduces the research of Monica Moore, who has been studying human dating behaviors in a manner similar to Jane Goodall's study of ape interactions. After watching 200 women over the course of two years, she has compiled a list of 52 behaviors women use—and a few used by men.

From "How to Handle Conflict"

P. Gregory Smith explains how to resolve tense situations in a "win-win" fashion, preserving respect for everyone involved. Notice the way in which he demonstrates that the alternative is effectively "lose-lose" for everyone.

About the Author

Thomas Lynch is both an undertaker and a poet whose work has appeared in the *Atlantic,* the *New York Times,* the *New Yorker,* and elsewhere. His book *The Undertaking* was the subject of an Emmy-award-winning PBS documentary

Excerpt from THE UNDERTAKING by Thomas Lynch. Copyright (c) 1998 by Thomas Lynch. Used by permission of W. W. Norton, Inc.

From *The Undertaking*
by Thomas Lynch

1   Last Monday morning Milo Hornsby died. Mrs. Hornsby called at 2 A.M. to say that Milo had *expired* and would I take care of it, as if his condition were like any other that could be renewed or somehow improved upon. At 2 A.M., yanked from my REM sleep, I am thinking, put a quarter into Milo and call me

5   in the morning. But Milo is dead. In a moment, in a twinkling, Milo has slipped irretrievably out of our reach, beyond Mrs. Hornsby and the children, beyond the women at the Laundromat he owned, beyond his comrades at the Legion Hall, the Grand Master of the Masonic Lodge, his pastor at First Baptist, beyond the mailman, zoning board, town council, and Chamber of Commerce; beyond us all,

10   and any treachery or any kindness we had in mind for him. . . .

Milo's dead. . . .

Which is why I do not haul to my senses, coffee and quick shave, Homburg and great coat, warm up the Dead Wagon, and make for the freeway in the early o'clock for Milo's sake. . . . I go for her—for she who has become, in the same

15   moment and the same twinkling, like water to ice, the Widow Hornsby. I go for her—because she still can cry and care and pray and pay my bill.

The hospital that Milo died in is state-of-the-art. There are signs on every door declaring a part or a process or a bodily function. I like to think that, taken together, the words would add up to The Human Condition, but they never do.

20   What's left of Milo, the remains, are in the basement, between SHIPPING & RECEIVING and LAUNDRY ROOM. Milo would like that if he were still liking things. Milo's room is called PATHOLOGY. . . .

I sign for him and get him out of there. . . .

Back at the funeral home, upstairs in the embalming room, behind a door

25   marked PRIVATE, Milo Hornsby is floating on a porcelain table under fluorescent lights. Unwrapped, outstretched. Milo is beginning to look a little more like himself—eyes wide open, mouth agape, returning to our gravity. I shave him, close his eyes, his mouth. We call this *setting the features*. These are the features—eyes and mouth—that will never look the way they would have looked in life when they

Vocabulary

REM
a restful stage of sleep characterized by rapid eye movement

Dead Wagon
a term used by Lynch's neighbors for his business's panel van

pathology
the study of diseases

embalming
treatment to prevent decay

agape
wide open

were always opening, closing, focusing, signaling, telling us something. In death, 30
what they tell us is that they will not be doing anything anymore. The last detail
to be managed is Milo's hands—one folded over the other, over the umbilicus, in
an attitude of ease, of repose, of retirement.

They will not be doing anything anymore, either.

I wash his hands before positioning them. 35

When my wife moved out some years ago, the children stayed here, as did
the dirty laundry. It was big news in a small town. There was the gossip and the
goodwill that places like this are famous for. And while there was plenty of talk, no
one knew exactly what to say to me. They felt helpless, I suppose. So they brought
casseroles and beef stews, took the kids out to the movies or canoeing, brought 40
their younger sisters around to visit me. What Milo did was send his laundry van
around twice a week for two months, until I found a housekeeper. Milo would pick
up five loads in the morning and return them by lunchtime, fresh and folded. I
never asked him to do this. I hardly knew him. I had never been in his home or
his Laundromat. His wife had never known my wife. His children were too old to 45
play with my children.

After my housekeeper was installed, I went to thank Milo and pay the bill.
The invoices detailed the number of loads, the washers and the dryers, detergent,
bleaches, fabric softeners. I think the total came to sixty dollars. When I asked
Milo what the charges were for pick-up and delivery, for stacking and folding and 50
sorting by size, for saving my life and the lives of my children, for keeping us in
clean clothes and towels and bed linen, "Never mind that" is what Milo said. "One
hand washes the other."

I place Milo's right hand over his left hand, then try the other way. Then
back again. Then I decide that it doesn't matter. One hand washes the other either 55
way.

The embalming takes me about two hours.

Vocabulary

umbilicus
navel

installed
in this case, settled into the
home

Think Critically Consider the final paragraph on the previous page. Why do you
think Lynch uses words like "agape" and "umbilicus" instead of "wide open" and
"navel"?

(AWV) The words "agape" and "umbilicus" portray the language of the writer's

profession. They are words that would more often come up when preparing a body

than in other scenes in life. Finally, they express a more appropriate tone and specificity

than "belly button" and "wide open" would.

About the Author

Geraldine Baum is a staff writer and New York Bureau Chief for the *Los Angeles Times*.

Geraldine Baum, "Flirting Fundamentals," LOS ANGELES TIMES, October 3, 1994. Reprinted by permission.

From "Flirting Fundamentals: A Glance, a Smile— So Sexy, So Subtle . . . So Scientific" by Geraldine Baum

1   You probably shouldn't know about Monica Moore's research.

You *think* you want to know, but really you don't. If you did, you'd be too self-conscious to do what comes naturally. For while the rest of us fumble through life clutching our hearts and throats, this woman observes us and simply knows.

5   For almost 20 years, Moore, an experimental **psychologist**, has been studying flirting. In fact, she has spent a career turning an immensely subtle art into science. Which is a little like reducing Mona Lisa's smile into a **neurological** tic.

Moore, a professor at St. Louis' Webster University, and her teams of graduate students spent hundreds of hours in bars and student centers covertly watching

10   women and men court, and **painstakingly** recording every smile and laugh.

After feeding all the data into a computer, Moore came up with a catalogue of 52 gestures women use to signal their interest in men. Think of it as L. L. Bean's Love Collection.

This is one of those studies congressmen like to rail against when it involves

15   a federal grant. But Moore, the Jane Goodall of human courtship, is quite serious about her work.

"People see flirting as so **frivolous**," she says. "But I'd argue that to know about all this is very important because it helps explain human relations."

Like Charles Darwin, Moore began with the **premise** that women make the

20   initial choice of a mate. And from there the courtship process begins. Western cultures wrongly assume men control the process, she says, because they focus on the far more obvious second stage of courtship: The approach. But Moore contends it all begins when girl eyes boy—and smiles or smooths her skirt or licks her lips. And study after study showed that how attractive a woman is is less important

25   than her flirting skills.

Vocabulary

psychologist
a scientist who studies the mind

neurological
having to do with the nervous system

painstakingly
carefully, attentively

frivolous
lacking seriousness or importance

premise
proposed idea

WAC

Compare this essay with a similar essay in the social sciences: "Study Says Flirtatious Women Get Fewer Raises" by Del Jones (pages 439–440). How does reading one essay affect your interpretation of the other?

Vocabulary

excruciatingly
torturously intensive

ipsilateral
on the same side of the body

scintillating
exciting, engaging

instituted
put into practice

ethics
having to do with moral duty

dissertation
a final report to achieve a doctorate

anthropologist
person who studies human beings as a species

objective
unopinionated

"So she gets the first turn, then he gets a turn. Each time one signals the other they are reaffirming their choice. Either one can opt out at any time along the way."

In fact, Moore's studies decode the obvious. The only surprise is that such **excruciatingly** erotic behavior can sound so boring. 30

Listen to her description of "neck presentation":

"The woman tilted her head sideways to an angle of approximately 45 degrees. This resulted in the ear almost touching the **ipsilateral** shoulder, thereby exposing the opposite side of the neck. Occasionally the woman stroked the exposed neck area with her fingers. . . ." 35

But Moore isn't writing for *True Romance*. Rather, she publishes in such **scintillating** academic journals as *Semiotica* and *Ethology and Sociobiology*.

The best part of her study on gestures, which included observing 200 women over two years, is the list.

To attract a man, women most often smile, glance, primp, laugh, giggle, toss 40 their heads, flip their hair and whisper. Sometimes they hike their skirts, pat a buttock, hug, request a dance, touch a knee and caress.

Moore's description of one of the most frequent signals—"solitary dancing"— would make anyone who has ever been in a singles bar squirm.

"While seated or standing, the woman moved her body in time to the music. 45 A typical male response was to request a dance."

In fact, there is something risky about Moore's work and she knows it. And so after one of her students came back from spring break boasting that it took 12 minutes of signaling to get a man to her side at an airport bar—and then she ignored him—Moore **instituted** an **ethics** policy for her graduate students. 50

"I didn't want them to misuse their knowledge," Moore says.

Moore began her research in flirting in the late 1970s when she herself was a graduate student in search of a **dissertation** topic. Her adviser suggested she pick something fun, and all she could think was: "Food, sex, food, sex, food, sex."

Later Moore heard an **anthropologist** lecture about biological theories of 55 human female choice, which started Moore wondering how women made decisions about who they choose.

Moore interviewed 100 women asking what it was about the men they were seeing that made them sexy. But interviewing techniques presented too many problems, so she decided she had to make **objective** observations of women making 60 choices. In other words, she wasn't as interested in when Harry met Sally as what Sally was doing with her hands at the time.

"I had to make a list," she says.

Moore doesn't have a similar list of men's gestures. All she knows is that men send out undirected signals of power and attractiveness by puffing up their 65 chests or checking their watch or smoothing their ties. "But they don't do what women do," she says. "Once a woman looks around the room, she settles on one or two men and starts sending out the signals."

It's amazing how intricate her research is.

Once in a bar her teams of graduate students—always one man and one woman because couples are rarely noticed when there are singles around—would randomly select a female subject. Then one member of the team would talk into a small tape recorder and keep track of her every movement. The other member of the team would keep track of all the responses made by men.

In the next few years Moore hopes to use her catalogue to find out more about women's choices, and she wants to explore whether flirting drops off after marriage.

"I don't think so, but it will be fascinating to find out," says Moore, who is 41 and married with a child.

She says there are only six other academics that she knows of in the world who have done human courtship studies. Most are **sexologists**.

"Whenever I presented my work at meetings of psychologists, I was always in a room packed with voyeurs," she says. "I had no one to talk to until I found the Society for the Scientific Study of Sex."

52 Ways Women Flirt
(in descending order of occurrence)

Facial/Head Patterns
- Smile
- Room-encompassing glance
- Laugh
- Short, darting glance
- Fixed gaze
- Hair flip
- Head toss
- Head nod
- Giggle
- Whisper
- Neck presentation

- Lip lick
- Pout
- Coy smile
- Face to face
- Kiss
- Eyebrow flash
- Lipstick application

Posture Patterns
- Solitary dance
- Lean
- Point
- Dance (acceptance)
- Parade
- Aid solicitation

- Play
- Brush
- Knee touch
- Shoulder hug
- Thigh touch
- Placement
- Approach
- Foot to foot
- Request dance
- Hug
- Frontal body contact
- Breast touch
- Hang
- Lateral body contact

Gestures
- Gesticulation
- Caress (object)
- Primp
- Caress (leg)
- Caress (arm)
- Hand hold
- Palm
- Caress (back)
- Arm flexion
- Caress (torso)
- Buttock pat
- Tap
- Caress (face/hair)
- Hike skirt

Think Critically How would you sum up this report? What process do you find embedded within it?

(AWV) The reporter breaks down a new study that lists the gestures women use to flirt.

Embedded in the article is not only the process of courtship between men and women

but also the process of running an academic study.

Vocabulary

sexologist
person who studies sexual relations

About the Author

P. Gregory Smith is a regular contributor to *Career World* magazine, where this essay was originally published.

P. Gregory Smith, "How to Handle Conflict," CAREER WORLD, November-December 2003. Special permission granted by Weekly Reader, published and copyrighted by Weekly Reader Corporation. All rights reserved.

From "How to Handle Conflict"
by P. Gregory Smith

Conflicts are a normal part of life. It's how you deal with them that makes all the difference. [1]

"Hey, college boy," Mr. Jefferson smirked as Ramon walked into the supermarket, "a lady just dropped a bottle of grape juice in aisle six. Do you think you could lower yourself enough to mop it up?" [5]

Ramon was **seething** inside as he grabbed the mop and headed off to clean up the spill. Ever since he told some of his co-workers that he had applied to the state university, Mr. Jefferson, the night manager, had teased and taunted him.

Ramon was tired of being called "college boy." He was sick of hearing the **sarcastic** remarks, and he was getting fed up with being assigned all the dirty [10] jobs.

Aggression Causes Trouble

As Ramon mopped up the purple mess, he thought about taking the dripping mop down to the front of the store, handing it to Mr. Jefferson, and saying, "Here you go, boss man. Clean up your own spills. I'm sick of your teasing and your dirty [15] work. Yeah, I'm going to college, and maybe I'll come back someday as your boss. Then we'll see how funny you are!"

As much as that might make him feel better for a few moments, Ramon realized that quitting his job would be just about the worst possible thing he could do, now that he needed every cent he could earn for college. Besides, he reasoned, [20] Mr. Jefferson might figure that he was right all along—that Ramon thought he was too good to clean up spills.

Vocabulary

seething
boiling with anger

sarcasm
bitter humor intended to cause pain

416

Passive Gets You Less Than Nowhere

Once the spill was mopped up and Ramon had calmed down, he thought
that maybe he should just keep his mouth shut and tough it out for the next few
months. But he caught himself. He realized that if he didn't stand up to his boss,
the teasing would probably continue. There would only be more mops and more
spills and more anger.

Asserting Your Rights

As Ramon returned to the front of the store, he remembered the
presentation his guidance counselor, Mrs. Chang, gave last week on something
called assertiveness. It is a way of standing up for your own rights without
creating conflict. As Ramon walked toward Mr. Jefferson, the main points of the
presentation started to come back to him.

- **The Right Time and Place.** Mr. Jefferson was talking with a customer
  when Ramon reached the front of the supermarket. Ramon waited until
  Mr. Jefferson was finished and then asked, "Can I talk with you in your
  office when you have a moment?"

  Mr. Jefferson looked up curiously and said slowly, "Sure, Ramon, I
  guess I have a few minutes now. Let's go."

  By waiting for the right time, Ramon was likely to have Mr. Jefferson's
  attention. Also, by asking to speak with him in private, Ramon reduced
  the chances that Mr. Jefferson would feel that he had to impress others,
  protect his reputation, or save face.

- **Posture, Eye Contact, Relaxed Stance.** Before Ramon said the first
  word, he reminded himself of a few important things. If he was going to
  stand up for himself, he needed to stand up straight! He also knew that it
  was important to make eye contact.

  Ramon also knew the importance of relaxing his hands and keeping
  a comfortable distance from Mr. Jefferson. He did not want to appear
  hostile or threatening.

- **Tone of Voice, Emotion, Rate of Speech.** Even though he was angry,
  Ramon reminded himself that he must speak calmly, clearly, and slowly if
  he was going to get his point across. If he let his anger creep in, he would
  probably get an angry or defensive response from Mr. Jefferson. Even
  worse, if he hid his feelings behind a quiet tone or rapid speech, then Mr.
  Jefferson would probably doubt his seriousness.

- **"I" Statements.** Mr. Jefferson closed the office door, folded his arms, and
  looked at Ramon questioningly. Ramon took a deep breath and began,
  "Mr. Jefferson, I really feel embarrassed when you call me 'college boy.' I
  like it a lot better when people call me Ramon."

  Mr. Jefferson nodded his head slightly and said, "Go on."

  "I don't mind doing my fair share of the dirty jobs around here," Ramon
  continued, "but I feel like I'm getting a lot more mop time than anyone else."

Workplace

This essay deals with conflict resolution—a crucial skill for workplace communication, productivity, and even survival. What tip here will be most helpful for you in the workplace? Why?

Vocabulary

assertiveness
presenting oneself with confidence

By using a statement that began with "I," Ramon was able to state his 65
feelings honestly, without accusing Mr. Jefferson. "I" statements usually
can't be considered false or cause an argument because they're a simple
statement of feelings.

- **Cooperative Statements.** Ramon kept going, "We used to get along
fine until everybody started talking about me going to college next year. I 70
haven't changed, and I'd like to go back to the way things were."

Cooperative statements—or statements that connect you with the
other person—create common ground for further discussion. They also
serve as a subtle reminder that you share experiences and values with
the other person. 75

It's All About Self-Respect

"Remember that standing up for your personal rights, or being assertive,
is very important," explains Betty Kelman of the Seattle University School of
Nursing. "Standing up for your rights involves self-respect—respect for your
rights and the other person's rights. Respecting ourselves is the ability to make 80
our own decisions involving relationships, how you spend your time, and whom
you spend it with."

Kelman also explains what assertiveness is not. "Standing up for yourself
does not mean that you express yourself in an aggressive, angry, or mean way."
She sums it up this way: "Think of standing up for yourself as being in a win-win 85
situation. You win and they win."

Some Other Ideas

Clinical psychologist Clare Albright offers some other suggestions for dealing
with conflict. "Wait a few days to cool down emotionally when a situation makes
you feel wild with intense feelings. As time passes, you will be more objective 90
about the issues." She also recommends face-to-face communication for resolving
conflicts. "E-mails, answering machine messages, and notes are too impersonal for
the delicate nature of negative words. What feels like a bomb on paper may feel
like a feather in person."

But wait—what happened to Ramon and Mr. Jefferson? 95

Mr. Jefferson looked down at the floor briefly and then up at Ramon. "Are you
finished now, college b . . . I mean, Ramon?"

Ramon nodded.

"Well, I'm sorry," Mr. Jefferson said. "I didn't have a chance to go to college,
and it's kept me from getting some good jobs and moving up in this company." He 100
shook his head. "I didn't realize that it was bothering you that much . . . and I
guess my personal problem shouldn't be your problem."

For a moment neither of them said anything. Then Ramon stuck out his
right hand. Mr. Jefferson shook his hand and said, "Let's get back to work, Ramon.
And no more mopping—for tonight anyway." 105

Analyze What process does this selection describe? Fill in the time line below with the steps of this process.

Process: How to handle conflict

Step 1: Meet at the right time and place.

Step 2: Have straight posture, eye contact, and relaxed stance.

Step 3: Use appropriate tone of voice, emotion, and rate of speech.

Step 4: Use "I" statements.

Step 5: End with cooperative statements.

Evaluate Do you agree with the information in the essay? Why or why not? Which points seem more valid or less valid?

Answers will vary.

Apply Consider the advice in the essay. How might you handle a past conflict differently today?

Answers will vary.

LO2 Writing a Process Essay

Prewrite Brainstorm a cluster to identify processes you are interested in explaining. List possible topics in the spaces below. (Add more circled spaces if necessary.)

Make an Idea Cluster

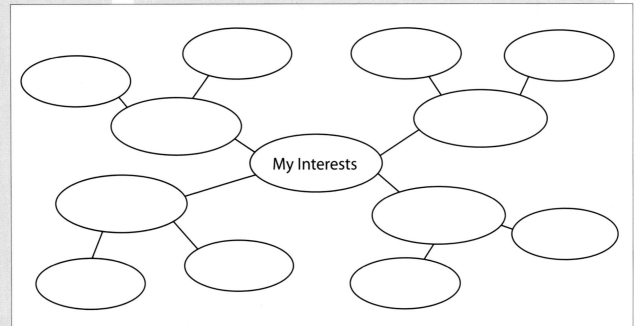

Choose one: Put a star next to the process that you would most like to write about.

Number the Steps

List the steps in your process from beginning to end. If the steps do not follow time order, list them in order of importance.

1. _____
2. _____
3. _____
4. _____
5. _____
6. _____
7. _____
8. _____
9. _____
10. _____

Draft Create a strong opening, middle, and closing for your process essay. Use the supports below as you create each part.

Opening Paragraph

Capture your reader's attention in the first line of your process essay. Consider why others should care about this process. Then use one of the following strategies:

- **Connect to the reader:** "For those of us living in the United States' smoggiest cities, air pollution is more than a nuisance. It's a health hazard."
- **Ask a question:** "Have you ever considered designing a game for a smart phone?"
- **Begin with action:** "Mack Boxley had no way of knowing that his first day on the construction site would put his new CPR training to the test."

Once you have your reader's attention, share information that effectively introduces the thesis statement. Here is a formula for creating your thesis statement.

Traits

As you draft your essay, focus on getting your ideas down, creating a three-part organizational structure. When you revise and edit, you will review these traits as well as voice, words, sentences, and conventions.

Process	Importance to Reader	Thesis Statement
Writing a résumé	**+** improves chances of getting an interview	**=** By following a few simple résumé-writing steps, you can vastly improve your chances of getting an interview.

Process

Importance to Reader _____

_____

_____

Thesis Statement

_____

_____

_____

Middle Paragraphs

In your middle paragraphs, expand upon your thesis statement:
- Present the steps of the process.
- Define any special terms.
- Explain any needed equipment and how to use it.
- Identify any safety issues.

Closing Paragraph

The final paragraph should "set" the process in the reader's mind. To accomplish this, review the most important details and restate your thesis. You may also conclude by strongly emphasizing the significance of the process.

Revise Take a break from your writing. Then come back to it with fresh eyes. If possible, have a friend or family member read the essay and then perform the process while you watch. Look for points and steps that are not clear to your reader. Then review your writing with the following checklist. Keep polishing until you can check off each item in the list.

Ideas

- [ ] **1.** Do I explain a process that is important or interesting to other people?
- [ ] **2.** Do I include all the needed details about steps, equipment, special terms, and safety issues?

Organization

- [ ] **3.** Does my opening grab the reader's attention and present a clear thesis?
- [ ] **4.** Do my middle paragraphs fully explain the steps in the process?
- [ ] **5.** Are the steps clearly presented in time order or order of importance?
- [ ] **6.** Does my closing restate the thesis and remind the reader of the significance of the process?

Voice

- [ ] **7.** Is my voice both friendly and professional?

Edit Prepare a clean copy of your process essay and use the following checklist to look for errors. Continue working until you can check off each item in the list.

Words

- [ ] **1.** Have I used specific nouns and verbs? (See page 103.)
- [ ] **2.** Have I used more action verbs than "be" verbs? (See page 73.)

Sentences

- [ ] **3.** Have I varied the beginnings and lengths of sentences? (See pages 226–231.)
- [ ] **4.** Have I combined short choppy sentences? (See page 232.)
- [ ] **5.** Have I avoided shifts in sentences? (See page 278.)
- [ ] **6.** Have I avoided fragments and run-ons? (See pages 261–266, 270–271.)

Conventions

- [ ] **7.** Do I use correct verb forms *(he saw,* not *he seen)*? (See pages 320, 324.)
- [ ] **8.** Do my subjects and verbs agree *(she speaks,* not *she speak)*? (See pages 245–260.)
- [ ] **9.** Have I used the right words *(their, there, they're)*?
- [ ] **10.** Have I capitalized first words and proper nouns and adjectives? (See page 386.)
- [ ] **11.** Have I used commas after long introductory word groups? (See page 358.)
- [ ] **12.** Have I carefully checked my spelling?

Allan Baxter/Photodisc/gettyimages

36

Comparison-Contrast Essays

When you describe something, you often tell what it is like, comparing it to other things. Sometimes you tell what it is *not* like, contrasting it with other things. By drawing comparisons and contrasts, you develop a deeper understanding of a subject.

This chapter includes three comparison-contrast essays, each showing the similarities and differences between two subjects. It also guides you through the process of writing your own comparison-contrast essay.

Learning Outcomes

LO1 Understand, read, and analyze comparison-contrast essays.

LO2 Write your own comparison-contrast essay.

What do you think?

What comparison details (similarities) can you find in this photo? How does the Goethe quotation affect the photo's meaning?

Answers will vary.

LO1 Understanding Comparison Essays

A comparison-contrast essay looks at the similarities and differences between two subjects. This chapter contains three comparison-contrast essays, along with tools—a graphic organizer and some questions—for analyzing each reading. The chapter concludes with guidelines for writing a comparison-contrast essay, as well as revising and editing checklists.

SQ3R

When you read, become involved with the text by using the SQ3R approach.

Survey: Skim the essay, noting the title and author, reading "About the Author," considering the photo, and scanning the vocabulary words.

Question: Ask yourself what subjects are being compared and contrasted and how the details are organized. Here are three common patterns of organization:

Point-by-Point		Subject-to-Subject	Similarities-Differences
Beginning		Beginning	Beginning
Point 1	Subject 1		
	Subject 2	Subject 1	Similarities
Point 2	Subject 1		
	Subject 2		
Point 3	Subject 1	Subject 2	Differences
	Subject 2		
Ending		Ending	Ending

Read: Take time to read the essay carefully, finding answers to your questions and studying the vocabulary terms.

Recite: Stop to repeat important points, either silently or aloud.

Review: Analyze the essay by filling in the graphic organizer and answering the questions provided.

Traits

As you read these selections, focus first on ideas. Then reread the beginning and ending and skim the middle, noting organization. Afterward, think about the voice of the author, and how it reflects the writer's personality, subject, and purpose.

Essay List

Two Views of the Same News Find Opposite Biases:

Shankar Vedantam shows how partisans are likely to feel that neutral coverage of news is biased against them.

Los Chinos Discover el Barrio:

Luis Torres describes how his former neighborhood, primarily Latino, has transitioned into a mixed Hispanic and Asian one.

Two Ways to Belong in America:

Bharati Mukherjee contrasts herself with her sister, both of whom moved from India to America but chose different paths after that.

About the Author

Shankar Vedantam is a staff writer for the *Washington Post* and author of the book *The Hidden Brain*.

Two Views of the Same News Find Opposite Biases
by Shankar Vedantam

1   You could be forgiven for thinking the television images in the experiment were from 2006. They were really from 1982: Israeli forces were clashing with Arab **militants** in Lebanon. The world was watching, charges were flying, and the air was thick with grievance, hurt and outrage.

5   There was only one thing on which pro-Israeli and pro-Arab audiences agreed. Both were certain that media coverage in the United States was hopelessly biased in favor of the other side.

The endlessly **recursive** conflict in the Middle East provides any number of instructive morals about human nature, but it also offers a psychological window into the world of **partisan** behavior. Israel's 1982 war in Lebanon sparked some of the earliest experiments into why people reach dramatically different conclusions about the same events.

The results say a lot about partisan behavior in general—why Republicans and Democrats love to hate each other, for example, or why Coke and Pepsi fans clash. Sadly, the results also say a lot about the newest conflicts between Israel and its enemies in Lebanon and the Palestinian territories, and why news organizations are being **besieged** with angry complaints from both sides.

Partisans, it turns out, don't just arrive at different conclusions; they see entirely different worlds. In one especially telling experiment, researchers showed 144 observers six television news segments about Israel's 1982 war with Lebanon.

Pro-Arab viewers heard 42 references that painted Israel in a positive light and 26 references that painted Israel unfavorably.

Pro-Israeli viewers, who watched the very same clips, spotted 16 references that painted Israel positively and 57 references that painted Israel negatively.

25   Both groups were certain they were right and that the other side didn't know what it was talking about.

The tendency to see bias in the news—now the **raison d'etre** of much of the **blogosphere**—is such a reliable indicator of partisan thinking that researchers coined a term, "hostile media effect," to describe the sincere belief among partisans that news reports are painting them in the worst possible light.

Were pro-Israeli and pro-Arab viewers who were especially knowledgeable about the conflict immune from such distortions? Amazingly, it turned out to be

Vocabulary

militant
a person aggressively active in supporting a cause, often violently

recursive
returning upon itself

partisan
a strong supporter of a cause, often biased

besieged
surrounded by attackers

raison d'etre
French phrase for "reason for being"

blogosphere
the world of Web logs ("blogs")

exactly the opposite, Stanford psychologist Lee D. Ross said. The best-informed partisans were the most likely to see bias against their side.

Ross thinks this is because partisans often feel the news lacks context. *35* Instead of just showing a missile killing civilians, in other words, partisans on both sides want the news to explain the history of events that prompted—and could have justified—the missile. The more knowledgeable people are, the more context they find missing.

Even more curious, the hostile media effect seems to apply only to news *40* sources that strive for balance. News reports from obviously biased sources usually draw fewer charges of bias. Partisans, it turns out, find it easier to **countenance** obvious **propaganda** than news accounts that explore both sides.

"If I think the world is black, and you think the world is white, and someone comes along and says it is gray, we will both think that person is biased," Ross *45* said.

The experiment, of course, did not address whether news reports were in fact biased—who would decide?—or how the media ought to cover conflicts. Partisans argue that assigning equal weight to both sides is wrong when one side (theirs) is right. In any event, psychologists such as Ross are less interested in rating the *50* news or in which side is right than in the curiosities of human perception: Why are partisans invariably blind to how news coverage might help their side?

If someone says several nice things about you and one **derogatory** thing, what sticks in your mind? People who are deeply invested in one side are quicker to spot and remember aspects of the news that hurt than they are to see aspects that *55* help, said Richard Perloff, a Cleveland State University political communication researcher.

Perloff **elicited** the same clashing perceptions of bias from pro-Israeli and pro-Arab audiences when he showed them news clips with equal amounts of violence.

Ross and Perloff both found that what partisans worry about the most is *60* the impact of the news on neutral observers. But the data suggest such worry is misplaced. Neutral observers are better than partisans at seeing flaws and virtues on both sides. Partisans, it turns out, are particularly susceptible to the general human belief that other people are **susceptible** to propaganda.

"When you are persuaded by something, you don't think it is propaganda," *65* Ross said. "Israelis know they see the world the way they do because they are Israelis, and Arabs, too. The difference is people think in their case, their special identities are a source of enlightenment, whereas other people's source of enlightenment is a source of bias."

Analyze Review the article by doing the following:

1. Create a Venn diagram (see page 434) to compare and contrast pro-Israeli and pro-Arab audiences as described in this article.

2. Create a second Venn diagram to compare and contrast "partisans" and "neutral observers," as described in the article.

3. Which Venn diagram shows more similarities? Which shows more differences? Where do you fall on these diagrams? Why?

WAC

In addition to tackling a thorny issue in the social sciences, this essay gets at a fundamental difficulty in communication—objectivity and (perceived or actual) bias. What can consumers of information do to avoid bias in their interpretation of information?

Vocabulary

countenance
put up with

propaganda
information spread to support a particular viewpoint

derogatory
negative or insulting

elicit
draw a response

susceptible
open to or vulnerable

Photo by Ilpo Koskinen

Los Chinos Discover el Barrio
by Luis Torres

1   There's a colorful mural on the asphalt playground of Hillside Elementary School, in the neighborhood called Lincoln Heights. Painted on the beige handball wall, the mural is of life-sized youngsters holding hands. Depicted are Asian and Latino kids with bright faces and ear-to-ear smiles.

5   The mural is a mirror of the makeup of the neighborhood today: Latinos living side by side with Asians. But it's not all smiles and happy faces in the Northeast Los Angeles community, located just a couple of miles up Broadway from City Hall. On the surface there's harmony between Latinos and Asians. But there are indications of simmering ethnic-based tensions.

10   That became clear to me recently when I took a walk through the old neighborhood—the one where I grew up. As I walked along North Broadway, I thought of a joke that comic Paul Rodriguez often tells on the stage. He paints a picture of a young Chicano walking down a street on L.A.'s East Side. He comes upon two Asians having an animated conversation in what sounds like babble.

15   "Hey, you guys, knock off that foreign talk. This is America—speak Spanish!"

When I was growing up in Lincoln Heights 30 years ago, most of us spoke Spanish—and English. There was a sometimes uneasy **coexistence** in the neighborhood between brown and white. Back then we Latinos were moving in and essentially displacing the working-class Italians (to us, they were just *los*

20   *gringos*) who had moved there and thrived after World War II.

Because I was an extremely fair-skinned Latino kid, I would often overhear remarks by gringos in Lincoln Heights that were not intended for Latino ears, **disparaging** comments about "smelly wetbacks," and worse. The transition was, for the most part, a gradual process and, as I recall—except for the slurs that

25   sometimes stung me directly—a process marked only occasionally by outright hostility.

A trend that began about 10 years ago in Lincoln Heights seems to have hit a critical point now. It's similar to the ethnic tug-of-war of yesteryear, but different colors, different words are involved. Today Chinese and Vietnamese

30   are displacing the Latinos who, by choice or circumstance, had Lincoln Heights virtually to themselves for two solid generations.

Evidence of the transition is clear.

About the Author

Luis Torres is an American writer who grew up in a mostly Latino neighborhood in Northeast Los Angeles. In this essay, Torres compares the "barrio" neighborhood of his childhood with the same neighborhood today. He also compares the current arrival of Asian families to the past arrival of Latino families. The picture he paints of this change is as much about new friendships as it is about ethnic tension.

Luis Torres, "Los Chinos Discover El Barrio," LOS ANGELES TIMES, November 14, 1987. Reprinted by permission of the author.

Vocabulary

coexistence
living side by side without major conflict

gringos
Spanish term for white people

disparaging
insulting, criticizing

The bank where I opened my first **meager** savings account in the late 1950s has changed hands. It's now the East-West Federal Bank, an Asian-owned enterprise. 35

The public library on Workman Street, where I checked out *Charlotte's Web* with my first library card, **abounds** with signs of the new times: It's called "La Biblioteca del Pueblo de Lincoln Heights," and on the door there's a notice advising that the building is closed because of the October 1 earthquake; it's written in Chinese. 40

The white wood-frame house on Griffin Avenue that I once lived in is now owned by a Chinese family.

What used to be a Latino-run **mortuary** at the corner of Sichel Street and North Broadway is now the Chung Wah Funeral Home.

A block down the street from the funeral home is a *panaderia*, a bakery. As I 45 would listen to radio reports of the U.S. war in faraway Indochina while walking from class at Lincoln High School, I often used to drop in the *panaderia* for a snack.

The word *panaderia,* now faded and chipped, is still painted on the shop window that fronts North Broadway. But another sign, a gleaming plastic one, 50 hangs above the window. The sign proclaims that it is a Vietnamese-Chinese bakery. The proprietor, Sam Lee, bought the business less than a year ago. With a wave of his arm, he indicates that *La Opinion,* the Spanish-language daily newspaper, is still for sale on the counter. Two signs stand side by side behind the counter announcing in Spanish and in Chinese that cakes are made to order for 55 all occasions.

Out on North Broadway, Fidel Farrillas sells *raspadas* (snow cones) from his pushcart. He has lived and worked in Lincoln Heights "for 30 years and a pinch more," he says, his voice nearly whistling through two gold-framed teeth. He has seen the neighborhood change. Twice. 60

Like many older Latinos, he remembers the tension felt between *los gringos y las raza* years ago—even though most people went about their business **ostensibly** coexisting politely. And others who have been around as long will tell an inquiring reporter scratching away in his notebook, "We're going out of our way to treat the chinos nice—better than the gringos sometimes treated us back then." But when 65 the notebook is closed, they're likely to whisper, "But you know, the thing is, they smell funny, and they talk behind your back, and they are so arrogant—the way they're buying up everything in our neighborhood."

Neighborhood transitions can be tough to **reconcile**.

It isn't easy for the blue-collar Latinos of Lincoln Heights. They haven't 70 possessed much. But they had the barrio, "a little chunk of the world where we belonged," as one described it. There may be some hard times and hard feelings ahead as *los chinos* continue to make **inroads** into what had been an exclusively Latino **enclave**. But there are hopeful signs as well.

On one recent Saturday afternoon a Latino fifth grader, wearing the same 75 type of hightop tennis shoes I wore as a 10-year-old on that same street corner, strode up to Senor Farrillas' snow-cone pushcart. The kid pulled out a pocketful of dimes and bought two *raspadas*—one for himself, and one for his school chum, a Vietnamese kid. He was wearing hightops, too. They both ordered strawberry, as I recall.

Vocabulary

meager
small, poor, insufficient

abounds
overflows, is full of

mortuary
funeral home

ostensibly
apparently, according to appearances

reconcile
adapt to, accept

inroads
points of access, advances

enclave
living place for a specific group

Analyze Complete the following T-graph by writing descriptions of the barrio during Torres's childhood and the barrio 30 years later. An example has been provided for you.

Speaking & Listening
Complete this activity with a partner. One of you searches the essay and names a condition in "the barrio then," and the other responds with the corresponding condition in "the barrio now." Switch roles and keep going.

The Barrio Then	The Barrio Now
– Torres lived in a wood-frame house.	– Now a Chinese family owns the house.
– Most people in the neighborhood spoke Spanish and English.	– Chinese and Vietnamese outnumber the Spanish.
– The neighborhood was mostly a mix of Latinos and Italians.	– Bank is now an Asian-owned East-West enterprise.
– Torres went to the public library.	– The library is now called Biblioteca del Pueblo de Lincoln Heights.
– A Latino-run mortuary sat on Sichel Street.	– The Chung Wah Funeral Home now sits on Sichel Street.
– Torres used to eat at the *panaderia*.	– The *panaderia* sign is now faded and chipped; a sign for a Vietnamese-Chinese bakery hangs above it.

Think Critically In the essay, Fidel Farrillas remembers the neighborhood changing twice—once from gringo (Italian) to Latino, and now from Latino to Asian. How are these two periods of change similar, and how are they different?

(AWV) During Torres' youth, the neighborhood transitioned from a mostly Italian population to Latino. Spanish and English became the dominant languages, and many of the new businesses catered to Latinos. Thirty years later the neighborhood transitioned from a mostly Latino population to a mix of Latino and Chinese and Vietnamese. In fact, many of the businesses that catered to Latinos were replaced with Chinese and Vietnamese institutions. Both periods of change were similar in that they dealt with the clash between the two very different cultures.

About the Author

Bharati Mukherjee was born in India. During her childhood, her family moved to Europe for a time, and then to Canada and the United States. She has lived in North America since the mid-1960s. As a result, her five novels, including *The Tiger's Daughter* and *Jasmine*, deal with the struggle of leaving one's homeland and finding an identity in a new land. In the following essay, Mukherjee tells how she and her sister followed different paths to find their places in the New World.

Bharati Mukherjee, "Two Ways to Belong in America," NEW YORK TIMES, September 22, 1996. Reprinted by permission of the author's agent, Janklow & Nesbit Associates.

Two Ways to Belong in America
by Bharati Mukherjee

This is a tale of two sisters from Calcutta, Mira and Bharati, who have lived in the United States for some 35 years, but who find themselves on different sides in the current debate over the status of immigrants.

I am an American citizen and she is not. I am moved that thousands of long-term residents are finally taking the oath of citizenship. She is not.

Mira arrived in Detroit in 1960 to study child psychology and preschool education. I followed her a year later to study creative writing at the University of Iowa. When we left India, we were almost identical in appearance and attitude. We dressed alike, in **saris**; we expressed identical views on politics, social issues, love and marriage in the same Calcutta convent-school accent. We would endure our two years in America, secure our degrees, then return to India to marry the grooms of our father's choosing.

Instead, Mira married an Indian student in 1962 who was getting his business administration degree at Wayne State University. They soon acquired the labor certifications necessary for the green card of hassle-free residence and employment.

Mira still lives in Detroit, works in the Southfield, Michigan, school system, and has become nationally recognized for her contributions in the fields of preschool education and parent-teacher relationships. After 36 years as a legal immigrant in this country, she clings passionately to her Indian citizenship and hopes to go home to India when she retires.

In Iowa City in 1963, I married a fellow student, an American of Canadian parentage. Because of the accident of his North Dakota birth, I bypassed labor-certification requirements and the race-related "quota" system that favored the applicant's country of origin over his or her merit. I was prepared for (and even welcomed) the emotional strain that came with marrying outside my ethnic community. In 33 years of marriage, we have lived in every part of North America. By choosing a husband who was not my father's selection, I was opting for fluidity,

1

5

10

15

20

25

Vocabulary

sari
traditional woman's robe from India, often brightly colored and made of silk

self-invention, blue jeans and T-shirts, and renouncing 3,000 years (at least) of
30 caste-observant, "pure culture" marriage in the Mukherjee family. My books have
often been read as unapologetic (and in some quarters overenthusiastic) texts for
cultural and psychological "**mongrelization**." It's a word I celebrate.

Mira and I have stayed sisterly close by phone. In our regular Sunday
morning conversations, we are unguardedly affectionate. I am her only blood
35 relative on this continent. We expect to see each other through the looming
crises of aging and ill health without being asked. Long before Vice President
Gore's "Citizenship U.S.A." drive, we'd had our polite arguments over the ethics of
retaining an overseas citizenship while expecting the permanent protection and
economic benefits that come with living and working in America.

40 Like well-raised sisters, we never said what was really on our minds, but we
probably pitied one another. She, for the lack of structure in my life, the erasure
of Indianness, the absence of an unvarying daily core. I, for the narrowness of
her perspective, her uninvolvement with the mythic depths or the superficial pop
culture of this society. But, now, with the **scapegoating** of "aliens" (documented or
45 illegal) on the increase, and the targeting of long-term legal immigrants like Mira
for new scrutiny and new self-consciousness, she and I find ourselves unable to
maintain the same polite discretion. We were always unacknowledged adversaries,
and we are now, more than ever, sisters.

"I feel used," Mira raged on the phone the other night. "I feel manipulated
50 and discarded. This is such an unfair way to treat a person who was invited to
stay and work here because of her talent. My employer went to the I.N.S. and
petitioned for the labor certification. For over 30 years, I've invested my creativity
and professional skills into the improvement of this country's preschool system.
I've obeyed all the rules, I've paid my taxes, I love my work, I love my students, I
55 love the friends I've made. How dare America now change its rules in midstream?
If America wants to make new rules **curtailing** benefits of legal immigrants, they
should apply only to immigrants who arrive after those rules are already in
place." To my ears, it sounded like the description of a long-enduring, comfortable
yet loveless marriage, without risk or recklessness. Have we the right to demand,
60 and to expect, that we be loved? (That, to me, is the subtext of the arguments by
immigration advocates.) My sister is an **expatriate**, professionally generous and
creative, socially courteous and gracious, and that's as far as her **Americanization**
can go. She is here to maintain an identity, not to transform it.

I asked her if she would follow the example of others who have decided to
65 become citizens because of the anti-immigration bills in Congress. And here, she
surprised me. "If America wants to play the **manipulative** game, I'll play it too,"
she snapped. "I'll become a U.S. citizen for now, then change back to Indian when
I'm ready to go home. I feel some kind of irrational attachment to India that I
don't to America. Until all this **hysteria** against legal immigrants, I was totally
70 happy. Having my green card meant I could visit any place in the world I wanted
to and then come back to a job that's satisfying and that I do very well."

WAC

This essay and "Los Chinos
Discover el Barrio" both
deal with immigration—
but from two different
perspectives. One essay
describes what it is
like to be displaced by
immigrants, and the
other, what it is like to be
an immigrant trying to
fit into a new place. Both
have strong social-science
content.

Vocabulary

mongrelization
the process of creating or
producing mixed breeds

scapegoating
the practice of blaming social
ills on one person or group of
people

curtailing
ending, cutting off

expatriate
a person who willingly leaves
his or her home country to
live elsewhere

Americanization
the process of becoming
American; adopting the
culture and worldview of the
United States

manipulative
controlling in an unfair way

hysteria
public uproar, craziness

In one family, from two sisters alike as peas in a pod, there could not be a wider divergence of immigrant experience. America spoke to me—I married it—I embraced the demotion from expatriate **aristocrat** to immigrant nobody, surrendering those thousands of years of "pure culture," the saris, the delightfully *75* accented English. She retained them all. Which of us is the freak?

Mira's voice, I realize, is the voice not just of the immigrant South Asian community but of an immigrant community of the millions who have stayed rooted in one job, one city, one house, one ancestral culture, one **cuisine**, for the entirety of their productive years. She speaks for greater numbers than I possibly can. *80* Only the fluency of her English and the anger, rather than fear, born of confidence from her education, differentiate her from the seamstresses, the domestics, the technicians, the shop owners, the millions of hardworking but effectively silenced documented immigrants as well as their less fortunate "illegal" brothers and sisters. *85*

Nearly 20 years ago, when I was living in my husband's ancestral homeland of Canada, I was always well-employed but never allowed to feel part of the local Quebec or larger Canadian society. Then, through a Green Paper that invited a national **referendum** on the unwanted side effects of "nontraditional" immigration, the government officially turned against its immigrant communities, particularly *90* those from South Asia.

I felt then the same sense of betrayal that Mira feels now.

I will never forget the pain of that sudden turning, and the casual racist outbursts the Green Paper elicited. That sense of betrayal had its desired effect and drove me, and thousands like me, from the country. *95*

Mira and I differ, however, in the ways in which we hope to interact with the country that we have chosen to live in. She is happier to live in America as expatriate Indian than as an immigrant American. I need to feel like a part of the community I have adopted (as I tried to feel in Canada as well). I need to put roots down, to vote and make the difference that I can. The price that *100* the immigrant willingly pays, and that the exile avoids, is the **trauma** of self-transformation.

Yuriy Chaban, 2010/used under license from www.shutterstock.com

Role-play

With a partner, act out a debate between Mira and Bharati. "Mira" can tell why she prefers to keep her Indian identity, and "Bharati" can tell why she has given up 3,000 years of tradition to become Americanized.

Vocabulary

aristocrat
a member of the upper class, a privileged person

cuisine
the types of food commonly eaten within a certain culture

referendum
an official vote taken on an issue to decide a matter of public policy

trauma
pain and suffering

Analyze Complete the following Venn diagram. In the center section, write similarities between Mira and Bharati. In the outer sections, write differences between Mira and Bharati.

Work with a partner to fill in this Venn diagram.

Bharati

an American citizen, married an American, favors America's immigration policy

Similarities

live in the United States, appearance, love for each other, both felt betrayed by immigration policies

Mira

an Indian citizen, married an Indian, disagrees with America's immigration policy

Think Critically At the end of the sixth paragraph, Mukherjee says that she celebrates "cultural and psychological 'mongrelization.'" What evidence from the essay shows her enthusiasm for mixing cultures?

(AWV) The author demonstrates her enthusiasm for mixing cultures by marrying

a man of different descent, renouncing the caste system of her homeland, and

expressing her desire to vote and become part of North American culture.

LO2 Writing a Comparison Essay

Prewrite Read the general lists below and select two specific people, places, or things to compare and contrast.

People	Places	Things
actors	buildings	animals
artists	businesses	books
athletes	cities	films
authors	countries	foods
explorers	forests	fuels
friends	houses	hobbies
heroes	lakes	jobs
inventors	landmarks	laws
leaders	mountains	machines
neighbors	neighborhoods	processes
relatives	parks	resources
scientists	restaurants	styles
singers	rivers	tools
soldiers	rooms	trees
teachers	schools	vehicles

Prewrite Complete the Venn diagram below. Write the name of each subject on the lines provided. In the center section, write similarities between the subjects. In the outer sections, write differences between the subjects.

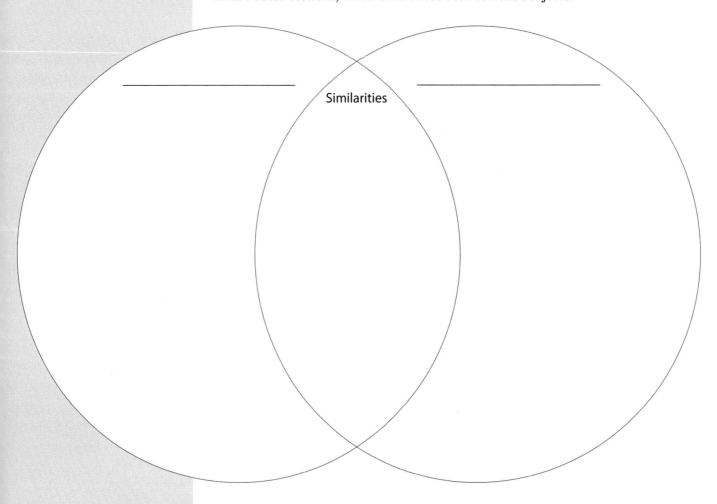

Similarities

Draft Create a strong opening, middle, and closing for your essay. Use the supports below as you create each part.

Opening Paragraph

Capture your reader's attention in the first line of your comparison-contrast essay. Then lead up to your thesis statement. Here is a formula for creating your thesis statement.

Two Subjects

Mount Saint Helens and Mount Rainier

+

Thought or Feeling

very similar mountains until 1980

=

Thesis Statement

Though Mount Saint Helens and Mount Rainier look very different now, their similarities were obvious before the big eruption of 1980.

Two Subjects

Thought or Feeling _____

_____

_____

_____

Thesis Statement

_____

_____

_____

_____

_____

Middle Paragraphs

In the middle paragraphs, compare the two subjects, using one of the organizational patterns shown in the right-hand column. Also use transitions to help the reader follow your ideas:

Transitions That Compare

as	as well	also	both	in the same way	much as
much like	one way	like	likewise	similarly	

Transitions That Contrast

although	even though	by contrast	but
on the one hand	on the other hand	otherwise	though
still	while	yet	however

Closing Paragraph

In your closing, share a final thought, pointing out a key similarity or difference between the subjects you have compared.

Traits

As you draft your essay, focus on getting your ideas down, creating a three-part organizational structure. When you revise and edit, you will review these traits as well as voice, words, sentences, and conventions.

Point-by-Point

Beginning

Point 1	Subject 1
	Subject 2
Point 2	Subject 1
	Subject 2
Point 3	Subject 1
	Subject 2

Ending

Subject-to-Subject

Beginning

Subject 1

Subject 2

Ending

Similarities-Differences

Beginning

Similarities

Differences

Ending

Revise Improve your writing. First ask a classmate to read your essay. Then discuss your work, using the following checklist. Continue making improvements until you can check off each item in the list

Ideas

- [ ] **1.** Do I compare and contrast two subjects??
- [ ] **2.** Do I include a variety of details (facts, quotations, anecdotes)?

Organization

- [ ] **3.** Do I get the reader's attention and introduce my subjects in the opening?
- [ ] **4.** Have I used a pattern of organization in the middle part?
- [ ] **5.** Have I used transitions to connect my sentences?
- [ ] **6.** Do I share a final thought about the comparison in my ending?

Voice

- [ ] **7.** Do I sound knowledgeable and interested in my subjects?

Edit Prepare a clean copy of your comparison essay and use the following checklist to look for errors. Continue working until you can check off each item in the list.

Words

- [ ] **1.** Have I used specific nouns and verbs? (See page 103.)
- [ ] **2.** Have I used more action verbs than "be" verbs? (See page 73.)

Sentences

- [ ] **3.** Have I varied the beginnings and lengths of sentences? (See pages 226–231.)
- [ ] **4.** Have I combined short choppy sentences? (See page 232.)
- [ ] **5.** Have I avoided shifts in sentences? (See page 278.)
- [ ] **6.** Have I avoided fragments and run-ons? (See pages 261–266, 270–271.)

Conventions

- [ ] **7.** Do I use correct verb forms (*he saw*, not *he seen*)? (See pages 320, 324.)
- [ ] **8.** Do my subjects and verbs agree (*she speaks*, not *she speak*)? (See pages 245–260.)
- [ ] **9.** Have I used the right words (*their, there, they're*)?
- [ ] **10.** Have I capitalized first words and proper nouns and adjectives? (See page 386.)
- [ ] **11.** Have I used commas after long introductory word groups? (See page 358.)
- [ ] **12.** Have I carefully checked my spelling?

37
Cause-Effect Essays

We live in a cause-effect world. One thing takes place, and another event unfolds as a result. However, the relationship between cause and effect isn't always so clear. Sometimes many small causes lead to one great effect. On the other hand, a single cause can have multiple results. Nor does sequence necessarily equate cause and effect: Philosophers once believed that maggots were born spontaneously from rotting food, until someone took the time to test the theory and show that flies first had to lay eggs.

The essays in this chapter present a number of cause-effect claims. As a reader, you'll have the opportunity to judge their strength for yourself.

> "We can evade reality, but we cannot evade the consequences of evading reality."
> —Ayn Rand

Learning Outcomes

LO1 Understand, read, and analyze cause-effect essays.

LO2 Write your own cause-effect essay.

What do you think?

Study the image and quotation. What does each say to you about cause and effect?

Answers will vary.

LO1 Understanding Cause-Effect Essays

Within this chapter you will find three example essays using a cause-effect approach. You will also find questions and graphic organizers for analyzing each reading. At the end of the chapter are writing guidelines for creating a cause-effect essay of your own.

SQ3R

When you read, become involved with the text by using the SQ3R approach.

Survey: Prepare by reading "About the Author," skimming the essay, and noting any vocabulary words.

Question: Ask yourself what cause-effect relationships you predict from the essay.

Read: Read the essay, noting the causes leading to or the effects resulting from the main topic.

Recite: Repeat aloud the main details of the cause-effect relationship the author provides.

Review: Answer the questions provided and use the graphic organizers to help you analyze the essay.

Essay List

"Study Says Flirtatious Women Get Fewer Raises"

Del Jones says that contrary to the advice of Donald Trump, women who attempt to capitalize on their sexuality in the workplace actually suffer for it.

"What Adolescents Miss When We Let Them Grow Up in Cyberspace"

Columnist Brent Staples argues that because of Internet communication, today's teens are missing out on essential social skills.

"Why We Crave Horror Movies"

Renowned horror novelist Stephen King reasons that human beings are all a little insane, and that scary movies act as a safety valve for the uncivilized portions of our brains.

Traits

As you read these selections, focus first on ideas. Then reread the beginning and ending and skim the middle, noting organization. Afterward, think about the voice of the author, and how it reflects the writer's personality, subject, and purpose.

About the Author

Del Jones is a journalist for *USA Today*.

Del Jones, "Study Says Flirtatious Women Get Fewer Raises," USA TODAY, August 4, 2005. Reprinted by permission.

Study Says Flirtatious Women Get Fewer Raises
by Del Jones

1   Women who send flirtatious e-mail, wear short skirts or massage a man's shoulders at work win fewer pay raises and promotions, according to a Tulane University study to be presented Monday at the Academy of Management annual meeting in Honolulu.

5   In the first study to make plain the negative consequences of such behavior, 49% of 164 female MBA graduates said in a survey that they have tried to advance in their careers by sometimes engaging in at least one of 10 sexual behaviors, including crossing their legs provocatively or leaning over a table to let men look down their shirts.

10   The other half said they never engaged in such activity, and those women have earned an average of three promotions, vs. two for the group that had employed sexuality. Those who said they never used sexuality were, on average, in the $75,000–$100,000 income range; the others fell, on average, in the next-lowest range, $50,000–$75,000.

15   The women in the study ranged in age from their mid-20s to 60. The average woman was 43 and had received an MBA 12 years ago.

Academic experts have not studied the use of sexual behavior in the workplace. After searching managerial literature, Tulane professor Arthur Brief and colleagues Suzanne Chan-Serafin, Jill Bradley and Marla Watkins found no
20   evidence showing such behavior to be effective or ineffective.

Brief said the research has been limited in scope to sexual harassment. This study is groundbreaking, he said, probably because the topic of workplace sexuality is considered taboo. "It's too lurid for some and too politically incorrect for others," he said.

25   That has created a vacuum filled by those such as Donald Trump, who has advised women to "use those God-given assets" and be sexy, at least to a point.

Such statements are not unchallenged, and Dianne Durkin, president of management consulting firm Loyalty Factor, says any unprofessional behavior is detrimental to a career. "Cleavage is not a plus," she says.

30   The Tulane study's findings are statistically significant to professional

Vocabulary

MBA
a Master of Business Administration degree

provocative
provoking or causing excitement

lurid
causing shock or horror

politically correct
accepted language and attitudes that avoid discrimination

detrimental
harmful

women looking for career advancement, Brief said.

The 10 questions, including, "I allow men to linger at certain places of my body while hugging them," were developed from a focus group of women in **pharmaceutical** sales who said they either employed or witnessed such behavior.

Brief said the study goes so far as to suggest that women should even be 35 careful about letting men open doors or lift boxes that aren't particularly heavy, because **chivalry** is "**benevolent** sexism" that advances the **stereotype** that women are vulnerable and weak.

"Our story is really a **feminist** story, because we argue that there are negative consequences for women who use sexuality in the workplace," Brief says. 40

But Durkin says the pendulum can swing too far, and she praises men for opening doors, says hugs between longtime business friends are OK, and is happy that more feminine attire has replaced the female suit and tie.

Almost all the women in the Tulane study who said they used sexual behavior said they did so infrequently. But executive coach Debra Benton, who has long 45 asked business leaders about the pros and cons of sexuality in the workplace, said that if a similar survey were given to men, they would say that women use sexuality "all the time." Women need to be aware that when they say "It's a nice day," men will often conclude "She wants me," Benton says.

Analyze What effects are identified in or implied by the essay? List them below. Then list possible causes mentioned in the essay. Do you believe the causes lead to the effects in this case? What other explanations might you imagine?

Causes	Effects
flirtatious behavior	lower income
revealing clothing	fewer promotions

About the Author

Brent Staples was born the son of a truck driver in 1951 in Chester, PA. He went on to receive a Ph.D., teach psychology at colleges in Pennsylvania and Chicago, become a reporter for the *Chicago Sun-Times*, and finally become an editorial writer for the *New York Times*.

What Adolescents Miss When We Let Them Grow Up in Cyberspace
by Brent Staples

1   My 10th-grade **heartthrob** was the daughter of a fearsome steelworker who struck terror into the hearts of 15-year-old boys. He made it his business to answer the telephone—and so always knew who was calling—and grumbled in the background when the conversation went on too long. Unable to make time by 5 phone, the boy either gave up or appeared at the front door. This meant submitting to the intense scrutiny that the girl's father soon became known for.

He greeted me with a crushing handshake, then leaned in close in a transparent attempt to find out whether I was one of those bad boys who smoked. He retired to the den during the visit, but cruised by the living room now and then 10 to let me know he was watching. He let up after some weeks, but only after getting across what he expected of a boy who spent time with his daughter and how upset he'd be if I disappointed him.

This was my first sustained encounter with an adult outside my family who needed to be convinced of my worth as a person. This, of course, is a crucial part of 15 growing up. Faced with the same challenge today, however, I would probably pass on meeting the girl's father—and **outflank** him on the Internet.

Thanks to e-mail, online chat rooms, and instant messages—which permit private, real-time conversations—**adolescents** have at last succeeded in shielding their social lives from adult scrutiny. But this comes at a cost: teenagers nowadays 20 are both more connected to the world at large than ever, and more cut off from the social encounters that have historically prepared young people for the move into adulthood.

The Internet was billed as a revolutionary way to enrich our social lives and expand our civic connections. This seems to have worked well for elderly people 25 and others who were isolated before they got access to the World Wide Web. But a

Vocabulary

heartthrob
an object of teenaged romantic attraction

outflank
a military maneuver to avoid face-to-face confrontation and instead attack from the side

adolescent
a person who has begun to mature sexually but is not yet an adult

growing body of research is showing that heavy use of the Net can actually isolate younger socially connected people who unwittingly allow time online to replace face-to-face interactions with their families and friends.

Online shopping, checking e-mail, and Web surfing—mainly solitary activities—have turned out to be more isolating than watching television, which 30 friends and family often do in groups. Researchers have found that the time spent in direct contact with family members drops by as much as half for every hour we use the Net at home.

This should come as no surprise to the two-career couples who have seen their domestic lives taken over by e-mail and wireless tethers that keep people working 35 around the clock. But a startling body of research from the Human-Computer Interaction Institute at Carnegie Mellon has shown that heavy Internet use can have a **stunting** effect outside the home as well.

Studies show that **gregarious**, well-connected people actually lost friends and experienced symptoms of loneliness and depression, after joining discussion 40 groups and other activities. People who communicated with **disembodied** strangers online found the experience empty and emotionally frustrating but were nonetheless seduced by the novelty of the new medium. As Prof. Robert Kraut, a Carnegie Mellon researcher, told me recently, such people allowed low-quality relationships developed in **virtual reality** to replace higher-quality relationships in 45 the real world.

No group has embraced this socially impoverishing trade-off more enthusiastically than adolescents, many of whom spend most of their free hours cruising the Net in sunless rooms. This **hermetic** existence has left many of these teenagers with nonexistent social skills—a point widely noted in stories about the 50 computer geeks who rose to prominence in the early days of **Silicon Valley**.

Adolescents are drawn to cyberspace for different reasons than adults. As the writer Michael Lewis observed in his book *Next: The Future Just Happened,* children see the Net as a transformational device that lets them discard **quotidian** identities for more glamorous ones. Mr. Lewis illustrated the point with Marcus 55 Arnold, who, as a 15-year-old, adopted a **pseudonym** a few years ago and posed as a 25-year-old legal expert for an Internet information service. Marcus did not feel the least bit guilty, and wasn't **deterred**, when real-world lawyers discovered his secret and accused him of being a fraud. When asked whether he had actually read the law, Marcus responded that he found books "boring," leaving us to conclude 60 that he had learned all he needed to know from his family's big-screen TV.

Marcus is a child of the Net, where everyone has a pseudonym, telling a story makes it true, and adolescents create older, cooler, more socially powerful selves any time they wish. The ability to slip easily into a new, false self is tailor-made for emotionally fragile adolescents, who can consider a bout of acne or a few 65 excess pounds an unbearable tragedy.

But teenagers who spend much of their lives hunched over computer screens miss the socializing, the real-world experience that would allow them to leave adolescence behind and grow into adulthood. These vital experiences, like much else, are simply not available in a virtual form. 70

WAC

How does the Internet shape your life, in school and out? What opportunities does it provide you? What problems does it create?

Vocabulary

stunting
preventing growth

gregarious
sociable, comfortable in the presence of other people

disembodied
not in a physical body

virtual reality
a computer simulation of the real world

hermetic
sealed away from outside influence

Silicon Valley
an area south of San Francisco famous for computer developments

quotidian
everyday

pseudonym
a fictitious name, used to disguise a writer's true identity

deter
to prevent or discourage

Analyze Which of the following cause-effect diagrams best illustrates the essay? Why?

This article follows the second cause-effect diagram because it begins with the main cause (the Internet) and then goes on to describe the different effects the Internet has had on adolescents' social development.

Explain What is the main effect or main cause in the essay?

The Internet allows adolescents to skirt certain face-to-face interactions, isolating them from important social development and personal relationships.

Analyze On what points do you agree or disagree with the author? Why?

Answers will vary.

Describe Explain how the Internet affects your own daily life. What social technologies do you use most often and least often? What shapes your online habits?

Answers will vary.

About the Author

Stephen King is a well-known American fiction author, with a particular bent for horror and science-fiction tales. Many of his stories have been adapted for screen and television.

Vocabulary

squinch
to squint the eyes or flinch

hysteria
emotional excess

province
a country or region under the control of another government

reactionary
ultraconservative

voyeur
someone who receives stimulation from watching (often secretly) instead of taking part

lynching
lawlessly put to death by a mob, typically by hanging

Why We Crave Horror Movies
by Stephen King

I think that we're all mentally ill; those of us outside the asylums only hide it a little better—and maybe not all that much better, after all. We've all known people who talk to themselves, people who sometimes **squinch** their faces into horrible grimaces when they believe no one is watching, people who have some **hysterical** fear—of snakes, the dark, the tight place, the long drop . . . and, of course, those final worms and grubs that are waiting so patiently underground.

When we pay our four or five bucks and seat ourselves at tenth-row center in a theater showing a horror movie, we are daring the nightmare.

Why? Some of the reasons are simple and obvious. To show that we can, that we are not afraid, that we can ride this roller coaster. Which is not to say that a really good horror movie may not surprise a scream out of us at some point, the way we may scream when the roller coaster twists through a complete 360 or plows through a lake at the bottom of the drop. And horror movies, like roller coasters, have always been the special **province** of the young; by the time one turns 40 or 50, one's appetite for double twists or 360-degree loops may be considerably depleted.

We also go to re-establish our feelings of essential normality; the horror movie is innately conservative, even **reactionary**. Freda Jackson as the horrible melting woman in *Die, Monster, Die!* confirms for us that no matter how far we may be removed from the beauty of a Robert Redford or a Diana Ross, we are still light-years from true ugliness.

And we go to have fun.

Ah, but this is where the ground starts to slope away, isn't it? Because this is a very peculiar sort of fun, indeed. The fun comes from seeing others menaced—sometimes killed. One critic has suggested that if pro football has become the **voyeur's** version of combat, then the horror film has become the modern version of the public **lynching**.

1

5

10

15

20

25

It is true that the mythic "fairy-tale" horror film intends to take away the shades of grey. . . . It urges us to put away our more civilized and adult penchant for analysis and to become children again, seeing things in pure blacks and whites. It may be that horror movies provide psychic relief on this level because this invitation to lapse into simplicity, irrationality and even outright madness is extended so rarely. We are told we may allow our emotions a free rein . . . or no rein at all.

If we are all insane, then sanity becomes a matter of degree. If your insanity leads you to carve up women like Jack the Ripper or the Cleveland Torso Murderer, we clap you away in the funny farm (but neither of those two amateur-night surgeons was ever caught, heh-heh-heh); if, on the other hand, your insanity leads you only to talk to yourself when you're under stress or to pick your nose on your morning bus, then you are left alone to go about your business . . . though it is doubtful that you will ever be invited to the best parties.

The potential lyncher is in almost all of us (excluding saints, past and present; but then, most saints have been crazy in their own ways), and every now and then, he has to be let loose to scream and roll around in the grass. Our emotions and our fears form their own body, and we recognize that it demands its own exercise to maintain proper muscle tone. Certain of these emotional muscles are accepted—even exalted—in civilized society; they are, of course, the emotions that tend to maintain the **status quo** of civilization itself. Love, friendship, loyalty, kindness—these are all the emotions that we applaud, emotions that have been immortalized in the couplets of Hallmark cards and in the verses (I don't dare call it poetry) of Leonard Nimoy.

When we exhibit these emotions, society showers us with positive reinforcement; we learn this even before we get out of diapers. When, as children, we hug our rotten little puke of a sister and give her a kiss, all the aunts and uncles smile and twit and cry, "Isn't he the sweetest little thing?" Such coveted treats as chocolate-covered graham crackers often follow. But if we deliberately slam the rotten little puke of a sister's fingers in the door, **sanctions** follow—angry **remonstrance** from parents, aunts and uncles; instead of a chocolate-covered graham cracker, a spanking.

But anticivilization emotions don't go away, and they demand periodic exercise. We have such "sick" jokes as, "What's the difference between a truckload of bowling balls and a truckload of dead babies?" (You can't unload a truckload of bowling balls with a pitchfork . . . a joke, by the way, that I heard originally from a ten-year-old.) Such a joke may surprise a laugh or a grin out of us even as we recoil, a possibility that confirms the thesis: If we share a brotherhood of man, then we also share an insanity of man. None of which is intended as a defense of either the sick joke or insanity but merely as an explanation of why the best horror films, like the best fairy tales, manage to be reactionary, **anarchistic**, and revolutionary all at the same time.

Insight

Is the phenomenon described here uniquely a product of the United States, or do all cultures share a love of horror movies? Do different cultures have different cravings for or tolerance of horror?

Vocabulary

status quo
existing state of affairs

sanctions
group actions to coerce a misbehaving member

remonstrance
earnest correction

anarchistic
in rebellion against authority

The **mythic** horror movie, like the sick joke, has a dirty job to do. It deliberately 70
appeals to all that is worst in us. It is **morbidity** unchained, our most base instincts
let free, our nastiest fantasies realized . . . and it all happens, fittingly enough, in
the dark. For those reasons, good liberals often shy away from horror films. For
myself, I like to see the most aggressive of them—*Dawn of the Dead,* for instance—
as lifting a trap door in the civilized **forebrain** and throwing a basket of raw meat 75
to the hungry alligators swimming around in that **subterranean** river beneath.

Why bother? Because it keeps them from getting out, man. It keeps them
down there and me up here. It was Lennon and McCartney who said that all you
need is love, and I would agree with that.

As long as you keep the gators fed. 80

Analyze Which of the following
cause-effect diagrams best illustrates
the essay? Why?

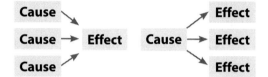

The first diagram best illustrates the essay because the author spends the majority
of the essay describing the ways our subconscious makes us crave scary movies.

Explain What is the main effect or main cause in the essay?

(AWV) The essay concludes that the repressed portion of our subconscious needs a
periodic outlet, which can be created by watching horror films.

Analyze Are you a fan of horror movies? How does your experience match or
counter Mr. King's opinion?

Answers will vary.

446

LO2 Writing a Cause-Effect Essay

Prewrite Start by thinking of a cause-effect relationship you're interested in. Do you wonder how most forest fires are started? Are you interested in the effects of jogging on the joints? List possible topics on the lines below.

Make a List

_____   _____

_____   _____

_____   _____

_____   _____

_____   _____

_____   _____

_____   _____

Choose one: Put a star next to the topic that you would most like to write about.

Research and Organize

Find out all you can about the topic you have chosen. Then fill in one of the diagrams below with details to include in your essay. Add more boxes if you need them.

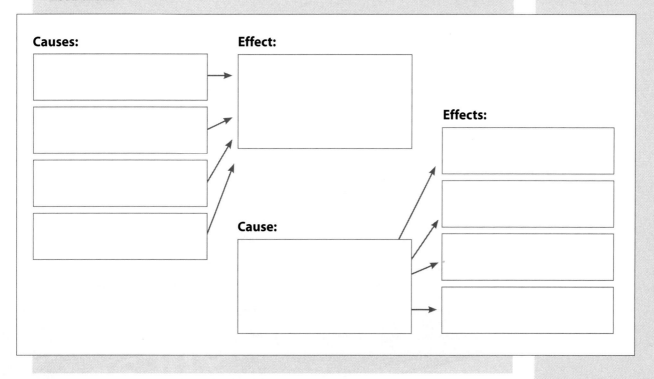

Causes:

Effect:

Cause:

Effects:

Opening Paragraph

The opening of your cause-effect essay should grab your reader's attention and clearly introduce the topic. It must present your claim that *this* cause results in *these* effects, or *these* causes yield *this* effect. Use one of the following strategies:

- **Ask a question:** "Have you ever wondered why some people like to jump from airplanes?"
- **Begin with action:** "At first, it seemed wonderful that morning to spot deer crossing the yard. Then we smelled smoke from the woods behind our house."
- **Connect to the reader:** "Though nowadays our worries about nuclear weapons are limited to suitcase bombs, there was a time when it seemed the entire nuclear arsenals of the U.S.A. and the Soviet Union might take flight, destroying all life on the planet."

Once you have your reader's attention, lead up to your thesis statement. Here is a formula for creating your thesis statement.

Main Point		**Causes or Effects**		**Thesis Statement**
A two-party system is virtually inevitable.	**+**	People naturally gravitate toward either liberalism or conservatism.	**=**	Because people naturally gravitate toward either liberalism or conservatism, a two-party system is virtually inevitable in a democracy.

Main Point

Causes or Effects _____

_____

_____

Thesis Statement

_____

_____

_____

Traits

As you draft your essay, focus on getting your ideas down, creating a three-part organizational structure. When you revise and edit, you will review these traits as well as voice, words, sentences, and conventions.

Feverpitch, 2010/used under license from www.shutterstock.com

Draft Create the middle paragraphs of your cause-effect essay.

Middle Paragraphs

In your middle paragraphs, support your thesis statement by fully explaining each cause and effect. You may write about a single cause with multiple effects, or multiple causes with a single effect. Here are two organizational patterns to consider:

Cause-Focused	Effect-Focused
Opening	Opening
Cause	Effect
Effect	Cause
Effect	Cause
Effect	Cause
Closing	Closing

Draft Create the closing paragraph of your cause-effect essay.

Closing Paragraph

The final paragraph of your essay should summarize the cause-effect relationship. You might also emphasize an important point or leave the reader with an intriguing final thought.

Draft Create a title for your essay, using one of the following strategies.

- **Start with the word "Why":** Why We Crave Horror Movies
- **Use a line from the essay:** Disembodied Strangers
- **Play with words:** Flirting with Disaster

Revise Take a break from your writing. Then come back to it with fresh eyes. If possible, have a friend or family member read the essay and make suggestions. Then review your writing with the following checklist. Keep polishing until you can check off each item in the list.

Ideas

☐ **1.** Is the cause-effect relationship clear?

☐ **2.** Do I cover all the important causes or effects of the main topic?

Organization

☐ **3.** Does my opening grab the reader's attention and present a clear thesis?

☐ **4.** Do the middle paragraphs fully explain all the causes or effects?

☐ **5.** Are the details presented in the best order?

☐ **6.** Does my ending summarize the cause-effect relationship and leave the reader with something more to think about?

Voice

☐ **7.** Is the voice both friendly and professional?

Edit Prepare a clean copy of your cause-effect essay and use the following checklist to look for errors. Continue working until you can check off each item in the list.

Words

☐ **1.** Have I used specific nouns and verbs? (See page 103.)

☐ **2.** Have I used more action verbs than "be" verbs? (See page 73.)

Sentences

☐ **3.** Have I varied the beginnings and lengths of sentences? (See pages 226–231.)

☐ **4.** Have I combined short choppy sentences? (See page 232.)

☐ **5.** Have I avoided shifts in sentences? (See page 278.)

☐ **6.** Have I avoided fragments and run-ons? (See pages 261–266, 270–271.)

Conventions

☐ **7.** Do I use correct verb forms (*he saw*, not *he seen*)? (See pages 320, 324.)

☐ **8.** Do my subjects and verbs agree (*she speaks*, not *she speak*)? (See pages 245–260.)

☐ **9.** Have I used the right words (*their, there, they're*)?

☐ **10.** Have I capitalized first words and proper nouns and adjectives? (See page 386.)

☐ **11.** Have I used commas after long introductory word groups? (See page 358.)

☐ **12.** Have I carefully checked my spelling?

"If you would persuade, you must appeal to interest rather than intellect."

—Benjamin Franklin

360b 2010/used with permission from www.shutterstock.com

38
Argument Essays

Anyone can spout an opinion. Some people can even support theirs with evidence. *Persuasion* goes a step further, however, connecting with the reader by addressing opposing viewpoints. It analyzes an issue from all sides before making a conclusion. This makes persuasion a tool of reasoned people seeking the truth, not just pressing their own agenda. Don't be surprised, then, if your opinion changes when reading an argument essay or when writing your own.

Learning Outcomes

LO1 Understand, read, and analyze argument essays.

LO2 Write your own argument essay.

What do you think?

Study the image and the quotation. What persuasive message does each communicate to you? What do they communicate together?

Answers will vary.

451

LO1 Understanding Argument Essays

Within this chapter you will find three example argument essays. Each is followed by questions and graphic organizers for analyzing the reading. At the end of the chapter are writing guidelines for creating an argument essay of your own.

SQ3R

When you read, become involved with the text by using the SQ3R approach.

Survey: Prepare by reading "About the Author," skimming the essay, and noting any vocabulary words.

Question: Ask yourself to predict what the writer hopes to convince you of.

Read: Read the essay, noting the value of supporting arguments and concessions the author makes.

Recite: Repeat aloud the main points of the argument.

Review: Answer the questions provided and use the graphic organizers to help you analyze the essay.

Essay List

"When Greed Gives Way to Giving"

Ana Veciana-Suarez shines a light on an unusual business person who upon retirement shared the wealth with everyone who worked for him.

"Shouldn't Men Have 'Choice' Too?"

In writing about the rights of men in unplanned pregnancies, Meghan Daum pursues a position in opposition to her own, in order to more fully understand the issue of abortion.

"In Praise of the F Word"

As a teacher in an adult-literacy program, Mary Sherry argues that by removing the possibility of a failing grade in public school, teachers and parents destine many students to fail in life.

Traits

As you read these selections, focus first on ideas. Then reread the beginning and ending and skim the middle, noting organization. Afterward, think about the voice of the author, and how it reflects the writer's personality, subject, and purpose.

About the Author

Ana Veciana-Suarez is a family columnist for The *Miami Herald*.

Ana Veciana-Suarez, "Giving Beyond Expectations Is All Too Rare," MIAMI HERALD, September 28, 1999. Reprinted by permission.

When Greed Gives Way to Giving
by Ana Veciana-Suarez

1   In the **flurry** of life, you probably missed this story. I almost did. And that would have been too bad.

    Over in Belleville, Minnesota, a 67-year-old man named Bob Thompson sold his road-building company for $422 million back in July. He did not, as we would

5   expect, buy himself a jet or an island, not even a new home. Instead, Thompson decided to share the wealth.

    He divided $128 million among his 550 workers. Some checks exceeded annual salaries. And for more than 80 people, the bonus went beyond their wildest expectations: They became millionaires. Thompson even included some retirees

10 and widows in his plan. What's more, he paid the taxes on those proceeds—about $25 million.

    Employees were so **flabbergasted** that the wife of an area manager tearfully said: "I think the commas are in the wrong place."

    The commas were right where they belonged. Thompson had made sure of

15 that, had made sure, too, that not one of the workers would lose their jobs in the buyout.

    I sat at the breakfast table stunned. I just don't know too many people or companies that would do something like that. Sure, many employers offer profit-sharing and stock-option plans. But outright giving? Nah.

20 Employees rarely share in the bounty when the big payoff comes. In fact, many end up losing their jobs, being demoted, seeking transfers or taking early retirement. Insecurity—or better yet, the concept of every man for himself—is a **verity** of work life in America.

    Yet, here is one man defying all the stereotypes. I search for clues in his

25 life, but find nothing out of the ordinary, nothing that stands out. He started the business in his basement with $3,500, supported by his schoolteacher wife. He has owned the same modest house for 37 years. His wood-paneled office has no

Vocabulary

flurry
a period of intense activity

flabbergast
stun with surprise

verity
a truth

Persian rugs or oil paintings, only photos of three children and five grandchildren. He admits to an indulgence or two: a Lincoln and an occasional Broadway show.

Yet, he possesses something as priceless as it is rare: generosity. And he seems to be sheepishly modest even about that. 30

"It's sharing good times, that's really all it is," he told a reporter. "I don't think you can read more into it. I'm a proud person. I wanted to go out a winner, and I wanted to go out doing the right thing."

We all want to do the right thing. But blessed by a **windfall**, would we have done as Thompson did? Maybe . . . I don't know . . . Honestly, I'm embarrassed to say I'm not sure I would have. 35

Perhaps, however, the more appropriate question is this: In our own more limited circumstances, do we share with others in the same spirit Thompson showed? Do we give beyond expectations? 40

For most of us, generosity comes with limits. It is, by and large, a sum without sacrifice, a respectable token. Some might say that Thompson's **munificence** was token-like. After all, the $153 million is less than a third of his $422 million payoff.

That kind of reasoning, however, misses the mark. Few of us give away even 10 percent, and even as our income increases, the tendency is not to share more but to buy more, to hoard more. Not Thompson. After finishing with his employees, he plans to continue giving away much of what's left of the $422 million. 45

I suspect he is on to something. In a society where success tends to be measured in what we can acquire, this guy instead is preaching and practicing the opposite. Success, he's telling us, is in the giving back. 50

He seems to have mastered what many of us have yet to understand: the difference between need and want, between the basic essentials and our **inchoate** desires. He has, by golly, defined ENOUGH.

Maybe that's all the wealth he needs. 55

Vocabulary

windfall
an unexpected gain, as if ripe fruit blown down from a tree

munificence
generosity

inchoate
imperfectly or only partially formed

Respond What do you think motivated Bob Thompson to give away so much from the sale of his business?

Answers will vary.

About the Author

Meghan Daum is an American author, essayist, and journalist who currently writes a weekly column for the *Los Angeles Times*.

Meghan Daum, "Shouldn't Men Have 'Choice' Too?" LOS ANGELES TIMES, December 10, 2005. Reprinted by permission of the author's agent, Janklow & Nesbit Associates.

Shouldn't Men Have "Choice" Too?
by Meghan Daum

1   For pro-choicers like myself, Supreme Court nominee Samuel A. Alito Jr.'s position regarding spousal consent for abortion seems like one more loose rock in the ongoing erosion of **Roe vs. Wade**. Even those of us who are too young to remember the pre-Roe era often see any threat to abortion rights as a threat to
5   our very destinies. We are, after all, the generation that grew up under **Title IX**, singing along to "Free to Be You and Me" (you know, the 1972 children's record where Marlo Thomas and Alan Alda remind us that mommies can be plumbers and boys can have dolls). When it comes to self-determination, we're as determined as it gets.

10   But even though I was raised believing in the **inviolability** of a woman's right to choose, the older I get, the more I wonder if this idea of choice is being fairly applied.

Most people now accept that women, especially teenagers, often make decisions regarding abortion based on educational and career goals and whether
15   the father of the unborn child is someone they want to hang around with for the next few decades. The "choice" in this equation is not only a matter of whether to carry an individual fetus to term but a question of what kind of life the woman wishes to lead.

But what about the kind of life men want to lead? On December 1, Dalton
20   Conley, director of the Center for Advanced Social Science Research at New York University, published an article on the **Op-Ed** page of the *New York Times* arguing that Alito's position on spousal consent did not go far enough.

Describing his own experience with a girlfriend who terminated a pregnancy against his wishes, Conley took some brave steps down the slippery slope of this
25   debate, suggesting that if a father is willing to assume full responsibility for a child not wanted by a mother, he should be able to obtain an **injunction** stopping her from having an abortion—and he should be able to do so regardless of whether or not he's married to her.

Conley freely acknowledges the many obvious **caveats** in this position—the
30   most **salient** being the fact that regardless of how "full" that male responsibility

Vocabulary

Roe vs. Wade
a landmark 1973 case in which the Supreme Court ruled that privacy protects a woman's right to choose abortion

Title IX
a law forbidding gender discrimination in educational programs

inviolability
the state of not being able to be violated or revoked

Op-Ed
a newspaper page "opposite the editorials" page

injunction
a court order

caveat
a cautionary exception

salient
significant or notable

might be, the physical burden of pregnancy and childbirth will always put most of the **onus** on women. But as much as I shudder at the idea of a man, husband or not, obtaining an injunction telling me what I can or cannot do with my own body, I would argue that it is Conley who has not gone far enough.

Since we're throwing around radical ideas about abortion rights, let me raise this question: If abortion is to remain legal and relatively unrestricted—and I believe it should—why shouldn't men have the right during at least the first **trimester** of pregnancy to terminate their legal and financial rights and responsibilities to the child?

As Conley laments, the law does not currently allow for men to protect the futures of the fetuses they help create. What he doesn't mention—indeed, no one ever seems to—is the degree to which men also cannot protect their own futures. The way the law is now, a man who gets a woman pregnant is not only powerless to force her to terminate the pregnancy, he also has a complete legal obligation to support that child for at least 18 years.

In other words, although women are able to take control of their futures by choosing from at least a small range of options—abortion, adoption, or keeping the child—a man can be forced to be a father to a child he never wanted and cannot financially support. I even know of cases in which the woman **absolves** the man of responsibility, only to have the courts demand payment anyway. That takes the notion of "choice" very far from anything resembling equality.

I realize I've just alienated feminists (among whose ranks I generally count myself) as well as pro-lifers, neither of whom are always above **platitudes** such as "You should have kept your pants on." But that reasoning is by now as **reductive** as suggesting that a rape victim "asked for it." Yes, people often act irresponsibly and yes, abortion should be avoided whenever possible. But just as women should not be punished for choosing to terminate a pregnancy, men should not be punished when those women choose not to.

One problem, of course, is that the child is likely to bear the **brunt** of whatever punishment remains to be **doled** out. A father who terminates his rights, although not technically a deadbeat dad, has still helped create a kid who is not fully supported. And (in case you were wondering) there are dozens of other holes in my theory as well: What if a husband wants to terminate his rights—should that be allowed? What if a father is underage and wants to terminate, but his parents forbid him? Should a father's decision-making time be limited to the first trimester? Should couples on first dates discuss their positions on the matter? Should Internet dating profiles let men check a box saying "will waive parental rights" next to the box indicating his astrological sign?

There's also the danger that my idea is not just a slippery slope but a major mudslide on the way to Conley's idea. If a man can legally **dissociate** himself from a pregnancy, some will argue, why couldn't he also bind himself to it and force it to term? That notion horrifies me, just as my plan probably horrifies others. But that doesn't mean these ideas aren't worth discussing. Though it may be hard to find an adult male who's sufficiently undiplomatic to admit out loud that he'd like to have the option I'm proposing, let alone potentially take it, I know more than a few parents of teenage boys who lose sleep over the prospect of their sons landing

35
40
45
50
55
60
65
70
75

Traits

The ideas in this essay are especially strong because of the way that they seem to surprise even the writer. Daum follows a logical argument to conclusions she herself might not wish. How does this use of logic strengthen or weaken her persuasive power?

Vocabulary

onus
obligation

trimester
a three-month period of time

absolve
set free from an obligation

platitude
a dull, unoriginal truism

reductive
explained in an overly simplistic manner

brunt
the main force of a blow

dole
portion out bit by bit

dissociate
separate from association with

in the kind of trouble from which they'll have no power to **extricate** themselves.

And although the notion of women "tricking" men into fatherhood now sounds **arcane** and sexist, we'd be blind not to recognize the extent to which some women
80 are capable of tricking themselves into thinking men will stick around, despite all evidence to the contrary. Allowing men to legally (if not always gracefully) bow out of fatherhood would, at the very least, start a conversation for which we haven't yet found the right words.

Actually, there's one word we've had all along: choice. We just need to broaden
85 its definition.

Vocabulary

extricate
free from entanglements

arcane
obscure

Analyze In your own words, state the argument Ms. Daum is making.

(AWV) The ruling of Roe vs. Wade allows women to take control of their futures in regard to childbirth, but the ruling provides no protections for men to decide their own futures. The author argues that, in the spirit of fairness and equality, men should be provided the choice to terminate their legal and financial responsibilities to children at an early stage in pregnancy.

Weight It List the essay's main supporting details and concessions.

Supporting Details:
- If women are afforded the right to choose, men should have the same right.
- The current law leaves men who get women pregnant powerless to force a termination.
- The law also forces men to financially support the child for 18 years.
- Even if the woman absolves the man, the courts demand payment.

Concessions:
- Women have to shoulder the physical burden of pregnancy and childbirth.
- People often act irresponsibly.
- Abortion should be avoided when possible.
- A child will be harmed by a father who terminates his rights.
- Men could potentially force the woman to have the baby.

About the Author

Mary Sherry is a teacher of adult literacy programs. She lives near Minneapolis, Minnesota.

Mary Sherry, "In Praise of the F Word." From Newsweek, May 6, 1991. Copyright (c) 1991 Newsweek, Inc. All rights reserved. Used by permission and protected by the Copyright Laws of the United States. The printing, copying, redistribution, or retransmission of the Material without express written permission is prohibited.

In Praise of the F Word
by Mary Sherry

Tens of thousands of 18-year-olds will graduate this year and be handed meaningless diplomas. These diplomas won't look any different from those awarded their luckier classmates. Their validity will be questioned only when their employers discover that these graduates are semiliterate. [1]

Eventually a fortunate few will find their way into educational-repair shops—adult-literacy programs, such as the one where I teach basic grammar and writing. There, high-school graduates and high-school dropouts pursuing graduate-equivalency certificates will learn the skills they should have learned in school. They will also discover they have been cheated by our educational system. [5]

As I teach, I learn a lot about our schools. Early in each session I ask my students to write about an unpleasant experience they had in school. No writers' block here! "I wish someone would have made me stop doing drugs and made me study." "I liked to party, and no one seemed to care." "I was a good kid and didn't cause any trouble, so they just passed me along even though I didn't read and couldn't write." And so on. [15]

I am your basic do-gooder, and prior to teaching this class I blamed the poor **academic** skills our kids have today on drugs, divorce, and other **impediments** to concentration necessary for doing well in school. But, as I rediscover each time I walk into the classroom, before a teacher can expect students to concentrate, he has to get their attention, no matter what distractions may be at hand. There are many ways to do this, and they have much to do with teaching style. However, if style alone won't do it, there is another way to show who holds the winning hand in the classroom. That is to reveal the **trump** card of failure. [20]

I will never forget a teacher who played that card to get the attention of one of my children. Our youngest, a **world-class** charmer, did little to develop his intellectual talents but always got by. Until Mrs. Stifter. [25]

Our son was a high-school senior when he had her for English. "He sits in

Vocabulary

academic
having to do with learning in a school setting

impediment
obstruction or hindrance

trump
in some card games, a suit that wins over all other suits

world-class
capable of competing against others from all over the world

the back of the room talking to his friends," she told me. "Why don't you move
him to the front row?" I urged, believing the embarrassment would get him to
settle down. Mrs. Stifter looked at me steely-eyed over her glasses. "I don't move
seniors," she said. "I flunk them." I was **flustered**. Our son's academic life flashed
before my eyes. No teacher had ever threatened him with that before. I regained
my **composure** and managed to say that I thought she was right. By the time
I got home I was feeling pretty good about this. It was a radical approach for
these times, but, well, why not? "She's going to flunk you," I told my son. I did not
discuss it any further. Suddenly English became a priority in his life. He finished
out the semester with an A.

I know one example doesn't make a case, but at night I see a parade of
students who are angry and resentful for having been passed along until they
could no longer even pretend to keep up. Of average intelligence or better, they
eventually quit school, concluding they were too dumb to finish. "I should have
been held back," is a comment I hear frequently. Even sadder are those students
who are high-school graduates who say to me after a few weeks of class, "I don't
know how I ever got a high-school diploma."

Passing students who have not mastered the work cheats them and the
employers who expect graduates to have basic skills. We excuse this dishonest
behavior by saying kids can't learn if they come from terrible environments. No
one seems to stop to think that—no matter what environments they come from—
most kids don't put school first on their list unless they perceive something is at
stake. They'd rather be sailing.

Many students I see at night could give expert testimony on unemployment,
chemical dependency, abusive relationships. In spite of these difficulties, they
have decided to make education a priority. They are motivated by the desire for a
better job or the need to hang on to the one they've got. They have a healthy fear
of failure.

People of all ages can rise above their problems, but they need to have a reason
to do so. Young people generally don't have the maturity to value education in the
same way my adult students value it. But fear of failure, whether economic or
academic, can motivate both. Flunking as a regular policy has just as much merit
today as it did two generations ago. We must review the threat of flunking and
see it as it really is—a positive teaching tool. It is an expression of confidence by
both teachers and parents that the students have the ability to learn the material
presented to them. However, making it work again would take a dedicated, caring
conspiracy between teachers and parents. It would mean facing the tough reality
that passing kids who haven't learned the material—while it might save them
grief for the short term—dooms them to long-term illiteracy. It would mean that
teachers would have to follow through on their threats, and parents would have
to stand behind them, knowing their children's best interests are indeed at stake.
This means no more doing Scott's assignments for him because he might fail. No
more passing Jodi because she's such a nice kid.

WAC

Imagine that you were flunking a class. Would you prefer to have the instructor give you a failing grade or let you just barely pass? What effects would either choice have on your future?

Vocabulary

fluster
to make someone confused or agitated

composure
calmness

chemical dependency
need for alcohol or drugs

Summarize Write a one-sentence summary of each paragraph in this essay.

1. _A student can be awarded a high school diploma without being fully literate._

2. _Adult literacy programs are necessary for students who have been cheated by a flawed educational system._

3. _Students don't hold back when writing about unpleasant school experiences._

4. _A teacher must gain the attention of the students before they will learn, and the best way to do that is to use a trump card—failure._

5. _A former teacher of the author's son introduced this idea._

6. _The teacher threatened to flunk her son, and it made him worker harder._

7. _Too many teachers pass students even if they didn't show any aptitude in class, and students later regret passing._

8. _Passing students who have not mastered basic skills cheats students and employers._

9. _Students who fear failure make school a priority._

10. _Fear of failing motivates students of all ages, meaning flunking those who are not proficient has merit._

Analyze Which paragraphs do you believe make up the opening? The middle? The closing? List the numbers for each section, and then compare your answers with a fellow student's and discuss each other's reasoning.

Opening paragraphs: _____

Middle paragraphs: _____

Closing paragraphs: _____

L○2 Writing an Argument Essay

Prewrite To select a topic for an argument essay, start by making a cluster of subjects you have opinions about.

Make a Cluster

Add more circled spaces and lines as needed. Continue clustering until an idea intrigues you. Put a star next to that idea.

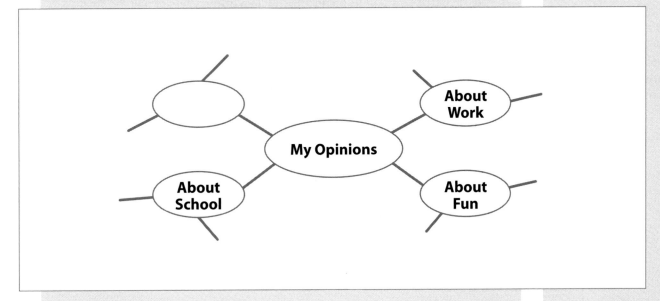

Freewrite

Prepare to write your argument essay by freewriting. Write until you run out of ideas for supporting your position. Then freewrite about arguments *against* your position. (Continue on your own paper.)

_____

_____

_____

_____

_____

_____

_____

_____

Opening Paragraph(s)

The opening of an argument essay should catch your reader's attention, provide any necessary background information about the topic, and then make your main point, or thesis statement. Use one of the following strategies:

- **Make a logical claim:** "Compare the food pyramid with the pyramid of agricultural subsidies, and you can see our priorities are all wrong."
- **Present yourself as an authority:** "In a dozen years of training small dogs, I've never seen a behavior problem that couldn't be solved by a disciplined owner."
- **Appeal to the reader's emotion:** "No child should have to feel ashamed for wearing unfashionable clothing."

Once you have your reader's attention, lead up to your thesis statement. Here is a formula for creating your thesis statement.

Your Topic		**Your Feeling About It**		**Thesis Statement**
China's cautious attitude toward the West	**+**	It's understandable given Great Britain's colonial aggression.	**=**	China's cautious attitude toward the West is understandable given Great Britain's colonial aggression.

Your Topic

Your Feeling About It _____

_____

_____

Thesis Statement

_____

_____

_____

Middle Paragraphs

In your middle paragraphs, defend your thesis statement by providing supporting reasons. Follow the approach you opened with, making a logical claim, speaking as an authority, or appealing to your reader's emotion or feelings. To strengthen your position, also address opposing viewpoints and make concessions if necessary.

Closing Paragraph(s)

Your closing should make a firm conclusion based on the support presented in your middle paragraphs. You may also call the reader to action or point out related subjects for discussion.

Revise Take a break from your writing. Then come back to it with fresh eyes. Also ask a friend or family member to read the essay and make suggestions. Finally, review your writing with the following checklist. Keep polishing until you can check off each item in the list.

Ideas

☐ **1.** Have I presented a clear position on an interesting topic?

☐ **2.** Do I include the most persuasive reasons for taking this position?

Organization

☐ **3.** Does the opening grab the reader's attention and state my position?

☐ **4.** Do the middle paragraphs convincingly present support, address opposing viewpoints, and make necessary concessions?

☐ **5.** Does the ending include a firm conclusion and call the reader to action if appropriate?

Voice

☐ **6.** Is my voice authoritative and convincing?

Edit Prepare a clean copy of your argument essay and use the following checklist to look for errors. Continue working until you can check off each item in the list.

Words

☐ **1.** Have I used specific nouns and verbs? (See page 103.)

☐ **2.** Have I used more action verbs than "be" verbs? (See page 73.)

Sentences

☐ **3.** Have I varied the beginnings and lengths of sentences? (See pages 226–231.)

☐ **4.** Have I combined short choppy sentences? (See page 232.)

☐ **5.** Have I avoided shifts in sentences? (See page 278.)

☐ **6.** Have I avoided fragments and run-ons? (See pages 261–266, 270–271.)

Conventions

☐ **7.** Do I use correct verb forms (*he saw,* not *he seen*)? (See pages 320, 324.)

☐ **8.** Do my subjects and verbs agree (*she speaks,* not *she speak*)? (See pages 245–260.)

☐ **9.** Have I used the right words (*their, there, they're*)?

☐ **10.** Have I capitalized first words and proper nouns and adjectives? (See page 386.)

☐ **11.** Have I used commas after long introductory word groups? (See page 358.)

☐ **12.** Have I carefully checked my spelling?

Index

M

N

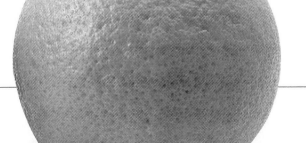

HomeStudio, 2010/used under license from www.shutterstock.com

Naira,2010 / Used under license from Shutterstock.com

Simple predicate, 196, 197

Simple sentence, 211–213

    with compound subjects, 214–215

    with compound verbs, 216–217

    direct/indirect object of, 212

    modifiers in, 212

Simple subject, 196, 197

Singular noun, 286–287, 368

Singular pronoun, 252–256, 304–305

Singular verb, 246, 248, 250

Slippery slope, 173

Smith, P. Gregory, 410, 416–418

Solon, 245

Sources, research, 41

Southey, Robert, 73

Spatial order, 44

Specific nouns, 72, 73, 103

Specific verbs, 73, 103

SQ3R

    argument essay and, 452

    cause-effect essay and, 438

    comparison-contrast essay and, 424

    narrative essay and, 398

    process essay and, 410

Staples, Brent, 398, 399–400, 438, 441–442

Statistics, as supporting information, 169

Stein, Gertrude, 2

Steinbeck, John, 54

STRAP strategy, 18–19, 36–37

Strategies

    for avoiding writer's block, 53

    for choosing a topic, 39

    for college-level assignments, 17–22

    for editing, 76

    for gathering details, 40

    for organizing supporting details, 46–48

    for reading, 9, 10–13, 17–22

    STRAP, 18–19, 36–37

    writing-to-learn, 3

Straw man, 155

Structure, 54, 184–185. *See also* Drafting; Organization

"Study Says Flirtatious Women Get Fewer Raises" (Jones), 438, 439–440

Subject, 162

    agreement of verb and, 118–119, 120, 245–255

    complete, 196, 197

    compound, 119, 198, 199, 248–249, 252

    delayed, 264

    double, 258, 259, 302–303

    gerund as, 198, 199

    implied, 131, 162, 196, 262, 264

    infinitive as, 198, 199

    inverted order of predicate and, 196

    noun clause as, 198–199, 208–209

    simple, 196, 197

    STRAP strategy and, 18–19, 36–37

Subject-to-subject pattern of organization, 424

Subject-verb agreement, 118–119, 120, 245–255

Subjective pronoun, 258

Subordinate clause, 348

Subordinating conjunction, 234–235, 348–349

    in adverbial clause, 230

    comma splice and, 268–269

    in complex sentence, 220–221

    run-on sentences and, 270–271

Summarizing, 13

Superlative adjective, 332–333

Superlative adverb, 338–339

Supporting information, 40–43, 183

    in argument paragraph, 168, 169

    in cause-effect paragraph, 155

    in classification paragraph, 113

    in comparison-contrast paragraph, 141

    levels of detail and, 58–59

    in narrative paragraph, 99

    organizing, 44–48

    in process paragraph, 127

Synonyms, 73

Reading-Writing Connection

To succeed in college, students must approach writing and reading not as assignments to complete, but rather as opportunities to learn and to think. In this way, writing and reading are means to an end, rather than ends unto themselves. Students also must appreciate the unique relationship between the two tasks. Writing aids reading; reading provides ideas for writing.

Writing to Learn (page 2-3)

Writing to learn is ungraded writing, carried out to help students understand concepts introduced in lectures, discussions, lab work, and readings. Essentially, writing to learn consists of having students write freely about the subjects and concepts they are studying. In these writings, students can explore topics under discussion, argue for or against particular points of view, reflect on their work on specific projects, and so on. Writing as a learning strategy is part of the larger writing-across-the-curriculum movement.

Writing to Share Learning (page 4)

The focus of *WRITE 1* and *WRITE 2* is writing to share learning—the paragraphs, essays, and reports students turn in for evaluation. Both texts cover the writing process, writing paragraphs, writing essays, the conventions of the language, and so on. While writing to learn helps students explore and form their thoughts, writing to share learning helps them clarify and fine-tune them. In this way, both types of writing stimulate thinking and learning.

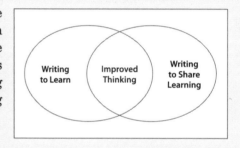

Reading to Learn (pages 8-13)

Reading to learn is an approach that leads to more productive academic reading. It includes, among other things, previewing the text, reading the text, making annotations, engaging in exploratory writing during the reading, and summarizing the text after the reading. Employing such strategies helps students take control of their college-level reading.

Reading Graphics (pages 14-15)

In college-level texts, significant portions of information is communicated via charts, tables, and diagrams. As a result, students need to understand how to read a graphic: scanning it, studying the specific parts, considering and questioning the image, and reflecting on its effectiveness. This skill is often overlooked in developmental and introductory courses.

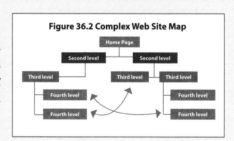

Figure 36.2 Complex Web Site Map

Understanding Assignments (pages 18-19)

Students, too often, approach their writing and reading assignments without the proper forethought, and as a result, they don't carry out their work in the appropriate way. So students must be made aware that understanding the dynamics of each assignment is critical: Are they expected to inform or to persuade in a writing assignment? Who is the intended audience in the material they are reading? *WRITE 1* and *WRITE 2* introduce students to the STRAP strategy, which helps them identify the dynamics of both writing and reading assignments. (*See the back of this card.*)

Students use the STRAP strategy to analyze their writing and reading assignments. The strategy consists of answering questions about these five features: *subject, type, role, audience,* and *purpose*. Once they answer the questions, they'll be ready to get to work. This chart shows how the strategy works:

For Writing Assignments		For Reading Assignments
What specific topic should I write about?	**Subject**	What specific topic does the reading address?
What form of writing *(essay, article)* will I use?	**Type**	What form *(essay, text chapter, article)* does the reading take?
What position *(student, citizen, employee)* should I assume?	**Role**	What position *(student, responder, concerned individual)* does the writer assume?
Who is the intended reader?	**Audience**	Who is the intended reader?
What is the goal *(to inform, to persuade)* of the writing?	**Purpose**	What is the goal of the material?

Using the Traits (pages 20-21)

Students sometimes struggle to understand why a text works or does not work. Without this understanding, they have a hard time developing their own writing, discussing the writing of their peers, and/or analyzing reading material. *WRITE 1* and *WRITE 2* use the traits of writing as a guide to effective prose. A working knowledge of the traits helps students become more thoughtfully involved in their writing and reading. (Traits side notes appear throughout the text.)

- **Ideas** The main points and supporting details in writing and reading material
- **Organization** The overall structure of the material
- **Voice** The personality of the writing—how the writer speaks to the reader
- **Word Choice** The writer's use of words and phrases
- **Sentence Fluency** The flow of the sentences
- **Conventions** The correctness or accuracy of the language
- **Design** The appearance of the writing

Using Graphic Organizers (pages 22-23)

Struggling students find visuals such as graphic organizers helpful when they are writing and learning. Graphic organizers work well for collecting details during the prewriting stage; they also work well when students are gleaning key concepts and ideas from essays and articles they are assigned to read.

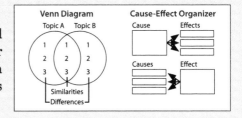

Further Readings

To learn more about writing to learn and the traits of writing, refer to the following publications.

Collins, James L. *Strategies for Struggling Writers.* Guilford Press, 1998.
Mayher John S., Nancy Lester, and Gordon M. Pradl. *Learning to Write / Writing to Learn.* Heinemann, 1983.
Spandel, Vickie. *Creating Writers Through 6-Trait Writing.* Allyn & Bacon, 2008.

Writing Process

Educators Donald M. Murray and Donald H. Graves led a group of others in shifting the focus of writing from product to process. They explored the "moves" that different writers made at different stages as they developed a piece of writing. Though the steps in the process have had various names throughout time, the terms used in *WRITE 1* and *WRITE 2* are prewriting, writing, revising, editing, and publishing.

Prewriting

This phase begins when the writer first starts to think about an idea. Prewriting may begin with a formal writing assignment (as is often the case in academic writing), or it may begin with inspiration, or even a niggling idea that won't let go. During prewriting, the writer focuses on ideas and organization and does the following:

- **Analyzes the rhetorical situation**—the writer's role, the subject of the writing, the purpose, the medium or form, the audience, and the context. In terms of academic writing, this task involves understanding the assignment.

- **Selects a topic** by brainstorming possible ideas and narrowing them down to a specific topic that fits all parts of the rhetorical situation.

- **Gathers information about the topic** through personal reflection, questioning, and research. At this stage, graphic organizers, lists, and notes help writers generate or discover ideas and keep track of them.

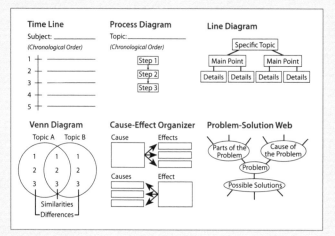

- **Finds a focus,** deciding which specific thought or feeling about the topic that the writer wants to explore. Finding a focus involves sizing the project, making sure it is not too large or too small to be covered in the form required.

- **Organizes details** by creating a quick list or a more formal topic or sentence outline. The organizational structure is often dictated by the writer's purpose (to inform, persuade, entertain, reflect) and by the form of the writing.

Writing

This phase involves creating a first draft—pouring words onto a page or into a computer. The writing phase is informed and guided by the prewriting work, but the writer should feel free to innovate and experiment. At this phase, the writer should focus on ideas, organization, and voice while creating a three-part structure:

- **Opening:** The opening should catch the reader's attention and identify the writer's subject and focus. In a paragraph, the opening is the topic sentence. In an essay, the opening is the first paragraph or so, providing background and introducing the topic.

- **Middle:** The middle should support the opening. In a paragraph, the middle consists of sentences of different levels, presenting main points and supporting details. In an essay, the middle consists of paragraphs, each of which focuses on a main point and develops it.

- **Closing:** The closing should bring the writing to an effective end, perhaps by revisiting the opening, by summing up the main points, or by providing an important final thought. In a paragraph, the closing is a final sentence, and in an essay, it is a paragraph.

Revising

Revising involves making large-scale changes to writing, improving it in the most important ways. A peer review at this stage can help the writer discover what is working and what could work better in a specific piece of writing. During revising, the writer (and peer reviewers) should focus on the "Big Three" traits: ideas, organization, and voice. There are four basic revising moves:

- **Adding**—providing answers to some of the 5 W's and H, or adding engaging, surprising, or varied details to bolster a claim
- **Cutting**—removing ideas that are off topic, redundant, obvious, or otherwise unhelpful in conveying the writer's message
- **Rearranging**—putting it in a more effective order or creating a smoother flow of thought, often using transition words and phrases
- **Rewriting**—experimenting to find the best way to express each idea, and reworking parts that did not convey the message in the first draft

Editing

Editing involves making small-scale changes to improve style and correctness. During editing, the writer should focus on the "Little Three" traits:

- **Words**—using specific nouns, active verbs, and modifiers that clarify, and avoiding wordiness, deadwood, and clichés
- **Sentences**—varying sentence beginnings, lengths, and style
- **Conventions**—correcting punctuation, capitalization, usage, spelling, and grammar

Correction Marks	
⌐	delete
d̲	capitalize
∅	lowercase
∧	insert
⌃	add comma
? ⌃	add question mark
word ∧	add word
⊙	add period
⬭	spelling
⎍	switch

Publishing

Publishing is simply the act of sharing writing, whether in an official publication or simply by reading it aloud to classmates or family members. Publishing is the step in which writing becomes true communication, the ideas in the writer's mind entering the minds of a real audience.

A Recursive Process

Writing rarely moves straight forward through this process. Instead, writers in one stage may go back to a previous stage, or jump ahead to a later one. The needs of the rhetorical situation dictate the order of steps.

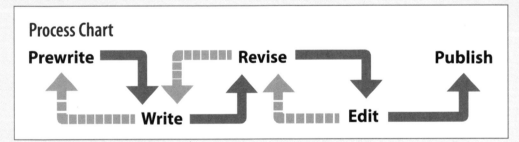

Process Chart

Prewrite → Write → Revise → Edit → Publish

Further Readings

For further readings into the writing process, see the following publications.

Graves, Donald H. *Writing: Teachers & Children at Work.* Heinemann, 2003.
Murray, Donald M. *Learning by Teaching.* Boyton/Cook Heinemann, 1982.
VanderMey, Randall et al. *COMP: Write.* Wadsworth Cengage Learning, 2010.

History of the Traits of Writing

The writing traits date back to the 1960s, when researcher Paul Diederich gathered a group of 50 professionals to determine what elements make up strong writing. In reviewing numerous student papers, the group uncovered a common pattern of characteristics, or traits, that made some papers more effective than others. Years later a group of teachers in Beaverton, Oregon, and Missoula, Montana, replicated Diederich's work and settled on a similar set of traits. Since then, the traits—ideas, organization, voice, word choice, sentence fluency, correctness—have become a cornerstone of writing instruction in schools throughout the world. *WRITE 1* and *WRITE 2* describe the six traits in detail, as well as adding a seventh trait—appropriate design.

The Traits of Writing

Strong Ideas

Good writing starts with an interesting idea. A writer should include plenty of effective ideas and details in his or her writing. And all of the information needs to hold the reader's interest.

Logical Organization

Effective writing has a clear overall structure—with a beginning, a middle, and an ending. Each paragraph should have a topic sentence, and transitions should link the ideas.

Fitting Voice

In the best writing, the writer's voice comes through. Voice is a writer's unique way of saying things. It shows that he or she cares about the writing. Furthermore, voice should fit the form. A personal essay should convey a different voice than a formal expository essay.

Well-Chosen Words

In strong writing, nouns and verbs are specific and clear, and modifiers add important information. The word choice should also fit the purpose and audience.

Smooth Sentences

The sentences in good writing should read smoothly from one to the next. Sentence variety gives the writing flow and energy, while each sentence carries the meaning of the essay or article.

Correct Copy

Strong writing is easy to read because it follows the conventions or rules of the language.

Appropriate Design

The design should follow the guidelines established by the instructor.

Connecting the Process and the Traits

The writing process makes writing easy by breaking the job into five recursive steps. The traits identify the key elements to consider at each step. Together the process and the traits help writers assess and improve their writing. The first three traits—ideas, organization, and voice—deal with big issues and thus dominate the early stages of the writing process (prewriting and writing). Meanwhile, words, sentences, conventions, and design become important later in the process (revising, editing, and publishing). See how the process and traits connect in the chart below.

Process	Traits
Prewriting	**Ideas:** selecting a topic, collecting details about it, forming a thesis **Organization:** arranging the details **Voice:** establishing your stance (objective, personal)
Writing	**Ideas:** connecting your thoughts and information **Organization:** following your planning **Voice:** sounding serious, sincere, interested, . . .
Revising	**Ideas:** reviewing for clarity and completeness **Organization:** reviewing for structure/arrangement of ideas **Voice:** reviewing for appropriate tone
Editing	**Word choice:** checking for specific nouns, verbs, and modifiers **Sentences:** checking for smoothness and variety **Conventions:** checking for correctness
Publishing	**Design:** evaluating the format

Traits Across the Spectrum

The writing traits work well with all writing forms and disciplines. Each discipline has its own specific ideas and organizational structures that writers should follow. And any form of writing benefits from strong words, smooth sentences, correctness, and effective design.

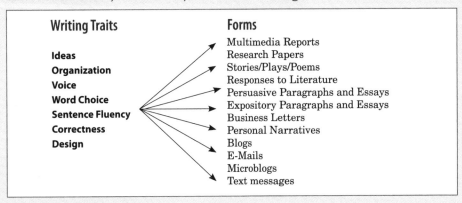

Writing Traits

Ideas
Organization
Voice
Word Choice
Sentence Fluency
Correctness
Design

Forms

Multimedia Reports
Research Papers
Stories/Plays/Poems
Responses to Literature
Persuasive Paragraphs and Essays
Expository Paragraphs and Essays
Business Letters
Personal Narratives
Blogs
E-Mails
Microblogs
Text messages

Further Readings

For further readings into the traits of writing, see the following publications.

Diederich, Paul B. *Measuring Growth in English*. National Council of Teachers of English, 1974.
VanderMey, Randall et al. *COMP: Write*. Wadsworth Cengage Learning, 2010.

Paragraph Patterns

Before writers can throw themselves into the drafting stage, they must first find a focus and consider the various patterns of organization. In college-level writing, students will need to introduce their focus in the form of a thesis statement (or in a topic sentence if they are writing a paragraph). A strong thesis statement states a particular feeling, feature, or part of a specific topic.

Forming a Thesis Statement

| A specific topic | + | A particular feeling, feature, or part | = | An effective thesis statement or topic sentence |

Once students establish a thesis, they should identify an appropriate pattern of organization to organize the information that supports it. As a result, students will begin drafting with a sense of purpose, focus, and organization.

Patterns of Organization

- Use **chronological order** (time) when you are sharing a personal experience, telling how something happened, or explaining how to do something.
- Use **spatial order** (location) for descriptions, arranging information from left to right, top to bottom, from the edge to the center, and so on.
- Use **order of importance** when you are taking a stand or arguing for or against something. Either arrange your reasons from most important to least important or the other way around.
- Use **deductive organization** if you want to follow your thesis statement with basic information—supporting reasons, examples, and facts.
- Use **inductive organization** when you want to present specific details first and conclude with your thesis statement.
- Use **compare-contrast organization** when you want to show how one topic is different from and similar to another one.

Choosing a Pattern of Organization

How do students decide on an appropriate pattern of organization? Here are two strategies they can use:

1. **Study the thesis statement or topic sentence.** It will indicate how to organize the ideas.

2. **Review the information or research gathered during prewriting.** Decide which ideas support the thesis and arrange them according to the appropriate method of organization.

Forming a Meaningful Whole

A meaningful whole in writing means the writer connects all of his or her thoughts and feelings about a specific topic into a complete draft—one with clear beginning, middle, and ending parts. Forming a meaningful whole for a paragraph means including a topic sentence, body sentences, and a closing sentence. For an essay, it means including an opening part (including a thesis statement), a number of supporting paragraphs, and a closing paragraph.

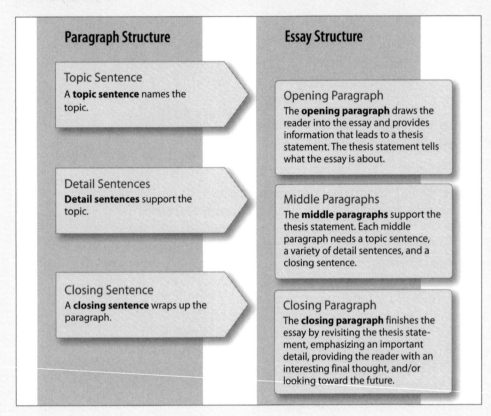

Paragraph Structure

Topic Sentence
A **topic sentence** names the topic.

Detail Sentences
Detail sentences support the topic.

Closing Sentence
A **closing sentence** wraps up the paragraph.

Essay Structure

Opening Paragraph
The **opening paragraph** draws the reader into the essay and provides information that leads to a thesis statement. The thesis statement tells what the essay is about.

Middle Paragraphs
The **middle paragraphs** support the thesis statement. Each middle paragraph needs a topic sentence, a variety of detail sentences, and a closing sentence.

Closing Paragraph
The **closing paragraph** finishes the essay by revisiting the thesis statement, emphasizing an important detail, providing the reader with an interesting final thought, and/or looking toward the future.

Levels of Detail

College writing requires students use a certain level of depth in their writing. When they make a point, they should fully explain it with specific examples and details before they move to the next point. The process of making important points and supporting them with details is at the core of most writing. To write with depth, students should include different levels of detail. Here are three basic levels:

- **Level 1:** A **controlling sentence** (usually a topic sentence) names a topic or makes a main point.
- **Level 2:** A **clarifying sentence** explains a level 1 sentence.
- **Level 3:** A **completing sentence** adds details to complete the point.

Exceptional writers may add a fourth level of detail, elaborating on the point with anecdotes, examples, quotations, and so on.

Teaching Complete Sentences

Students learn less from worksheets about identifying and correcting sentences than from writing and correcting their own sentences. As a result, many of the activities in this book prompt students to write their own simple, compound, and complex sentences, to create their own prepositional and participial phrases, and so on. Real writing is key.

Subjects and Verbs

At base, every sentence is the connection between a subject and verb. The instruction in the "Sentence Basics" chapter thus focuses on subjects and verbs, and then on special types of subjects and special types of verbs. The other words in the sentence either complete these words (as is the case with direct and indirect objects and object complements) or modify them.

Adjectives and Adverbs

Adjectives, of course, modify nouns and words that function as nouns. Adverbs modify verbs, adjectives, and other adverbs or words that function as such. These definitions might seem a bit esoteric to students, so instead of focusing on definitions, focus on function. Adjectives and adverbs answer basic questions.

Adjective Questions	Adverb Questions
Which?	*How?*
What kind of?	*When?*
How many?/How much?	*Where?*
	Why?
	To what degree?
	How often?/How long?

Impress on students that words that answer these questions are functioning as adjectives or adverbs. These questions become important not so much for identifying words and phrases in writing, but for helping students expand their sentences and create deeper, more thought writing.

Simple, Compound, and Complex Sentences

A simple sentence is a subject and a verb that express a complete thought. A compound sentence is a pair of simple sentences joined with a comma and a coordinating conjunction *(and, but, or, nor, for, so, yet.)* The conjunction coordinates the sentences by showing they are of equal importance. A complex sentence is a pair of simple sentences joined with a subordinating conjunction. The conjunction subordinates one sentence to another by making one sentence into a dependent clause.

The chapter "Simple, Compound, and Complex Sentences" goes into detail about these sentence structures, giving students practice forming each type. Students should then apply their learning in the writing they are doing elsewhere.

Subordinating Conjunctions	
after	so that
although	that
as	though
as if	till
as long as	unless
because	until
before	when
even though	whenever
if	where
in order that	whereas
provided that	while
since	

Avoiding Sentence Fragments

A sentence must have a subject and verb and must express a complete thought. To check sentences, have students find the subject (single underline) and the verb (double underline) and then determine if the words express a complete thought. A fragment is missing one or more of these features, but it can be fixed by supplying what is missing.

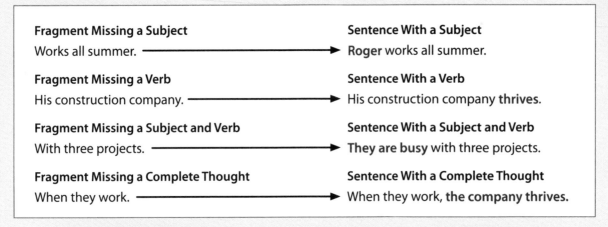

Fragment Missing a Subject
Works all summer. ⟶ **Sentence With a Subject**
Roger works all summer.

Fragment Missing a Verb
His construction company. ⟶ **Sentence With a Verb**
His construction company **thrives**.

Fragment Missing a Subject and Verb
With three projects. ⟶ **Sentence With a Subject and Verb**
They are busy with three projects.

Fragment Missing a Complete Thought
When they work. ⟶ **Sentence With a Complete Thought**
When they work, **the company thrives**.

Note: When a subject and verb are present but a complete thought is not, usually the words are a dependent clause. A dependent clause begins either with a subordinating conjunction *(after, because, though, etc.)* or with a relative pronoun *(who, which, that)*.

Avoiding Run-On Sentences and Comma Splices

Just as fragments can result from splitting up a complex sentence, run-ons and comma splices can result from incorrectly creating a compound sentence. A run-on is a pair of sentences joined without a comma and coordinating conjunction. A comma splice occurs when only a comma is used to join sentences. Either error can be corrected by supplying **both** a comma and a coordinating conjunction (or by joining the sentences with a semicolon).

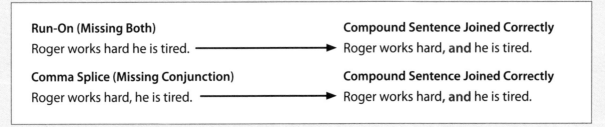

Run-On (Missing Both)
Roger works hard he is tired. ⟶ **Compound Sentence Joined Correctly**
Roger works hard, **and** he is tired.

Comma Splice (Missing Conjunction)
Roger works hard, he is tired. ⟶ **Compound Sentence Joined Correctly**
Roger works hard, **and** he is tired.

Note: Fragments, run-ons, and comma splices in student writing may be signs that students are experimenting with sentences, trying to combine them in compound and complex forms. Treat these errors, then, as signs of growth. Help students recognize and correct them, but do so in the context of authentic writing.

Teaching Sentence Variety

Variety is more than just the spice of life. The reason the Food and Drug Administration recommends a varied diet is not for sake of spice, but because our bodies need different types of nutrients from different sources. Sentence variety is similar. Yes, varied sentences spice up writing and read more smoothly, but the deeper reason for variety is that different types, kinds, and structures of sentences convey different kinds of thoughts. Sentence variety makes for deeper and more "nutrient-rich" thinking.

Simple, Compound, and Complex

Simple, compound, and complex sentences are covered in their own chapter, which focuses on creating these structures rather than identifying them. Students need to understand that these three structures work well for different kinds of thinking:

- **Simple sentences** provide ideas in a straightforward way.
- **Compound sentences** connect simple sentences equally. Different coordinating conjunctions create different connections.

  additions: *and*   contrasts: *but, yet*

  options: *or, nor*   causes: *for, so*

- **Complex sentences** connect simple sentences in a more nuanced way, making one depend on the other. Note the relationships created by the subordinating conjunctions in complex sentences.

  time: *after, as, as long as, before, since, until, when, whenever, while*

  contrasts: *although, as if, even though, though, unless, until, whereas, while*

  causes: *as, as long as, because, if, in order that, since, so that, when, whenever*

Medium, Long, and Short

Just as different sentence structures create special relationships between ideas, different sentence lengths are suited to different sizes of ideas. Students should not vary the length of sentences randomly. Instead, they should use different lengths for different purposes in their writing.

- **Medium sentences** (10-20 words) work well to express most ideas.

  When I read the advertisement online, I wrote my résumé and cover letter and sent them in.
- **Long sentences** (over 20 words) work well to express complex ideas.

  After waiting anxiously to hear from the employer, I received a call requesting an interview, went in to meet the department manager, toured the facility, and completed a test.
- **Short sentences** (under 10 words) work well to make a point.

  I got the job!

Varied Beginnings

On the surface, the reason to vary the beginnings of sentences is to keep them from sounding repetitive and predictable. At a deeper level, varying beginnings provides the chance to insert a transition word, phrase, or clause that helps make clear the connection between a sentence and what has come before.

- Transition word: However, I won't start work until July.
- Transition phrase: With all the arrangements, I won't start work until July.
- Transition clause: Though I am eager to begin, I won't start work until July.

Varying the Kinds of Sentences

Throughout *WRITE 1* and *WRITE 2,* students are prompted to create statements, questions, commands, and conditional sentences. These kinds of sentences are taught in context—for example, using command verbs when teaching the reader how to perform a process. Additional instruction in the kinds of sentences appear in the online bonus chapters "End Punctuation" and "Sentence Analysis." The key point is for students to understand the uses of the different kinds of sentences in their writing:

- **Statements** provide information about the subject. Use them most often.
  I was one of 25 applicants for the job.

- **Questions** ask for information about the subject. Use them to engage the reader.
  What made me stand out from the other applicants?

- **Exclamations** express strong emotion. Use them sparingly in academic writing.
  I had the best attitude!

- **Commands** tell the reader what to do. (They have an implied subject—*you.*) Use them to call the reader to act.
  Show a positive attitude when you interview.

- **Conditional** sentences show that one situation depends on another.
  If you have a good attitude and résumé, then the interviewer will notice.

Note: Each of these kinds of sentences represents a different kind of thinking. Using a variety of sentence kinds in writing stimulates deeper and broader thought.

Modifying Phrases and Clauses

The "Sentence Basics" chapter deals with creating sentence style by adding modifying phrases and clauses. Instead of focusing on the daunting names of such word groups—participial phrases, infinitive phrases, subordinate clauses—the exercises focus on the function of these groups. Do they answer an adjective question or an adverb question?

Adjective Questions	Adverb Questions
Which?	*How?*
What kind of?	*When?*
How many?/How much?	*Where?*
	Why?
	To what degree?
	How often?/How long?

If you ask one of these questions, students will likely respond verbally with a modifying phrase or clause that you could identify but they could not. Identification is not as important as use. Help students see that if the words answer an adjective or adverb question, those words can be used like an adjective or adverb.

Combining Sentences

Sentence combining is a proven strategy for improving sentence style, especially among struggling writers, who often produce short, choppy, repetitive sentences. *WRITE 1* and *WRITE 2* focus on three main approaches to combining sentences. The first two approaches, coordination and subordination, help writers make new connections between ideas. The third approach, moving and deleting, helps writers remove accidental repetition and create sentences with greater meaning.

Coordination

The word "coordinate" means "make equal" or "place in the same rank." A coordinating conjunction places two ideas on an equal footing. Coordinating conjunctions can connect words, phrases, or clauses in an equal way.

Coordinating Conjunctions						
and	but	or	nor	for	so	yet

When a coordinating conjunction is used to create a compound sentence, a comma should precede the conjunction.

Choppy sentences:	The book is late. I need to turn it in.
Combined sentences:	The book is late, **so** I need to turn it in.

If the sentences are joined without a conjunction and comma, a run-on sentence results. If the sentences are joined with the comma but without the conjunction, a comma-splice results. Compound sentences require both the comma and the conjunction (or just a semicolon).

Subordination

The word "subordinate" means "make unequal" or "place in a lower rank." A subordinating conjunction makes one idea depend upon another idea. The subordinating conjunction appears before the clause that is less important, making it dependent.

Choppy sentences:	The book is due. The library is closed.
Combined sentences:	**Though** the book is due, the library is closed.
Combined sentences:	The book is due **though** the library is closed.

If the dependent clause comes first, it should be followed by a comma.

Subordinating Conjunctions	
after	so that
although	that
as	though
as if	till
as long as	unless
because	until
before	when
even though	whenever
if	where
in order that	whereas
provided that	while
since	

Moving and Deleting

When sentences repeat content, the best way to combine them is to delete the repetition and merge the rest. The "Sentence Style" chapter includes instruction and exercises for combining by moving and deleting. Again, students should select the combining strategy that improves their thinking rather than one that just improves the flow of words.

Repetitive sentences:	I plan to be a nurse. I want to work in a hospital.
Combined sentences:	I plan to be a nurse **in a hospital**.

Expanding Sentences

Often struggling writers create sentences that provide little information. A writer who has eked out four say-nothing sentences does not need to combine them into two say-nothing sentences. Instead, the writer should expand the sentences. The best way to get writers to expand sentences is to have them answer the 5 W's and H about a sentence and add some of their answers to the original. This approach taps into spoken English, which is much more fluent for most struggling writers than written English is. For that reason, expanding works well as a partner or group activity.

Say-nothing sentence:	She works there.
Who works there?	my friend Stacy
What does she do?	She's a pediatrics nurse.
Where does she work?	at Lakeside Memorial Hospital
When does she work?	She works nights.
Why does she work?	to support her son
How does she work?	cheerfully
Expanded sentence:	My friend Stacy cheerfully works nights as a pediatrics nurse at Lakeside Memorial Hospital.

Modeling Sentences

Sentence modeling is similar to copying a masterpiece, stroke for stroke. The focus required to replace each word in a sentence makes students think about how the original sentence was built. Modeling explores word choice, syntax, and semantics. Students can construct participial phrases, absolute phrases, and appositives without being frightened by the difficult names of these structures. When students build appositives and understand their use, they may well ask, "What is this thing called?" That's the point at which the word *appositive* is meaningful to the student.

Original Sentence:	Storms are sensual feasts—the cold wet touch of rain, the smell of damp soil, the percussive crack of thunder, the brilliant flashes of lightning.
	—Eli King
Modeled Sentence:	Morning on the lake was a languid treat—the soft wet slap of oars, the coils of rising mist, the watery murmur of waves, the dark, welling depths.

The "Sentence Style" chapter includes a number of sentences from literary figures, and these are valuable to model. However, students may find it even more valuable to model sentences from their areas of study. An engineer builds a sentence in a different way than an accountant or a nurse or a social worker. Encourage students to submit "great sentences" they find outside the classroom, perhaps from their area of study. You might even give them an extra credit point for each sentence they bring in. At the start of class, then, you can write such a sentence on the board, discuss what makes it great, and have everyone in class model the sentence.

Noun

The distinction between common and proper nouns is mainly an issue for ensuring correct capitalization. However, forming the plurals of nouns can be challenging, especially given the special rules for nouns ending in *s, ch, f,* and *y,* as well as irregular plurals such as *children.* It's important to directly teach these issues to those who have trouble with them, but the only way students will internalize these rules is to use them consistently in authentic writing.

The "Noun" chapter also provides instruction about count and noncount nouns as well as articles and noun markers. Native speakers of Standard English often use these parts of speech correctly without even being aware of their existence, while those who speak English as a second language may be aware of them but may struggle with them. Provide direct instruction and practice as needed.

Pronoun

Pronouns may be just stand-ins for nouns, but these little words carry a lot of information. Personal pronouns must match their antecedents in person, number, and gender and have the correct case for their role in the sentence. Here is a chart of these forms of personal pronouns.

Person	Singular			Plural		
	Nom.	Obj.	Poss.	Nom.	Obj.	Poss.
First (speaking)	I	me	my/mine	we	us	our/ours
Second (spoken to)	you	you	your/yours	you	you	your/yours
Third (spoken about) masculine	he	him	his	they	them	their/theirs
feminine	she	her	her/hers	they	them	their/theirs
neuter	it	it	its	they	them	their/theirs

With indefinite pronouns, agreement errors are common. The material in the "Pronoun" chapter provides direct instruction on these issues, but mastery will come in authentic writing.

Verb

Verbs come in three basic classes—action, linking, and helping verbs. Understanding the uses of each class will help students form better sentences. Verbs also reflect number, voice, and tense, as shown in the chart below.

	Active Voice		Passive Voice	
	Singular	Plural	Singular	Plural
Present Tense	I see you see he/she/it sees	we see you see they see	I am seen you are seen he/she/it is seen	we are seen you are seen they are seen
Past Tense	I saw you saw he saw	we saw you saw they saw	I was seen you were seen it was seen	we were seen you were seen they were seen
Future Tense	I will see you will see he will see	we will see you will see they will see	I will be seen you will be seen it will be seen	we will be seen you will be seen they will be seen
Present Perfect Tense	I have seen you have seen he has seen	we have seen you have seen they have seen	I have been seen you have been seen it has been seen	we have been seen you have been seen they have been seen
Past Perfect Tense	I had seen you had seen he had seen	we had seen you had seen they had seen	I had been seen you had been seen it had been seen	we had been seen you had been seen they had been seen
Future Perfect Tense	I will have seen you will have seen he will have seen	we will have seen you will have seen they will have seen	I will have been seen you will have been seen it will have been seen	we will have been seen you will have been seen they will have been seen

Adjective and Adverb

Adjectives modify nouns, and adverbs modify verbs, adjectives, and other adverbs. Once students understand adjectives and adverbs, they will better understand word groups that function like adjectives and adverbs. Instead of loading writers down with the names of phrases and clauses, teach them the adjective and adverb questions. If a word, phrase, or clause answers one of these questions, it is probably functioning as an adjective or adverb.

Adjective Questions	Adverb Questions
Which?	*How?*
What kind of?	*When?*
How many?/How much?	*Where?*
	Why?
	To what degree?
	How often?/How long?

The chapter "Adjective and Adverb" includes an activity on teaching the order of adjectives. This is, once again, a feature of language that native English speakers use without thought, but that may need to be directly taught to ESL students.

Conjunction

Conjunctions show the relationships between ideas. Here are the three types of conjunctions and the relationships they show:

- **Coordinating conjunctions** connect ideas in an equal way, showing the following:
  Additions: *and*
  Contrasts: *but, yet*
  Options: *or, nor*
  Causes: *for, so*
- **Correlative conjunctions** stress the equality of two ideas, showing the following:
  Inclusion: *both / and, not only / but also*
  Exclusion: *neither / nor*
  Options: *whether / or*
- **Subordinating conjunctions** make one idea depend on another, showing the following:
  Time: *after, as, as long as, before, since, until, when, whenever, while*
  Contrasts: *although, as if, even though, though, unless, until, whereas, while*
  Causes: *as, as long as, because, if, in order that, since, so that, that, when, whenever*

Preposition

Prepositions create special relationships between nouns and other words in the sentences. The preposition and its object (a noun or pronoun) form a prepositional phrase, which functions as an adjective or adverb. As such, the prepositional phrase can answer the adjective or adverb questions listed above.

The chapter "Conjunction and Preposition" features four small prepositions that are used very frequently in English—*by, at, on,* and *in*. Native speakers of English use these words correctly without knowing the rules for them, but often ESL writers will need to learn the rules through direct instruction and then apply them to their writing.